Contested Images

Women of Color in Popular Culture

Edited by Alma M. García

ALTAMIRA
PRESS

A division of
ROWMAN & LITTLEFIELD PUBLISHERS, INC.
Lanham • New York • Toronto • Plymouth, UK

Published by AltaMira Press
A division of The Rowman & Littlefield Publishing Group, Inc.
A wholly owned subsidiary of The Rowman & Littlefield Publishing Group, Inc.
4501 Forbes Boulevard, Suite 200, Lanham, Maryland 20706
www.rowman.com

10 Thornbury Road, Plymouth PL6 7PP, United Kingdom

British Library Cataloguing in Publication Information Available

Library of Congress Cataloging-in-Publication Data
Contested images : women of color in popular culture / edited by Alma M. García.
p. cm.
Includes bibliographical references.
ISBN 978-0-7591-1961-1 (cloth : alk. paper) — ISBN 978-0-7591-1962-8 (pbk. : alk. paper) — ISBN 978-0-7591-1963-5 (electronic)
1. Minorities in mass media. 2. Minority women—United States. 3. Women in popular culture—United States. 4. Women in mass media. I. García, Alma M.
P94.5.M552U6273 2012
305.48'8—dc23
2012018802

The paper used in this publication meets the minimum requirements of American National Standard for Information Sciences Permanence of Paper for Printed Library Materials, ANSI/NISO Z39.48-1992.

Printed in the United States of America

In loving memory of my beloved mother, Alma Araiza Garcia
(November 13, 1920–April 2, 2011)

Thank you for the miracle of the hummingbird.

Contents

Acknowledgments

I would like to offer my sincere thanks to the following without whose support I could not have completed this project:

Don Dodson, Special Assistant to the President, Santa Clara University, and Diane Jonte Pace, Vice Provost for Academic Affairs, Santa Clara University, for awarding me an Office of Faculty Development's Writing for Publication Grant;

Jack Meinhardt, formerly of AltaMira Press, and Marissa Parks of Alta-Mira Press, for their support during the early stages of this publication;

Wendi Schnaufer, Executive Editor, Acquisitions, AltaMira Press, for her patience and understanding during the final stages in completing this publication;

Swati and Harish Negi and the entire staff at Copy Craft, Santa Clara, California, for their invaluable assistance and technical support; and

Josie Rosas, my *amiga*, for her steadfast friendship.

I would like to acknowledge Pancho Jiménez (http://www.jimenez art.com) for allowing me to use his artwork for the book cover. The intersecting circles in his piece perfectly capture the theoretical framework of intersectuality used by the articles in this anthology. Pancho Jiménez received his Masters of Fine Arts from San Francisco State. He has exhibited extensively in the San Francisco Bay Area and nationally at museums, colleges, universities, private galleries, and civic spaces. His work is part of the permanent collection at the University of San Francisco and has been featured in *Ceramics Monthly* and in three Lark Book publications, *The Ceramic Design Book*, *Extruded Ceramics*, and *500 Ceramic Sculptures*. He is currently a lecturer in the Art and Art History Department and an academic advisor in the Drahmann Academic Advising and Learning Resources Center at Santa Clara University.

I would like to give a special acknowledgment and sincere thanks to Francisco Jiménez, Modern Languages and Literature, Santa Clara University, my colleague and friend, for supporting this project from the very beginning and during the difficult family time that I experienced as I completed this project.

Credits

The following were reprinted with permission for this anthology:

Frances R. Aparicio, "Jennifer as Selena: Rethinking Latinidad in Media and Popular Culture," pp. 99–105 in *Latino Studies* 1 (1) (2003). Reproduced with permission of Palgrave Macmillan.

S. Elizabeth Bird, "The Burden of History: Representations of American Indian Women in Popular Media," in *Women in Popular Culture: Representation and Meaning* edited by Marian Meyers (Cresskill, NJ: Hampton Press, 2008), 185–207. Reprinted with permission of Hampton Press Inc.

Jacqueline Bobo, "Black Women's Films: Genesis of a Tradition," in *Black Women Film and Video Artists*," edited by Jacqueline Bobo (New York: Routledge, 1998), 3–19. Reproduced with permission of Taylor and Francis Group LLC-Books.

Yen Le Espiritu, "Ideological Racism and Cultural Resistance: Constructing Our Own Images," in *Asian American Women and Men* by Yen Le Espiritu (Thousand Oaks, CA: AltaMira Press, 1997), 97–120. Reproduced with permission of AltaMira Press.

Rayna Green, "The Pocahontas Perplex: The Image of Indian Women in American Culture," pp. 698–714. *Massachusetts Review* 16 (4) (Autumn 1975). Reprinted by permission from *Massachusetts Review*.

Yasmin Jiwani, "The Eurasian Female Hero(ine): Sydney Fox as Relic Hunter," pp. 182–191. *Journal of Popular Film and Television* 32 (4) (2005). Reprinted by permission of Taylor and Francis Group, http://www.informaworld.com.

M. Elise Marubbio, "Ghosts and Vanishing Indian Women: Death of the Celluloid Maiden in the 1990s," in *Killing the Indian Maiden: Images of the Native American in Film* by M. Elise Marubbio (Lexington: University of Kentucky Press, 2006), 197–226. Reproduced by permission of University of Kentucky Press.

Evelyn Nakano Glenn, "Yearning for Lightness: Transnational Circuits in the Marketing and Consumption of Skin Lighteners," pp. 281–302 in *Gender & Society* 22 (3) (2008). © 2008 Sociologists for Women in Society. Reprinted by permission of SAGE Publications.

Frances Negrón-Muntaner, "Barbie's Hair: Selling Out Puerto Rican Identity in the Global Market," in *Latino/a Popular Culture*, edited by Michelle Habell-Pann and Mary Romero (New York: New York University Press, 2002), 38–60. © 2002 by New York University Press. Reprinted with permission of New York University Press.

Jane C. H. Park, "Cibo Matto's *Stereotype A*: Articulating Asian American Hip Pop," in *East Main Street: Asian American Popular Culture*, edited by Shilpa Dave, LeiLani Nishime, and Tasha G. Oren (New York: New York University Press, 2005), 292–312. Reprinted with permission of New York University Press.

Tracey Owens Patton, "Hey Girl, Am I More than My Hair?: African American Women and Their Struggles with Beauty, Body Image, and Hair," pp. 24–51 in *Feminist Formations* (formerly *NWSA Journal*) 18 (2) (2006). ©2006 NWSA Journal. Reprinted with permission of John Hopkins University Press.

Domino Renee Pérez, "Lost in the Cinematic Landscape: Chicanas as Lloronas in Contemporary Film," in *Velvet Barrios: Popular Culture of Chicana/o Sexualities* edited by Alicia Gaspar de Alba (New York: Palgrave Macmillan, 2003), 229-247. Reprinted with Permission of Taylor and Francis Group LLC-Books.

"Puamana" written by Irmgard Aluli. Used by permission of Criterion Music Corporation. All Rights Reserved. International Copyright Reserved.

Tricia Rose, "Bad Sistas . . . ." This essay is an abridged version of a chapter titled "Bad Sistas: Black Women Rappers and Sexual Politics in Rap Music," in *Black Noise: Rap Music and Black Culture in Contemporary America*, by Tricia Rose (Middletown, CT: Wesleyan University Press, 1994), 146–55.

Beretta E. Smith-Shomade, "The Maddening Business of Show," in *Shaded Lives: African-American Women and Television*, by Beretta E. Smith-Shomade (Piscatawy, NJ: Rutgers University Press, 2002), 8–23. Reprinted by permission of Rutgers University Press.

Introduction

Contested Images: Women of Color in Popular Culture is a collection of essays about the representations in popular culture of African American, Asian American, Latina, and Native American women. The anthology is divided into four parts: film images, beauty images, music, and television. The idea for *Contested Images* developed from my experiences teaching an undergraduate course on race, class, and gender. Over the years, I saw that students would gain a deeper understanding of the impact of race, class, and gender by examining popular culture. I wanted them to understand the process through which popular culture shapes and is shaped by the social construction of race, class, and gender. I also wanted students to learn how to analyze the relationship between cultural representations and power relations in society. In addition, I wanted students to understand personal and collective audience resistance to such representations in popular culture. After several years, I began to include in my course many articles that focused on women of color. My students analyzed films, advertising, music, and other forms of cultural production using a race, class, and gender analysis. Women began to "see and read" beauty advertisements with a critical eye while women of color contested their "invisibility" and their stereotypical representations in popular culture. Men began to question the "John Wayne" film icon as the ideal representation of masculinity. Men of color, specifically African American men, questioned their depiction in films and television as hypersexualized men. A couple of years after incorporating readings that analyzed popular culture, one student concluded to the class by commenting, "I finally get it. We need to really analyze a movie and not just watch it." Another student's comment illustrates how she was moving from visceral reactions in response to cultural productions to an analytical understanding of the world of popular culture and its social construction:

I can't pick up a fashion magazine and just flip through the pages anymore. I
am now really looking at the ads to see what they say about me as a woman
instead of checking out the new fashion trends. My roommate keeps telling me
to just look at the ads without analyzing them. I told her that this was impossible for me. I want to analyze everything.

OVERVIEW OF THE ANTHOLOGY

The seventeen articles selected for this anthology share two intellectual traditions. First, the authors use an intersectionality perspective in their analysis
of popular culture and the representation of women of color. Second, the
authors identify popular culture as a site of conflict and contestation. An
intersectionality perspective has been instrumental in revising gender analysis across academic disciplines and, as a result, represents a major contribution to feminist scholarship. Scholars who are women of color have been
critical of a gender analysis that did not fully account for the diversity of
women's experiences. This intellectual debate can be traced back to the
political struggles of activists who were women of color. In 1977, for example, the Combahee River Collective, a black feminist organization in Boston,
published the *Combahee River Collective Statement*. The document remains
a hallmark of the activism of women of color and an early articulation of an
intersectionality perspective:

> The most general statement of our politics at the present time would be that we
> are actively committed to struggling against racial, sexual, heterosexual, and
> class oppression, and see as our particular task the development of integrated
> analysis and practice based upon the fact that the major systems of oppression
> are interlocking.[1]

Similarly, the essays, personal narratives, and creative writings collected by
Cherríe Moraga and Gloria Anzaldúa (1981) in their path-breaking anthology
This Bridge Called My Back: Writings by Radical Women of Color stressed
the need to use an intersectionality perspective to understand the impact of
race, class, gender, and sexual orientation.[2] These essays, personal narratives, and creative writings further contributed to the development of an
intersectionality perspective. The essays in *All the Women Are White and All
the Men Are Black, but Some of Us Are Brave*, edited by Hull, Scott, and
Smith (1982), use an intersectionality perspective to explore the affects of
living at the "intersections" of race, class, gender, sexual orientation, religion, age, and other social locations that "still matter."[3] Baca Zinn and Thornton Dill (1994) added to this debate by criticizing a gender analysis that used
an "additive approach" to study race, class, and gender. Zinn and Dill viewed
the concepts of "double jeopardy" and "triple jeopardy" as a reflection of an

additive approach that obscures how race, class and gender form a "matrix of domination."[4] Lisa Bowleg (2008) also criticizes gender analysis for its reliance on an additive approach. Bowleg gives an example of how an intersectionality perspective is conceptualized. She explains how the use of the term "Black lesbian women" instead of "Black and lesbian and women" best captures the impact of race, sexual orientation, and gender by omitting the word "and."[5] Patricia Hill Collins (1990) further explains the limitations of an additive approach:

> Black feminist thought fosters a fundamental paradigmatic shift that *rejects additive approaches* to oppression. Instead of starting with gender and then adding in other variables such as age, sexual orientation, race, social class, and religion, Black feminist thought sees these distinctive systems of oppressions being part of one overarching structure of domination.[6]

Kimberley Crenshaw (1991) uses the concept of "representational intersectionality" to explore the ways in which women of color are represented in popular culture and the relationship between such images and power hierarchies. Crenshaw shows how popular culture reinforces a matrix of domination, power relations and the development of oppositional cultural sites.[7] As Hill Collins (1990) concludes,

> The very notion of the intersections of race, class and gender as an area worthy of study emerged from the recognition of practitioners of each distinctive theoretical tradition that inequality could not be explained, let alone challenged, via a race-only, or a gender-only framework. No one had all of the answers and no one was going to get all of the answers without attention to two things. First, the notion of interlocking oppressions refers to the macro-level connections linking systems of oppression such as race, class and gender. This is a model describing the social structures that create social positions. Second, the notion of *intersectionality* describes micro-level processes— namely, how each individual and group occupies a social position within interlocking structures of oppression described by the metaphor of *intersectionality*. Together they shape oppression.[8]

An intersectionality perspective explores the affects of living at the "intersections" of race, class, gender, sexual orientation, religion, age and other social locations that "still matter."

A second theme that cuts acros, buts the articles in *Contested Images: Women of Color in Popular Culture* is that popular culture is a site of conflict and contestation. The representations of, in this case, women of color embedded in forms of popular culture reinforce existing power relations that legitimate different levels of inequality. Cultural messages, images, and codes are produced, distributed, and reinvented within popular culture. Specific types of popular culture are not randomly constructed but rather reflect ongoing tensions within a given society and, above all, the ability of dominant groups to construct stereotypes. Quite simply, popular culture matters. It matters because it legitimizes a system of social stratification based on race, class, gender, sexual orientation, and other social locations. Stuart Hall (1981) sees popular culture as "one of the sites where this struggle for and against a culture of the powerful is engaged. . . . It is the arena of consent and resistance."[9] Hegemonic cultural productions have a legacy of distorting the lived experiences of women of color. Women of color, for example, view popular culture scripts, images, and messages, but not in a passive manner. Like other subaltern groups, women of color develop resistance to the wide array of representations that have erased or distorted their historical and contemporary experiences.[10] Mimi Thi Nguyen and Thuy Linh Nguyen (2007) explain the role of popular culture in constructing images of Asian American women:

> As phantasmic constructs of Asian and Asian America, over a century's worth of dragon ladies, lotus blossoms, . . . have entered the American popular imaginary, often in a discordant cacophony of sounds and images. By examining these images in the historical specificity of their production, circulation, and consumption, scholars and critics have demonstrated the salience of popular culture as a realm of political conflict and an important force in shaping the material and social realities.[11]

While the authors of the articles in *Contested Images* focus on long-standing stereotypes in popular culture of women of color, they also examine the development of resistance to such stereotypes. Most follow in the tradition of what Catharine Stimpson (1986) calls "acts of defiance."[12] Hill Collins (1991) explains how a "culture of resistance" enables those women of color who are able to "talk back" as either cultural producers and/or audiences (hooks 1989; Hill Collins, 1991).[13] Interestingly, Joyce Antler (1997), like bell hooks, selected the title *Talking Back* for her anthology on popular culture and Jewish women. Jewish women, like other women, have created a legacy of contesting false representations.[14] The creation of oppositional images underscores how women who have the opportunity to create cultural productions become subversive. As "cultural rebels," Jewish women writers, confronted "dramas of subordination" and, indeed, talked back. Antler (1997) concludes that "an understanding of these images, as they developed across several generations, can restore the voices of Jewish women to the cultural record, modifying myths and stereotypes and shaping new images."[15] The same can be said for women of color as the essays in this anthology will demonstrate. The articles in *Contested Images* deconstruct the power relations inherent in cultural productions produced by dominant groups about women of color. Authors explore the ways in which women of color engage in "acts of defiance" through their construction of counter forms of popular culture, what Lisa Lowe (1996) calls "cultural counter sites."[16]

CONTENTS OF THE ANTHOLOGY

Each of the four parts—film images, beauty images, music, and television—of *Contested Images* includes articles on African American women, Asian American women, Latinas, and Native American women.

Part I. Film Images: Out of Focus

Part I of *Contested Images* "focuses" on film as a form of cultural production that create images, many of which become a dominant narrative of the "other." These narratives are firmly rooted in historical contexts that are closely linked to the surrounding political climate. In her essay "Ideological Racism and Cultural Resistance: Constructing Our Own Images," Yen Le Espiritu discusses the changing nature of stereotypes of Asians in relation to the role they play within the context of specific U.S. foreign policy. Before the Chinese Revolution of 1949, when the United States did not view China as a threat, films depicted Chinese men as noble farmers and Chinese women as long-suffering. Later, when the United States viewed the Chinese Revolution as a threat, the image of the Chinese as depicted in the 1937 film *The Good Earth* was transformed. The development of changing film images of Asian men and women reflected changes in the geopolitical climate of the United States in its relationship with Japan. Asian women were portrayed as hyper-sexualized "Dragon Ladies" and Asian men as villains, security threats, and lustful of white women.

Jacqueline Bobo's "Black Women's Films: Genesis of a Tradition" examines the historical and contemporary contributions of black women filmmakers. Black women produced films as a form of resistance to the widely distributed films that contributed to the distorted images of the social realities of black women. Bobo analyzes the production, distribution, and audience reception of these films and the racial barriers that confronted black women artists. These artists created cultural sites of struggle and resistance against social oppression and marginalization. Bobo views such oppositional cultural sites as places where black women can "see" their social worlds depicted realistically. For Bobo, these films also have the potential to motivate black women "toward activism, thereby strengthening their ability as a potent social force."

M. Elise Marubbio's essay, "Ghosts and Vanishing Indian Women: Death of the Celluloid Maiden in the 1990s" is a "starting point for understanding how deeply embedded the Native American woman is in violent and romantic images of American nation building." Marubbio compares and contrast films responsible for the creation of stereotypical image of the "celluloid princess and the sexualized maiden" within the context of different historical periods. She examines films produced in the 1990s that attempted to reconcile U.S. national identity with the historical legacy of genocide. Films depicted Native American women as "noble" princesses, the exoticized objects for white males. Marubbio contrasts the images of the "Indian maiden" with that of white women. Although white males in these films were portrayed as being attracted to Native American women, they usually did not put them in the same category as white women whom they revered on a pedestal. Films also portrayed the Native American woman as a hybrid "celluloid maiden" who was both a docile princess and an eroticized, highly sexualized temptress. In recent films, Native American women are often depicted as a martyr figure: a throwback to the Indian princess film icon. Marubbio points out the difficulty in eliminating gendered racializations in films even in those meant to be ones that tried to replace stereotypes of Native American women.

In "Lost in the Cinematic Landscape: Chicanas as *Lloronas* in Contemporary Film," Domino Renee Pérez analyzes the representation of Chicanas in five films. Pérez discusses how the Latina protagonist depicted in each film can be seen as modern day version of *La Llorona* (the Weeping Woman), one of the most iconic figures in Chicano/Mexican legends. It has been passed down through the generations in both Mexico and the United States. *La Llorona* is a mother who drowns her children after learning that her husband has forsaken her for another woman. She appears at night and can be heard crying as she searches for her children along the river. Pérez links the figure of *La Llorona* with the Chicanas represented in each of the following films: *Mi Vida Loca* (1994), *Mi Familia* (1995), *Lone Star* (1996), *Fools Rush In* (1997), and *Mulholland Drive* (2001). She explores how the representations of Chicanas in these films provide a new perspective on the iconic figure of *La Llorona*. Pérez also examines the role of Chicanas who view these films. As members of an audience exposed to film representations, Chicanas can bring what Pérez calls a "subversive" reading that enables them to "reclaim texts that are read by mainstream culture as palatable 'otherness.'"

In "Chasing Fae: *The Watermelon Woman* and Black Lesbian Possibility," Laura L. Sullivan focuses on the distorted representation of black women in Hollywood films. She analyzes Cheryl Dunye's 1996 film *The Watermelon Woman*, the first film made by a black lesbian filmmaker. The film's main character Cheryl, played by the filmmaker, is producing a film about Fae Richards, an actor who appeared in the 1930s film *Plantation Memories* and other Hollywood films in the 1930s and 1940s. Richards is actually a fictional person created by the filmmaker herself. These films cast Richards in the role of the stereotypical "mammy" figure. Dunye's movie is a film about a film produced by the movie's fictional producer named Cheryl. Sullivan analyzes how this film documents the life and film career of Fae Richards. Sullivan analyzes how Cheryl, during the making of the film, is forced to come to terms with her relationships with her black woman friend and her white lesbian lover. Cheryl uncovers that Fae Richards also had to come to terms with her relationship with her white lover who produced the film. Through the fictional character of Cheryl, Dunye, the writer/director, raises several issues related to the intersections of identity of black women lesbians. Tensions exist within both white and black communities over the question of "authenticity" of black women lesbians. Similarly, the two black women in the film find themselves questioning each other's racial "authenticity." Similar tensions also exist within both white and black communities over the question of sexual orientation. Dunye's film examines how these black lesbian women eventually confront their black male employers who make overt references to the women's sexuality. Cheryl Dunye explains what she wanted her film to accomplish: "*The Watermelon Woman* came from the real lack of any information about the lesbian and film history of African-American women. Since it wasn't happening, I invented it."

Part II. Beauty Images: Mirror, Mirror, On Whose Wall?

This section examines how beauty images depicted in various forms of popular culture contain unattainable images of what society, in any given historical period, defines as beautiful. The essays in this section examine the origins and development of socially constructed beauty images and their consequences for women of color. Authors also discuss the ways in which women of color resist and challenge unattainable beauty images. In "Hey Girl, Am I More Than My Hair?: African American Women and Their Struggles with Beauty, Body Image, and Hair," Tracey Owens Patton addresses the impact of hegemonically created expectations of beauty, body images, hair color, hair texture, and skin color for African American women. Using standpoint, intersectionality and Afrocentric theories, Patton explores the link between unattainable beauty images and identity formation for black women. Patton discusses the impact of a hegemonic image of beauty in the relationships between African American women and African American men, between African American and white women, and African American women and Latinas. Patton examines the ways in which black women have creatively resisted the imposition of white beauty images within black communities, specifically through the development of the "Black is Beautiful" movement that rejected a hegemonic white beauty standard. Patton concludes that "a Womanist Black is Beauty Liberation campaign would encompass a Black or woman of color whose beauty issues . . . are brought in from the margin to the center in an attempt to honor the beauty in her that has been reviled, rebuffed."

Frances Negrón-Muntaner focuses on the impact of hair, specifically hair texture, as a site of conflict and contestation by analyzing the impact of U.S. and Puerto Rican politics and culture. The overarching theme in "Barbie's Hair: Selling Out Puerto Rican Identity in the Global Market" is that Mattel's Puerto Rican Barbie doll, introduced in 1997, is not merely a doll. It is a space where Puerto Ricans engage in a contentious debate over ethnic nationalism and identity. For Negrón-Muntaner, the Puerto Rican Barbie represents a marketable transnational icon. Its distribution in Puerto Rico as part of Mattel "Dolls of the World" represents an attempt to increase its profits on a global scale. The creation of these "ethnic" Barbie doll collections opened a market by transforming the white Barbie doll with her long legs, straight blonde hair, blue eyes, exaggerated body proportions of a wasp-like waist and large breasts into Mattel's concept of an "ethnic" Barbie. Negrón-Muntaner argues that in Puerto Rican communities, hair, specifically hair texture, becomes the focal point of the public debate surrounding the Puerto Rican Barbie doll. Hair texture, more than skin color, becomes the target of such debate. This doll is essentially white beneath the plastic cultural icon. Negrón-Muntaner sees the Puerto Rican Barbie doll as a consumer item whose acceptance has triggered a heated debate over Puerto Rican identity. The doll's Anglicized straight hair is seen by some groups as an imposed standard of beauty and held up as a contentious symbol of Puerto Rican assimilation, "Americanization," and upward mobility. Others see the doll as compatible with Puerto Rican beauty standards. For Negrón-Muntaner, the struggle to deconstruct the Puerto Rican Barbie represents "the real and perceived power of different Puerto Ricans to invent, control, and deploy their cultural specificity within hostile or relatively auspicious contexts."

Rayna Green's essay, "The Pocahontas Perplex: The Image of Indian Women in American Culture" analyzes the socially constructed image of the Pocahontas Princess and the Squaw. Green provides a historical overview of the origins and development of the Pocahontas image by identifying her as a symbol of the Western gaze of the "New World." The rescue narrative of Pocahontas and John Smith constructed the image of the naive Native American Princess who falls in love with John Smith. The creation of the Indian woman as princess image can best be understood in relation to her counterpart: the Indian woman as squaw. Both the Princess and the Squaw "perplex" is at the core of European expansionism. European settlers held up the Indian princess as a metaphor for the inhabitants of the "virgin lands" they occupied. The image of Indian males as "savages" and the Indian women as "squaws" became contrasting images to the Indian woman as princess. Green deconstructs ballads, paintings, poetry, and other forms of popular culture to illustrate the personifications of all three stereotypes. She identifies the myth of the Indian Princess as a key narrative played in development of a U.S. national imagination. As Green concludes, Pocahontas "offers an intolerable metaphor for the Indian-white experience. Perhaps if we explore the meaning of Native American lives outside the boundaries of the stories, songs, and pictures given us in tradition, we will find a more humane truth."

Evelyn Nakano Glenn addresses the issue of white skin as the normative skin color in her essay "Yearning for Lightness: Transnational Circuits in the Marketing and Consumption of Skin Lighteners." Nakano Glenn discusses the multinational, multi-billion dollar skin lightener industry as it reaches across the globe. She views skin color as an individual's social capital used to secure privileges through the ability to cosmetically lighten one's skin to avoid discrimination based on dark skin color. Women across the globe consume various types of products produced, marketed, and sold by multinational corporations. Ironically, women of color are increasingly becoming consumers of whitening products as a result of aggressive global marketing campaigns. Nakano Glenn analyzes the direct connection between the legacy of European colonization and the politics of skin color. White skin becomes a symbol of civilization; darkness, a mark of inferiority. With the booming market around the world for skin lighteners, women of color are subject to the deafening mantra that "white makes right." A woman with light skin, either natural or processed, becomes a prize, a more marketable commodity in many countries, usually those that continue to have arranged marriages. As the Internet reaches more women across the globe through online advertising, marketing, and chat rooms, the skin-lightening multinational business will continue to expand at the expense of the women of color. Nakano Glenn concludes that "the yearning for lightness evident in the widespread and growing use of skin bleaching around the globe can rightfully be seen as a legacy of colonialism, a manifestation of 'false consciousness' and the internalization of 'white is right' values by people of color, especially women."

Part III. Music: What Key?

The authors in this section examine the world of music about and by women of color. Their essays raise key questions about music as a site of oppression and one of contested identity. Debates continue about the relationship between the text of music and the affect on not only women of color but also other social groups. The essay "Bad Sistas: Black Women Rappers and Sexual Politics in Rap Music" is nearly the full chapter from Tricia Rose's book, *Black Noise: Rap Music and Black Culture in Contemporary America*.[17] Rose contributes to discussions within popular culture discourse regarding the cultural space and voice occupied by black women rappers. She analyzes rap music as an unfolding process through which various groups, such as black male and female rappers, engage in a historically contextualized discourse about rap music and its impact on women's oppression through representation in rap music lyrics and music videos. Rose positions black women's rap music by examining 1) their dialogue with male rappers, specifically their music's sexual contexts, and 2) their dialogue with other groups outside of rap music, such as white women feminists. Her discussion shows how black women rappers, who occupy multiple identity positions and boundaries, navigate through the world of male rappers, their black women friends, and other groups of "audiences."

In her study, "Jennifer as Selena: Rethinking Latinidad in Media and Popular Culture," Frances R. Aparicio raises questions about identity formation among diverse groups covered by the term *Latinidad*. Her analysis stresses the need to redefine *Latinidad* by focusing on interethnic group relations among Latinos. Aparicio explores the concept of *Latinidad* in order to "explore moments of convergences and divergences in the formation of Latino/a (post)colonial subjectivities and in hybrid cultural expressions among various Latino national groups." Her essay traces the emergence onto the "stage" of two musical icons in Latina/o culture: the Mexican American Selena and the Puerto Rican Jennifer Lopez, whose tremendous musical success followed her depiction of Selena in the 1997 movie *Selena*. Aparicio shows how Selena's body and the body of Jennifer Lopez in the movie about Selena were inscribed through a non-Latino gaze and discusses its cultural and political implications. Aparicio weaves a narrative that focuses on issues of beauty images, physical appearances, fashion, and musical styles of Selena and Lopez as Selena and later as herself.

Amy Kuʻuleialoha Stillman's "Passed into the Present: Women in Hawaiian Entertainment" traces the historical development of hula music and the role of Native Hawaiian women as safe keepers of this tradition as an authentic source of cultural pride. Stillman contextualizes the role played by Hawaiian women in the contestation of American missionary attempts, in the early 1880s, to suppress hula performances because they viewed such musical performances as manifestations of a pagan religion. Beginning in the early 1900s, the famous hula shows emerged as a staple form of entertainment targeted at tourists who were all too eager to witness "native" dance. As a form of tourist commodification, women hula dancers became objectified as the exotic "other." Stillman argues that Native Hawaiian women, as "matriarchs of tradition," retained the integrity of this cultural production by preserving and teaching the musical and dance skills from one generation to the next. Stillman documents the rise of Native Hawaiian women as composers and performers, particularly featured soloists. Stillman concludes that "women's contributions to Hawaiian entertainment have been absolutely crucial to its perpetuation. Women have been involved in a broad spectrum of roles, not only as singers and dancers, but as composers, instrumentalists, teachers, educators, scholars and policymakers."

In her essay, "Cibo Matto's *Stereotype A*: Articulating Asian American Hip Pop," Jane C. H. Park traces the development of the hip pop band, Cibo Matto, started in 1996 by two Japanese-born women, Yuka Honda and Miho Hatori. *Cibo matto* is Italian for "food madness." Honda and Hatori integrate food metaphors throughout their songs. Park explores the strategies that the artists use to respond to existing gender and racial stereotypes in hip pop music. Through a combination of music lyrics, grounded in food themes and imagery and postmodern music arrangements, Honda and Hatori transgress the boundaries in the hip pop musical world that they encountered both in Japan and the United States. These artists broke through the constraints placed on them by marketers and audiences. When they released their album, *Stereotype A*, they self-identified as "Asian Americans." Park sees such identity formation as an outcome of the group's occupying a transnational space of culture, gender, and nation. Through their combination of innovative lyrics, arrangements, and synthesis of divergent musical forms, Honda and Hatori challenge the racial, gender, and nation stereotypes of Asian American women.

Part IV. Television: Changing Channels

This last section includes essays that examine the portrayal of women of color in television programs. The essays by Rosa E. Soto and S. Elizabeth Bird also integrate an analysis of films with their discussion of Latinas and Native American women, respectively. In "'Made to be the Maid'?: An Examination of the Latina as Maid in Mainstream Film and Television," Soto analyzes the character of the Latina domestic worker, usually referred to by her employers as the "maid." This character represents the ubiquitous "other" in relation to the Anglo family who employs her. The Anglo employers, specifically the woman employer, are depicted as benevolent and culturally sensitive persons. The Latina maid is depicted in a variety of ways. She appears as a hypersexual woman who poses a threat to the Anglo family. Latina domestic workers are simultaneously depicted as docile, subservient workers who are grateful for the paternalistic treatment of their Anglo family. For the Anglo family, the Latina domestic worker is a one-dimensional character whose last name is rarely known. Her life outside the home is hardly a concern for her employer. The Latina adds an "ethnic flavor" to the Anglo household. The depiction of her intimate relationship with her Anglo employers serves as a subterfuge for economic exploitation. Soto concludes that Latinas are "made to be the maid" in television programs and films so that the Anglo characters see themselves—and the audience sees them—as "altruistic, and good moral individuals who care for their communities and are worthy of all the privileges that come with their race and class."

In "The Burden of History: Representations of American Indian Women in Popular Media," S. Elizabeth Bird analyzes the portrayal of Native American men and women in television programs and films. Bird's study shows that Native American Indian women are "conspicuous by their absence" in programs such as *Dr. Quinn Medicine Woman* and *Northern Exposure*. American Indian women are usually depicted in relation to white women and men. American Indian women remain in the shadows while their male counterparts appeared, with only a few exceptions, in the usual stereotypical roles such as "noble savages." Native American women and men became "props" for white actors, often only appearing briefly and rarely speaking. Bird concludes her essay with a discussion of Canadian television programs and films, many produced by Native Americans. Even in these innovative productions, Native American women did not appear as central to films such as the buddy road trip film *Smoke Signals*. Some television documentaries, such as *Lakota Woman*, portray Native American women as main characters. Bird concludes that cultural productions such as television programs, films, and documentaries must undertake a concerted movement to "cast off the old imagery" of Native American women.

In her essay "The Eurasian Female Hero(ine): Sydney Fox as Relic Hunter," Yasmin Jiwani examines the representation of a biracial woman action character in a Canadian television program. Jiwani considers Sydney Fox as the adventure-seeking "relic hunter" whose appearance in a prime-time slot as a complex moment in popular culture and the representation of women of color. Despite her central role in the television series, Sydney Fox remains the exotic "other." Jiwani examines the historical representations of women of color in television programs. The European colonial and postcolonial gaze led to women of color being seen as "exotic, erotic and dangerous" while white women were depicted as "virginal or sexually repressed." Jiwani argues that Sydney Fox as a Eurasian female "*hero*(ine)"—the daughter of an Asian mother and a white father—has replaced the "Dragon Lady" with the "Warrior Woman" in the tradition of such heroes as Indiana Jones. Sydney Fox represents the "quintessential assimilated Asian American woman" but one whose image continues to be constructed as the exotic "other."

In "The Maddening Business of Show," Beretta E. Smith-Shomade studies the historical process through which representations of African American women and men move from glaring invisibility to problematic visibility. She links these representations to the political climate within which they emerged. Smith-Shomade discusses the role of program sponsors and producers in deciding what television programs that featured African Americans would be the most profitable and least likely to offend white audiences.

During the civil rights movement of the 1960s, African Americans were cast in roles in a variety of television programs and anchors on newscasts. Smith-Shomade analyzes how these new images "sanitized" the lives of African Americans in an attempt to reach a mainly white, middle-class audience. The program *Julia* cast the first African American woman who was not depicted as a domestic worker. *Julia* aired in prime time and depicted an African American woman as a successful woman who was impervious to the pernicious affects of racism, sexism, and classism in the her life and those of other African American women. These programs revolved around the common tropes of successful assimilation and contentment despite the everyday struggles of the majority of African American women whose precarious economic situations made them all but content. As Smith-Shomade concludes, "[t]his alternative image was mandated in part by broadcast images and practices departments, who policed all material for broadcast. *Julia*, in particular, operated fully within the American safe, white, and middle-class mainstream."

NOTES

1. The Combahee River Collective, "A Black Feminist Statement," in Gloria T. Hull, Patricia Bell Scott, and Barbara Smith eds., *All the Women Are White, All the Blacks Are Men, but Some of Us Are Brave: Black Women's Studies* (Old Westbury, NY: Feminist Press, 1982), 13–22.

2. Cherríe Moraga and Gloria Anzaldúa, eds., *This Bridge Called My Back: Writings by Radical Women of Color* (Watertown, MA: Persephone Press, 1981).

3. Hull, Scott, and Smith eds., *All the Women Are White, All the Blacks Are Men, but Some of Us Are Brave: Black Women's Studies.*

4. Maxine Baca Zinn and Bonnie Thornton Dill, "Difference and Domination," in *Women of Color in U.S. Society*, ed. Maxine Baca Zinn and Bonnie Thornton Dill (New York, Routledge, 1994), 3–12.

5. Lisa Bowleg, "When Black + Lesbian + Woman = Black Lesbian Woman: The Methodological Challenges of Qualitative and Quantitative Intersectionality Research," *Sex Roles* 59 (2008): 312–325.

6. Patricia Hill Collins, *Black Feminist Thought: Knowledge, Consciousness and the Politics of Empowerment* (New York: Routledge, 1990), 222.

7. Kimberley Crenshaw, "Mapping the Margins: Intersectionality, Identity Politics, and Violence against Women of Color," *Stanford Law Review* 43, no. 6 (July 1991), 1241–1249.

8. Hill Collins, *Black Feminist Thought*, 228.

9. Stuart Hall, "Notes on Deconstructing 'The Popular,'" in *People's History and Socialist Theory*, ed. Raphael Samuel (Boston: Routledge and Kegan Paul, 1981), 239.

10. Roland Barthes, *Mythologies* , translated by Annette Lavers (New York: Farrar, Straus and Giroux, 1972); Kenneth Burke, *A Rhetoric of Motives* (Berkeley: University of California Press, 1969).

11. Mimi Thi Nguyen and Thuy Linh Nguyen, eds., *Alien Encounters: Popular Culture in Asian America* (Durham, NC Duke University Press, 2007), 6.

12. Catharine Stimpson, "Female Insubordination and the Text," in *Women of Culture and Politics: A Century of Change*, ed. Judith Freelander, Blanche Wiesen Cook, Alice Kessler-Harris and Carroll Smith-Rosenberg (Bloomington: Indiana University Press, 1986), 165–169.

13. bell hooks, *Talking Back: Thinking Feminist, Thinking Black* (Toronto, ON: Between the Lines, 1989); Hill Collins, *Black Feminist Thought*, 10.

14. Joyce Antler, ed., *Talking Back: Images of Jewish Women in American Popular Culture* (Hanover, NH: Brandeis University Press, 1997).

15. Antler, *Talking Back*, 3.

16. Lisa Lowe, *Immigrant Acts: On Asian American Cultural Politics* (Durham, NC: Duke University Press, 1996).

17. Tricia Rose, *Black Noise: Rap Music and Black Culture in Contemporary America* (Hanover, CT: Wesleyan University Press, 1994).

Part I

Film Images

Out of Focus

Chapter One

Ideological Racism and Cultural Resistance

Constructing Our Own Images

Yen Le Espiritu

Racist and gendered immigration policies and labor conditions have worked in tandem to keep Asian Americans in an assigned, subordinate place. But as is evident from the stereotypes listed above, besides structural discrimination, Asian American women and men have been subject to ideological assaults. Focusing on the ideological dimension of Asian American oppression, this chapter examines the cultural symbols—or what Patricia Hill Collins (1991) called "controlling images" (pp. 67–68)—generated by the dominant group to help justify the economic exploitation and social oppression of Asian American women and men over time. Writing on the objectification of black women, Collins (1991) observed that the exercise of political-economic domination by racial elites "always involves attempts to objectify the subordinate group" (p. 69). Transmitted through cultural institutions owned, controlled, or supported by various elites, these "controlling images" naturalize racism, sexism, and poverty by branding subordinate groups as alternatively inferior, threatening, or praiseworthy. These controlling images form part of a larger system of what Donald G. Baker (1983) referred to as "psychosocial dominance" (p. 37). Along with the threat and occasional use of violence, the psychosocial form of control conditions the subject minority to become the stereotype, to "live it, talk it, embrace it, measure group and individual worth in its terms, and believe it" (Chin and Chan, 1972, pp. 66–67). In so doing, minority members reject their own individual and group identity and accept in its stead "a white supremacist complex that establishes the primacy of Euro-American cultural practices and social institutions"

3

(Hamamoto, 1994, p. 2). But the objectification of Asian Americans as the exotic and inferior "other" has never been absolute. Asian Americans have always, but particularly since the 1960s, resisted race, class, and gender exploitation not only through political and economic struggles but also through cultural activism. This chapter surveys the range of oppositional projects in which Asian American cultural workers have engaged to deconstruct the conceptual apparatus of the dominant group and to defend Asian American manhood and womanhood. My goal is to understand how the internalization and renunciation of these stereotypes have shaped sexual and gender politics within Asian America. In particular, I explore the conflicting politics of gender between Asian American women and men as they negotiate the difficult terrain of cultural nationalism—the construction of an anti-assimilationist, native Asian American subject—and gender identities. This chapter draws heavily from the fields of cultural studies and literary criticism.

YELLOW PERIL, CHARLIE CHAN, AND SUZIE WONG

A central aspect of racial exploitation centers on defining people of color as "the other" (Said, 1979). The social construction of Asian American "otherness"—through such controlling images as the Yellow Peril, the model minority, the Dragon Lady, and the China Doll—is "the precondition for their cultural marginalization, political impotence, and psychic alienation from mainstream American society" (Hamamoto, 1994, p. 5). As indicated by these stereotypes, representations of gender and sexuality figure strongly in the articulation of racism. These racist stereotypes collapse gender and sexuality: Asian men have been constructed as hyper-masculine, in the image of the "Yellow Peril," but also as effeminate, in the image of the "model minority," and Asian women have been depicted as super-feminine, in the image of the "China Doll," but also as castrating, in the image of the "Dragon Lady" (Mullings, 1994, pp. 279–80; Okihiro, 1995). As Mary Ann Doane (1991) suggested, sexuality is "indissociable from the effects of polarization and differentiation, often linking them to structures of power and domination" (p. 217). In the Asian American case, the gendering of ethnicity—the process whereby white ideology assigns selected gender characteristics to various ethnic "others"—cast Asian American men and women as simultaneously masculine and feminine but also as neither masculine nor feminine. On the one hand, as part of the Yellow Peril, Asian American women and men have been depicted as a masculine threat that needs to be contained. On the other hand, both sexes have been skewed toward the female side: an indication of the group's marginalization in U.S. society and its role as the compliant "model minority" in contemporary U.S. cultural ideology. Although an apparent disjunction, both the feminization and masculinization of Asian men and women exist to define and confirm the white man's superiority (Kim, 1990).

THE YELLOW PERIL

In the United States, Asia and America—East and West—are viewed as mutually exclusive binaries (Kim, 1993, p. viii). Within this exclusive binary system, Asian Americans, even as citizens, are designated Asians, not Americans. Characterizing Asian Americans as "permanent house guests in the house of America," Sau-Ling Cynthia Wong (1993) stated that "Asian Americans are put in the niche of the 'unassimilable alien': . . . they are alleged to be self-disqualified from full American membership by materialistic motives, questionable political allegiance, and, above all, outlandish, overripe, 'Oriental' cultures" (p. 6). Sonia Shah (1994) defined this form of "cultural discrimination" as a "peculiar blend of cultural and sexist oppression based on our accents, our clothes, our foods, our values and our commitments" (p. 182). This cultural discrimination brands Asians as perpetual foreigners and thus perpetuates the notion of their alleged racial unassimilability.

As the unassimilable alien, Asian Americans embody for many other Americans the Yellow Peril—the threat that Asians will one day unite and conquer the world. This threat includes military invasion and foreign trade from Asia, competition to white labor from Asian labor, the alleged moral degeneracy of Asian people, and potential miscegenation between whites and Asians (Wu, 1982, p. 1). Between 1850 and 1940, U.S. popular media consistently portrayed Asian men as a military threat to the security and welfare of the United States and as a sexual danger to innocent white women (Wu, 1982). In numerous dime novels, movies, and comic strips, Asians appeared as feral, rat-faced men lusting after virginal white women. Arguing for racial purity, these popular media depicted Asian-white sexual union as "at best, a form of beastly sodomy, and, at worst, a Satanic marriage" (Hoppenstand, 1983, p. 174). In these popular depictions, the white man was the desirable sexual partner and the hero who rescued the white woman from "a fate worse than death" (Hoppenstand, 1983, pp. 174–75). By the mid-1880s, hundreds of garishly illustrated and garishly written dime novels were being disseminated among a wide audience, sporting such sensational titles as *The Bradys and the Yellow Crooks, The Chase for the Chinese Diamonds, The Opium*

Den Detective, and *The Stranglers of New York*. As portrayed in these dime novels, the Yellow Peril was the Chinatown district of a big city "in which decent, honest white folk never ventured" (Hoppenstand, 1983, p. 177).

In twentieth-century U.S. popular media, the Japanese joined the Chinese as a perceived threat to Europe and the United States (Wu, 1982, p. 2). In 1916, William Randolph Hearst produced and distributed *Petria*, a movie about a group of fanatical Japanese who invade the United States and attempt to rape a white woman (Quinsaat, 1976, p. 265). After the Japanese bombing of Pearl Harbor on December 7, 1941, the entire Yellow Peril stereotype became incorporated in the nation's war propaganda, quickly whipping white Americans into a war fever. Along with the print media, Hollywood cranked up its anti-Japanese propaganda and produced dozens of war films that centered on the Japanese menace. The fiction of the Yellow Peril stereotype became intertwined with the fact of the United States war with Japan, and the two became one in the mind-set of the American public (Hoppenstand, 1983, pp. 182–83). It was fear of the Yellow Peril—fear of the rise of nonwhite people and their contestation of white supremacy—that led to the declaration of martial law in Hawaii on December 7, 1941, and to the internment of over 110,000 Japanese on the mainland in concentration camps (Okihiro, 1994, p. 137). In subsequent decades, reflecting changing geopolitical concerns, U.S. popular media featured a host of new Yellow Peril stereotypes. During the 1950s Cold War years, in television programs as well as in movies, the Communist Chinese evildoers replaced the Japanese monster; during the Vietnam War of the 1970s, the Vietnamese Communists emerged as the new Oriental villains.

Today, Yellow Perilism takes the forms of the greedy, calculating, and clever Japanese businessman aggressively buying up U.S. real estate and cultural institutions and the super achieving but non-assimilating Asian Americans (Hagedorn, 1993, p. xxii). In a time of rising economic powers in Asia, declining economic opportunities in the United States, and growing diversity among America's people, this new Yellow Perilism—the depiction of Asia and Asian Americans as economic and cultural threats to mainstream United States—supplies white Americans with a united identity and provides ideological justification for U.S. isolationist policy toward Asia, increasing restrictions against Asian (and Latino) immigration, [1] and the invisible institutional racism and visible violence against Asians in the United States (Okihiro, 1994, pp. 138–39).

THE RACIAL CONSTRUCTION OF ASIAN AMERICAN MANHOOD

Like other men of color, Asian American men have been excluded from white-based cultural notions of the masculine. Whereas white men are depicted both as virile and as protectors of women, Asian men have been characterized both as asexual and as oversexed. As Viet Thanh Nguyen (2002) explains, legislation and popular rhetoric at the turn of the twentieth century reflected fears about the "threats" of Chinese immigrant men's non-normative sexuality: "The asexuality of Chinese immigrants, an aspect of their inhuman dedication to work, threatened white labor, while their contradictory voracious sexuality threatened white womanhood and white patriarchy" (p. 90). It is important to note the historical contexts of these seemingly divergent representations of Asian American manhood. The racist depictions of Asian men as "lascivious and predatory" were especially pronounced during the nativist movement against Asians at the turn of the century (Frankenberg, 1993, pp. 75–76). The exclusion of Asian women from the United States and the subsequent establishment of "bachelor societies" eventually reversed the construction of Asian masculinity from "hypersexual" to "asexual" and "homosexual." The contemporary model-minority stereotype further emasculates Asian American men as passive and malleable. As David Eng (2001) writes, "feminization is a crucial issue that plagued Asian American male subjectivity throughout the nineteenth and twentieth centuries" (p. 210). Disseminated and perpetuated through the popular media, these stereotypes of the emasculated Asian male construct a reality in which social and economic discrimination against these men appears defensible. As an example, the desexualization of Asian men naturalized their inability to establish conjugal families in pre-World War II United States. Gliding over race-based exclusion laws that banned the immigration of most Asian women and antimiscegenation laws that prohibited men of color from marrying white women, these dual images of the eunuch and the rapist attributed the "womanless households" characteristic of prewar Asian America to Asian men's lack of sexual prowess and desirability.

A popular controlling image applied to Asian American men is that of the sinister Oriental—a brilliant, powerful villain who plots the destruction of Western civilization. The tales of Fu Manchu, popularized in books and in the comics, and on film, television, and the radio over a forty-year span, "harnessed the great tradition of Orientalism to the purposes of Yellow Peril hysteria" (Lee, 1999, p. 114). The archetype of villainy, Fu Manchu combines Western science with Eastern magic and commands an army of devoted assassins (Hoppenstand, 1983, p. 178). Though ruthless, Fu Manchu lacks masculine heterosexual prowess (Wang, 1988, p. 19). Frank Chin and

Jeffrey Chan (1972), in a critique of the desexualization of Asian men in Western culture, described how the Fu Manchu character undermines Chinese American virility:

> Dr. Fu, a man wearing a long dress, batting his eyelashes, surrounded by muscular black servants in loin cloths, and with his habit of caressingly touching white men on the leg, wrist, and face with his long fingernails is not so much a threat as he is a frivolous offense to white manhood. (p. 60)

In another critique that glorifies male aggression, Frank Chin (1972) contrasted the neuterlike characteristics assigned to Asian men to the (hetero) sexually aggressive images associated with other men of color: "Unlike the white stereotype of the evil black stud, Indian rapist, Mexican macho, the evil of the evil Dr. Fu Manchu was not sexual, but homosexual" (p. 66). Asian American feminist and queer commentators have long challenged these strict and inflexible notions of Asian American male identity. As David Eng (2001) writes, by staking their cultural nationalist project on the recuperation of a "strident Asian American masculinity and a 'pure,' heroic, Asian martial tradition," Frank Chin, Jeffrey Chan, and other critics unwittingly reinscribe "a dominant system of compulsory heterosexuality with all its attendant misogyny and homophobia" (p. 210). Moreover, the critiques of the desexualization of the Fu Manchu character failed to note that Fu Manchu's power and his sexual attractiveness lie in his ambiguous sexuality—his simultaneous heterosexuality and homoeroticism (Lee, 1999, p. 116).

Whereas the evil Oriental stereotype marks Asian American men as the white man's enemy, the stereotype of the sexless Asian sidekick—Charlie Chan, the Chinese laundryman, the Filipino houseboy—depicts Asian men as devoted and impotent, eager to please. William Wu (1982) reported that the Chinese servant "is the most important single image of the Chinese immigrants" in American fiction about Chinese Americans between 1850 and 1940 (p. 60). More recently, such diverse television programs as *Bachelor Father* (1957–1962), *Bonanza* (1959–1973), *Star Trek* (1966–1969), and *Falcon Crest* (1981–1990) all featured the stock Chinese bachelor domestic who dispenses sage advice to his superiors in addition to performing traditional female functions within the household (Hamamoto, 1994, p. 7). By trapping Chinese men (and by extension, Asian men) in the stereotypical "feminine" tasks of serving white men, American society erases the figure of the Asian "masculine" plantation worker in Hawaii or railroad construction worker in the western United States, thus perpetuating the myth of the androgynous and effeminate Asian man (Goellnicht, 1992, p. 198). This feminization, in turn, confines Asian immigrant men to the segment of the labor force that performs "women's work."

The motion picture industry has been key in the construction of Asian men as sexual deviants. In a study of Asians in U.S. motion pictures, Eugene Franklin Wong (1978) maintained that the movie industry filmically castrates Asian males to magnify the superior sexual status of white males (p. 27). As on-screen sexual rivals of whites, Asian males are neutralized, unable to sexually engage Asian women and prohibited from sexually engaging white women. By saving the white woman from sexual contact with the racial "other," the motion picture industry protects the Anglo-American, bourgeois male establishment from any challenges to its hegemony (Marchetti, 1993, p. 218). At the other extreme, the industry has exploited one of the most potent aspects of the Yellow Peril discourses—the sexual danger of contact between the races—by concocting a sexually threatening portrayal of the licentious and aggressive Yellow Man lusting after the White Woman (Marchetti, 1993, p. 3). Heedful of the larger society's taboos against Asian male-white female sexual union, white male actors donning "yellow face"—instead of Asian male actors— are used in these "love scenes." Nevertheless, the message of the perverse and animalistic Asian male attacking helpless white women is clear (Wong, 1978). Though depicting sexual aggression, this image of the rapist, like that of the eunuch, casts Asian men as sexually undesirable. As Wong (1978) succinctly stated, in Asian male-white female relations, "There can be rape, but there cannot be romance" (p. 25). Thus, Asian males yield to the sexual superiority of the white males who are permitted filmically to maintain their sexual dominance over both white women and women of color. A young Vietnamese American man describes the damaging effect of these stereotypes on his self-image:

> Every day I was forced to look into a mirror created by white society and its media. As a young Asian man, I shrank before white eyes. I wasn't tall, I wasn't fair, I wasn't muscular, and so on. Combine that with the enormous insecurities any pubescent teenager feels, and I have no difficulty in knowing now why I felt naked before a mass of white people. (Nguyen, 1990, p. 23)

White cultural and institutional racism against Asian males is also reflected in the motion picture industry's preoccupation with the death of Asians—a filmic solution to the threats of the Yellow Peril. In a perceptive analysis of Hollywood's view of Asians in films made from the 1930s to the 1960s, Tom Engelhardt (1976) described how Asians, like Native Americans, are seen by the movie industry as inhuman invaders, ripe for extermination. He argued that the theme of the nonhumanness of Asians prepares the audience to accept, without flinching, "the leveling and nearobliteration of three Asian areas in the course of three decades" (Engelhardt, 1976, p. 273). The industry's death theme, though applying to all Asians, is mainly focused on Asian males, with Asian females reserved for sexual purposes (Wong, 1978, p. 35).

Especially in war films, Asian males, however advantageous their initial position, inevitably perish at the hands of the superior white males (Wong, 1978, p. 34).

THE RACIAL CONSTRUCTION OF ASIAN AMERICAN WOMANHOOD

Like Asian men, Asian women have been reduced to one-dimensional caricatures in Western representation. The condensation of Asian women's multiple differences into gross character types—mysterious, feminine, and non-white—obscures the social injustice of racial, class, and gender oppression (Marchetti, 1993, p. 71). Both Western film and literature promote dichotomous stereotypes of the Asian woman: either she is the cunning Dragon Lady or the servile Lotus Blossom Baby (Tong, 1994, p. 197). Though connoting two extremes, these stereotypes are interrelated: both eroticize Asian women as exotic "others"—sensuous, promiscuous, but untrustworthy. Whereas American popular culture denies "manhood" to Asian men, it endows Asian women with an excess of "womanhood," sexualizing them but also impugning their sexuality. In this process, both sexism and racism have been blended together to produce the sexualization of white racism (Wong, 1978, p. 260). Linking the controlling images of Asian men and women, Elaine Kim (1990) suggested that Asian women are portrayed as sexual for the same reason that men are asexual: "Both exist to define the white man's virility and the white man's superiority" (p. 70).

As the racialized exotic "others," Asian American women do not fit the white-constructed notions of the feminine. Whereas white women have been depicted as chaste and dependable, Asian women have been represented as promiscuous and untrustworthy. In a mirror image of the evil Fu Manchu, the Asian woman was portrayed as the castrating Dragon Lady who, while puffing on her foot-long cigarette holder, could poison a man as easily as she could seduce him. "With her talon-like six-inch fingernails, her skin-tight satin dress slit to the thigh," the Dragon Lady is desirable, deceitful, and dangerous (Ling, 1990, p. 11). In the 1924 film *The Thief of Baghdad*, Anna May Wong, a pioneer Chinese American actress, played a handmaid who employed treachery to help an evil Mongol prince attempt to win the hand of the Princess of Baghdad (Tajima, 1989, p. 309). In so doing, Wong unwittingly popularized a common Dragon Lady social type: treacherous women who are partners in crime with men of their own kind. The publication of *Daughter of Fu Manchu* (1931) firmly entrenched the Dragon Lady image in white consciousness. Carrying on her father's work as the champion of Asian hegemony over the white race, Fah Lo Sue exhibited, in the words of

American studies scholar William F. Wu, "exotic sensuality, sexual avail-
ability to a white man, and a treacherous nature" (cited in Tong, 1994, p.
197). A few years later, in 1934, Milton Caniff inserted into his adventure
comic strip *Terry and the Pirates* another version of the Dragon Lady who
"combines all the best features of past moustache twirlers with the lure of the
handsome wench" (Hoppenstand, 1983, p. 178). As such, Caniff's Dragon
Lady fuses the image of the evil male Oriental mastermind with that of the
Oriental prostitute first introduced some fifty years earlier in the dime novels.
In the 1870s and 1880s, newspapers, magazines, and public officials in Western cities characterized the Chinese or Japanese prostitute as a conduit of
disease and social decay, thereby providing a major weapon for those supporting the prohibition of Asian immigration to the United States (Lee, 1999,
p. 89).

At the opposite end of the spectrum is the Lotus Blossom stereotype,
reincarnated throughout the years as the China Doll, the Geisha Girl, the War
Bride, or the Vietnamese prostitute—many of whom are the spoils of the last
three wars fought in Asia (Tajima, 1989, p. 309). Demure, diminutive, and
deferential, the Lotus Blossom Baby is "modest, tittering behind her delicate
ivory hand, eyes downcast, always walking ten steps behind her man, and,
best of all, devot[ing] body and soul to serving him" (Ling, 1990, p. 11).
Interchangeable in appearance and name, these women have no voice; their
"nonlanguage" includes uninterpretable chattering, pidgin English, giggling,
or silence (Tajima, 1989). These stereotypes of Asian women as submissive
and dainty sex objects not only have impeded women's economic mobility
but also have fostered an enormous demand for X-rated films and porno-
graphic materials featuring Asian women in bondage, for "Oriental" bath-
house workers in U.S. cities, and for Asian mail-order brides (Kim, 1984, p.
64).

SEXISM, RACISM, AND LOVE

The racialization of Asian manhood and womanhood upholds white masculine hegemony. Cast as sexually available, Asian women become yet another
possession of the white man. In motion pictures and network television programs, interracial sexuality, though rare, occurs principally between a white
male and an Asian female. A combination of sexism and racism makes this
form of miscegenation more acceptable: Race mixing between an Asian male
and a white female would upset not only racial taboos but also those that
attend patriarchal authority as well (Hamamoto, 1994, p. 39). Whereas Asian
men are depicted as either the threatening rapist or the impotent eunuch,
white men are endowed with the masculine attributes with which to sexually

attract the Asian woman. Such popular television shows as *Gunsmoke* (1955–1975) and *How the West Was Won* (1978–1979) clearly articulate the theme of Asian female sexual possession by the white male. In these shows, only white males have the prerogative to cross racial boundaries and to choose freely from among women of color as sex partners. Within a system of racial and gender oppression, the sexual possession of women and men of color by white men becomes yet another means of enforcing unequal power relations (Hamamoto, 1994, p. 46).

The preference for white male–Asian female is also prevalent in contemporary television news broadcasting, such as in the successful 1993–1995 pairing of Dan Rather and Connie Chung as coanchors of the *CBS Evening News*. Moreover, while female Asian American anchorpersons are popular television news figures, there is a near total absence of Asian American men. A 2002 study by the University of California's Annenberg School of Journalism of twenty-five major markets identified about one hundred Asian American reporters and anchors, only twenty of them men. In other words, Asian American women outnumbered men by five to one (Geisler, 2004). Critics argue that this is so because the white male hiring establishment, and presumably the larger American public, feels more comfortable (i.e., less threatened) seeing a white male sitting next to a minority female at the anchor desk than the reverse. Stephen Tschida of WDBJ-TV (Roanoke, Virginia), one of only a handful of male Asian American television news anchors, was informed early in his career that he did not have the proper "look" to qualify for the anchorperson position. Other male broadcast news veterans have reported being passed over for younger, more beauteous, female Asian Americans (Hamamoto, 1994, p. 245). This gender imbalance sustains the construction of Asian American women as more successful, assimilated, attractive, and desirable than their male counterparts.

To win the love of white men, Asian women must reject not only Asian men but also their culture. Many Hollywood narratives featuring romances between Anglo American men and Asian women follow the popular Pocahontas mythos: the Asian woman, out of devotion for her white American lover, betrays her own people and commits herself to the dominant white culture by dying, longing for, or going to live with her white husband in his country. For example, in the various versions of Miss Saigon , the contemporary version of Madame Butterfly, the tragic Vietnamese prostitute eternally longs for the white boy soldier who has long abandoned her and their son (Hagedorn, 1993, p. xxii). These tales of interracial romance inevitably have a tragic ending. The Asian partner usually dies, thus providing a cinematic resolution to the moral lapse of the Westerner. The Pocahontas paradigm can be read as a narrative of salvation; the Asian woman is saved either spiritually or morally from the excesses of her own culture, just as she physically saves her Western lover from the moral degeneracy of her own people (Marchetti, 1993, p. 218). For Asian women, who are marginalized not only by gender but also by class, race, or ethnicity, the interracial romance narratives promise "the American Dream of abundance, protection, individual choice, and freedom from the strictures of a traditional society in the paternalistic name of heterosexual romance" (Marchetti, 1993, p. 91). These narratives also carry a covert political message, legitimizing a masculinized Anglo American rule over a submissive, feminized Asia. The motion picture *China Gate* (1957), by Samuel Fuller, and the network television program *The Lady from Yesterday* (1985), for example, promote an image of Vietnam that legitimizes American rule. Seduced by images of U.S. abundance, a feminized Vietnam sacrifices herself for the possibility of future incorporation into America, the land of individual freedom and economic opportunities. Thus, the interracial tales function not only as a romantic defense of traditional female roles within the patriarchy but also as a political justification of American hegemony in Asia (Marchetti, 1993, p. 108).

Fetishized as the embodiment of perfect womanhood and genuine exotic femininity, Asian women are pitted against their more modern, emancipated Western sisters (Tajima, 1989). In two popular motion pictures, *Love Is a Many-Splendored Thing* (1955) and *The World of Suzie Wong* (1960), the white women remain independent and potentially threatening, whereas both Suyin and Suzie give up their independence in the name of love. Thus, the white female characters are cast as calculating, suffocating, and thoroughly undesirable, whereas the Asian female characters are depicted as truly "feminine"—passive, subservient, dependent, and domestic. Implicitly, these films warn white women to embrace the socially constructed passive Asian beauty as the feminine ideal if they want to attract and keep a man. In pitting white women against Asian women, Hollywood affirms white male identity against the threat of emerging feminism and the concomitant changes in gender relations (Marchetti, 1993, pp. 115–16). As Robyn Wiegman (1991) observed, the absorption of women of color into gender categories traditionally reserved for white women is "part of a broader program of hegemonic recuperation, a program that has at its main focus the reconstruction of white masculine power" (p. 320). It is also important to note that as the racialized exotic "other," Asian women do not replace but merely substitute for white women, and thus will be readily dismissed once the "real" mistress returns.

The controlling images of Asian men and Asian women, exaggerated out of all proportion in Western representation, have created resentment and tension between Asian American women and men. Given this cultural milieu, many American-born Asians do not think of other Asians in sexual terms (Fung, 1994, p. 163). In particular, due to the persistent desexualization of the Asian male, many Asian females do not perceive their ethnic counterparts as desirable marriage partners (Hamamoto, 1992, p. 42). In so doing, these women unwittingly enforce the Eurocentric gender ideology that objectifies both sexes and racializes all Asians (see Collins, 1991, pp. 185–86). In a column to *Asian Week*, a weekly Asian American newspaper, Daniel Yoon (1993) reported that at a dinner discussion hosted by the Asian American Students Association at his college, the Asian American women in the room proceeded, one after another, to describe how "Asian American men were too passive, too weak, too boring, too traditional, too abusive, too domineering, too ugly, too greasy, too short, too . . . Asian. Several described how they preferred white men, and how they never had and never would date an Asian man" (p. 16). Partly as a result of the racist constructions of Asian American womanhood and manhood and their acceptance by Asian Americans, intermarriage patterns are high, with Asian American women intermarrying at a much higher rate than Asian American men. Moreover, Asian women involved in intermarriage have usually married white partners (Agbayani-Siewert and Revilla, 1995, p. 156; Min, 1995, p. 22; Nishi, 1995, p. 128). In part, these intermarriage patterns reflect the sexualization of white racism that constructs white men as the most desirable sexual partners, frowns on Asian male–white women relations, and fetishizes Asian women as the embodiment of perfect womanhood. Viewed in this light, the high rate of outmarriage for Asian American women is the "material outcome of an interlocking system of sexism and racism" (Hamamoto, 1992, p. 42).

CULTURAL RESISTANCE: RECONSTRUCTING OUR OWN IMAGES

"One day/I going to write/about you," wrote Lois-Ann Yamanaka (1993) in "Empty Heart" (p. 548). And Asian Americans did write—"to inscribe our faces on the blank pages and screens of America's hegemonic culture" (Kim, 1993, p. xii). As a result, Asian Americans' objectification as the exotic aliens who are different from, and other than, Euro-Americans has never been absolute. Within the confines of race, class, and gender oppression, Asian Americans have maintained independent self-definitions, challenging controlling images and replacing them with Asian American standpoints. The civil rights and ethnic studies movements of the late 1960s were training grounds for Asian American cultural workers and the development of oppo-sitional projects. Grounded in the U.S. black power movement and in antico-lonial struggles of Third World countries, Asian American antihegemonic projects have been unified by a common goal of articulating cultural resis-tance. Given the historical distortions and misrepresentations of Asian Americans in mainstream media, most cultural projects produced by Asian American women and men perform the important tasks of correcting histories, shaping legacies, creating new cultures, constructing a politics of resistance, and opening spaces for the forcibly excluded (Kim, 1993, p. xiii; Fung, 1994, p. 165).

Fighting the exoticization of Asian Americans has been central in the ongoing work of cultural resistance. As discussed above, Asian Americans, however rooted in this country, are represented as recent transplants from Asia or as bearers of an exotic culture. The Chinese American playwright Frank Chin noted that New York critics of his play *Chickencoop Chinaman* complained in the early 1970s that his characters did not speak, dress, or act "like Orientals" (Kim, 1982, p. xv). Similarly, a reviewer described Maxine Hong Kingston's *The Woman Warrior* as a tale of "East meets West" and praised the book for its "myths rich and varied as Chinese brocade"—even though *The Woman Warrior* is deliberately antiexotic and antinostalgic (quoted in Kim, 1982, p. xvi). In both of these examples, the qualifier American has been blithely excised from the term Asian American.

Asian American cultural workers simply do not accept the exotic, one-dimensional caricatures of themselves in U.S. mass media. In the preface of *Aiiieeeee!*, a landmark collection of Asian American writers (in this case, Chinese, Japanese, and Filipinos), published in the mid-1970s, the editors announced that the anthology, and the title *Aiiieeeee!* itself, challenged the exoticization of Asian Americans:

> The pushers of white American culture . . . pictured the yellow man as something that when wounded, sad, angry, or swearing, or wondering whined, shouted, or screamed "aiiieeeee!" Asian America, so long ignored and forcibly excluded from creative participation in American culture, is wounded, sad, angry, swearing, and wondering, and this is his AIIIEEEEE!!! It is more than a whine, shout, or scream. It is fifty years of our whole voice. (Chan et al., 1974, p. xii)

The publication of *Aiiieeeee!* gave Asian American writers visibility and credibility and sparked other oppositional projects. Jessica Hagedorn, a Filipina American writer, described the legacy of *Aiiieeeee!*: "We could not be ignored; suddenly, we were no longer silent. Like other writers of color in America, we were beginning to challenge the long-cherished concepts of a xenophobic literary canon dominated by white heterosexual males" (Hagedorn, 1993, p. xviii). Inspired by *Aiiieeeee!* and by other "irreverent and blasphemous" American writers, Hagedorn created an anthology of contemporary Asian American fiction in 1993—"a book I wanted to read but had never been available to me" (Hagedorn, 1993, p. xxx). In the tradition of *Aiiieeeee!*, the title of Hagedorn's anthology, *Charlie Chan Is Dead*, is vigorously political, defying and stamping out the vestiges of a "fake Asian pop icon" (Hagedorn, 1993, p. xxi). In the anthology's preface, Elaine Kim

(1993) contested the homogenization of Asian Americans by juxtaposing the one-dimensional Charlie Chan to the many ways of being Asian American in the contemporary United States:

> Charlie Chan is dead, never to be revived. Gone for good his yellow face asexual bulk, his fortune-cookie English, his stereotypical Orientalist version of "the [Confucian] Chinese family," challenged by an array of characters, some hip and articulate, some brooding and sexy, some insolent and others innocent, but all as unexpected as a Korean American who writes in French, a Chinese-Panamanian-German who longs too late to know her father, a mean Japanese American grandmother, a Chinese American flam-dive, or a teen-aged Filipino American male prostitute. Instead of "model minorities," we find human beings with rich and complex pasts and brave, often flamboyant dreams of the future. (p. xiii)

Taking up this theme, Wayne Wang's commercial film *Chan Is Missing* (1981) offers a range of Chinatown characters who indirectly convey the message that Chinese Americans, like other Americans, are heterogeneous (Chan, 1994, p. 530). "Portraying Asian Americans in all our contradictions and complexities—as exiled, assimilated, rebellious, noble—Asian American cultural projects reveal heterogeneity rather than "producing regulating ideas of cultural unity or integration" (Lowe, 1994, p. 53). In so doing, these projects destabilize the dominant racist discourse that constructs Asians as a homogeneous group who are "all alike" and readily conform to "types" such as the Yellow Peril, the Oriental mastermind, and the sexy Suzie Wong (Lowe, 1991).

During the late 1960s and early 1970s, the first Asian American theatre companies—Los Angeles's East-West Players, Seattle's Northwest Asian American Theatre and New York's Pan Asian Repertory—emerged as a manifestation of the larger Asian American and Third World political/artistic movements. For many Asian American theater activists, the very act of casting an Asian American actor on stage in a leading role was a political statement in itself—an ideological challenge to mainstream theater actors, producers, and audiences (Shimakawa, 2000, p. 286). Asian American theaters also attempt to subvert and reappropriate "Oriental" stereotypes. For example, rather than ignoring the theatrical power stereotypes possess, Philip Kan Gotanda's 1992 play *Yankee Dawg You Die* and David Henry Hwang's 1998 *M. Butterfly* reproduce the grotesque villain or submissive tragic female in order to "rob the stereotype of its power to substitute for the natural or essential being and reveal it as a social construct, the product of specific historical and social circumstances" (Lee, 1997, p. 30). Solo performance, as an alternative theatre, has also become an indispensable part of Asian American culture. Working beyond and oftentimes against the conventions of established theatre companies, Asian American solo performers incorporate multimedia techniques, autobiography, storytelling, ethnicity, gender, and sexuality in their shows. In Lane Nishikawa's 1990 solo show, *I'm on a Mission from Buddha*, he subverted undesirable stereotypes of Asian men and replaced them with a range of real characters as a tribute to actual Asian American men he had known (Lee, 2003, pp. 296–97). In the same way, in Jude Narita's acclaimed one-woman show, *Coming Into Passion/Song For a Sansei*, she calls attention to the intersection of racism, sexism, and imperialism by taking on the personas of six different Asian women, including a Vietnamese bar girl, a Filipino mail-order bride, a Cambodian refugee, and a troubled Sansei teenager—all of whom have experienced abuse, loneliness, and suffering by the actions of Western men (Lee, 2003, p. 297).

Asian American cultural projects also deconstruct the myth of the benevolent United States promised to women and men from Asia. Carlos Bulosan's *America Is in the Heart* (1943/1973), one of the core works of Asian American literature, challenges the narrative of the United States as the land of opportunity. Seduced by the promise of individual freedom through education, the protagonist Carlos discovers that as a Filipino immigrant in the United States, he is denied access to formal schooling. This disjunction between the promise of education and the unequal access of different racial and economic groups to that education—reinforced by Carlos's observations of the exploitation, marginality, and violence suffered by his compatriots in the United States—challenges his faith in the promise of U.S. democracy and abundance (Lowe, 1994, p. 56). John Okada's *No-No Boy* (1957) is another searing indictment of U.S. racist hysteria. In this portrayal of the aftermath of the internment of Japanese Americans during World War II, the protagonist, Ichiro, angrily refuses to adjust to his postinternment and postimprisonment circumstances, thus dramatizing the Asian American subject's refusal to accept the subordinating terms of assimilation (Lowe, 1994, p. 59). In the poem by Cao Tan, "Tomorrow I Will Be Home," a Vietnamese refugee describes the emasculating effect of U.S. society.

To reject the myth of a benevolent United States is also to refute ideological racism: the justification of inequalities through a set of controlling images that attribute physical and intellectual traits to racially defined groups (Hamamoto, 1994, p. 3). In the 1980 autobiographical fiction *China Men*, Maxine Hong Kingston smashed the controlling image of the emasculated Asian man by foregrounding the legalized racism that turned immigrant Chinese "men" into "women" at the turn of the century. In his search for the Gold Mountain, the novel's male protagonist Tang Ao finds instead the Land of Women, where he is caught and transformed into an Oriental courtesan. Because Kingston reveals at the end of the legend that the Land of Women was in North America, readers familiar with Chinese American history will readily see that "the ignominy suffered by Tang Ao in a foreign land symbolizes the emasculation of Chinamen by the dominant culture" (Cheung, 1990, p. 240).

Later in the novel, the father's failure as a provider—his emasculation—inverts the sexual roles in the family. His silence and impotent rage deepen as his wife takes on active power in the family and assumes the "masculine" traits of aggressiveness and authority. As a means of releasing his sense of frustration and powerlessness in racist America, the father lapses into silence, screams "word-less male screams in his sleep," and spouts furious misogynistic curses that frighten his daughter (Sledge, 1980, p. 10). The author/narrator Maxine traces her father's abusive behavior back to his feeling of emasculation in America: "We knew that it was to feed us you had to endure demons and physical labor" (cited in Goellnicht, 1992, p. 201). Similarly, in Louis Chu's 1961 novel *Eat a Bowl of Tea*, protagonist Ben Loy s sexual impotence symptomizes the social powerlessness of generations of segregated Chinatown bachelors prevented by anti-Asian immigration and antimiscegenation laws from establishing a traditional family life—a prerequisite for integration into the U.S. nation-state (Kim, 1982, p. xviii). Foregrounding this long history of institutionalized racism and disenfranchisement that socially emasculated Chinese male immigrants, David Eng (2001, p. 181) reads Loy's impotence not as a personal failure but as a testament to the deliberate and emphatic exclusion of Asian men from U.S. national ideals of a proper masculine citizenry. More recently, Steven Okazaki's film *American Sons* (1995)[2] tells the stories of four Asian American men who reveal how incidents of prejudice and bigotry shaped their identity and affected the way they perceived themselves and society. About his film, Okazaki (1995) explained, "Prejudice, bigotry, and violence twist and demean individual lives. *American Sons* looks at difficult issues, such as hate and violence, in order to show this intimate and disturbing examination of the deep psychological damage that racism causes over generations" (n. p.). Asian American men's increasing involvement in hip-hop—a highly masculinized cultural form and a distinctly American phenomenon—is yet another contemporary denouncement of the stereotype of themselves as "effeminate, nerdy, asocial foreigners" (Choe, 1996). By exposing the role of the larger society in the emasculation and oppression of Asian men, Kingston, Chu, and Okazaki denaturalized and denormalized Asian men's asexuality in U.S. popular culture.

Finally, Asian American cultural workers reject the narrative of salvation: the myth that Asian women (and a feminized Asia) are saved, through sexual relations with white men (and a masculinized United States), from the excesses of their own culture. Instead, they underscore the considerable potential for abuse in these inherently unequal relationships. Writing in Vietnamese, transplanted Vietnamese writer Tran Dieu Hang described the gloomy existence of Vietnamese women in sexist and racist U.S. society—an accursed land that singles out women, especially immigrant women, for oppression and violence. Her short story "Roi Ngay Van Moi" ("There Will Come New Days," 1986) depicts the brutal rape of a young refugee woman by her American sponsor despite her tearful pleas in limited English (Tran, 1993, pp. 72–73). Marianne Villanueva's short story "Opportunity" (1991) also calls attention to the sexualization and racialization of Asian women. As the protagonist Nina, a "mail-order bride" from the Philippines, enters the hotel lobby to meet her American fiance, the bellboys snicker and whisper *puta*, whore: a reminder that U.S. economic and cultural colonization of the Philippines always forms the backdrop to any relations between Filipinos and Americans (Wong, 1993, p. 53). Characterizing Filipino American literature as a "literature of exile," Oscar Campomanes (1992) underscored the legacy of U.S. colonization of the Philippines: "The signifiers 'Filipinos' and 'Philippines' evoke colonialist meanings and cultural redactions which possess inordinate power to shape the fates of the writers and of Filipino peoples everywhere" (p. 52). Theresa Hak Kyung Cha's *Dictee* (1982), a Korean American text, likewise challenges the myth of U.S. benevolence in Asia by tracing the impact of colonial and imperial damage and dislocation on the Korean subject (Lowe, 1994, p. 61). *Sa-I-Gu*, an independent video about the aftermath of the 1992 Los Angeles race riots, further illuminates the failure of immigration for first-generation Korean women. Consisting of taped interviews with six first-generation Korean women, all of whom had their businesses destroyed during the 1992 riots, the video details how immigration has brought them financial loss, not gain; how their businesses were funded with capital from the homeland, not resources amassed in the United States; and how their family life has deteriorated as a result of immigration (James, 1999, p. 166). As Sau-Ling Cynthia Wong (1993) suggested, "To the extent that most typical cases of Asian immigration to the United States stem from an imbalance of resources writ large in the world economy, it holds in itself the seed of exploitation" (p. 53).

CONTROLLING IMAGES, GENDER, AND CULTURAL NATIONALISM

Cultural nationalism has been crucial in Asian Americans' struggles for self-determination. Emerging in the early 1970s, this unitary Asian American identity was primarily racial, male, and heterosexual. Asian American literature produced in those years highlighted Chinese and Japanese American male perspectives, obscuring gender and other intercommunity differences (Kim, 1993). Asian American male writers, concerned with recuperating their identities as men and as Americans, objectified both white and Asian women in their writings (Kim, 1990, p. 70). In a controversial essay titled "Racist Love," Frank Chin and Jeffrey Paul Chan (1972) pointed to the stereotype of the emasculated Asian American man:

> The white stereotype of the Asian is unique in that it is the only racial stereo-
> type completely devoid of manhood. Our nobility is that of an efficient house-
> wife. At our worst we are contemptible because we are womanly, effeminate,
> devoid of all the traditionally masculine qualities of originality, daring, physi-
> cal courage, creativity. (p. 68)

In taking whites to task for their racist debasement of Asian American men,
however, Chin and Chan succumbed to the influence of Eurocentric gender
ideology, particularly its emphasis on oppositional dichotomous sex roles
(Collins, 1991, p. 184). As Nguyen (2002) argues, Chin frequently collapses
emasculation into feminization: "for Chin, there is little difference between
being less than a man and being a woman" (p. 104). In a critique of "Racist
Love," King-Kok Cheung (1990) contended that Chin and Chan buttressed
patriarchy "by invoking gender stereotypes, by disparaging domestic effi-
ciency as 'feminine,' and by slotting desirable traits such as originality, daring, physical courage, and creativity under the rubric of masculinity" (p.
237). Similarly, Wong (1993) argued that in their influential "Introduction"
to *Aiiieeeee! An Anthology of Asian American Writers* (1974), Chan, Chin,
Inada, and Wong operated on the premise that a true Asian American sen-
sibility is "non-Christian, nonfeminine and nonimmigrant" (p. 8).

Though limited and limiting, a masculinist cultural nationalist agenda
appealed to Asian American activists because of its potential to oppose and
disrupt the logic of racial domination. In the following excerpt, Elaine Kim
(1993), a pioneer in the field of Asian American literature, explained the
appeal of cultural nationalism:

> Certainly it was possible for me as a Korean American female to accept the
> fixed masculinist Asian American identity posited in Asian American cultural
> nationalism, even when it rendered invisible or at least muted women's op-
> pression, anger, and ways of loving and interpreted Korean Americans as
> imperfect imitations of Chinese Americans; because I could see in everyday
> life that not all material and psychic violence to women of color comes from
> men, and because, as my friends used to say, "No Chinese [American] ever
> called me a 'Gook.'" (p. x)

Kim's statement suggests that for Asian American women, and for other
women of color, gender is only a part of a larger pattern of unequal social
relations. Despite the constraints of patriarchy, racism inscribes these wom-
en's lives and binds them to Asian American men in what Collins (1991)
called a "love and trouble" tradition (p. 184).

Because the racial oppression of Asian Americans involves the "feminization" of Asian men (Said, 1979), Asian American women are caught
between the need to expose the problems of male privilege and the desire to
unite with men to contest the overarching racial ideology that confines them

both. As Cheung (1990) suggested, Asian American women may be simultaneously sympathetic and angry toward the men in their ethnic community: sensitive to the men's marginality but resentful of their sexism (p. 239). Maxine Hong Kingston's writings seem to reflect these conflicting emotions. As discussed above, in the opening legend of *China Men*, the male protagonist Tang Ao is captured in the Land of Women (North America), where he is forced to become a woman—to have his feet bound, his ears pierced, his eyebrows plucked, his cheeks and lips painted. Cheung (1990) argued that this legend is double-edged, pointing not only to the racist debasement of Chinese Americans in their adopted country but also to the subjugation of Chinese women both in China and in the United States (p. 240). Although the effeminization suffered by Tang Ao is brutal, it is the same mutilation that many Chinese women were for centuries forced to bear. According to Goellnicht's (1992) reading of Kingston's work, this opening myth suggests that the author both deplores the emasculation of her forefathers by mainstream America and critiques the Confucian patriarchal practices of her ancestral homeland (p. 194). In *China Men*, Kingston also showed no acceptance of sexist practices by immigrant men. The father in this novel/autobiography is depicted as a broken man who attempts to reassert male authority by denigrating those who are even more powerless—the women and children in his family (Cheung, 1990, p. 241; Goellnicht, 1992, p. 200).

Along the same lines, Maxine Hong Kingston's *The Woman Warrior* (1977) reveals the narrator's contradictory attitudes toward her childhood "home," which is simultaneously a site of "woman hatred" and an area of resistance against the racism of the dominant culture. The community that nourishes her imagination and suffuses her with warmth is the same community that relegates women to an inferior position, limiting them to the role of serving men (Rabine, 1987, pp. 477–78). In the following passage, the narrator voices her mixed feelings toward the Chinese American community:

> I looked at their ink drawings of poor people snagging their neighbors' flotage with long flood hooks and pushing the girl babies on down the river. And I had to get out of hating range. . . . I refuse to shy my way anymore through our Chinatown, which tasks me with the old sayings and the stories. The swordswoman and I are not so dissimilar. May my people understand the resemblance so that I can return to them. (Kingston, 1977, p. 62)

Similarly, in a critique of Asian American sexual politics, Kayo Hatta's short video *Otemba* (1988) depicts a girl's-eye view of the final days of her mother's pregnancy as her father hopes and prays for the birth of a boy (see Tajima, 1991, p. 26).

Stripped of the privileges of masculinity, some Asian American men have attempted to reassert male authority by subordinating feminism to nationalist concerns. Lisa Lowe (1991) argued that this identity politics displaces gender differences into a false opposition of "nationalism" and "assimilation." From this limited perspective, Asian American feminists who expose Asian American sexism are cast as "assimilationist," as betraying Asian American "nationalism." Maxine Hong Kingston's *The Woman Warrior* (1977) and Amy Tan's *The Joy Luck Club* (1989) are the targets of such nationalist criticisms. Frank Chin, Ben Tong, and others have accused these and other women novelists of feminizing Asian American literature by exaggerating the community's patriarchal structure, thus undermining the power of Asian American men to combat the racist stereotypes of the dominant white culture. For example, when Kingston's *The Woman Warrior* received favorable reviews, Chin accused her of attempting to "cash in on the feminist fad" (Chan, 1994, p. 528). Another Asian American male had this to say about the movie *The Joy Luck Club*:

> The movie was powerful. But it could have been powerful and inclusive, if at least one of the Asian male characters was portrayed as something other than monstrously evil or simply wimpy. We are used to this message coming out of Hollywood, but it disturbed me deeply to hear the same message coming from Amy Tan and Wayne Wang—people of my own color. (Yoon, 1993)

Whereas Chin and others cast this tension in terms of nationalism and assimilationism, Lisa Lowe (1991) argued that it is more a debate between nationalist and feminist concerns in Asian American discourse. This insistence on a fixed masculinist identity, according to Lowe (1991), "can be itself a colonial figure used to displace the challenges of heterogeneity, or subalternity, by casting them as assimilationist or anti-ethnic" (pp. 33–34).

But cultural nationalism need not be patriarchal. Rejecting the ideology of oppositional dichotomous sex roles, Asian American cultural workers have also engaged in cross-gender projects. In a review of Asian American independent filmmaking, Renee Tajima (1991) reported that some of the best feminist films have been made by Asian American men. For example, Arthur Dong's *Lotus* (1987) exposes women's exploitation through the practice of footbinding (Tajima, 1991, p. 24). Asian American men have also made use of personal documentary, in both diary and autobiographical form—an approach known to be the realm of women filmmakers. Finally, there is no particular gender affiliation in subject matters: just as Arthur Dong profiles his mother in *Sewing Woman*, Lori Tsang portrays her father's life in *Chinamans Choice* (Tajima, 1991, p. 24).

CONCLUSION

Ideological representations of gender and sexuality are central in the exercise and maintenance of racial, patriarchal, and class domination. In the Asian American case, this ideological racism has taken seemingly contrasting forms: Asian men have been cast as both hypersexual and asexual, and Asian women have been rendered both superfeminine and masculine. Although in apparent disjunction, both forms exist to define, maintain, and justify white male supremacy. The racialization of Asian American manhood and womanhood underscores the interconnections of race, gender, and class. As categories of difference, race and gender relations do not parallel but intersect and confirm each other, and it is the complicity among these categories of difference that enables U.S. elites to justify and maintain their cultural, social, and economic power. Responding to the ideological assaults on their gender identities, Asian American cultural workers have engaged in a wide range of oppositional projects to defend Asian American manhood and womanhood. In the process, some have embraced a masculinist cultural nationalism, a stance that marginalizes Asian American women and their needs. Though sensitive to the emasculation of Asian American men, Asian American feminists have pointed out that Asian American nationalism insists on a fixed masculinist identity, thus obscuring gender differences. Though divergent, both the nationalist and feminist positions advance the dichotomous stance of man or woman, gender or race or class, without recognizing the complex relationality of these categories of oppression. It is only when Asian Americans recognize the intersections of race, gender, and class that we can transform the existing hierarchical structure.

NOTES

1. In recent years, Asian Americans' rising consciousness, coupled with their phenomenal growth in certain regions of the United States, has led to a significant increase in inter-Asian marriages (e.g., Chinese Americans to Korean Americans). In a comparative analysis of the 1980 and 1990 Decennial Census, Larry Hajimi Shinigawa and Gin Young Pang (1996) found a dramatic decrease of interracial marriages and a significant rise of inter-Asian marriages. In California (where 39 percent of all Asian Pacific Americans reside), inter-Asian marriages increased from 21.1 percent in 1980 to 64 percent in 1990 of all intermarriages for Asian American husbands, and from 10.8 percent to 45 percent for Asian American wives during the same time period.

2. I thank Takeo Wong for calling my attention to this film.

REFERENCES

Agbayani-Siewert, P., and L. Revilla. 1995. Filipino Americans. In P. G. Min (ed.), *Asian Americans: Contemporary trends and issues* (pp. 134–68). Thousand Oaks, CA: Sage.

Baker, D. G. 1983. *Race, ethnicity, and power: A comparative study.* New York: Routledge.

Bulosan, C. 1973. *America is in the heart: A personal history.* Seattle: Washington University Press. (Original work published 1946).

Campomanes, O. 1992. Filipinos in the United States and their literature of exile. In S. G. Lim and A. Ling (eds.), *Reading the literatures of Asian America* (pp. 49–78). Philadelphia: Temple University Press.

Cha, T. H. K. 1982. *Dictee.* New York: Tanam.

Chan, J. P., F. Chin, L. F. Inada, and S. Wong. 1974. *Aiiieeeee! An anthology of Asian American writers.* Washington, DC: Howard University Press.

Chan, S. 1994. The Asian American Movement, 1960–1980s. In S. Chan, D. H. Daniels, M. T. Garcia and T. P. Wilson (eds.) *Peoples of Color in the American West* (pp. 525–33). lexington, MA: D. C. Heath.

Cheung, K.-K. 1990. The woman warrior versus the Chinaman pacific: Must a Chinese American critic choose between feminism and heroism? In M. Hirsch and E. F. Keller (eds.), *Conflicts in feminism* (pp. 234–51). New York: Routledge.

Chin, F. 1972. Confessions of the Chinatown cowboy. *Bulletin of Concerned Asian Scholars* 4 (3), p. 66.

Chin, F., and J. P. Chan. 1972. Racist love. In R. Kostelanetz (ed.), *Seeing through shuck* (pp. 65–79). New York: Ballantine.

Choe, L. 1996. "Versions": Asian Americans in hip hop. Paper presented at the California Studies Conference, Long Beach, CA. February 10.

Chu, L. 1961. *Eat a bowl of tea.* Seattle: University of Washington Press.

Collins, P. H. 1991. *Black feminist thought: Knowledge, consciousness, and the politics of empowerment.* New York: Routledge.

Doane, M. A. 1991. *Femme fatales: Feminism, film theory, psychoanalysis.* New York: Routledge.

Dong, A. (dir). 1982. *Sewing woman* [Film]. San Francisco: DeepFocus Productions.

Eng, D. L. 2001. *Racial castration: Managing masculinity in Asian America.* Durham, NC: Duke University Press.

Engelhardt, T. 1976. Ambush at Kamikaze Pass. In E. Gee (ed.), *Counterpoint: Perspectives on Asian America* (pp. 270–79). Los Angeles: University of California at Los Angeles, Asian American Studies Center.

Frankenberg, R. 1993. *White women, race matters: The social construction of whiteness.* Minneapolis: University of Minnesota Press.

Fung, R. 1994. Seeing yellow: Asian identities in film and video. In K. Aguilar-San Juan (ed.), *The state of Asian America* (pp. 161–71). Boston: South End.

Geisler, J. 2004. A few good (Asian American) men. Poynteronline, http://www.poynter.org/content/content_view.asp?id=64151 January 9, 2007.

Goellnicht, D. C. 1992. Tang Ao in America: Male subject positions in China men. In S. G. Lim and A. Ling (eds.), *Reading the literatures of Asian America* (pp.192–212). Philadelphia: Temple University Press.

Hagedorn, J. 1993. Introduction: Role of dead man require very little acting. In J. Hagedorn (ed.), *Charlie Chan is dead: An anthology of contemporary Asian American fiction* (pp. xxi–xxx). New York: Penguin.

Hamamoto, D. Y. 1992. Kindred spirits: The contemporary Asian American family on television. *Amerasia Journal* 18 (2), (pp. 35–53).

———. 1994. *Monitored peril: Asian Americans and the politics of representation.* Minneapolis: University of Minnesota Press.

Hoppenstand, G. 1983. Yellow devil doctors and opium dens: A survey of the Yellow Peril stereotypes in mass media entertainment. In C. D. Geist and J. Nachbar (eds.), *The popular culture reader* (3rd ed., pp. 171–85). Bowling Green, OH: Bowling Green University Press.

James, D. 1999. Tradition and the movies: The Asian American avant-garde in Los Angeles. *Journal of Asian American Studies* 2 (pp. 157–80).

Kim, E. 1982. *Asian American literature: An introduction to the writings and their social context.* Philadelphia: Temple University Press.

———. 1984. Asian American writers: A bibliographical review. *American Studies International* 22 (p. 2).

———. 1990. "Such opposite creatures": Men and women in Asian American literature. *Michigan Quarterly Review* 29 (pp. 68–93).

———. 1993. Preface. In J. Hagedorn (ed.), *Charlie Chan is dead: An anthology of contemporary Asian American fiction* (pp. vii–xiv). New York: Penguin.

Kingston, M. H. 1977. *The woman warrior.* New York: Vintage.

———. 1980. *China men.* New York: Knopf.

Lee, E. 2003. Between the personal and the universal: Asian American solo performance from the 1970s to the 1990s. *Journal of Asian American Studies* 6 (pp. 289–312).

Lee, J. 1997. *Performing Asian America: Race and ethnicity on the contemporary stage.* Philadelphia: Temple University Press.

Lee, R. G. 1999. *Orientals: Asian Americans in popular culture.* Philadelphia: Temple University Press.

Ling, A. 1990. *Between worlds: Women writers of Chinese ancestry.* New York: Pergamon.

Lowe, L. 1991. Heterogeneity, hybridity, multiplicity: Marking Asian American difference. *Diaspora* 1 (pp. 22–44).

———. 1994. Canon, institutionalization, identity: Contradictions for Asian American studies. In D. Palumbo-Liu (ed.), *The ethnic canon: Histories, institutions, and interventions* (pp. 48–68). Minneapolis: University of Minnesota Press.

Marchetti, G. 1993. *Romance and the "Yellow Peril": Race, sex, and discursive strategies in Hollywood fiction.* Berkeley: University of California Press.

Min, P. G. 1995. Korean Americans. In P. G. Min (ed.), *Asian Americans: Contemporary trends and issues* (pp. 199–231). Thousand Oaks, CA: Sage.

Mullings, L. 1994. Images, ideology, and women of color. In M. Baca Zinn and B. T. Dill (eds.), *Women of color in U.S. society* (pp. 265–89). Philadelphia: Temple University Press.

Nguyen, V. 1990. Growing up in white America. *Asian Week*, December 7, p. 23.

Nguyen, V. T. 2002. *Race and resistance: Literature and politics in Asian America.* New York: Oxford University Press.

Nishi, S. M. 1995. Japanese Americans. In P. G. Min (ed.), *Asian Americans: Contemporary trends and issues* (pp. 95-133). Thousand Oaks, CA: Sage.

Okada, J. 1957. *No-no boy.* Rutland, VT: Charles E. Tuttle.

Okazaki, S. 1995. *American Sons.* Promotional brochure.

Okihiro, G. Y. 1991. *Cane fires: The anti-Japanese movement in Hawaii, 1865–1945.* Philadelphia: Temple University Press.

———. 1994. *Margins and mainstreams: Asians in American history and culture.* Seattle: University of Washington Press.

———. 1995. *Reading Asian bodies, reading anxieties.* Paper presented at the University of California, San Diego Ethnic Studies Colloquium, La Jolla, November.

Quinsaat, J. 1976. Asians in the media: The shadows in the spotlight. In E. Gee (ed.), *Counterpoint: Perspectives on Asian America* (pp. 264–69). Los Angeles: University of California at Los Angeles, Asian American Studies Center.

Rabine, L. W. 1987. No lost paradise: Social gender and symbolic gender in the writings of Maxine Hong Kingston. *Signs: Journal of Women in Culture and Society* 12 (pp. 471–511).

Said, E. 1979. *Orientalism.* New York: Random House.

Shah, S. 1994. Presenting the Blue Goddess: Toward a national, Pan-Asian feminist agenda. In K. Aguilar-San Juan (ed.), *The state of Asian America: Activism and resistance in the 1990s* (pp. 147–58). Boston: South End.

Shimakawa, K. 2000. Asians in America: Millenial approaches to Asian Pacific American performance. *Journal of Asian American Studies* 3 (pp. 283–99).

Shinagawa, L. H., and G. Y. Pang. 1996. Asian American panethnicity and intermarriage. *Amerasia Journal* 22 (pp. 127–52).

Sledge, L. C. 1980. Maxine Kingston's *China Men:* The family historian as epic poet. *MELUS* 7 (pp. 3–22).
Tajima, R. 1989. Lotus blossoms don't bleed: Images of Asian women. In Asian Women United of California (ed.), *Making waves: An anthology of writings by and about Asian American women* (pp. 308–17). Boston: Beacon.
———. 1991. Moving the image: Asian American independent filmmaking 1970–1990. In R. Leong (ed.), *Moving the image: Independent Asian Pacific American media arts* (pp. 10–33). Los Angeles: University of California at Los Angeles, Asian American Studies Center, and Visual Communications, Southern California Asian American Studies Central.
Tan, A. 1989. *The Joy Luck Club.* New York: Putnam.
Tong, B. 1994. *Unsubmissive women: Chinese prostitutes in nineteenth-century San Francisco.* Norman: University of Oklahoma Press.
Tran, Q. P. 1993. Exile and home in contemporary Vietnamese American feminine writing. *Amerasia Journal* 19 (pp. 71–83).
Villaneuva, M. 1991. *Ginseng and other tales from Manila.* Corvallis, OR: Calyx.
Wang, A. 1995. Maxine Hong Kingston's reclaiming America: The birthright of the Chinese American male. *South Dakota Review* 26 (pp. 18–29).
Wiegman, R. 1991. Black bodies/American commodities: Gender, race, and the bourgeois ideal in contemporary film. In L. D. Friedman (ed.), *Unspeakable images: Ethnicity and the American cinema* (pp. 308–28). Urbana: University of Illinois Press.
Wong, E. F. 1978. *On visual media racism: Asians in the American motion pictures.* New York: Arno.
Wong, S.-L. C. 1993. *Reading Asian American literature: From necessity to extravagance.* Princeton, NJ: Princeton University Press.
Wu, W. F. 1982. *The Yellow Peril: Chinese Americans in America fiction 1850–1940.* Hamden, CT: Archon.
Yamanaka, L. A. 1993. Empty heart. In J. Hagedorn (ed.), *Charlie Chan is dead: An anthology of contemporary Asian American fiction* (pp. 544–50). New York: Penguin.
Yoon, D. D. 1993. Asian American male: Wimp or what? *Asian Week,* p. 16, November 26.

Chapter Two

Black Women's Films

Genesis of a Tradition

Jacqueline Bobo

My earliest introduction to the work of black women filmmakers occurred at several venues—an insightful paper given by Gloria Gibson at the 1989 Society for Cinema Studies Conference and, next, during Zeinabu irene Davis's challenging advocacy at the Twelfth Annual Ohio University Film Conference in 1990. These presentations stimulated my interest in and confirmed the need for more information about this vital aspect of black women's creative contributions. Not only had these papers whetted the research appetite of those at the conferences, but also Gloria and Zeinabu had continued a tradition of insuring that the work of black women filmmakers would be given their deserved critical attention.[1] Archivist and programmer Pearl Bowser had previously presented the work of black women in a retrospective of black American Independent Cinema 1920–1980 at a festival in Paris in 1980. Fortuitously, the event was preserved through the publication of a very useful document of the same title which is available through Third World Newsreel.[2]

Other events showcasing the films and videos of black women kept the work in public view. Pearl Bowser was involved in yet another research endeavor critical for outlining the history of not only black women filmmakers, but, as the title confers, *In Color: Sixty Years of Images of Minority Women in the Media.*[3] Groundbreaking essays included in the publication were written by Kathleen Collins, Christine Choy, Renee Tajima, Ada Gay Griffin, and Toni Cade Bambara, among others. Throughout the early 1980s, articles were written about black women filmmakers in publications such as *Heresies, Jump Cut, Black Film Review,* and elsewhere.[4] In 1987, Valerie Smith curated a showing of black women's films, "The Black Woman Inde-

27

pendent: Representing Race and Gender," at the Whitney Museum of American Art in New York City. Later, Smith published an overview and analysis of black women's work in *Callaloo*.[5]

I was fortunate to meet several of the filmmakers in the summer of 1992 at a conference exploring ways to effectively distribute the product of black independent film/videomakers.[6] I made contact with O. Funmilayo Makarah, Linda Gibson, Cheryl Fabio Bradford, and Jacqueline Shearer, and reconnected with Pearl Bowser and Zeinabu irene Davis. An earlier chance encounter with filmmaker, programmer, and later marketer Michelle Materre proved to be a godsend for my research on *Daughters of the Dust* (1991). I was a participant in the Black Popular Culture Conference[7] in New York City in December 1991 and decided to take advantage of the time there to preview black women's films at the independent distribution organization Women Make Movies. Fortunately, Michelle, who worked there at the time, approached me about having a look at a video copy of *Daughters of the Dust*. I was impressed with the sheer power of Julie Dash's film. From Michelle I obtained a preview videotape copy of the film to show to groups of black women I was interviewing for my book *Black Women as Cultural Readers* (1995). The women in my research group were even more taken with the film than I, incredible as that may have seemed at the time, for the earliest reviews posited that *Daughters of the Dust* would test the patience and comprehension of untutored audiences. Michelle also introduced me to Julie Dash, setting up an interview in Los Angeles that proved pivotal in my analysis of the film.

By this time black women scholars and artists were teaching courses about black female makers at several universities in the country: Claire Andrade Watkins at Wellesley College, Carmen Coustaut at Howard University and later at the University of Maryland, College Park; Gloria Gibson at Indiana University, and Michelle Parkerson was keeping the topic vibrant at Temple, Northwestern, Howard, and in early articles detailing the artists' history and significance.[8]

I started teaching courses on black women filmmakers about five years ago, and have continued to do so at three universities: the University of California, Santa Cruz; the University of North Carolina at Chapel Hill; and at my present location, the University of California, Santa Barbara. I encountered the same impediments that others faced, regardless of whether they taught courses devoted exclusively to the topic or incorporated the films with complementary subject matter within other courses. I considered these obstacles to be challenges rather than problems, but I also understood how those less involved in the subject would be intimidated by the lack of accessible background information about the films' production history and the relative absence of material about the filmmakers themselves. Also, many of the later films, and especially the videos and interactive media, were experimental works, in which some form of background material would enhance students' understanding.

To redress the issue in my courses, I began to invite many of the makers—Cheryl Fabio Bradford, Cauleen Smith, Aarin Burch, Linda Gibson, O. Funmilayo Makarah, Yvonne Welbon, Crystal Griffith, and programmer Margaret Daniel—to speak about their works in my classes. The students were enormously impressed with the women's knowledge, skill, and training. The women not only provided astute analyses of black women's films and videos but also contextualized the works within the broader spectrum of film and video production and criticism. I was reminded of the three days at the independent distribution conference, when, even in a casual setting, O. Funmilayo Makarah and Zeinabu Davis expertly explicated the works shown to the participants.

These events made me acutely aware that further information about the history of black women film and video makers would fill an egregious void within cinema scholarship. This was reaffirmed in Jacqueline Shearer's keynote address at the independent distributor's conference. Shearer's documentary *The Massachusetts 54th Colored Infantry* (1991) had just recently aired on public broadcasting as part of the prestigious *American Experience* series. Although she recognized the valuable opportunity for such a national presentation, Shearer reminded us that more work needed to be done to insure greater opportunities for more exhibition of the works of black independent makers. She detailed her experiences with distribution, including her first production, *A Minor Altercation* (1977). Shearer was at that time a founding member of the Boston Newsreel Collective, which operated with a political intent—that media could augment people's understanding of the social matrices in which they were involved. The collective held community screenings, which led to discussions and interactions with audiences, and brought the images that people viewed into perspective with their daily lives. Shearer related that

> it became clear to me that a film had no political merit gathering dust on the shelf. It was only in interaction with an audience that it had power. This is a very simpleminded truth but one that is still stunning to me in its significance and consequences. So a longstanding cornerstone of my understanding about media is that the production of a piece is not finished until and unless it plays to its audience.[9]

Despite the tremendous success of *A Minor Altercation* (which dealt with the desegregation conflicts in Boston in the early 1970s) through the grassroots efforts of the Boston Collective, the film was rejected by distributors. The early incarnation of Women Make Movies dismissed the film as not being feminist, even though the makers were women and the protagonists in the story were two teenage girls and their working-class mothers. Other organizations considered the film not polished enough, asserting that it lacked sophisticated production aesthetics. *A Minor Altercation* has since gone on to be distributed by the present Women Make Movies and is regarded as a classic early black feminist work.

There is a substantial body of work created by black women film/video makers, extending back to the early part of this century. Unfortunately, the work is overlooked not only by many distributors, but also by critical reviews and scholarly analyses, with the notable exception of those by black women scholars, have been few and far between. The success of filmmaker Julie Dash's *Daughters of the Dust* (1991), due in large measure to the fervent support of black female audiences, underscores the critical role of black women's films within this far-reaching creative tradition. Through the aid of other women filmmakers and an independent publicity campaign, *Daughters of the Dust* circumvented traditional venues to be placed before receptive audiences hungry for depictions of their history long missing from mainstream white productions. The film chronicles a loving, though complicated, multigenerational black family at the turn of the century. They struggle, yet eventually triumph over the oppressive legacies of forced removal from their homeland and the tortuous regimens of enslavement. Dash's piece is historic; it proved, yet again, that there was a large untapped market for creative work that seriously examined black women's experiences.

The demonstrated interest in *Daughters of the Dust* notwithstanding, widespread recognition of black women film and video artists lags behind their extensive history. Documentation exists of black women producing and directing films during the prolific interim of black film production from 1910 through the 1920s. Archivist and film scholar Pearl Bowser notes that black women worked behind the camera on numerous films during this time on what were known as "race" films, that is, independent films produced by black filmmakers, rather than white-controlled films about black life. [10]

Historical records show that two women were especially noteworthy in filmmaking during this period. Madame C. J. Walker, one of the first black millionaires, made her fortune manufacturing and distributing cosmetics and hair-care products for black women. In addition to her retail business, Walker owned the Walker Theater in Indianapolis, and produced training and promotional films about her cosmetics factory. These films, Bowser declares, "offered a visual record of women's work history" and the "development of cottage industries." [11] Bowser also points to the importance of Madam Toussaint Welcome, Booker T. Washington's personal photographer, who produced at least one film about black soldiers who fought in World War I.

Film scholar Gloria J. Gibson-Hudson provides further evidence of black women's production background. Gibson-Hudson's research fills out important details on earlier black women filmmakers, but she also works to restore, in conjunction with the Library of Congress, the films of Eloyce Gist. Gist was a traveling evangelist, who toured the country in the 1920s with her religious folk dramas, exhibiting them in churches to black audiences. [12] Her two known films, *Hell Bound Tram* and *Verdict Not Guilty* are considered to be as rich and provocative as those of her more studied contemporaries such as Oscar Micheaux and the brothers Noble and George Johnson.

Other pioneer black female filmmakers examined in Gibson-Hudson's study include folklorist Zora Neale Hurston, who made ethnographic films in the 1930s. Hurston earned an MA in cultural anthropology, working with Franz Boas at Columbia University. Currently, several reels of Hurston's film footage are available for viewing at the Library of Congress. Similarly, footage exists of the films shot by Eslanda Goode Robeson (whose husband was Paul Robeson), but its fragile condition renders it inaccessible for public screening. Robeson, who held a PhD in Anthropology, made ethnographic films in the 1940s. Alice B. Russell, another key person, worked with and was perhaps the driving force behind many of the films of Oscar Micheaux. [13]

Confronted with the dearth of scholarship about early black female film-makers, these activist researchers—Bowser, Gibson-Hudson, and others—retrieved the history of a long-neglected body of films that dealt substantively with important issues. The works addressed an array of matters crucial to understanding various facets of black life and culture, including the role of religion in black people's lives, the contributions of black soldiers fighting for a country that afforded them little honor, and black women's work and business history. Certainly, an even more bountiful cache will surface once scholars begin to uncover the largely obscured output of black women filmmakers from the 1950s and early 1960s. Pearl Bowser is currently compiling information about black female photographers who were involved in film-making at that time.

That black women filmmakers were active in every decade of this century is not insignificant. The newly discovered films increase the opportunities to advance an understanding of black women's cultural history and the social determinants molding black women's lives. Furthermore, these texts demonstrate the ways in which filmmakers within the social group present stories that have an effect on altering these conditions for the better.

Concomitantly, exposure of their existence links the present to the past, outlining the expansive contours of a fertile lineage of creativity. We can now enlarge the process of assessing commonalities, pervasive themes, and preoccupations, as well as dissimilarities, discontinuities, and interruptions.

Such prominent patterns are recognizable in recent films and offer insight into black women's perspectives on their ongoing efforts to better their lives. The contemporary film that is generally singled out as the first created by a black woman is *I am Somebody* (1970), directed by Madeline Anderson. It records the successful 113-day strike in 1969 by hospital workers in Charleston, South Carolina. Anderson's documentary is an empathetic portrait of black women and their supporters, including the Southern Christian Leadership Conference in its first mass demonstration after the death of Martin Luther King Jr. Also involved were the labor union organizations UAW and the AFL-CIO, along with white women who were members of the Spartanburg, South Carolina, chapter of ILGWU.[14] The importance of the strike (initiated by what later became local 1199B of the national union of hospital workers) was that lowly regarded women persevered in their struggle to demand what was their right—"recognition as human beings," as one striker stated at the end of the film.

Centering black women as subjects recognizable as human beings is paramount in black women's films. Starting with *I am Somebody*, the following works form a nucleus that shapes and gives definition to a com prehensive movement of black women film and video artists: *Valerie; A Woman, an Artist, a Philosophy of Life* (1975), directed by Monica Freeman, is a documentary about sculptor Valerie Maynard, who considers her art a vital part of her political impulse. Jacqueline Shearer's *A Minor Altercation* (1977) dramatizes the activities in Boston in the early 1970s surrounding the conflicts over busing. The film is based on interviews with participants and community members, but is a dramatic depiction of events. It is different from the other works created by black women during this period in that it is not a documentary, it is a narrative reconstruction.

Kathleen Collins, with her two feature narratives *The Cruz Brothers and Miss Malloy* (1980) and *Losing Ground* (1982), further extended the range of black women's films. Although *Losing Ground* was denied large-scale exhibition, it was among the first films created by a black woman deliberately designed to tell a story intended for popular consumption, with a feature-length narrative structure. Collins's film thus paved the way for *Daughters of the Dust* to become the first feature-length narrative film created by a black woman to be placed in commercial distribution. Finally, *Fundi: The Story of Ella Baker* (1981), directed by Joanne Grant, powerfully restores Ella Baker to the pantheon of civil rights organizers and thinkers. In conjunction with Michelle Parkerson's *Gotta Make This Journey: Sweet Honey in the Rock* (1983), the films are compelling examples of art transforming people's consciousness, facilely intertwining cultural expression with cogent political analysis.

These early makers successfully battled debilitating societal restraints of scarce resources and blocked access to production facilities to redress significant omissions within black women's history. Even in the face of continual rejection from established funding sources, and despite their films being refused exhibition by festival committees and alternative distribution centers, the women stayed true to their belief that stories about black women's lives merited creative representation. Their portfolios included, for example, films about overlooked cultural and political activists and social documentaries charting black women's essential contributions at pivotal historical moments. The filmmakers maintained contact with black audiences by personally carrying their films wherever people desired to see them. And they conscientiously tailored their works to match the requisites of audience understanding, traversing the spectrum of filmmaking, from documentary to fictional recreation, and moving onward toward the subversive potential of narrative cinema. This legacy was passed on to present-day filmmakers. Thus, the innovative forms and impressive content of the early films, the stories the makers selected to tell, combined with the social context governing the works' production and their eventual favorable reception over time, established a germinative foundation for black women film and videomakers who followed.

DOCUMENTING BLACK LIVES

Congruence between the personal histories of filmmaker and subject is a predominant feature of black women's biographical documentaries. The works are more than a distanced, voyeuristic examination of an isolated artist, but rather illustrate how both filmmaker and artist have overcome obstacles to create art that is meaningful for black audiences. Monica Freeman's *Valerie* was among the first of this kind. Other examples include Ayoka Chenzira's *Syvilla: They Dance to Her Drum* (1979); . . . *But Then, She's Betty Carter* (1980); and *Storme: The Lady of the Jewel Box* (1987) by Michelle Parkerson, as well as her later film codirected with Ada Gay Griffin *A Litany for Survival: The Life and Work of Audre Lorde* (1995); Carroll Parrott Blue's *Vamette's World: A Study of a Young Artist* (1979); *Miss Fluci Moses: A Video Documentary* (1987) by Alile Sharon Larkin; and Kathe Sandler's *Remembering Thelma* (1981).

Evident in Freeman's film about Valerie Maynard are the two women's affinities as black women and as artists. *Valerie* is a sensory, evocative examination of a printmaker and sculptor who is inspired by the people and the rhythms of her native Harlem. For her, Harlem is "continual conversation, continual change, continual movement." This sentiment emerges in the tightly structured film; it is dynamic and fluid, emulating Maynard's art and life as she works in her studio, interacts with the residents of her neighborhood, arranges an exhibit at the University of Massachusetts. As the documentary begins, the filmmaker draws the viewer into the artist's environment. There are lingering shots of Maynard's larger-than-life figures followed by slow camera movement along the length of a female form with its upraised arm and open palm. Accompanying the visuals are sounds of the artist using the tools of her craft: sanding, carving, pounding a mallet against a chisel. The voice-over consists entirely of Maynard speaking about her life and philosophy of art, and of her desire to display her work to as broad an audience as possible, including the conventional circles of galleries and university lectures, along with the less familiar turf of jails and people's homes. As much as Maynard's aesthetic draws from other's experiences, so does she seek to share her work with a vast and diverse audience.

Harlem forms the backdrop for Freeman's other two works as well: *A Sense of Pride: Hamilton Heights in Harlem* (1977) and *Learning Through the Arts: The Children's Art Carnival* (1979). Each documentary clearly functions to identify and preserve essential elements of black culture. Hamilton Heights is a neighborhood in New York City that has been recognized as a historic landmark. Acknowledgment of that designation is evidenced by several longtime residents, who validate the significance of the community. Roy Thomas, born in 1906, states that he was probably one of the first black people born in Harlem. He talks about black people needing collective memories of their heritage, housed in communities such as his. In the film, Thomas displays copies of family mementos, one being the receipt given to his great-great-grandfather as proof that he had bought his freedom from enslavement.

Another resident, Alston Harris, noticing the onset of deterioration in his neighborhood, began planting ferns, flowers, trees, and other vegetation throughout the area as a "garden of pleasure for people." He states that people live better if they take pride in their surroundings: "the air here smells different than from a block away." Harris's neighbors soon began to follow his example, keeping the area clean, guarding against litter and vandalism, and tending the community gardens.

Pride in Harlem's legendary status is demonstrated by other inhabitants who moved to the neighborhood's grand brownstones. At the time of the film's production, Eleanor Holmes Norton was New York City's Human Rights Commissioner and a longtime resident of Harlem Heights. She explains that, for her, the best way to protect the area was to live there and serve as an example to lure other potential residents. She felt that there was a feeling of cohesion as the communities pulled together to maintain what had been designated a valuable component of black people's past.

Harlem Heights was also the location of the Children's Art Carnival, a community-based arts school for children aged 4–18. The organization began as a summer program by the Museum of Modern Art in 1968 and later moved to Harlem. The film *Learning Through the Arts: The Children's Art Carnival* is an inspirational look at young people developing a variety of artistic skills: printmaking, silkscreen, animation, filmmaking, sewing and design, collage, and 3-D construction, among other disciplines. The narrator and director of the program, Betty Blayton Taylor, asserts that art is everywhere in people's lives and that an understanding of the arts motivates children in other aspects of their lives. One of the Carnival's programs, "Creative Reading Through the Arts," was used to stimulate children's curiosty about communication and used art as a bridge for verbal and written breakthroughs. The documentary illustrates how children, once they become curious, motivate themselves by wanting to read and communicate effectively. Because of their success, the Children's Art Carnival was cited as a model of arts education by the National Endowment for the Arts.

Monica Freeman's three 1970s documentaries all exemplify the skill and training of a committed cultural activist. Freeman studied with Madeline Anderson at Columbia University, earning an MFA in film production in 1977. She later served as mentor to other emerging filmmakers. Her film *A Sense of Pride* featured an all-woman crew who are now established filmmakers in their own right with noteworthy production credits. The women included Ayoka Chenzira, whose landmark film *Hair Piece: A Film for Nappyheaded People* (1984) is an animated satire that is shown frequently at colleges and festivals. Chenzira also directed *Alma's Rainbow* (1993), an ambitious and remarkably achieved 35mm feature-length narrative. Debra Robinson was another member of Freeman's crew. She would later direct the well-known documentary about black female comedians, *I Be Done Been Was Is* (1984), and a fictional feature story of a young black girl's turmoil, *Kiss Grandmama Goodbye* (1992).

BLACK WOMEN'S NARRATIVES

Exploration of social conditions through documentary is a first step for many beginning filmmakers. This is also true of black women filmmakers, but as their skills matured, the necessity for matching the format of their works with the theater-going experiences of specific audiences became a prime consideration. Even though the women were virtually shut out of the established film industry, the need to reach black people with responsible depictions of black life was imperative. One of the first to successfully achieve this goal was Kathleen Collins.

Collins understood that the effective use of cinema had the potential to evoke in the viewer a certain depth of response, similar to that experienced by other forms of art. In her films she was concerned with utilizing the grammar of film to resolve the structural and formal questions unique to film as a specific discipline. For independent makers, especially, this was necessary if audiences were to gain an appreciation of cinema as more than a commercial vehicle. [15]

Kathleen Collins embraced the principle that cinema has a literary parallel—not in any direct way, but in the sense that every element of composition is a specific convention that makes up a film language. Collins's first film conscientiously employed cinematic techniques in translating a literary story to film. *The Cruz Brothers and Miss Malloy* is based on one of a series of episodes in a longer literary work, *The Cruz Chronicle: A Novel of Adventure and Close Calls* (1989), by Henry H. Roth.[16] The film tells the story of three Puerto Rican brothers, orphaned after their father is killed by guards while attempting to rob a bank, who live as exiles in a small isolated town in upstate New York. They are hired by an elderly Irish widow, Edna Malloy, a longtime resident of the town, to restore her home to its former grandeur as she prepares to give one last party.

The film is coherent, with a consistent tone and style. The brothers have survived unfortunate circumstances, from living in an orphanage to existing by their wiles in a potentially hostile environment. In spite of the element of danger in their lives, there is a whimsical, fanciful ambience to the film. This is apparent from the outset as the dead father appears as a ghost at the beginning of the film, giving it a surreal dimension. The father's presence is shown through the perspective of a hand-held camera, with his voice heard off-camera as a disembodied voice-over. The story is told alternately by the father and by the oldest son, Victor, who provides background information on the family as he constructs their history by talking into an audiotape recorder. Victor is the only one of the brothers who is able to converse with the dead father.

The suspense of the film builds as it becomes obvious that someone, not shown on camera, is spying on the brothers as they go about their business in the town. From the unseen voyeur's point of view, the brothers are presented, in one scene, playfully making their way along an extremely high narrow crossing spanning an enormous chasm. The inference is that the brothers lead risky lives with vastly different experiences from their observer. The brothers soon become aware that the elderly woman is following them, but they do not know her intentions. The viewer is also kept wondering. That the brothers' future is uncertain and in possible jeopardy is maintained throughout Edna Malloy's first appearance in the film. The fender of her classic automobile slowly enters the frame, as the brothers are seen walking off down the road. The car door swings open; Miss Malloy steps out, filling up the frame with her back to the camera, as the boys are shown much smaller and vulnerable in the distance. The brothers' apprehension increases when she eventually approaches them. A canted camera angle indicates that the boys perceive her to be odd and unusual. This is reinforced by her statement about their passage across the bridge: "I saw your act a few times previously. And I caught it again today. Each time you cross that bridge you tempt fate. You're tempted to jump. But I think you are definitely survivors. I have been one for many years, but now I'm going to die."

The technical properties of *The Cruz Brothers and Miss Malloy* were overlooked at the time of its debut because more attention was given to the absence of black people in the film. However, Collins felt that any subject was open to black artists.[17] Thematically, in *The Cruz Brothers* she was dealing with the notion of happiness and whether a person has lived a full life or, as Edna Malloy relates to the brothers, whether she has traded the security of living her entire life in the town in which she was born, married to a man with whom she was unhappy, for taking risks with her fate in unknown circumstances.

Amplifying the potential of the medium was a prime consideration in Collins's work. She was trained in France in the mid-1960s, earning an MA in film theory and production from the Middlebury Graduate School. She was a faculty member at the City College of New York from 1974 to 1988, teaching courses on directing for film, scriptwriting, theory and aesthetics of cinema, and editing. Collins was considered by many filmmakers the finest film editor of her era. She learned her craft by working with John Carter, one of the first black union editors. Collins worked as an editor from 1967 to 1974 at WNET-NY.

The influence of Collins as one of the first contemporary black women working within the genre of narrative cinema is seen in subsequent films directed by black women. Commercially distributed films include *Daughters of the Dust,* Leslie Harris's *Just Another Girl on the IRT* (1992), and *I Like it Like That* (1994) by Darnell Martin.

Command of the fictional form raises black women makers to another level of visibility. Within the genre of dramatic narratives, a variety of films are represented: *A Minor Altercation* (1977) directed by Jacqueline Shearer; *A Powerful Thang* (1991) and *Mother of the River* (1995) by Zeinabu irene Davis; *Your Children Come Back to You* (1979) and *A Different Image* (1982), directed by Alile Sharon Larkin; Carmen Coustaut's *Extra Change* (1987); *Twice as Nice* (1989) by Jessie Maple; Daresha Kyi's *Land Where My Fathers Died* (1991); and *Rags and Old Love* (1986) by Ellen Sumter, among others.

There are also feature-length narratives, though not in wide-scale distribution, that have been directed by black women: Jessie Maple's *Will* (1981); *Love Your Mama* (1989) by Ruby Oliver; *Alma's Rainbow* (1993), directed by Ayoka Chenzira; *Naked Acts* (1995) by Bridgett Davis; *The Promised Land* (1995) by Monika Harris; *Medipaid Queens* (1995) by Karen Stone; and, *The Watermelon Woman* (1996), directed by Cheryl Dunye.

Although only three dramatic films created by black women—*Daughters of the Dust, I Like It Like That, Just Another Girl on the IRT*—have been exhibited theatrically, several others have been presented nationally. Helaine Head directed a CBS Schoolbreak Special, starring Whoopi Goldberg, that examined black students' participation in the sit-ins of the 1960s, *My Past Is My Own* (1989). Mary Neema Barnette, who has directed many network television programs including episodes of *The Cosby Show, Frank's Place, China Beach, A Different World,* among others, and one of the few black women to receive an Emmy Award in a nonacting category, directed Ruby Dee's play *Zora Is My Name* (1989), broadcast nationally on PBS. Finally, Dianne Houston's *Tuesday Morning Ride* (1995), produced as part of Showtime's short film series, was the first film directed by a black woman to be nominated for an Academy Award.

SOCIAL MOVEMENTS, CULTURAL MOVEMENTS

In the construction of narrative films or creating social documentaries, black women filmmakers have engaged questions of resistance and social oppression as a vital part of their work. Anderson's *I Am Somebody* led the way for examinations of black women's roles in major political movements, followed by Joanne Grant's *Fundi: The Story of Ella Baker* (1981) and Michelle Parkerson's *Gotta Make This Journey: Sweet Honey in the Rock* (1983). The films focus on the lives of extraordinary women, but the central issues they raise concern the political activities of these women as they sparked catalytic events within historic moments. Each film superbly achieves the desired effect of political films: they contain mutually reinforcing components of historical exegesis, inspiration, and a call to action.

Although her name may not be as readily recognized as some of the more visible activists, Ella Baker (1903–1986) influenced several generations of civil rights workers. In the 1940s she was a field organizer for the NAACP, traveling throughout the South six months of the year organizing membership drives and working with communities to help them recognize their potential for collective action. She was born in the South, graduated from Shaw University in Raleigh, North Carolina, and eventually moved to New York right before the Depression. Baker's participation in radical organizations in New York, along with her work with black groups in the South, nurtured her progressive ideas about social change.

Despite her impressive record of involvement and progressive initiatives in movement activities, Baker shunned being elevated to the status of a leader. She cautioned repeatedly against relying on a "charismatic leader," formulating instead the principle of participatory democracy: those involved in social movement organizations can be empowered to act on their own behalf if they participate in the decision-making process. It was Baker, rather than the white student leaders of the Students for a Democratic Society (as has been widely written about), who originated the underlying framework of participatory democracy. Movement scholar Carol Mueller insists that Baker was the primary impetus behind this powerful set of ideas that guided the organization she helped to found, the Student Nonviolent Coordinating Committee.[18]

Fundi: The Story of Ella Baker skillfully blends archival footage of Baker's public life promoting group-centered leadership with one-on-one interviews Baker gives in numerous settings: among her colleagues in the movement, including E. D. Nixon, the organizer of the 1955 Montgomery Bus Boycott; and Amzie Moore, who initiated the voter registration project in Mississippi in the 1960s. She is tenderly shown in the company of her extended family and friends and at a tribute arranged in her honor by those she inspired. These include activists such as Bob Moses, who heeded Baker's call for working and living in the communities where voter registration drives were conducted. Moses categorized Baker as the embodiment of Fundi: a designation of honor originating from Swahili, which refers to someone in a community who masters a craft, then passes on what they have learned by sharing it with others. Many renowned civil rights activists articulate their debt to Baker in the film, including Julian Bond, Ralph David Abernathy, Septima Clark, Bernice Johnson Reagon, Vincent Harding, and others who were politically active during the span of Baker's life.

One of the strengths of Grant's film is that it showcases Baker's speeches in such a powerful manner. She was a forceful, courageous person, tackling difficult issues forthrightly and honestly. A fundamental tenet of her life's work was that "no one will do for you that which you've had the power to do for yourself and did not." Ella Baker was also the organizer for the challenge mounted by the Mississippi Freedom Democratic Party in their bid to be seated at the 1964 Democratic National Convention in Atlantic City, New Jersey. During her keynote address to the delegation she referred to the sustained public outrage in the wake of the murders of the civil rights workers in Mississippi in 1964, two of whom were white workers from the North. Many black people were aware that as the authorities searched for the missing workers, they found bodies of murdered black men in the rivers of Mississippi that no one had previously investigated because they had not been killed along with white men. Baker expressed her anger with the following resolution: "Until the killing of black men, black mothers' sons, becomes as important to the rest of the country as a white mother's son, we who believe in freedom will not rest until it comes."

This declaration was responded to in a song by Bernice Johnson Reagon, "We Who Believe in Freedom" (also known as "Ella's Song") that is a part of the soundtrack sung by Reagon and Sweet Honey in the Rock for *Fundi.* Reagon had known and worked with Ella Baker since the beginnings of her own political transformation in Albany, Georgia, in the early 1960s. In her book, *We Who Believe in Freedom: Sweet Honey in the Rock Still On the Journey* (1993), Reagon emphasizes the importance of Baker and her over-riding philosophy that citizens are empowered through direct participation in social change.[19] It was this political privileging of "rank and file" members rather than the authoritarian head of an organization which placed Baker in conflict with the directors of the NAACP and, later, the group for which she was the first organizer, the Southern Christian Leadership Conference. With admirable foresight, Baker felt that the development of leadership capabil-ities within individuals would enhance their ability for long-term political action.

In yet another prescient endeavor that would accrue benefits in the years to come, Baker led the drive to recruit more women and young people into the SCLC. This constituency would ignite the push for a broader range of rights for a variety of social groups. Baker also initiated, in the late 1950s, the Crusade for Citizenship, composed of voter clinics, social action committees, and classes to teach basic reading and writing skills that would qualify black citizens to vote. Ella Baker understood the power of targeted, large-scale demonstrations and knew that, by utilizing the strategy of mass, direct action, combined with the power of the vote, the collective will of the group would exert considerable influence.[20]

In the film *Gotta Make This Journey: Sweet Honey in the Rock,* Bernice Johnson Reagon discusses the tremendous courage of those who participated in the voter registration drives. The American public was aware of the large protest marches because these were the events attracting national media cov-erage, but the local campaigns for the right to vote cost black people their lives. As a consequence, Reagon's first singing group, the SNCC Freedom Singers, became a "singing newspaper," keeping people at the grassroots level informed of the activities in the small cities and towns where black people were fighting for their constitutional rights.

Reagon refers to Ella Baker as her "political mother" and uses her exam-ple of recognizing the potential for resistance to oppression in every individ-ual. Her goal, in the formation of the singing group Sweet Honey in the Rock, was to provide the inspiration that motivated people toward collective action for social change. It was her participation in the freedom movement, Reagon states, that made her realize that songs can do more than make people feel good; they have the power to mobilize concentrated, large-scale opposition to varied manifestations of injustice.

Gotta Make This Journey: Sweet Honey in the Rock, produced by Michelle Parkerson, is a broadcast videotape of Sweet Honey's ninth anniversary concert held in 1982 at Gallaudet College in Washington, D.C.[21] It is a thoughtful documentary and much more than a typical concert tape. There is a compatibility between the programming of the concert and the structure of the videotape, so that the force of Sweet Honey builds throughout, not overwhelming the viewer. Careful attention is given to the rhythm and pacing of the video, matching the content of the songs with the narrative provided by the individual women as they are interviewed in the field segments of the documentary.

Each section of *Gotta Make This Journey* is intersected by quick fades to black, followed by a song from the concert. These musical bridges further articulate the ideas and sentiments expressed in interviews and commentary. Several narrative lines evolve: the origin of the group, its overall philosophy, and how each member's personal history contributes to the collective. As an example, the six then-current members of Sweet Honey—Yasmeen Williams, Evelyn Harris, Aisha Kahlil, Ysaye Barnwell, Shirley Johnson (the sign language interpreter), and the group's founder and leader, Bernice Johnson Reagon—are all committed to Sweet Honey's political mission of creating awareness of specific human rights issues. When Evelyn Harris conveys that singing with Sweet Honey allows her to work for black people through song, there is a juxtaposition with a clip of the Reverend Ben Chavis, who had been imprisoned as a member of the Wilmington Ten. Chavis speaks of his love for the group, and his gratitude to them for volunteering to provide the musical soundtrack for the film *The Wilmington Ten—U.S.A. Ten Thousand* (1978), created by director Haile Gerima. The song "You can break one human body, I see ten thousand Bikos" is then featured in the next segment of the anniversary concert. The song was composed by Bernice Johnson Reagon specifically for Gerima's documentary. In the film, the song accompanies a series of photographs of antiapartheid marches in South Africa. The comparison likens the repression in South Africa with the condition of those imprisoned in Wilmington, North Carolina, and, in turn, draws a parallel to acts of social injustice as they occur throughout the world.

After the forceful and impassioned rendition of "I See Ten Thousand Bikos," Bernice Johnson Reagon sets up a change of pace and introduces the title song inspired by the words of Ella Baker, "We Who Believe in Freedom." It imparts a quiet, understated resolve, matched in the next segment with comments from Angela Davis, speaking of the importance of the younger generation remembering the contributions of civil rights pioneers Fannie Lou Hamer and Ella Baker.

A comparison can be made between those who devoted their lives to the struggle for social equality and similarly dedicated black women filmmakers. Ella Baker presents a formidable, yet attainable example. Her life's work corresponds to the filmmakers' creative commitment. Baker believed that political action should empower people to solve their own problems and that social change is finally achieved through enabling people to act on their own convictions. As she states in Grant's film *Fundi:* "The natural [impulse toward] resistance is there already. No human being, I don't care how undeveloped he is, relishes being sat upon and beaten as if he were an animal without any resistance."

Mainstream cultural forms are replete with devastating representations of black women as victims, as pawns of systemic oppressive forces, lacking the will or agency to resist. Both *Fundi: The Story of Ella Baker* and *Gotta Make This Journey* present vastly different interpretations of black women as social agents within historic political periods. The films are instrumental in the effort by black women filmmakers to erase destructive ideologies affecting black women. With their body of socially conscious work, the filmmakers form an integral component of a cultural movement, a configuration of activists that seeks to transform the status of black women in popular imagination and in the minds of black women themselves. Through meticulous concentration on black women's history, faithfully representing their lives, black women's films magnify female viewers' perception of their material circumstances, motivating them toward activism, thereby strengthening their viability as a potent social force.

NOTES

1. Gloria Gibson, Zeinabu Davis, and I also presented a panel on "Black Women's Films" at the Modern Language Association Annual Convention in Toronto, Ontario in December 1993; and we were part of a panel on the same topic with Mable Haddock, Kathe Sandler, Lisa Kennedy, and Kass Banning at the Black Cinema: An International Celebration of Pan-African Film Conference, at the New York University Tisch School of the Arts, in March 1994.

2. Pearl Bowser and Valerie Harris, eds., *Independent Black American Cinema* (New York: Third World Newsreel, 1981).

3. Pearl Bowser and Ada Gay Griffin, eds., *In Color: Sixty Years of Images of Minority Women in Film* (New York: Third World Newsreel, 1984).

4. See Loretta Campbell, "Reinventing Our Image: Eleven Black Women Filmmakers," *Heresies* 4, 4 (1983): 58–62; Claudia Springer, "Black Women Filmmakers," *Jump Cut* 29 (1984): 34–37; and "The Special Section: Black Women Filmmakers Break the Silence," *Black Film Review* 2, 3 (Summer 1986).

5. Valerie Smith, "Reconstituting the Image: The Emergent Black Woman Director," *Callaloo; A Journal of Afro-American and African Arts and Letters* 11, 4 (Fall 1988): 710–19.

6. See the report of the conference in Jacqueline Bobo, ed., *Available Visions Improving Distribution of African American Independent Film and Video Conference Proceedings* (San Francisco: California Newsreel, 1993).

7. For an overview of the conference see Gina Dent, ed. *Black Popular Culture: A Project by Michele Wallace* (Seattle, WA: Bay Press, 1992).

8. See her articles, "Did You Say the Mirror Talks?" in Lisa Albrecht and Rose M. Brewer, eds., *Bridges of Power: Women's Multicultural Alliances* (Santa Cruz, CA: New Society Publishers, 1990), 108–17; and "Women Throughout the Diaspora Tackle Their Firsts," *Black Film Review* 6, 1: 10–11.

9. Jacqueline Shearer, "Random Notes of a Homeless Filmmaker," in Bobo, *Available Visions.*

10. Pearl Bowser, "The Existence of Black Theatres," *Take Two Quarterly* (Columbus, OH: National Black Programming Consortium), 1.

11. Bowser, "The Existence of Black Theatres," 19.

12. Gloria J. Gibson-Hudson, "Recall and Recollect: Excavating the Life History of Eloyce King Patrick Gist," *Black Film Review* 8, 2 (1995): 20–21.

13. Gibson-Hudson, "Recall and Recollect," 20.

14. Philip Foner, *Women and the American Labor Movement* (New York: The Free Press, 1980), 443.

15. See her comments in the following interviews: Oliver Franklin, "An Interview: Kathleen Collins," *Independent Black American Cinema* (conference program brochure published by Third World Newsreel, February 1981): 22–24; David Nicholson, "Conflict and Complexity: Filmmaker Kathleen Collins," *Black Film Review* 2, 3 (Summer 1986): 16–17; and David Nicholson, "A Commitment to Writing: A Conversation with Kathleen Collins Prettyman," *Black Film Review* 5, 1 (Winter 1988/1989): 6–15.

16. Collins was working from Roth's book in manuscript form before it was eventually published.

17. Nicholson, "A Commitment to Writing," 8.

18. Carol Mueller, "Ella Baker and the Origins of 'Participatory Democracy,'" in Vicki L. Crawford et al., eds., *Women in the Civil Rights Movement: Tratlblazers and Torchbearers, 1941–1965* (Bloomington: Indiana University Press, 1993), 53.

19. Bernice Johnson Reagon et al., eds., *We Who Believe in Freedom: Sweet Honey in the Rock Still On the Journey* (New York: Anchor Books, 1993), 20.

20. Mueller, "Ella Baker and the Origins of 'Participatory Democracy,'" 65.

21. Sweet Honey in the Rock was formed in 1973, taking its name from a parable of religious origin, though not found in the Bible. According to the parable, there was a land that was so rich that when you cracked the rocks, honey would flow from them. Over the course of the group's twenty-plus years of existence, twenty women have at various times been a member.

Chapter Three

Ghosts and Vanishing Indian Women

Death of the Celluloid Maiden in the 1990s

M. Elise Marubbio

The 1990s saw the celluloid Indian back in the saddle, literally. Multiculturalism became one of the buzzwords of the nineties, and Hollywood filmmakers
were ready to "set the record straight" on the American Indian.
—Jacquelyn Kilpatrick [1]

The complex forms of identificatory desire evoked by works such as Thunderheart . . . and Legends of the Fall . . . suggest that contemporary images of
Native America have become even more powerfully imbricated with the national Imaginary than in the past.
—Robert Burgoyne [2]

The Celluloid Maiden reappears in the 1990s, after a hiatus of seventeen
years, in a number of films that reaffirm this figure's ability to adapt to
changing cultural trends in representing Native Americans. The figure
emerges in a diversity of roles—including an avenging ghost, a political
activist, and a mixed-blood Princess who crosses genres and national film
boundaries—that reveals the complexity of the figure. Although more contemporary and, in some cases, quite different from past presentations, these
uses of the figure stimulate cultural memories of prior Celluloid Maidens
through the films' reliance on or reference to previous modes of depicting the
character as a Princess or a Sexualized Maiden type. As a result, a tension
exists between the various films' multiculturalist and revisionist angles and
the deeply imbedded system of stereotypes that continues to use the figure as
a palimpsest upon which American national myths are reinscribed. [3] Thus,
although the 1990s films use the Celluloid Maiden to promote a racially

diverse narrative, to a greater extent the character reproduces the social ruptures of an era when past national mythic identities and the ideologies of the
western become antithetical to the nation's racial and cultural diversity.[4]

The contemporary narratives that incorporate the Celluloid Maiden rely
on nostalgia marred by violence and racism in their articulations of the power
structures involved in maintaining an American national identity and Native-
white relations. Revisionist in intent, four films from the early 1990s promote a "realistic" image of the Native woman, and all reveal the underlying
racial tension inherent in Native American-white relations. These traits clearly mark the efforts of *Thunderheart* (1992), *Silent Tongue* (1993), and *Legends of the Fall* (1994) to "'set the record straight' on the American Indian,"
or at least to rethink it and modify it in some way.[5] All exhibit revisionist
disillusion with the myth of the frontier, which celebrates an idealized na-
tion-building process. *Thunderheart*, *Legends of the Fall*, and the Canadian
film *Legends of the North* (1995) critique the governing body of the nation-
state—the corruption of the mythic ideal—at the same time that they celebrate the individual hero figure. *Silent Tongue*, the clearest western of the
films, takes on the idealism of the genre itself through its portrayal of white
men as an ineffectual force on the frontier and Native American women as
effective reactionaries.

Through the efforts and contradictions that create them, these films participate in what Richard Slotkin suggests is a pattern of reciprocal influence
in which politics shape the concerns and imagery of movies, and movies in
turn question or promote current political and social attitudes.[6] Though not
necessarily westerns, these Celluloid Maiden films, as a part of their revisionism, reference some aspect of the myth of the frontier that informs the
genre. Their use of genre nostalgia and Hollywood western generic conventions also ties them to the Hollywood tradition of portraying the Celluloid
Maiden. Their reliance on well-known visual metaphors in describing the
Celluloid Maiden often contrasts with their revisionist narrative ideology.
The resulting conflict parallels the tensions between conservative and liberal
attitudes toward multiculturalism and the United States' national identity in
the 1990s. *Legends of the North* might be exempted from such a claim about
U.S. films on the basis of its national origin; however, the pattern of stress
related to the political moment in the United States in which revisionism
resurfaced in the 1990s also exists in this film.

The early 1990s witnessed the end of the Cold War, the fall of the Soviet
system, the drawing to a close of the conservative Republican presidential
reign, and an increase in the United States' imperial behavior overseas in
places such as Panama and the Middle East. The sudden collapse of the
Soviet Union "left the political leadership of the United States unprepared"
for its uncontested position as world leader. The nation was overextended in
military and economic aid to other countries and unready to deal with such a

monumental change. The fall of communism and the dissolution of the Soviet Union eliminated the United States' external Other—the group used since the 1940s as a measure of what Americans were not. President George H. W. Bush's "new world order," a quest for a new political Other and a justification of global U.S. government and economic investments, resulted in two wars—one in Panama and the other in the Persian Gulf. Both reflected the country's insecurity about its national identity and the belief in the need to reassert international dominance. Certainly the Gulf War, in connection with the ultraconservative religious mood of the nation, presented a message of continued U.S. supremacy and established U.S. control over Middle East oil resources. [7]

The resulting turmoil of the early 1990s culminated in an intense questioning on the part of many Americans of their national past and their imperial and neocolonial present. Howard Zinn explains that, in the United States, a "citizenry disillusioned with politics and with what pretended to be intelligent discussions of politics turned its attention (or had its attention turned) to entertainment, to gossip, to ten thousand schemes for self-help. Those at its margins became violent, finding scapegoats within one's group (as with poor-black on poor-black violence), or against other races, immigrants, demonized foreigners, welfare mothers, minor criminals (standing in for untouchable major criminals)." On the political scene, conservatives supporting Whiteness rhetoric and prowhite national agendas countered liberal groups recognizing and celebrating a multicultural nation. Many critiqued the ongoing system of color hierarchy and ultraconservative political agendas that targeted peoples of color and the poor as responsible for national economic, social, and religious regression. They were, however, confronted by the rise of the religious Right, family values, and Bush's new world order. Such movements reaffirmed the ideology of America as the conquering hero and the world's policeman and echoed the ideological message of the myth, so prominent in the western film, that European-derived "civilization . . . really is *better* than all other civilizations, past and present." This conservative trend, which had its roots in the mid-1970s backlash against 1960s and 1970s liberalism, supported an increasing intolerance toward immigrants of color, illegal aliens, and the nation's racial poor; differing religious views and political orientations; and nontraditional "family values." Also in the early nineties, Native Americans and those of European descent in both North and South America mobilized against European and American quincentenary celebrations of Columbus's arrival in the New World. [8] Multiple voices were heard during this period both questioning and defending the colonial past, often resulting in heated debate and violence that indicated the depth to which the United States' identity remained tied to memories of conquest.

The Celluloid Maiden films register the effects of these debates and tensions in varying degrees in their revisionist narrative approaches and, in the case of *Silent Tongue* and *Thunderheart*, their diverse, contemporary portrayals of Native Americans and Native American-white racial power struggles. *Legends of the Fall* and the joint French-Canadian production *Legends of the North* maintain a more traditional and familiar approach to the Celluloid Maiden. They are, in outcome and style, similar to the much-heralded *Dances with Wolves* (1990), which, with its romanticizing of Native Americans, remains a hallmark of the 1990s revisionist movement and is remembered as the second western ever to win the Academy Award for Best Picture.[9] *Silent Tongue*, a western that follows more closely the approach of *Unforgiven* (1992)—also an Academy Award winner—challenges the conventions of the western and clearly questions the dominant racial and masculine order of the genre.[10] *Thunderheart* does not frame its narrative as a western; rather, it relies on the criminal investigation genre to inform its overarching narrative structure. Yet the film's location in the West, the positioning of Native Americans as the primary group within the narrative, and the narrative allusions to the western genre tie it to that tradition. This group of films offers a lens through which to view the legacy of almost ninety years of filmic presentation. In addition, these films maneuver the genre to speak to the political and media presence of Native Americans during the nineties, the demand for less racializing images in media, and, as Richard Slotkin suggests, the ongoing disillusionment of many Americans about the national government and "fundamental principles of national ideology."[11]

THE ACTIVIST, THE GHOST, THE HEALER, AND THE MARTYR

A chronological analysis of the 1990s Celluloid Maiden characters reveals a marked shift in their uses of the figure. The maiden metamorphoses from a highly revisionist and political manifestation of the Native woman as an activist against colonialism to a conservative martyr figure reminiscent of the silent-period Princess. Though *Thunderheart* and *Silent Tongue* focus on different eras in U.S. history, each creates a character who resists the white power structures manipulating her world. *Thunderheart*'s Maggie Eagle Bear and *Silent Tongue*'s Awbonnie embody the spirit of Native agency, their interactions with western European culture laying bare the often violent reality of the colonial experience for Native American women. In contrast, *Legends of the Fall* and *Legends of the North* retain a nostalgic tone most closely related to the silent-period films and display characteristics reminiscent of the various eras of Princess figures. *Legends of the Fall* relies on the "going native" theme prevalent in the 1970s films; *Legends of the North* reverts to a figure whose self-sacrifice harks back to the early depictions of the Celluloid Princess. The conservative construction of the Celluloid Maiden in these films is juxtaposed to the liberal agenda that underlies *Thunderheart* and *Silent Tongue*.

Thunderheart is one of the most poignant of the revisionist works because of its contemporary setting and focus on Native activism. The film, Michael Apted's mainstream fictional remake of his documentary *Incident at Oglala* (1992), places contemporary Native issues about land rights and political sovereignty squarely in front of the viewer.[12] It remains one of the few films that confront the audience with a realistic and complex picture of Native Americans, women's roles in tribal society, and the daily realities that many Native communities face. In addition, as Robert Burgoyne's work on *Thunderheart* and the national imaginary suggests, the film presents an internally colonized group pitted against the dominant nation from the point of view of the subjugated.[13] Thus this film undermines a particular idea of national unity by basing its narrative on examples of national discontinuity that result in political, social, and cultural differences.

Called to aid a murder investigation on the Bear Creek Sioux reservation in South Dakota, FBI agent Ray Lavoi (Val Kilmer), who is one-quarter Sioux, finds himself struggling between his loyalty to the bureau and western European culture and his awakening tribal identity. Well-trained in racializing poverty and nonconformity as signs of moral weakness, Ray initially blames the people of Bear Creek for their third-world status. Prompted by tribal police officer Walter Crow Horse (Graham Greene) to question his superior Frank Coutelle's (Sam Shepard) theory about the murder, Ray delves deeper into the incident, only to be drawn into a situation that forces him to confront the disturbing reality of Native-federal relations. As he learns more about the FBI-backed tribal governments "reign of terror" over the traditional and activist Sioux, Ray begins to wonder about his own heritage, to come to terms with his stereotypes about Indians, and to align himself with the traditionalists. Befriended by Walter, Maggie Eagle Bear (Sheila Tousey), and Grandpa Sam Reaches (Chief Ted Thin Elk), the traditionalist's medicine man, Ray begins to shed his white exterior and to take an interest in the problems of those living on the reservation. His interactions with Grandpa Reaches and Maggie initiate visions that link Ray to his Sioux heritage and bind him more closely to their cause. He eventually exposes the federal government's role in the terrorism, the uranium poisoning of the reservation's water source, and the murder at the heart of the film's plot.

Maggie Eagle Bear pays with her life for her political connections—her disruption of political order—and her interaction with Ray Lavoi. Her character is based on Anna Mae Aquash, an American Indian Movement activist who was allegedly killed by the FBI or by FBI supporters in 1976.[14] Maggie works for her people and against the dominant white culture represented by the FBI and Ray Lavoi. Her primary concern is to prove that the federal government has knowingly poisoned the reservation's only source of drinking water by illegally dumping uranium tailings into the river's source. A Dartmouth honors graduate, mother, and activist, and a force to be reckoned with, Maggie challenges Ray to "do his job," to investigate the many "suicides" and the "misappropriation of funds in school and health programs" on the reservation. In keeping with the reality of Anna Mae's death, the movie leaves the identity of Maggie's killer unknown, but the narrative implies that a federal plant within her community, the FBI, or the corrupt tribal government's vigilante squad aligned with the federal agents committed the crime.

Maggie's activism and militancy reach back into Celluloid Maiden history to revive the militant Native American Queen figure, whose resistance to encroaching Europeans is both sexually arousing and deadly. As discussed previously, the Native American Queen embodies the qualities of the feminized and premodern New World, including the danger awaiting the colonial forces there. As depicted in engravings and early accounts of colonial expansion, she figuratively represents the psychological reaction of the indigenous peoples to colonial action and the rape of their motherland, as well as the potential disruption of the colonial process. Her militant stance, with a "foot on the slain body of an animal or human enemy," suggests that she is capable of fighting back.[15] Similarly, Maggie's activities threaten the colonial order, in this case the U.S. government and the FBI. Though she is not a violent warrior like the Queen, Maggie's continual probing into the government's misconduct with the uranium mines, her relentless pursuit of justice for her people, who are being murdered, and her championing of Indian sovereignty cast her as a reactionary figure. Just as the Queen fought against the European invaders, she fights against the power structures that abuse the federal-Indian treaty relationship and for the rights of indigenous people. Within this context and because of the FBI's secret activities and infiltration of the tribal community, Maggie Eagle Bear's death, which recalls that of Sunshine's in *Little Big Man* (1970), symbolizes a history of governmentally sponsored military suppression of Native peoples and radically subversive elements in the nation's populace.

Thunderheart's narrative clearly criticizes the federal government's history of covert military intervention in tribal affairs for economic gain. Through Maggie's character, the film also highlights a tradition of Native community activism powered by women, including mothers and grandmothers. While some of this force gets channeled into education, symbolized in the film by Maggie's role as a teacher, a great deal emerges through political positions and organized demonstrations against treaty violations, destruction of sacred lands, and corruption in federal governmental programs that deal with Native American communities.[16]

Part of *Thunderheart*'s power lies in its open confrontation of several significant and controversial themes: colonialism, racism, and the violation of human rights. These are clearly summed up by various characters on both sides of the political struggle. Early in the film, Frank Coutelle explains to Ray that, while their assignment is a murder investigation, "it's also about helping people, helping people caught in the illusions of the past come to terms with the reality of the present." He explains this "reality" near the end of the film: "Let me tell you something. I feel for them, I really do, they're a proud people. But they're also a conquered people and that means their future is dictated by the nation that conquered them. Now rightly or wrongly, that's the way it works down through history." This patronizing, neoconservative perspective of U.S. dominance clashes with that of Jimmy Looks Twice (John Trudell), Maggie Eagle Bear, and the other traditionalists, who maintain their identity as a culturally and politically sovereign people. As Jimmy Looks Twice tells Ray, "We choose the right to be who we are. We know the difference between the reality of freedom and the illusion of freedom. There is a way to live with the earth and a way not to live with the earth. We choose earth. It's about power." Maggie Eagle Bear's position as an activist places her squarely in these cultural debates, and she initiates Ray into the power of the earth, reminding him at one point that evidence is not power: "Power is the rainstorm. That river right there—that's what I have to protect."

Thunderheart's narrative and its visual presentation connect Maggie to the land and water as its guardian. She fights against the uranium mines that are contaminating the water; she spreads offerings over the river and takes samples for testing; and she reminds Lavoi that the river needs her aid. Her death brings her full circle, back into the earth she protects. Well into the film, Ray and Walter Crow Horse go to the site of the first murder to investigate. The moon casts a pale light over the sand and rock formations of the badlands and the illegal, government- sponsored uranium mining pools. Startled by the sound of animals, Ray moves toward a shape in the sand. He finds Maggie partially buried, face down in the sand, only her denim jacket showing above the ground. Moaning with grief as he recognizes her, Lavoi turns Maggie over. Her sand-covered face, tinted a pale blue, stares back at him while her open eyes reflect the light of the moon. Maggie Eagle Bear dies in the Black Hills, the Sioux's sacred land and the river's source, near the uranium mines she fought against.

Maggie's character embodies the contemporary activist and ecologist at the same time that it relies on elements from the hybrid Celluloid Maiden history. The only primary Native woman character, she is depicted as a love interest for the white hero, betrays her own people by aiding Ray, and is metonymically connected to the landscape, all of which invoke memories of the Princess figures. These elements are reinforced by the film's tendency to romanticize Indian spirituality. This aspect emerges most clearly in visions Ray has in connection with Maggie and Grandpa Reaches. A number of times, while on Maggie's property or just after having spoken to Maggie, Ray sees dancers in full regalia across the river. Walter informs him later that he has seen the old ones performing the Ghost Dance in preparation for war against the whites.[17] He also dreams of "running with the old ones" at Wounded Knee as white soldiers mow down the unarmed women and children. Grandpa Reaches stimulates Ray's memories of a childhood with his drunken Sioux father and a single dream of the old ones, but the majority of Ray's visions occur in conjunction with Maggie, who, through association, links Ray to the physical sites in the dreams. Such subtle references do not overwhelm the film's pro-Indian angle, but they do render Maggie a capitulation to Hollywood marketing. As John Walton suggests, she takes on the "favorable stereotype" of the earth mother, the "Ecological Indian," and the sexually attractive love interest.[18]

As mentioned above, Maggie's character is based on the American Indian Movement activist Anna Mae Aquash. The character's connection to this well-known woman and her much-publicized death is an important component of the film's pro-Native stance. The connection between the two women also underscores the human rights and anticolonial themes highlighted throughout the film. By overlaying the earth mother and other "favorable" Hollywood stereotypes onto the core representative of Anna Mae Aquash, however, the film undermines the potential of Maggie's character to effectively symbolize the resistance movement and replaces it with the Celluloid Princess. As a result, the political position characterized by Maggie within the cultural debates discussed early in the film shifts. She initially uses her Dartmouth training against the system—to investigate it and to empower her own people. But her commitment to Ray weakens the effects of these actions and repositions her on the side of the debate that Frank Coutelle supports. The character recapitulates to the colonial system and reverts from the Native American Queen figure to the Princess figure. This move cancels out Maggie's intentions to use the dominant society against itself. Thus the use of the Celluloid Maiden figure in the film weakens the film's political agenda and positions age-old stereotypes on contemporary images of Native American women.

Maggie Eagle Bear's sand-covered face, pale and tinted slightly blue, eerily reappears in Sam Shepard's *Silent Tongue* as the face of Awbonnie. Sheila Tousey plays the decomposing woman-ghost Awbonnie. Her distraught white husband, Talbot Roe (River Phoenix), ties her to the land of the living through his relentless vigil over her corpse. In direct contrast to most of the Celluloid Maiden films, *Silent Tongue* challenges the idea of the young woman who falls in love with the white hero by suggesting that such love and devotion are illusions of the colonial mind. In addition, Shepard's film revises the connection between the Native woman and nature that plays such an important role in the Celluloid Maiden's tropic resonance.

The film enfolds the lives of three women—the Kiowa bone picker Silent Tongue (Tantoo Cardinal) and her two mixed-blood daughters, Awbonnie and Velada (Jeri Arredondo)—into the story of three white men who are bound to the women by violence and need. Awbonnie, whom Prescott Roe (Richard Harris) purchases from her father Eamon McCree (Alan Bates) for three horses with the hope that she will cure his son's melancholia, dies in childbirth. The heartbroken and selfish Talbot refuses to burn or bury her body, acts that would release her spirit; rather, he guards her decomposing form, battling the scavenging birds of prey and her angry ghost for its possession. Prescott travels across the desert in search of Eamon McCree to buy Awbonnie's sister Velada, believing that she will halt his son's increasing insanity. Eamon refuses only because Velada—the "Kiowa Warrior Princess"—is the main attraction of his traveling medicine show. Prescott kidnaps Velada, who eventually agrees to help for a large sum of money and many horses. As Prescott, Talbot, and Velada are preyed upon by Awbonnie's ghost, Eamon and his son Reeves (Dermot Mulroney) search for Velada, only to be hunted by Silent Tongue's people. Silent Tongue, so named when her tongue was cut out for lying to a chief, left Eamon and her girls to return to her people. But as one review points out, "Her brutal treatment at the hands of her own people is nothing to the way she and her daughters are treated by the new settlers."[19] Much like her daughter's ghost, Silent Tongue seeks revenge on the white man who forced her into marriage. As Eamon's nightmarish memories reveal, he came upon her in the desert while she collected bones, raped her while Reeves was forced to watch, and then took her as his wife.

Refusing an easy good/bad dichotomy between the Native women and their white husbands, Shepard's narrative hints at the affection felt by the white men for their captive wives. For example, Eamon covers the walls of his caravan with photographs of Silent Tongue and her daughters. The images add a level of intimacy and tenderness to the relationship that contradicts the visions of Silent Tongue's rape and Eamon's callous economic selfishness with respect to Velada. Similarly, Talbot remains tender to his wife's shrouded body, holding it protectively, kissing its face, arranging its covering, and viciously attacking all that attempt to approach it, even when under siege by her femme fatale ghost. His own mental breakdown at her death clarifies the genuine intensity of his love. Like the Celluloid Maidens of the 1970s, the living Awbonnie acted as the white hero's anchor, allowing him to "go native" to a limited arid safe extent.

While the film's insight into characters' emotional development leans toward the males, the women's activism refutes the western tradition of white-hero worship. The film achieves this in part by depicting the men as weak and atypical of the traditional western hero. In addition, the film underscores its revisionist agenda by giving the women agency through the acts of leaving or terrorism. Silent Tongue chooses to abandon her daughters and return to her people. She continues, however, to haunt her husband in his dreams. Awbonnie, depicted through Talbot's love as a Princess type during her life, metamorphoses into a femme fatale, much like Nita in *Arrowhead* (1953) and Hesh-ke in *Mackenna's Gold* (1969), whose physical connection to the hero turns violently against him. When Talbot thwarts her attempts to escape to the spirit world, Awbonnie's ghost carries on increasingly violent attacks on the bodies and minds of Talbot and Prescott Roe, until Prescott finally throws her body into the fire, an act that releases all parties involved. Prescott's actions allegorically suggest the need for white America to let go of its symbolic romantic notions of Native Americans. Early in the film, Awbonnie's ghost foregrounds the allegory by stating, "You keep me bound here out of your selfish aloneness." Her comment reinforces the traditional use of the Native American in western European culture as a symbolic racial and cultural Other that offers a psychological and political justification for the entrenchment of the American nation.

In keeping with the message above, *Silent Tongue* also inverts the traditional cinematic reliance on metaphorically linking the Native woman to images of nature. Although the beautiful Native woman remains tied to the landscape, stark and harsh images of the land replace all romanticism, as seen in Silent Tongue's bone picking, Awbonnie's physical decomposition, and the birds of prey that stalk Awbonnie's body. Nature takes on as violent a veneer as does the Celluloid Maiden. Reminiscent of the landscape in Cormac McCarthy's *Blood Meridian*, the desert of *Silent Tongue* never offers any oasis of beauty. Rather, the barren, dry land, punctuated by thirsty stands of trees, contains birds of prey, fields of sun-bleached animal bones, and a Greek tyle Fury whose presence haunts and physically harms the living.[20] Like this space, Awbonnie's body carries the marks of life and death. Half of her white-painted face is decomposed, and her milk-white eyes are bright with passionate anger. Feathers, vulture wings, bones, and cloth adorn the tree where she lies. Because the viewer never encounters the living Awbonnie, her persona emerges from these images. As a result, Awbonnie and the land she inhabits invoke the memory of a vengeful, beautiful, and dangerous Native American Queen and the femme fatale, more reminiscent of the Sexualized Maidens of the 1950s than of the Princess figure.

The commitment of *Silent Tongue* to reworking the western forces the viewer to confront the colonial process head-on. Its "stylized allegory of the white man's brutalization of Native Americans" refuses to allow the viewer any lapses into romanticism or nostalgia about America's evolution as a nation.[21] Although the film relies on stereotypes, such as the Princess figure and the Native femme fatale, to shore up its characterization of Native American women, these do not consume the character. Velada, the "Kiowa Warrior Princess" and rodeo queen, negotiates her own payment for helping Prescott Roe. Awbonnie, who "was [Talbot's] light," refuses the responsibility of that role, and her ghost takes her husband to task for his participation in her purchase and her death. The images of the Native American women fighting for their freedom are political and effective. The film's deemphasis of the Princess type in the characters of Awbonnie and Silent Tongue helps it push the boundaries of the figure more successfully than does *Thunderheart*.

The anticolonialist narratives in *Thunderheart* and *Silent Tongue* and the Celluloid Maiden's use within the films must also be placed within the context of the early 1990s' ultraconservative political atmosphere and the controversial quincentenary. The year of the quincentenary, 1992, marked a tumultuous moment in U.S. and Western history, a period that forced mainstream U.S. culture to reevaluate its historical narratives, its political heroes, and its heritage on this continent. Debates abounded regarding whether the quincentenary should celebrate Columbus and the "civilizing" of the Americas, the multicultural encounter, or five hundred years of indigenous survival in the wake of colonialism and genocide. A wide range of literary reactions illustrated the intense self-examination that academia and the American public underwent during this time.[22]

With respect to the post–Cold War global political positioning of the United States, one is struck by the complexity of these quincentenary debates in relation to U.S. nationalism. During 1992, Americans witnessed the third-greatest period of U.S. immigration, a rise in anti-illegal immigration measures, and a decline in employment opportunities. As Walter Zinn suggests, events such as rising unemployment, U.S. economic expansion overseas, and the U.S. military action in Iraq culminated in insecurity, causing many Americans to question their position in their own country and their role in global economic politics. The works of Michael Omi and Howard Winant and of Lauren Berlant point toward the various strategies used by groups to express these identity crises, including masking racist political agendas in multicultural rhetoric. Within this milieu, the quincentenary was, in the words of Stephen Summerhill and John A. Williams, "no longer an innocuous ethnic celebration of Columbus' discovery of America, it had become a battleground for our entire view of Western culture."[23]

Thunderheart and *Silent Tongue* represent what appear to be respectful efforts by the filmmakers to explore and participate in the deconstruction of the colonial process and these debates. *Thunderheart*, in particular, relied heavily on the input of Native Americans and the continued collaborative effort between Apted and the Native American participants from his documentary *Incident at Oglala* (1992). Both *Thunderheart* and *Silent Tongue* challenge the tenets of the western's pro-white and pro-nation formation agenda, illuminating in the process a darker side of American history and the nation's continuing actions as a colonizing force. However, both films also show how difficult it is for those working with representations of Native Americans to divorce themselves from racializing stereotypes. Both Maggie Eagle Bear and Awbonnie represent the possible destabilization of the Celluloid Maiden figure and the concrete reality that Native Americans continue to demand an identity and voice outside the national whole. At the same time, *Thunderheart* resorts to invoking the Celluloid Maiden figure, and *Silent Tongue* the Native American Queen component of it. In addition, by placing its narrative in the past, *Silent Tongue* perpetuates the tradition of depicting Native Americans as historical relics of a mythic space. The inability to completely abandon tropic references is not unique to the film community; it emerged as a problem facing many Americans attempting to come to terms with the politics of the quincentenary.

On the whole, *Silent Tongue* and *Thunderheart* remain the most progressive of the revisionist Celluloid Maiden films. Perhaps as a sign of the waning influence of the quincentenary debates of 1992, subsequent films fail to maintain the level of commitment *Silent Tongue* and *Thunderheart* display in deconstructing Hollywood's presentation of Native Americans and the Celluloid Maiden figure. Only one year after the release of *Silent Tongue*, a decidedly more conservative and nostalgic approach to revisionism and the western surfaces in Edward Zwick's *Legends of the Fall*, setting the tone for *Legends of the North*.

The World War I family melodrama *Legends of the Fall* (1994), as one critic described it, throws "the golden shadows of the waning Old West . . . across the big screen with full reverential treatment."[24] The film celebrates an American individualism and isolationism born of the frontier landscape and shaped by antigovernment rhetoric. Like the revisionist westerns of the 1970s, *Legends of the Fall* weaves nostalgia for ennobled Native Americans and their spiritual connection to the world into its ideology. The film's hero, Tristan Ludlow (Brad Pitt), bucks the mainstream way of life. More at home working cattle, hunting in the wilderness, or defying authority than existing in the cultural mainstream, he tracks bears just to touch them, sails the world as a game hunter and trader among the world's tribal communities, and makes his living running bootleg liquor. The Native American character One Stab (Gordon Tootoosis) provides a point of reference through which the story unfolds and, with Isabel Two (Karina Lombard), is a pivotal influence on Tristan's emergence as a legend—a man more at peace with the "savages" of the world than with "civilization." Jim Harrison's novella of the same name, the basis for the screenplay, also includes these characters and attaches meaning to Tristan's father-son relationship with One Stab. The film, however, clearly emphasizes the Native American angle of the story to suggest that Tristan's wildness and inner savagery come from One Stab's influence, rather than, as is the case in the novel, from a hereditary link to his Scottish grandfather. The film also plays down Harrison's focus on demythologizing "our romantic notions of Cowboys and Indians," instead enhancing such notions.[25]

The "reverential treatment" accorded the Old West also applies to the film's reliance on stereotypical symbolism in its coding of the two primary Native characters. One Stab and Isabel Two represent the environment Tristan really belongs to—the vanishing world of the Indian West. While he loves his brothers and Susannah Finncannon (Julia Ormond), Tristan clashes with the civilized and educated world of the East that they represent. "He had always lived in the border lands . . . somewhere between this world and the next." It is this liminal spirit that binds him to One Stab and Isabel Two, who instinctively understand his wild nature and embrace it.

One Stab is a wise Cree Indian elder who outlives the family and is thus able to perpetuate its legend. The narrative opens with One Stab sitting in a tepee speaking these words: "Some people hear their own inner voices and they live by what they hear. Such people become crazy or they become legend." He is referring to Tristan Ludlow, the middle son of One Stab's friend Colonel William Ludlow (Anthony Hopkins). The film depicts One Stab as Tristan's spiritual guide and the man who feels Tristan's presence through his dreams. One Stab's voiceovers also link Tristan to the land and Tristan's periodic lapses into savagery to "the bear's voice he heard deep inside him, growling low from dark, secret places."

Similar to that of One Stab, the characterization of Isabel Two relies on the now-familiar traditional images of the Celluloid Maiden, with an emphasis on the Princess figure. In an interesting evolution of the figure, Isabel Two is not established as a Princess by any one particular scene; rather, the image emerges out of an accumulation of narrative vignettes that places her within the tradition of the figure. Demonstrating how deeply solidified the figure is in the American memory, the film economically presents the traces of Celluloid Princess ancestry in Isabel Two, clearly depending on the audience's genre memories of past figures. Much as the films of the 1950s and the 1970s do, *Legends of the Fall* confines the Celluloid Maiden to an extremely small though important position on the edges of the narrative, where her world centers on the white hero. Reminiscent of Sonseeahray in *Broken Arrow* (1950), Isabel Two has the gift of prophecy—at least where her life with Tristan is concerned. She knows she will marry Tristan, a fact she relays at age twelve to the newly arrived Susannah. The film's introduction of her as a child establishes her innocence and absolute devotion to the white hero. Isabel Two's reappearance as a beautiful and intriguing young woman, whom Tristan finds captivating, opens the door for the possibility of assimilation through marriage. The figure also carries traces of the 1940s Sexualized Maiden in her mixed heritage as the daughter of Paul Decker (Paul Desmond) and his Cree wife Pet (Tantoo Cardinal), who work for Ludlow. Her mixed-blood status carries no sexual or psychological stigma and does nothing to diminish her Princess persona. Rather, it works to underscore the liberal and antiracist utopia of the Ludlow ranch in contrast to the external world.

The structure set up by the film's coupling of Tristan with Native America and the power of the wilderness references the Hollywood trend seen in the 1970s Celluloid Maiden films. His ability to "go native" without falling too deeply into insanity or savagery depends on the Native woman—a Princess type—with whom he finds spiritual and psychological balance. *Legends of the Fall* symbolically establishes Isabel Two in this role by placing her in relation to the two white women in the film, Isabel Ludlow and Susannah. Isabel Two takes her name from Mrs. Ludlow (Christina Pickles) and thus is metaphorically connected to Tristan's absent mother through her name and to his spiritual father, One Stab, through tribal affiliation. Mrs. Ludlow's character does not develop beyond a cameo appearance here and there, but her return to the family ranch with a wedding gown for Isabel after years of absence establishes the girl as the family's choice to marry Tristan. The film does develop Susannah's character, and in fact she exists as the primary love interest for all the Ludlow boys. Susannah initially arrives at the ranch as Samuel Ludlow's (Henry Thomas) fiancée. She quickly captivates all the Ludlow men, who are starved for the presence of a cultivated eastern woman like their mother, and falls in love with Tristan. After Samuel dies in war and Tristan abandons her to exorcise his demons, she marries Alfred (Aidan Quinn).

Isabel Two's Native heritage makes her more capable of understanding Tristan's savage instincts and "the bear inside" than is Susannah, whose fragile eastern spirit continually clashes with Tristan's wildness. Isabel Two and Tristan marry and, according to One Stab, "It was then that Tristan came into the quiet of his life. The Bear was sleeping." Like *Jeremiah Johnson's* Swan (1972), whose Christianity worked as a link for Jeremiah between the wilderness and the civilization he abandoned, Isabel Two is well equipped for the position of cultural mediator. Her combination of "Western" education and Native grounding in the earth allows Isabel Two to keep Tristan anchored to the white world and to cultivate in him a certain level of contentedness, something missing from Tristan's relationship with Susannah.

Following in the footsteps of *Jeremiah Johnson* and *Broken Arrow*, *Legends of the Fall* tenuously hints at the idea of an American Adam and Native American Eve through Tristan and Isabel Two's union. But the film resorts to an interesting permutation on the Adam and Eve narrative by killing both the Native American Eve and her competitor, Susannah, the white Eve whose mental instability results in her suicide. This allows the film to continue the tradition of idolizing the white male hero, whose wild soul and individualism, cultivated out of his love for a Native American way of life, leave little room for domestication. In addition, within a discourse on race, Isabel Two's Native-white heritage suggests a new image of the American Eve—a more culturally and racially "white" one. She is a multicultural allegory for a changing American identity, which, on the surface, appears a seductive one. Yet multiculturalism carries a less than idealized meaning within the film's nostalgia for the waning American past and through its presentation of Isabel Two as a child raised in a primarily white environment and isolated from the racism she would have encountered in town. Multiculturalism looks more like an assimilative process than an interaction of culturally and racially diverse groups. Subtly, the film suggests that an egalitarian interaction of many different cultures and heritages, an idealized assimilated culture, is still unrealistic.

Comparable to *Legends of the Fall* in its romantic nostalgia for a mythic West, *Legends of the North* attempts to critique extreme white paternalism while maintaining a high degree of romantic attachment to the symbolism the Celluloid Maiden figure resonates in the earlier films. Here, too, one finds an insular community founded by a patriarchal leader who has abandoned the cultural system he sees as responsible for the demise of the Native American. The least revisionist of all the 1990s films, *Legends of the North* simply transfers the markers of change seen in *Legends of the Fall*, such as creating an educated, mixed-blood Princess, to a traditional martyr figure, as seen in the silent-period films. In so doing, the film forgoes any in-depth reworking of the figure.

Legends of the North takes place in the Yukon in the early 1890s. Aristocrat Charles Bel-Air (Georges Corraface) and his deceased father's guide, Whip (Randy Quaid), set out on a journey to find Esperanza, a legendary gold treasure. They find the gold guarded by a remote tribe of primitive Indians under the authoritarian rule of a white man, McTavish (Serge Houde), who fancies himself their "great white hope." As he tells Bel-Air, "These people were on the edge of extinction. And as their white father, I gave them a sense of themselves and their community." His commitment to them extends far enough to ensure their entrapment in his idea of how Native American culture must remain in order to survive. He keeps the tribe mired in the past, and all intruders—threats to the community's lifestyle—are either killed or married into the tribe as captive participants. His mixed-blood daughter, Kanata (Sandrine Holt), falls in love with Bel-Air as the two recite and enact *Romeo and Juliet* and *Wuthering Heights*. She rejects her Native lover for the white outsider, whom she helps to escape. Their journey across the frozen north toward freedom in the south ends in tragedy as she gives up her rations to ensure Bel-Air's survival. He illustrates his love for her by vowing to stay with her dead body, a gesture that fails when Whip finds him and takes him back to civilization.

The film returns to the silent period for its narrative structure. As in the early Princess films, the aristocratic white male leaves the East; France takes the place of the earlier films' East Coast or England. Bel-Air journeys into the wilderness, where he must be rescued by the Princess figure. Kanata's character melds the Princess with the helper figure of that era, and for the first time in eighty years, the Princess does not marry the hero. Much as she did in *Iola's Promise* (1912) and *Red Wing's Gratitude* (1909), the Princess saves the hero when his culture clashes with her own. As in the romantic love narratives of the Princess films, the two lovers presumably would have wed once they reached civilization. Unlike the silent-period films, however, *Legends of the North* never quite melds its disparate elements into a satisfactory formula. It seems that the reliance on a *Romeo and Juliet*-style unrequited love theme, within a narrative that builds on the girl's exoticism, fails to hold the tensions found in the earlier films. Perhaps the structure simply no longer fits with the film's contemporaries, such as *Thunderheart* and *Silent Tongue*, and thus appears less successful. But it seems more likely that the addition of a white patriarchal and oppressive tribal ruler undermines the film's ability to maintain the tension between the vanishing American noble savage image and the manifest destiny of white cultural superiority.

The reliance of *Legends of the North* on the Princess as a martyr figure brings the historical trajectory of the Celluloid Maiden full circle, to its cinematic roots in the silent period. Kanata's mixed-blood heritage makes her a hybrid figure like Isabel Two. More overtly than does Isabel Two, however, Kanata retains the symbolic components of the first Princess figures, appearing as a beautiful and alluring chiefs daughter whose yearning for western European culture can be achieved only through a commitment to a white male patriarchal figure—either her father or Bel-Air. The film's most obvious reversion to the silent-period figures surfaces in Kanata's self-sacrifice, which reaffirms the primacy of western European culture.

Kanata's high tribal social standing, her Native sensuality, and the exoticism of her tribal existence are enhanced for the contemporary audience and her white lover by their contrast with her Western literary training. Both *Thunderheart* and *Legends of the Fall* use this narrative tool to reduce the difference between the Native American woman and the white male and to highlight the Celluloid Maiden's aura as a contemporary woman—an intellectually equal partner for the white hero. *Legends of the North* takes full advantage of this mechanism to underscore Kanata's exoticism and difference from her peers, who, while they are equal in beauty to Kanata, never captivate Bel-Air's romantic imagination. One scene in particular brings this into focus. The newly arrived Bel-Air and Kanata are framed in a medium long shot, standing in the snow near the village meat-drying racks. Bel-Air, dressed in his mountaineering gear, recites *Romeo and Juliet* to a fur-swathed Kanata. Her costume fits the environment and reinforces the "Indianness" of their surroundings. The mise-en-scene carries on the tradition of juxtaposing the "civilized" white outsider to the "savage" and "primitive" Native girl, but Kanata's reciting of Juliet's line from memory jars the image. Bel-Air, along with the viewer, reacts strongly to this seemingly incongruous moment: a "savage" girl in an isolated Indian village with little or no contact with the white world knows this literary classic by heart. His delight at finding such a well-read and intoxicating woman increases as she informs him of her knowledge of other works as well. From this moment forward, they take on the roles of their literary counterparts, enacting the taboo relationships of both *Romeo and Juliet* and *Wuthering Heights*'s Heathcliff and Catherine. Kanata will go so far as to die as tragically as these well-known female characters of Western literature.

Though in some ways the Celluloid Maiden's education appears a progressive step toward creating a more equal union and a less "primitive" character, her training carries symbolic weight as intellectual advancement only because it comes in the form of Western liberal arts rather than Native-centered teachings. In the case of *Legends of the North*, the film's textual overtones are accentuated through the contrast of Kanata's education with her father's commitment to containing his people in a tribal culture of the past. The film has little to do with supporting equal opportunity for minorities and more to do with perpetuating a society governed through the unquestioned power of a white elite. McTavish molds a daughter who will fulfill his need for intellectual stimulation but will not threaten his primitive utopia. Unlike *Thunderheart*, in which Maggie Eagle Bear utilizes Western education as a tool against the colonial system, *Legends of the North* wields it as a sign of the civilized savage that validates colonialism in the process. The film reaffirms the ideological dictum from the turn of the century that the only way to save the Indian was through a Western education, which would prepare him or her for entrance into white society. Unlike in the early films, however, assimilation does not appear as an option or a goal in McTavish's world. Rather, the patriarchal white father isolates his Native "children" in order to teach them how to be better Natives. As a result, the film appears to capitalize on the demand for multicultural revisionist narratives, yet it does not commit to abandoning the racializing practices inherent in filmic stereotypes.

The revitalization of such a conservative Celluloid Maiden figure in *Legends of the Fall* and *Legends of the North*, which rely heavily on the Princess aspect of the figure, reinforces the figure's traditional symbolic boundaries. In other words, by eliminating the more progressive trends of the last twenty years, these films depict the Princess primarily as a romanticized ideal of the nation's historical emergence and racial hierarchies. Kanata's depiction, in particular, offers a subtle overturning of any attempt by the film to question the role of paternalism as a historical and contemporary colonial force. In addition, Kanata's self-inflicted death, as is the case with those of the silent-period Princess figures, relieves white America of its cultural guilt over the colonization process—as does the tribe's eventual killing of her father. Furthermore, the mixed-blood Princess nods toward a multicultural nation without challenging a white national ideal that relegates racialized minorities to the periphery of society, banishing them from its political and social center.

All of the 1990s films utilize the Celluloid Princess figure as their basic reference point, incorporating to some degree the traits of noble spirit, high social standing, a primary connection to nature and the American landscape's primordial essence, a tie to the American hero (symbolic of Whiteness), and racial exoticism. *Legends of the Fall* and *Legends of the North* retain the additional qualifications of innocence and purity seen in the 1910s and 1950s films, which dates the figure. Such a reliance on the Princess rather than the Sexualized Maiden aspect of the figure comes as no surprise, considering the importance of the civil rights movement of the 1960s and the 1990s' attention to creating more sympathetic and contemporary images of Native Americans. The move away from Vietnam-era liberalism and activism toward the conservative mores of the 1990s, however, also results in a revival of elements of the Sexualized Maiden that do not surface in the 1970s films but reach back to the 1940s, 1950s, and 1960s. The 1940s figures combine eroticism, sexual aggression, and femme fatale violence in the body of a mixed-race woman. The 1950s films eliminate the mixed-race component but add the woman's desire to kill the white hero. On the whole, the 1990s films appear less overtly anti-Indian and racist than their predecessors for three reasons. They adapt only one or two of the older combination of characteristics; they eliminate the character's eroticism and sexual aggression; and they do not rely on sadism, as is the tendency of the older films. As a result, the elements they do choose to include—mixed-race parentage, femme fatale qualities, or Native American Queen-style resistance—seem to offer, but not guarantee, the possibility of a more complex representation of the figure, as seen in *Thunderheart* and *Silent Tongue*.

The 1990s films all register some degree of uncertainty over abandoning the Celluloid Maiden as a palimpsest through which the nation's "identificatory desire" for a mythic past continues to be considered.[26] Certainly, the Celluloid Maiden figure's return from a countercolonial symbol that throws white superiority into question to a symbol that reaffirms it indicates a waning commitment on the part of the film industry to vigorously challenging racial inequality. This comes as no surprise, considering the lackluster political commitment to addressing race in the 1990s. The year 1992 marked the end of the Republican presidencies and a move into a Democratic administration that ultimately failed to resurrect a strong antiracism agenda for the nation. Rather, there emerged a neoliberal project that sought to "rearticulate the neoconservative and new right racial projects of the Reagan-Bush years in [a] centrist framework of moderate redistribution and cultural universalism." Similarly, multiculturalism, which originally carried a liberal awareness of racial structures and racial inequality in the United States, became a buzzword for pacifying civil rights activists and minority groups.[27] The resulting ineffectuality of the term reflected the political and social reality of racial politics in the United States, as does the increasingly conservative image of the Celluloid Maiden in 1990s films. The trajectory formed by the 1990s films' changing applications of multiculturalism suggests that the film industry continues to be influenced by external social indicators when it deals with delicate issues of race. Whether a symbol of resistance to, or acceptance of, the power structures involved in the colonialism historically present in Native American-white relations, the Celluloid Maiden remains a textual index and a telling metaphor for ongoing national ambivalence regarding race, interracial mixing, and multiculturalism.

THE CELLULOID MAIDEN AS PALIMPSEST

This study of the representations of the Celluloid Maiden from the silent period through the mid-1990s reveals the complexity of the figure and its versatility as a metonym for interracial mixing and Native-white relations. It also highlights the continual remolding of the Celluloid Maiden to resonate with subsequent generations, indicating the extent to which our national myths continue to inform our sociopolitical present and our strong commitment to maintaining such an ambivalent image. The temporal distance of the 1970s and 1990s hybrid figure from the figure's blueprint in the 1910s, coupled with the increasing tendency to rely on genre memories of the subsequent adaptations, manifests itself in disunity between the ideological tenets behind the figure and revisionist intentions. Looking back over the past ninety years of images, one is struck by how often the figure chafes against the most liberal aims of a film. The variety of depictions of the Celluloid Maiden illustrates the difficulty of locating this symbol within a mythic system of representation that is increasingly scrutinized and yet continually maintained. This may be the reason the figure now emerges in cross-genre and Native-centered films that reference the western but also attempt to move past it.

Although the Celluloid Maiden figure resists rigidity, offering instead a degree of latitude for change, even in its malleability it remains contained within a particular racializing discourse of power, domination, and exotic pleasure that fixes it within a cultural, historical, and racial framework. Because the figure is constructed as an exotic Other, even its most elusive presence ensures a film's inculcation into a colonial discourse based on racializing stereotypes. Thus the films never completely reject the racial and colonial premises of American nation building and the myth of the frontier. Rather, the ambivalence ingrained in the figure allows it to continue as a palimpsest—a textual body erased and rewritten to fit each generation's idea of its place in American history and its image of the role of the Native American woman within that history.

The individual components of the figure—the Celluloid Princess and the Sexualized Maiden—underscore different manifestations of the ambivalence toward Native Americans and interracial mixing. Embodying the concept of the noble red man, the Princess represents the best of Native America and the idea of assimilation. Within the western's colonial discourse on American nation building, she symbolizes the notion of a virgin continent, an untamed wilderness that desires the white male colonizer and the progressive march of civilization. The pro-Indian films in which the figure emerges utilize it as a mitigating element between a liberal, utopian, mixed-race national image and the reality of cultural violence against those who are racially and culturally different from a national white norm. Although she is a by-product of the early Celluloid Princess figure, the Sexualized Maiden harbors none of the romanticism of her predecessor. Rather, she stands for the dangers of assimilation and functions to maintain a phobia and fetish about race that verges on sadistic fantasy, which even the films attempting to examine themes of race and sexuality continue to reinforce. When, as in *The Searchers* (1956), *In Cold Blood* (1967), and the 1990s films, the two sides of the figure merge into a hybrid figure, a balance must be found between the different ideological foci. That balance appears to have moved over the course of the century toward the romanticism of the Princess. Nonetheless, the underlying ideology of the figure remains the same. This ideology involves the Celluloid Maiden's accentuated racial and cultural difference from the white hero and her ultimate death, which underscores the politics of conquest and the reality of the nation's racial hierarchy. In addition, while each generation of media adapts the tropic components, a fundamental and unresolved ambivalence remains clearly embedded in each revision.

Even with the wane, and perhaps disappearance, of the western, and with the rise of Native-produced films, a beautiful young Native woman cinematically represented by particular images who is physically connected with the white hero and dies rekindles a memory of the Celluloid Maiden. The inability to completely escape the evocation of the Celluloid Maiden as a symbol of white dominance, historical violence, political power, and desire for a particular national identity resides in the strength of the system surrounding the figure. The racial formation of the Celluloid Maiden, to borrow from Omi and Winant, relies on a particular *"interpretation, representation, or expla-*

nation of racial dynamics." These racial dynamics connect "what race means in a particular discursive practice and the ways in which both social struc-tures and everyday experiences are racially organized, based upon that mean-ing."[28] The emergence of the Celluloid Maiden during moments of extreme national identity crisis and stress suggests the figure's ability to reinforce the familiar without completely alienating those trying to change the system; they too find value in its structure, as *Silent Tongue* makes evident. Additio-nally, the nation continues to rely on images from its myth of the frontier, particularly in times of war, economic stress, and changing population dy-namics. One simply need recall President Reagan's reliance on a cowboy persona, the ongoing cowboy-Indian rhetoric used in international and urban warfare, and the backlash to legal and illegal immigrants of color to realize that the nation consciously relies on the power of such dynamics. Likewise, the death of the Celluloid Maiden provides a specific nostalgic image of a heterogeneous white ideal and justifies the ordering and controlling of unruly Others. The Celluloid Maiden, particularly the Princess persona, engages an idea of a multiethnic and multiracial state while allowing us to romanticize or ignore the racial politics of our historical past and present.

Perhaps the most obvious evidence of the figure's power and resilience resides in its emergence in a cluster of films released from the late 1980s through the 1990s. These include *Powwow Highway* (1989), *Black Robe* (1991), *A River Runs Through It* (1992), *Dance Me Outside* (1994), *Grand Avenue* (1996), *Smoke Signals* (1998), and *Naturally Native* (1999). Of this group, the two historical dramas—*Black Robe* and *A River Runs Through It*—remain most closely tied to the Hollywood tradition of depicting Native Americans in the past. *Black Robe* presents a Princess-type figure who, like the hybrid Celluloid Maidens of the 1970s, woos her white lover away from his own culture and his religion. In contrast, *A River Runs Through It* briefly introduces a young Native woman into an otherwise non-Native narrative as a sexually active flapper. In both cases, the women simply disappear from the narratives. The remaining films also reference, but do not fully develop, the Celluloid Maiden figure. They include films that are Native centered (*Powwow Highway* and *Dance Me Outside*) and Native written, Native pro-duced, or both (*Grand Avenue*, *Smoke Signals*, and *Naturally Native*), and that highlight the racial realities in contemporary communities.

Dance Me Outside and *Grand Avenue*, the HBO production by Native American writer Greg Sarris, adhere most closely to the Celluloid Maiden figure. Of the cluster, only these two films kill off the young woman. *Dance Me Outside*'s Little Margaret (Tamara Podemski) appears in the first few minutes of the film as a young native Canadian woman whose poor judgment in asking a white thug to dance at a bar on the edge of the Native reserve results in her rape and death. She exists for no more than a few brief scenes, but her murder motivates the other young characters to avenge her death. The young women of the tribe eventually spearhead a national campaign against the young man's minimal sentence, but when the courts disregard their pleas and release him after one year, they kill him. Justine (Deeny Dakota) of *Grand Avenue* has a more substantial role as a teenage daughter in a dysfunctional family. Although, like Little Margaret, she is promiscuous, Justine does not die for her sexual activities per se, but when caught in the cross fire between rival gangs. Neither Little Margaret nor Justine appears consciously contrived as the Celluloid Maiden type, but their youth, physical look, interaction with non-Indian men, and sexuality trigger genre memories of past images in Hollywood films and their prescribed deaths.

The emergence of the Celluloid Maiden image in these films, whether intentional or not, underscores how deeply inscribed the figure and mainstream stereotypes are in American culture, and how successful the colonizing process has been in encouraging Native Americans to reaffirm such a figure. Native-centered and Native-produced films have the potential to disempower the figure by allowing the young girl to live and by creating more realistic images of Native women; certainly, the main characters in *Dance Me Outside* and *Grand Avenue* attest to this. But, even in their obvious retaliation against Hollywood stereotyping, the films contain the young woman in the figure through her typecasting or her death.

According to Robert K. Thomas's work on the internalization of colonialism by Native Americans, the legacy of colonialism is the interpolation of both the colonized and colonizing subject into the continual validation of the system.[29] This process results in a vicious cycle of internal and external racism. A case in point surfaces in the mainstream recognition of Irene Bedard (the voice of Pocahontas in Disney's 1995 release) as a Princess figure even in roles that do not utilize the figure, such as her character in *Smoke Signals*. It is simply her metonymical connection to Pocahontas, or her presentation as a beautiful young girl, that inscribes her as that figure. Bedard reenacts the conflict of such stereotyping in the film *Naturally Native* as the youngest of three sisters. Teased by her siblings for acting the part, she must confront the racism of that image when a date calls her an Indian princess and then attempts to rape her. His attack leaves her traumatized and in the hospital. This film, perhaps more than any other, demands that the viewer question the violence behind the Celluloid Maiden figure without fully enacting the figure. The young woman does not die!

The introduction of trauma as an alternative to death first surfaces in the Native-centered film *Powwow Highway*. A single mother of mixed-race children, Bonnie Redbow (Joannelle Nadine Romero) is framed for drug running, thrown in jail, and separated from her children. These experiences indicate her connection to the Sexualized Maiden figure, but she is also a Celluloid Princess in her goodness, honesty, and dedication to her children. The physical and psychological trauma she experiences foreshadows that of future Princess types: Pocahontas in the 1995 Disney film is left alone after her white lover leaves, and, as discussed above, Irene Bedard's *Naturally Native* character is hospitalized. While replacing death with trauma diffuses the racist and colonialist implications associated with the Celluloid Maiden figure, it does not erase them. Rather, a subtle shift occurs in these films that underscores Thomas's point about internal colonization. Even when it is an accurate description of the realities faced by Native Americans, the replay of violence onto the body of a Native woman who resembles the Celluloid Maiden reifies the figure.

A number of questions arise that need further investigation but are outside the limits of this work. In particular, over the last decade, the Native woman continually fades from the screen, seen mostly behind the main male figure or as an extra who creates a more realistic image of Native communities. While the early 1990s Hollywood films pay particular attention to creating more substantial Native male characters, why does the Native woman decline in her screen presence? The revisionist attempts of the 1990s pay no real attention to the Native woman. This leads me to wonder whether Hollywood simply cannot fathom the reality of a progressive Native female lead in these films, or whether the films are simply following social trends in relegating women and people of color to the role of accoutrement to the white hero. Second, a certain level of social sadism exists in reproducing the Celluloid Maiden figure. Why are the reproduction of this social violence against the body of a woman of color and the symbolic representation of a colonized people not challenged in the same way that similar representations of men of color have been? Third, what still legitimizes the use of this figure in the eyes of the viewing public? A number of films, including *Thunderheart* and *Silent Tongue*, attempt to get closer to the roots of these last two questions through their disruption of the Celluloid Maiden figure, yet even so, a satisfactory answer eludes them. Last, and in reference to the work of Robert K. Thomas and Homi Bhabha, how do we deprogram the effects of internalized colonialism and colonial rhetoric? How and when do we stop reinscribing violent silencing onto the body of the Native American woman?

As the first in-depth documentation of this particular depiction of Native American women in film, *Killing the Indian Maiden* offers a stepping stone for further investigations of the cinematic representations of Native American women. I have traced a trend in Hollywood of utilizing the Celluloid Maiden as a vehicle through which to explore and express the American ambiguity over Native American-white relations and interracial mixing. As my analysis shows, latitude for expression and manipulation of the figure exists, but her death remains a necessary component for "fixing," to borrow from Bhabha, the figure within the colonial and racializing discourse in which the films participate. In addition, this study's historical tracing indicates the significance of the Celluloid Maiden figure within American identity politics and an ongoing reestablishment of a particular American national image as a white patriarchal system of power. These findings, of course, lead to more questions than they answer, but the material presented here does offer a starting point for understanding how deeply imbedded the Native American woman is in violent and romantic images of American nation building.

NOTES

1. Jacqueline Kilpatrick, *Celluloid Indians: Native Americans in Film* (Lincoln: University of Nebraska Press, 1999), 124.

2. Robert Burgoyne, *Film Nation: Hollywood Looks at U.S. History* (Minneapolis: University of Minnesota Press, 1997), 39.

3. I refer to the reader to the words of David Mayer: "Historians of American culture have long and effectively argued that the identity of the Native American and Native American's encounters with European invaders constitutes a palimpsest upon which our current reoccupations and understandings and world-views are constantly reinscribed." (Mayer, 2000:192). See David Mayer, "The Broken Doll," in *The Griffith Project*, ed. Paolo Cherchi Usai. Vol. 4, *Films Produced in 1910*, (London: British Film Institute: 2000), 191–94.

4. Burgoyne, *Film Nation*, 10.

5. Kilpatrick, *Celluloid Indians*, 124.

6. Richard Slotkin, *Gunfighter Nation: The Myth of the Frontier in Twentieth-Century America* (Norman: University of Oklahoma Press, 1992). See especially the introduction, which offers a substantial description of patterns of reciprocal influence.

7. Howard Zinn, *A People's History of the United States, 1492–Present* (New York: HarperCollins, 1995), 580, 583.

8. Ibid., 552; Michael Omi and Howard Winant, *Racial Formation in the United States from the 1960s to the 1990s* (New York: Routledge, 1994); George Lipsitz, *Time Passages: Collective Memory and American Popular Culture* (Minneapolis: University of Minnesota Press, 1990); also see Ruth Frankenburg ed., *Displacing Whiteness: Essays in Social and Cultural Criticism* (Durham, NC: Duke University Press, 1997); Lauren Berlant, *The Queen of America Goes to Washington City: Essays on Sex and Citizenship* (Durham, NC: Duke University Press, 1997).

9. Wesley Ruggles's *Cimarron* (1931) was the first western to receive the Academy Award for Best Picture.

10. See Leighton Grist, "Unforgiven," pp. 294–301 in *The Book of Westerns*, Ian Cameron and Douglas Pye, eds. (New York: Continuum, 1996).

11. Slotkin, *Gunfighter Nation*, 655.

12. *Incident at Oglala*, also released in 1992, is narrated by Robert Redford. The film concentrates on the 1975 incident at Pine Ridge, South Dakota, in which two FBI agents and one Native American were killed. Apted negotiates this material by interviewing members of the community invaded by the FBI and their reaction, twenty years later, to the "reign of terror" during that period (1972–1975). In 1972, the American Indian Movement was called in by tribal traditionalists to protest and actively respond to the violent actions of the corrupt tribal government led by Dick Wilson, his Guardians of the Oglala Nation (the "GOON Squad"), and the federal government. A seventy-one day siege ended in the surrender of American Indian Movement members and continued military reign by Wilson and his group. Leonard Peltier was one of those arrested; he continues to be held in prison even after ample evidence has been found to suggest his innocence. For a detailed history of the events behind Apted's documentary, see Peter Matthiessen, *In the Spirit of Crazy Horse* (New York: Penguin, 1991).

13. Burgoyne, *Film Nation*, 35–56.

14. Ellen L. Arnold, "Reframing the Hollywood Indian: A Feminist Re-Reading of *Pow-wow Highway* and *Thunder Heart*," 356 in *American Indian Studies: An Interdisciplinary Approach to Contemporary Issues*, ed. Dane Morrison (New York: Lange, 1997): 347–62 According to Arnold, Aquash was found shot in the head with her hands cut off at the wrists.

15. Rayna Green, "The Pocohontas Perplex: The Image of Indian Women in American Culture," *Massachusetts Review* 16, no. 4 (1995): 698–714, quote on 702.

16. Winona LaDuke and Wilma Mankiller come to mind as two high-profile political figures. In addition, a close look at the fishing protests in the Northwest, the Navajo demonstration against the Black Mountain Coal Company, and the O'odham U.S.-Mexico border disputes reveals women as primary participants.

17. The Ghost Dance initially came in a vision to the Northern Paiute spiritual leader Wovoka while he was ill. During his vision, he saw former generations of Native Americans, and God told him to spread peace, honesty, and love among the people. God also gave him the Ghost Dance to take back to the people. The dance became the basis for the Ghost Dance religion among the Plains and Great Basin tribes. "Among the Teton Lakota, devastated by war, reservations, poverty, and disease, Wavoka's admonitions of peace are forgotten," Duane Champagne, ed., *Chronology of Native North American History from Pre-Colombian Times to the Present* (Detroit, MI: Gale Research, 1994), 184, 239.

18. John Walton, "Hollywood and the Indian Question: Political, Radical or Ecological Symbol," *Multicultural Education* 1, no. 2 (1993): 12–13.

19. Geoffrey Macnab, "Review of *Silent Tongue*," *Sight and Sound* 3 (1993): 54

20. Paul Streufurt makes a convincing case that Shepard relies on both Greek drama and Native oral tradition in composing the film's narrative structure. Paul D. Streufert, "The Revolving Western: American Guilt and the Tragically Greek in Sam Shepard's *Silent Tongue*," *American Drama* 8 no. 2 (1999): 27–41.

21. Kevin Thomas, "Shepard's 'Tongue' A Supernatural Western Tale," review of *Silent Tongue*, *Los Angeles Times*, 25 February 1994.

22. The following works indicate the range of responses. James Axtell, *Beyond 1492: Encounters in Colonial North America* (Oxford: Oxford University Press, 1992); Stephen J. Summerhill and John Alexander Williams, *Sinking Columbus: Contested History, Cultural Politics, and Mythmaking during the Quincentenary* (Gainesville: University Press of Florida, 2000); Paul Gray, "The Trouble with Columbus," *Time*, 7 October 1991, 52, 56; *Time*, "*Beyond the Year 2000*," special issue, fall 1992; Jose Barreiro, ed. "View from the Shore, American Indian Perspectives on the Quincentenary," special issue, *Northeast Indian Quarterly* (Fall 1990).

23. Summerhill and Williamson, *Sinking Columbus*, 114; K. R. Dark with A. L. Harris, *The New World and the New World Order: U.S. Relative Decline, Domestic Instability in the Americas, and the End of the Cold War* (New York: St. Martin's Press, 1996): 58; Zinn, *A People's History*, 600; Omni and Winant, *Racial Formations*; Berlant, *The Queen of America.*

24. John Miller-Monzon ed., *The Motion Picture Guide: 1995 Annual* (*Films of 1994*) (New York: Baseline, 1994) 208.

25. Patrick A. Smith, "Mythmaking and the Consequences of 'Soul History' in Jim Harrison's *Legends of the Fall*," *Studies in Short Fiction* 36, no. 4 (1999): 369–80. 370.

26. Burgoyne, *Film Nation*, 39.

27. Omni and Winant, *Racial Formations*, 147; Kilpatrick, *Celluloid Indians*, 124.

28. Omni and Winant, *Racial Formations*, 56.

29. Robert. K. Thomas, "Colonialism: Domestic and Foreign," *New University Thought* 4, no. 4 (1967): 1–7.

Chapter Four

Lost in the Cinematic Landscape

Chicanas as Lloronas in Contemporary Film

Domino Renee Pérez

La Llorona is the woman of our dreams and nightmares who wanders through the landscape of our imagination, crying, searching, nurturing, always calling out to us. She is the wronged mother, lover, or woman who murders or abandons her children, though she will never stop searching until her children are brought home. La Llorona's prominence within Chicano popular culture has given her iconographic status.[1] Corridos, plays, poetry, and art represent this mysterious figure in her numerous incarnations, but while her appearance in the literature and music of Chicanos and Chicanas has been analyzed, La Llorona's representation in film has yet to be explored, and this is my project here. No Chicano or Anglo mainstream filmmaker has overtly foregrounded this cultural figure or focused on the implications of her deep roots in Chicano consciousness, but I see distinct outlines of La Llorona in the narratives and depictions of Chicana characters in film. My approach, in part, is informed by Tey Diana Rebolledo, who offers that contemporary Lloronas are not only symbolic of women but of Chicano culture as a whole, "whose children are lost because of their assimilation into the dominant culture or because of violence or prejudice."[2] This reading accounts for those women and men who become lost in our racially charged, xenophobic world.

As the foundation of my argument, I rely on elements of traditional and contemporary Llorona folklore to inform a cultural reading of this figure in five contemporary, widely distributed films: Allison Anders's *Mi Vida Loca* (1994), Gregory Nava's *Mi Familia* (1995), John Sayles's *Lone Star* (1996), Andy Tennant's *Fools Rush In* (1997), and David Lynch's *Mulholland Drive* (2001). I have chosen these films because their principal narratives focus on

71

Chicanas whose depiction is suggestive of primary elements of La Llorona lore.[3] Tennant's film was billed as a mainstream romantic comedy that used culture clash (Chicano and Anglo) as its primary comedic theme; Sayles's generational border drama featured Chicana characters in an attempt to illustrate the diversity of a Texas town; Anders's film is in large part a "gangxploitation" film in which Chicanos and Chicanas are both the victims and perpetrators of violence; and Nava's lively Chicano epic spans four generations of one family. Lynch's surrealist drama, on the other hand, is the only one in which La Llorona is not only mentioned by name but appears as a character in the film.

Most of the films included in this analysis, with two exceptions, are not *about* Chicana/os; rather, they occupy the landscape and at times fill the frame only inasmuch as they serve the narrative of the white protagonists' quest for identity. Because these directors and the majority of the people involved in these productions were Anglos who may or may not have had any knowledge of La Llorona, I focus on what their characterizations might say to audiences who are familiar with her. To do this, I rely on viewer response theory, particularly Jacqueline Bobo's approach to film analysis in *Black Women as Cultural Readers* (1995). Bobo goes beyond textual analysis to examine how readers contextualize narratives in their own cultural frameworks. In her view, "members of a social audience—people who are actually watching a film or television program—will utilize interpretive strategies that are based upon their past viewing experiences as well as upon their personal histories, whether social, racial, sexual, or economic."[4] It is within a cultural framework, in particular one informed by the Greater Mexican legend of La Llorona, that I conduct my investigation of Chicana characters in the five films I have chosen to discuss. This is not to say that my readings are the "only," "true," or "authentic" readings of these films or that all Chicanas or Chicanos will interpret them as I do. Rather my analysis is derived from a reading of the filmic texts and their images of Chicanas as informed by the discourses—La Llorona folklore, specifically—surrounding and informing our viewing experiences.

Considered from the perspective of a cultural outsider, the self-identified Chicana or Mexican American characters featured in *Fools Rush In* (Isabel Fuentes, played by Salma Hayek), *Lone Star* (Pilar Cruz, played by Elizabeth Peña; and Mercedes Cruz, played by Miriam Colon), *Mi Vida Loca* (Mousie, played by Siedy Lopez; Sad Girl, played by Angel Aviles; and Giggles, played by Marlon Marron), and *Mulholland Drive* (Rita and Camilla Rhodes, played by Laura Elena Harring) can easily be read as exotic, highly sexualized others. However, Chicana/o viewers, I argue, bring different backgrounds to their reception of the films' portrayal of sexuality, mestizaje, dialects, and Chicano iconography. In fact, I contend that La Llorona folklore is a dynamic reconfiguration of the diversity of Chicano life and experiences, reflecting regional, economic, social, sexual, and political concerns. Just as I want to avoid arguing that my reading is "true" or "authentic," neither am I conducting a search for genuine "Chicana/o-ness" or "Llorona-ness" by investigating visible cinematic ethnicity, such as dress, sexuality, or manner of speech. To some extent, it is because some of the characters in these films are so painfully stereotypical that I am particularly interested in how these characters can be viewed through the lens of a Llorona tale.

From within this framework I read my understanding of Chicana female types across the characters and texts in a way that Tennant, Sayles, Anders, Nava, and Lynch may not have intended. My endeavor is to see beyond the familiar two-dimensionality of "Latin women" in these films to view these Chicana characters through a cultural construction of women informed by the story of La Llorona with its folkloric and allegorical components. Specifically, my analysis seeks to identify whether or not Chicana viewers are offered self affirming positions by contemporary directors, even Anglo ones, outside of the fixed binaries of creator/destroyer, virgin/whore, and good/evil. Additionally, my readings of the women characters in the aforementioned films are influenced by Rebolledo's alternate positing of the weeping woman as iconic representation of the entire Chicano people's marginality in European American culture and their state of being lost in contemporary society. If, as Rebolledo argues, contemporary Llorona figures are characterized by various degrees of lostness, then these women are Lloronas who are isolated or alienated from their own community and the dominant culture. The women here embody in particularly interesting ways various degrees of Llorona-like lostness, suffering either from prejudice, violence, abandonment, or assimilation into a racist society.

With an opening date of February 14, 1997, *Fools Rush In* attempted to profit from the manufactured romance of Valentine's Day. Billed as a romantic comedy, the film focuses on the hastily developed relationship between Alex Whitman (his last name one letter off from "white man") and Isabel Fuentes, which fulfills the "romance" portion of the category title. Interestingly enough, Alex, who is Anglo, is defined by his career, class (upper), and his cosmopolitan New York lifestyle, while Isabel is defined by her temperament, ethnicity, and "spirituality." From these descriptions, viewers know that culture clashes between the two will be the source of the comedy. Alex and Isabel meet while he is overseeing the construction of a new club in Las Vegas, Isabel's hometown. Subsequently they have sex, she gets pregnant, and they marry and separate, until Alex realizes that he might lose Isabel forever. Consumers of romantic comedies might view the film in accordance with the standard generic formula (boy-meets-girl, boy-loses-girl, boy-gets-girl-back) with an ethnic twist for added spice; however, many may not acknowledge the fact that the "spice" comes at the expense of exploring the real issues facing interracial couples. As bell hooks states, "ethnicity becomes spice, seasoning that can liven up the dull dish that is mainstream white culture."[5] Therefore, the appeal of this film is derived from bringing white male fantasies about brown women into the open by disguising them as "romantic" overtures.

The tendency for most critics who viewed this film was to dismiss it as a lightweight romantic comedy. In addition to being lightweight, the film suffers from other more obvious problems, such as skimpy plot, weak character development, and stereotyping. *Fools Rush In* is, in other words, a formulaic film that seeks to do little more than fulfill the expectations of the genre, with its straightforward narrative and seemingly nonexistent subtext. The reading I offer, then, is a subversive one that locates the text and characters outside the confines of their traditional generic boundaries within a Chicano framework that reveals constraints of another sort.

In our very first encounter with Isabel, for instance, she is associated with a river, the body of water along which La Llorona wails. Viewers see Isabel floating down the middle of the river on an inner tube while contemplating a marriage proposal from a childhood friend. Significantly, she is dressed in a cropped white shirt with a black printed wraparound skirt, while two boys watch her from the shore. Isabel's sexuality is heightened as she steps out of the river with her wet clothes clinging to the curves of her body. From this first scene, and throughout the film, Isabel's sexuality is one of her primary features and is frequently commented upon by the Anglo men in the film. That this is the first scene in which she appears is significant because water (and this is a film about the desert town of Las Vegas), borders, children, and marriage figure prominently in this film, and these are all central features of traditional La Llorona folklore.[6]

Other components of a La Llorona scenario are present in this film as well—a man from the upper class, a Chicana from the working class, a wealthy upper-class woman as sexual and social threat, and a pregnancy. Due to the comedic tone of the movie, the only missing element is the explicit death of a child, though, as I will explain, there is a symbolic death. Like La Llorona, Isabel becomes pregnant out of wedlock and is threatened with abandonment by her lover. She decides to keep the child regardless of Alex's reaction to the news, thus allowing for a reworking of the folktale. In freely choosing to raise a child alone, Isabel is framed alternatively to the folklore that often features La Llorona as a despairing, unwed, or abandoned mother, deeply regretful of her state.

There are problems with this stance of independence, for although situated on a border, *Fools Rush In* reflects little of the volatility of true border and cross-cultural conflicts. Characters' transgressions across physical, emotional, and psychological borders are seen as merely humorous obstacles to be overcome at the expense of their representative cultures. The implication is that while on the border between worlds, a woman can attempt to carve out a space for herself and be, in part, self-defining, but movement away from that viable space places Isabel either in danger or in a rigid female role. For example, prior to meeting Alex, Isabel, alone in the desert, passionately pursues her love of photography, a narrative point that's all but abandoned when Alex enters her life. This abandonment of her "love" of photography is trivialized by the fact that Isabel does not even seem to care when one love is replaced by another. In short, the self-defining space cannot be maintained.

By reading Isabel in a more independent, self-empowering role, however briefly, I read the film as allowing for a partial revisioning of the folklore. Later it seemingly collapses her back into a Llorona posture of despair when we see a distraught Isabel prone in a hospital bed after Alex publicly condemns her for his problems. Isabel then lies to Alex, telling him that the baby has died, which is suggestive of the infanticide of the original folktale. Ostensibly, Isabel reverts to being La Llorona after all. Later we discover that she has lied about the miscarriage and done so to release Alex, who has given her the impression he does not love her. His stereotypical assumptions about her sexuality, personal beliefs, and culture have hurt Isabel: He mocks the "Chicano" redecorating her family has done to their home; the bright primary colors and oversized crucifixes hanging on the walls remind him of the very different world he has married into; he questions the paternity of the child; he tries to pass Isabel off to his parents as his maid; and he blames Isabel for stifling his career. Alex, similar to the lover in many versions of the myth, abandons his partner to return to his own social sphere.

Isabel symbolically rejects Alex's Anglo world of business competition and snobbish prejudice by returning "home" to Mexico, but here again, cultural readers might see the film repositioning Isabel in traditional ways when we witness her depression at having lost the man she loves: Weeping to her grandmother, Isabel says, "I got lost." In symbolically killing her child to set Alex free, Isabel becomes the subject of her own Llorona narrative as she explains her confusion and loss to her grandmother. Although Isabel's disorientation is in part a reference to the loss of her cultural beliefs caused by Alex's insensitivity to her ethnic roots, it is also the traditional despair of a woman abandoned by her lover. Isabel awakens in the middle of the night as if from a nightmare, seemingly confirming the despair in the latter interpretation, but what she has actually had is an epiphany: She wants to return to her home in the United States, Las Vegas, although not necessarily to reconcile with Alex.

At the same time, in a modern twist to the traditional tale, Alex parallels Isabel's desire to salvage the relationship. He rejects the advances of a wealthy woman whom his family hopes he will marry and begins "reading the signs" that he belongs with Isabel. In symbolic articulation of this parallel movement, Alex too is associated with water when we see him standing at the edge of Hoover Dam, drenched from the rain. As a very pregnant Isabel approaches, he first declares his undying love for her and then notices she is about to go into labor on the exact spot where her desert world meets his Anglo world of Las Vegas. Their child is born on the spot, after Isabel's water breaks, in the rain, on the border of two cultures, on a bridge holding back a dammed-up river. The dam becomes symbolic of Isabel's Llorona narrative because it, like the river that once flowed through the canyon, has been stopped: She is rescued from her lost status when Alex responds to her cries, returning to restore her faith in love and reclaim her as his wife. Unlike the traditional ending of a Llorona narrative, this wealthy lover returns to the woman he has abandoned.

Here at this intersection of water and borderland, the couple muses about how their daughter will enjoy aspects of both Alex's and Isabel's worlds. An optimistic Chicana cultural reader might anticipate that through compromise on both Alex's and Isabel's parts, Isabel and her daughter will transcend the binaries to carve out a new space, which lies on some middle ground. Yet the movie does not end at this point. As the camera pans down and back for the final scene, we see their re-commitment to marriage, not on a border but on the rim of one side of a canyon. The sustaining final shot in the film is one of concession, not compromise. For Isabel, the implication is that while she may be "redeemed" from her status as a Llorona, there is no new place for her as a woman outside of the fixed binaries of Anglo/Mexican, unwed motherhood/marriage, working-class/upper-class. Despite her strength and sacrifice, she is merely "lifted up" through marriage to an Anglo man and placed on the other side of the binary or canyon.

As in *Fools Rush In*, sexual entanglements and the clash of cultures figure prominently in *Lone Star* but with a different outcome. *Lone Star* is an intricately woven murder mystery that includes the narratives of more than ten characters who are living in the border town of Rio County, Texas, formerly known as Perdido (which means "lost"). Each of the main characters is in some way affected by the death of the corrupt sheriff of the town, Charlie Wade. When his body is discovered partially unearthed on an abandoned military rifle range, a chain of events is set in motion that pulls together the past and present of each character, in particular Pilar and Mercedes Cruz, who are central to the narrative. As a cultural reader acquainted with La Llorona's story, I see these women as Lloronas who have raised children alone due to abandonment by men through death. In addition, they both experience the anguish of loves that are not socially sanctioned. Although these women are successful professionals—an independent, college-educated history teacher and an esteemed businesswoman respectively—they each harbor a sadness or anger that viewers are led to believe is the result of their unfulfilling personal lives.

To review briefly the central romance of the film, Pilar and Sam are reunited after a twenty-three year separation. After their first verbal encounter, Sam asks Pilar to go for a walk, which leads them to the river, an obvious physical boundary demarcating territories and another signifier of La Llorona's terrain. Making the latter connection clearer is Pilar's foregrounding in the shot with the river as backdrop. Its presence fills the soundtrack, but Pilar speaks at the same level as the current, so that her voice and the river become one. After Pilar has left Sam contemplating their youth by the river, he turns from her to the water's sound while the camera follows smoothly his line of sight. The shot is uninterrupted as the pan continues left, moving beyond the boundaries of the present into the past, where this time we see a young Pilar leaning over the water of the same river while a young Sam sits well above the shore. Pilar's positioning in the past as the one who is closest to the river and her voice merging with it serves to substantiate her as Llorona figure. That the river is the possible site for their initial lovemaking and for her rejection of the idea that premarital sex is a sin suggests a knowing disregard for cultural mores, constructing her as a sexual threat also consistent with La Llorona. Furthermore, the two teenaged lovers are from different cultural and economic backgrounds, thus casting Sam as the unattainable white male. As in La Llorona folklore, outside sources are working to keep Sam and Pilar apart, which is demonstrated in another flashback showing Pilar forcibly pulled from a car at the drive-in theater by a deputy and dragged away from Sam. She wails in the night air, marking her permanent separation, until adulthood, from her illegitimate love.

The initial introduction to Pilar's portion of the narrative begins in the classroom, seemingly establishing her first as a teacher but metaphorically associating her with La Llorona's terrain. Off camera we hear her voice as the camera focuses on a map of Texas. As she quickly walks into the frame, her body is laid across the map, conflating her with lost Mexican territory. Because of Pilar's residence in Rio (River) County and her personal and cultural loss, cultural readers might see her only as a Llorona. Despite her conforming to major aspects of La Llorona myth, Pilar emerges as an educated, autonomous, proud Tejana who has self-definition and has since learned more than wailing. Her own identity, then, is constructed from a historically, socially, culturally, and politically informed perspective.

Accordingly, Pilar transforms herself from a victim in a traditional La Llorona tale to the subject of her own new narrative with Sam by reshaping myth, surrendering the familiar, and moving beyond the colonial, which in the past has kept them apart. The final scene in the drive-in theater, the site where the lovers were torn apart the first time, completes the romance. Cultural anthropologist José Limon argues that the setting takes on added significance: "It is entirely appropriate that this final scene and decision takes place in the now decaying abandoned drive-in theater where they once made illicit teenaged love, the theater and the forbidden lovemaking symbols of another era, when the colonial order was still in full force."[7] Sam, moreover, has abandoned his wealthy Anglo wife because he cannot forget his love for a mestiza, thus revising the original story. Separated by another border, the incest taboo, they decide to stay together. The revelation by Sam that his father, Buddy, is Pilar's father also threatens to tear them apart. Once again, Pilar's response ("That's it, then? You're not gonna want to be with me anymore?") signals her refusal to regard that or any other cultural taboo. The lovers decide to forget the past, to forget, as Pilar poses in the final line of the film, "all that other stuff—that history—to hell with it, right?" In doing so, Pilar actively creates what Limon calls in a different context "a new social order" with her lover and half-brother, defying societal norms, both subverting and revising her position as a "Mexican" woman, especially when viewed through the lens of the folklore.[8] Although Pilar, who is now sterile, loses the opportunity of having any children with Sam, together they reclaim her previous children as theirs, and Sam has a direct blood relationship with them. Pilar and Sam have successfully written themselves out of the traditional folklore by removing the externally imposed obstacles between them to attempt to live happily ever after.

Mercedes, Pilar's mother and a contentious barrier between Pilar and the man she loves, is perhaps the most complicated character in the film because she embodies aspects of both a traditional Llorona and Malinche from the film's start.[9] However, for the scope of this analysis, I focus primarily on those features that allow her to be cast within La Llorona folklore. She is a self-proclaimed "Spanish" woman who lives in a bordertown with her Chicana daughter, yet viewers discover that Mercedes crossed "illegally" into the United States from Mexico as a girl. Again, in one of Sayles's seamless scenes, audiences see her future husband, Eladio, pluck her from the river to help her onto shore and welcome her to Texas. This scene positions Mercedes as an undocumented worker from Mexico, and she, like La Llorona, is directly associated with water. In addition, Mercedes uses money from her married, unattainable Anglo lover, Buddy, to buy a home on the river. Unlike her daughter, Mercedes is a Llorona whose lover will never leave his wife and join her and their illegitimate daughter. Moreover, Buddy Deeds's wife stands as a symbol of all Anglo women who must contend with their husbands' infidelity, and Mrs. Deeds is constantly referred to as "a saint," again positioning Mercedes as a Llorona and sexual threat to the white wife's saintly goodness.

Mercedes seeks to diffuse her own Llorona narrative by attempting to inflate her status within the community to equal that of her lover. By distancing herself from her own people, she externalizes her own self hatred and embeds herself in a privileged position within the established colonial hierarchy. In this way, Mercedes also emerges as a contemporary Llorona, assimilated and lost to herself and her own history. She betrays Mexicans at every turn. She forbids her workers to speak Spanish, for instance, and calls undocumented workers "wetbacks." She has the border patrol on her speed dial, which she uses from her palatial hacienda with her Cadillac parked out front. Denying her Mexican heritage and choosing to identify herself as Spanish, she has written a tainted rags-to-riches story, for without the affair with Buddy Deeds, she would not be in her wealthy position. It is her adulterous, unequal relationship with Buddy and the betrayal of her own people that forms the backdrop to Mercedes as a contemporary Llorona figure.

When Eladio plucks Mercedes out of the river, he unknowingly sets in motion a chain of events that contributes to the future isolation of his wife and her mestiza daughter, and each of these women's narratives ends with an overt suggestion that they are permanently marked by their losses. However, Pilar transcends her personal loss to fashion a future for herself and her new family. Finally, like Pilar, Mercedes has lost a husband in death, but Eladio's death is a violent one perpetrated at the hands of the racist Anglo sheriff Charlie Wade, making her love for another Anglo sheriff, Buddy, an even greater betrayal of her heritage. La Llorona mythology plays itself out in Mercedes's life as she sits alone on her patio by the riverbank.

LLORONAS IN THE URBAN LANDSCAPE

The image of Mercedes alone on the banks of the Rio Grande appears at first consideration to have little relation to the Chicanas who populate the urban landscape of gangxploitation films. Yet by reading La Llorona folklore across these different cinematic landscapes, a broader delineation of modern Chicana identities and experiences emerges. Allison Anders's film, shot in documentary style and including "real" East Los Angeles gang members and a predominantly Chicano cast, seeks to provide a space for Chicanas and their voices within gang- life discourse. Based, in part, on her observations of her one-time Echo Park neighbors, Anders attempts to present a feminist view of her protagonists, Sad Girl/Mona and Mousie/Maribel, who have been best friends since childhood, as they struggle to support themselves and their children after the death of Ernesto, the man they battled over and reluctantly shared. During the film's opening credits, Anders includes icons from Chicano culture, including the Virgen de Guadalupe, but while the filmmaker may have attempted to reflect women's points of view, she unwittingly evokes stereotypes that reinscribe Sad Girl and Mona into the roles of Chicana "welfare" mothers abandoned by their lover. The positioning of these women in this manner does little to help cultural audiences see these women in positive ways.

Traditional and contemporary elements of La Llorona folklore, such as a body of water, abandonment, violence, and loss, resonate in the lives of these women. For example, the film takes place within a contemporary urban landscape, Echo Park, that has a lake as its central feature. Although the lake does not figure directly in their narratives, the lives of the characters revolve around the park. Because of the violence and turmoil in the neighborhood, these characters literally haunt the landscape surrounding the lake. An additional reading of these women as Lloronas results from their status as mothers. Sad Girl and Mousie are single, devoted women who care for their children, but they are highly sexualized within the context of their situational lives as female gang members because each knows that Ernesto is sleeping with the other. This blatant disregard for social mores underscores their cinematic identities as women outside of social boundaries. The film does attempt to dismantle this stereotype with a brief sequence featuring Mousie's narration of the loss of her virginity to Ernesto, indicating she is neither promiscuous nor oversexed. Yet the continuous quarrel between Mousie and Sad Girl, even after Ernesto's death, overshadows both women's loyalty to their dead adulterous partner and positions each as a sexual threat consistent with the narrative features of La Llorona folklore.

Of the two women, Sad Girl is the most visually affected by Ernesto's murder as evidenced by her visible despair and constant references to her dead lover. While she obviously concerns herself with the welfare of her child, she remains obsessed with Ernesto and laments over how different her life would be economically and physically if he had not died. Despite her character's adherence to several features of the folkloric figure here, Mona's positioning as a Llorona actually begins much earlier when her fellow gang members rename her Sad Girl. (Sad Girl's life is, indeed, fraught with difficult responsibilities, such as caring for her father after her mother's death, grieving for the death of her baby's father, and raising the child alone.) Mona reveals through voiceover narration that prior to the adoption of her new name, she laughed so much that the others thought the name Sad Girl inappropriate, but she eventually assumes the characteristics of her new identity, losing her gregarious nature. Both the names Mona and Sad Girl evoke the weeping and moaning of a traditional Llorona. Significantly, Sad Girl does not choose this legacy of despair for herself; it is instead bestowed upon her by others.

Mousie's figuration in La Llorona folklore is even more pronounced than Sad Girl's. When Mousie becomes pregnant, her father throws her out of the house, punishing her for her sexual behavior and the shame she brings on the family. The punishment at the hands of the patriarchal order parallels versions of the folktale that emphasize La Llorona's sexual transgression. Later, just as Mousie leaves for a potentially fatal altercation with Sad Girl, she emphasizes an often primary element of the lore. She threatens her infant son, telling him that she will come back and "haunt [his] macho ass" if she ever hears about his gangbanging, to which the child nods, as if he understands. Ironically, Mousie symbolizes as a gang member the difficulty of breaking the cycle of violence: She does not want to abandon her son, but she feels compelled to fight Sad Girl to eliminate the immediate sexual threat she poses to her own relationship with Ernesto. In her threat to return as a ghost to her son, she becomes the admonishing Llorona, wailing and bemoaning not only her own fate, but the fate of her child as well should he choose to follow in her footsteps. She wants her son to have a better life, yet she does not have the means to create one herself.

Although the film focuses chiefly on the female characters, the primary narrative is directly tied to their reactions to the behavior of the male gang members, underscoring Sad Girl's and Mousie's subservient positions and loss of agency, and further positioning them as Lloronas. This disempowering positionality is made more disconcerting due to the fact that throughout the film, the women are on the brink of overcoming their subjugated states to a achieve a positive agency denied La Llorona. But Anders restricts female movement toward transcendence by placing her women characters in situations in which they must always react to the actions of men. For example, when Ernesto dies during a drug sale to an Anglo woman, Mousie and Sad Girl, with no visible means of support, must raise their children alone. This modification, then, is consistent with versions of La Llorona tales that feature women from higher stations, in this case a white woman, who take men away from their legitimate partners. Ernesto does not willfully abandon his family, but Mousie and Sad Girl still become widows, literally lloronas (weepers), who are left behind to care for their children alone.

The majority of female characters featured in Anders's film are negative stereotypes, painting a grim picture of Chicanas. Yet one character, Giggles, emerges as an alternate image, one that demonstrates the potential of La Llorona to become a redemptive figure. In her youth, Giggles participated in gang life and was eventually sent to jail for an unspecified gang-related crime, leaving behind her daughter in the care of a family member. Having lost a part of her youth, her husband, and her child, Giggles does not succumb to La Llorona's despair. Instead, she works actively to change her life. When she is finally released from prison, the young women of the barrio anticipate Giggles will impart the vast wisdom she has gained as a result of her jail time. To their surprise, she emerges from incarceration with a plan for her future. She tells the other women, much to their chagrin, that they have to acquire new skills so that they can take care of themselves and their children. She reinvents herself to include a larger vision of the world and returns to reclaim the child she left behind. Later, when Big Sleepy offers to take care of Giggles and her daughter, she refuses his offer, determined to depend only on herself. In successfully organizing the female gang members,

Giggles does indeed impart a new wisdom that facilitates female self suffi-
ciency. By reclaiming her daughter and helping to shape the consciousness of
a new generation of women, she becomes a redemptive Llorona who never
stopped searching or caring about the welfare of her family or people. Giggles is a catalyst for change, presenting new options for cinematic Chicanas
beyond binaristic constructions.

At the same time, although Giggles emerges as a transcendent heroine,
her portrayal is in some ways unrealistic and problematic. As a convicted
felon, for instance, Giggles is unlikely to secure a job, yet we see her filling
out job applications. Although visibly discouraged, she clings to the belief
that she will get the job she hopes for. Furthermore, while Giggles transcends
a traditional Llorona narrative by calling for female agency and economic
independence, at the conclusion of the film, Sad Girl tells viewers that the
women now carry weapons and control their own drug businesses. These
women have digested the message of self-sufficiency but only by adopting
the methods of men. By treating so superficially the important subjects of
achieving economic independence, breaking the cycle of violence, and
crawling out from under economic, social, political, and racial oppression,
Anders reinforces the very boundaries that restrict Chicanas' abilities to succeed. Therefore, the film actually depicts a generation of contemporary Lloronas who will continue to lose their children, freedom, and lives.

In *Mi Vida Loca*, Anders attempts to provide a range of female characters,
from active and reformed gang members to college students. Had she chosen
to focus more on the latter characters, their representation would have signified a marked change in the construction of Chicanas in film, positioning
us in potentially affirming roles. While this Anglo filmmaker does make a
feminist statement in reference to female agency, she neglects the opportunity to capitalize on Chicanas in positive positions of self-empowerment.
Instead, she reinscribes female subordination by privileging images of moth-
erhood and dependence on welfare. The conclusion of the film does stress the
need for social change in the lives of these women, but as contemporary
Lloronas in the urban landscape, they remain lost and disempowered.

Of the films I have discussed, *Mi Familia* is the only one directed by a
Chicano; therefore, reading Nava's film through the lens of Jacqueline
Bobo's theoretical framework may appear contradictory to its subversive
intent. For example, one could argue that identifying María Sanchez as a
traditional Llorona figure is, by now, an obvious reading of Chicana types in
film, but no evidence exists that Nava knowingly inscribed his characters
onto a specifically "Chicano" cinematic landscape. Also, since Nava, who
defines himself as primarily a filmmaker rather than a Chicano filmmaker,
and his work are only minimally influenced by his cultural underpinnings,
we cannot assume that he knowingly presents cinematic Lloronas to his

audience. However, her presence in his film, especially in the character María, the matriarch of the family, constitutes a sophisticated construction that transcends that of the other films discussed.

María's position as a traditional Llorona is initiated when she is forcibly deported to rural Mexico in an INS roundup targeting people of Mexican descent who are being blamed by Anglo politicians for the economic crisis of the 1930s (seen in an extended flashback). As in some renderings of the folktale, through no fault of her own, María is separated from her family and, like La Llorona, fated to lose her child. In this case, María does not have the opportunity to go home or tell her family what is happening, and they have no explanation for her disappearance. Prior to her deportation, María enthusiastically informs her husband José that they are going to have another child, and he responds by telling her that he knows the child will be a boy, a very special boy, because the day the child was conceived José saw an angel pass by in the sky. María, in response, looks uneasily at José, sensing the omen might not be a good one, an interpretation reinforced by Old Gomez's crashing his car into the river. The convergence of these three events—the appearance of the angel, the baby's impending birth, and the car crash into the river—foreshadows the fate of the child, Chucho, and María's destiny to weep over her lost son. This doomed future is reinforced when María's aunt warns her that María's plan to return to the United States only after her child is born is "impossible": "You will die before you get there. And your child will die too."

The traditional Llorona narrative plays itself out when María, ignoring her aunt's advice, walks toward the border in the rain, with her child in her arms. In the scenes marking her movement northward, she is framed with water as Paco, the oldest son and narrator, says, "The rains came early that year." María, standing with her baby, sees that the river is raging; nevertheless, she begs the ferryman, an obvious symbol of death, to take her across, even though he warns her against doing so. Before stepping into the boat, María tells her infant, "Hold on to me, Chucho. The spirit of the river is evil and powerful." Whether the evil María speaks of is a direct reference to La Llorona or one of her Aztec precursors often associated with water, the river stands as a physical symbol demarcating danger and La Llorona's terrain. A white owl—which in some American Indian cultures forebodes death—perches as the final signifier of impending harm.

Insider audiences are not likely to miss all of these symbols, so María's and Chucho's being swept away in the violent current is no surprise. She struggles to hold onto her baby as they are tossed through the rapids, but for all of her effort, she loses him in the water swells. Miraculously, he stays afloat until she reaches him and then fights her way to shore. Safely on the other side of the river, María cradles the infant in her arms. As the camera cuts from the scene to the white owl, we are aware that death has temporarily been cheated. Further emphasizing this point is that in an effort to save the gravely ill boy, María takes him to some *curanderas* who tell her that "the river spirit wants [her] baby."

Although the child survives, his placement in the myth is complete when Chucho is murdered by a racist Anglo police officer twenty-five years later. The officer's arrival in the barrio signifies the frequendy cited man of higher social or economic position who causes La Llorona's despair. María completes her role in the Llorona narrative, which began in rural Mexico and concludes in East Los Angeles, by wailing under the bridge for the son she has lost through no fault of her own. Because the story concludes in an urban setting, the Llorona narrative is modified from its traditional rural framework to reflect contemporary concerns, such as "lost-ness."

As Paco retells this particular portion of his family's narrative, he carefully privileges Mexican American cultural and familial beliefs over the Anglo/ colonial discourse surrounding Chucho's death. María's refusal to believe that Chucho has died at the hands of white men illustrates the power and influence of cultural myth. She would rather view his death as an inescapable fate within the context of her beliefs (informed arguably in part by La Llorona folklore) than accept that her son was murdered in cold blood. Paco tells viewers, "Everybody said that the police killed Chucho, but my mother never believed that. She knew that he was meant to die by the river. Chucho's life had been on borrowed time. But you can't cheat fate forever. The spirit of the river had come back to claim what was rightfully his." Fully inscribed in a tragic scenario, María, unlike La Llorona, does not collapse from despair, in part because of her obligations to the family, particularly to her five other children. She endures forced separation, sickness, murder, and violence to demonstrate that one can overcome these obstacles without succumbing to bitterness and regret. In the final scenes of the movie, María momentarily ponders how different all of their lives might have been had Chucho only lived, but she decides, along with José, that their lives have indeed been "good."

While the previous films have depicted both traditional and contemporary Lloronas, none are as well drawn as María in Nava's generational epic. This is in part because the film spans four generations so viewers can see her evolution, and by extension that of La Llorona, from the tragic female of legend in a rural landscape to contemporary signifier of the effects on Chicanos of violence, prejudice, and assimilation in the urban world. In weaving together Aztec mythology and Chicano folklore, Nava illustrates the power of La Llorona as a complex symbol of abandonment and loss. For the characters in Nava's film, folklore provides a lens through which to view the world, and it has the power to provide an explanation for its inescapable horrors, such as the murder of a child by an agent of a racist, xenophobic oppressor.

OUT OF THE SHADOWS AND INTO THE SPOTLIGHT

To a Chicana/o cultural reader, outlines of La Llorona are clearly evident in the previously discussed films, although she is not directly mentioned by name. However, there are a few instances where a "llorona" is evoked within a film that does not include Chicanas as central characters. For example, in Steven Spielberg's *Jurassic Park: The Lost World* (1997), a Costa Rican man is crushed under the foot of a Tyrannosaurus rex shortly after listening to a song on his Walkman about a llorona. While this may seem like a mere coincidence, the images and symbols included in the events that proceed and follow this jungle scene lend themselves to a distinct cultural reading. A fellow dinosaur hunter named Stark (Peter Stormare) tells Roland Carter (Thomas Rosales) that he is "Going to the ladies room." As Stark descends toward a river, Carter sings, "Mi llorona, mi llorona."[10] The white man becomes lost in the jungle fog and cries out for help. Neither Carter nor anyone else in the group hears him. Abandoned and alone, Stark stumbles into a riverbed, La Llorona's territory, where he meets his fate at the hands of a pack of small scavenger-like dinosaurs that fill the river with Stark's blood. Minutes later Carter also dies, literally falling "under foot" of the larger-than-life predator, T. Rex. Clearly the elements of a La Llorona tale are present, yet in terms of the folklore, this scene is self-contained in that it fails to speak to the larger filmic narrative as a whole. Nevertheless, it does suggest to the cultural reader that dinosaurs are not the only threat on Isla Sorna (Isle of Cunning).

Similarly, *Dr. T and the Women* (2000) by Robert Altman includes an allusion to a Llorona-like figure known as the "lady of the lake." Dr. T's daughter, DeeDee (Kate Hudson) recounts the tale for her former partner Marilyn (Liv Tyler), whom DeeDee has abandoned for a heterosexual relationship. The two estranged lovers sit by the side of a fountain that has a statue of a woman who appears to be watching over the pair. Relishing this time alone, DeeDee tells Marilyn that if they sit by the waterside long enough, the lady of the lake might appear. When Marilyn admits her unfamiliarity with the tale, DeeDee recounts it for her: "It's a famous legend. Okay, well, this woman in this flowing white exotic negligee . . . she drowned because of a broken heart and she appears to couples who hang out around the lake who are really in love and she either cries for help or she just cries this sad mournful cry. . . . And I believe it. People swear it's true." Marilyn also believes in the truth of the tale. The story that DeeDee tells to her lover could easily be written off as another haunted-woman story, for the lady of the lake does not appear, but when tied to the fact that DeeDee abandons her fiance at the altar for her bridesmaid, Marilyn, one has to rethink the casual placement of the lady-of-the-lake story in the film. Moreover, the story DeeDee tells does inform the narrative as a whole because her father Dr. T (Richard Gere) spends his entire life in the service of women, professionally as a gynecologist and personally as a father to his daughters and husband to his mentally ill wife. In doing so, this patriarch slowly realizes that women control and dictate his life, leading to his disempowerment and emasculation. As Dr. T attempts to flee this space controlled by women, he is blown by a tornado "south of the border" to a town seemingly inhabited only by women. There he successfully delivers a male child and gains an ally in a new landscape, where he believes the patriarchal order can flourish, thus freeing him of women's power.

In the absence of Chicana characters, these allusions and references suggest that La Llorona is no longer the exclusive domain of Chicanas. Moving La Llorona away from her parent culture and its representatives may indicate nothing more than a kind of cultural tourism, where souvenirs such as folktales and legends are collected for later use as "flavor" for film narratives. Whether or not this is the case, we have to acknowledge that women's suffering, the kind that La Llorona experiences, is not particular to Chicanas. While writers' and directors' divorcing of La Llorona from her parent culture provides sound evidence of appropriation, perhaps filmmakers are beginning to understand the profound power of this cultural image to articulate the pain and oppression of not only Chicanas but of women in general. Still, if this is the case, David Lynch in *Mulholland Drive* provides, perhaps, an interesting caveat for women—white women in particular—who choose to appropriate La Llorona's legend and rework the power structure in the tale to suit their own needs, desires, and obsessions. Specifically, Lynch seems more than willing to bring La Llorona out of the shadows to allow her to play a pivotal role for Chicanas and speak to them in a way that they can understand. In Lynch's film, La Llorona is not simply spice or even window dressing; she is not merely an allusion, nor do we have to read her into the film. Lynch allows La Llorona to stand on her own, fully realized, articulating pain, loss, and the power of redemption. We no longer have to search for her outline. She calls to us, sings to us, and asks us to listen so that we might ease our own suffering and hers as well.

To present clearly the analysis that follows, I divide the film into two distinct parts and narratives. The first part of the film, with its vivid colors and drawn- out fantastical moments, visually articulates the dream of Betty Elm (played by Naomi Watts), who arrives in Hollywood with the vision of becoming a famous motion-picture actor. Upon arriving at her Aunt Ruth's apartment, Betty discovers a light-skinned Chicana, who is the victim of a car crash, living in Ruth's home. This too is a part of the dream. Although the Chicana has no memory of her identity, she adopts the name "Rita" after seeing in the apartment a movie poster of the 1946 film Gilda, which starred Rita Hayworth. Like Hayworth, who was born Margarita Carmen Cansino, the daughter of a Spanish- born father and a European American mother, Rita (played by Laura Elena Harring), "selects" a name that masks her ethnicity. Together, Betty and Rita attempt to uncover Rita's "true" identity. In the second part of the film, best described as its "cinematic reality," Camilla Rhodes (also played by Laura Elena Harring) is a successful Hollywood actor who has an affair with Diane Selwyn (also played by Naomi Watts), an aspiring actor. Camilla's decision to terminate the affair leaves Diane distraught and desiring revenge for her heartache.

La Llorona serves as a guardian to the gateway between two narratives where power, seduction, love, and loss intersect to leave someone "llorando." Her cry rouses dreamers from sleep, as with Rita. While dreaming, Rita speaks as though in a trance: "Silencio. Silencio. Silencio. No hay banda. No hay banda. No hay orquesta. Silencio . . . Silencio. No hay banda. No. No." Her rather cryptic mutterings suggest that while she has experienced silence and oppression, Rita has the capacity to break that silence, but she must first awaken from her dream state, psychologically and physically. The power of articulation, the ability to speak for oneself, is embedded in Rita's subconscious, though the fact that the voice reaches her in the vulnerable state of sleep suggests that someone else controls her narrative. Also, the location of which Rita dreams has no band or orchestra; it is a place devoid of music and life. Rita must go there; she may no longer linger idly in bed with Betty while somebody else takes control of her story. Clearly, Rita would like to resist, as indicated by her refusal, "No. No." After Betty awakens Rita from her dream, telling her that everything is "okay," Rita responds, "No, it's not okay. Go with me somewhere." Only Rita knows where they must travel, for La Llorona calls to Rita alone. Rita then guides Betty, a cultural outsider who does not hear La Llorona's wailing, into the darkness.

The journey toward Club Silencio begins with a cab ride over a river, a traditional boundary used to demarcate territory or neighborhoods, and one that in Los Angeles separates Anglos from Chicanos. This situates the club on culturally specific terrain, one inhabited by La Llorona de Los Angeles. Once inside the club, Betty, dressed in red and black, and Rita, donning a blonde wig and dressed only in black, descend into a theater, holding hands. The red and black colors included in this scene are used to identify binaries and archetypes, such as seduction and death respectively. While Rita's fate is suggested by her black apparel, Betty's future is undetermined, for she signifies both seduction and death. Once seated, the two witness a performance, or a simulation of performance, emceed by a man who states: "No hay banda. There is no band. [. . .] This is all a tape recording. No hay banda, and yet we hear a band. [. . .] It's all recorded. No hay banda. It is all a tape. [. . .] It is an illusion. Listen!" Rita begins to understand the source of her spoken dream and learns that disembodied sound and illusion permeate Club Silencio.

As if in violent recognition of her outsider status, Betty starts to convulse in her chair after the emcee's command and finally calms down when the announcer, Cookie, a Chicano, comes out dressed in red to introduce La Llorona de Los Angeles, Rebekah del Rio. Underscoring Betty's connection to La Llorona, she too is dressed in red and black with a painted tear underneath her right eye. La Llorona's wrenching ballad disrupts the stillness of the club, her voice a powerful means of breaking the symbolic and literal "silencio." Specifically, del Rio will reveal both Rita's past and her future. As La Llorona sings a version of Roy Orbison's "Crying," "Llorando," both Rita and Betty start to weep, overcome by the pain in del Rio's voice. In the middle of her performance La Llorona swoons, but her song continues, suggesting that a woman's voice is not exclusively her own. Although La Llorona mimes to a tape recording, the "mimicry of passion [is] enough to fell her."[11] Articulation, even mimicking the act, has profound consequences, for as Trinh T. Minh-ha states: "In trying to tell something, a woman is told, shredding herself into opaque words while her voice dissolves on the walls of silence."[12] Instead of allowing La Llorona's words to dissolve on the walls of Club Silencio, Rita internalizes them and visibly changes in some way as Cookie and the emcee drag del Rio off stage. Betty, who continues to weep, reaches over and discovers a blue box in her purse, where she may have been hiding it all along. Rita eventually takes possession of the box to which she literally and symbolically holds the key.

It is no mistake that at this point, after relinquishing the box, Betty disappears from the narrative. Rita calls out Betty's name. When she does not respond, Rita asks, "Donde 'stas?" Betty becomes lost to Rita, who despite this sudden loss opens the mysterious blue box with her key and takes us into the darkness of self, other, and sexual containment. The box functions as a portal, transporting viewers from one narrative to another. With La Llorona's work partially done, Rita must continue the search for her identity alone. In this way, she is a contemporary Llorona, lost to herself as the result of some forgotten or suppressed violence.

As we move into the second narrative and part of the film, we see Rita, now as Camilla Rhodes, write herself out of containment. Instead of continuing her lesbian relationship with Betty (now Diane) Camilla ends the affair by telling Diane that she is leaving her for a man. In this way, Camilla will not assume the role of La Llorona, the one abandoned for another lover of a higher station. She refuses the mantle of weeping and wandering for lost love. Instead, Camilla abandons her lover to perform heterosexually with not just any man, but the first man—Adam. Keenly aware of the kind of power and protection this relationship can offer her, Camilla knowingly pairs herself with Adam, who in previous scenes has been in contact with God, a cowboy in Lynch's imagination. The appearance of God- and Adam-like figures speaks to the omnipresence and omnipotence of the patriarchy to dictate women's lives. It may seem that Camilla has sacrificed one way of life for perceived heteronormative behavior, but she has in fact done nothing of the kind. Camilla simply attaches herself to the ultimate representative of the patriarchy while maintaining and pursuing other lesbian affairs. In other words, she willfully and successfully manipulates the patriarchal order to suit her needs. As Camilla passionately kisses her new lover in front of her ex, while Adam's back is turned, Diane is faced with the realization that she is the abandoned one. To emphasize Diane's new status as lost, viewers learn that Diane is a once again a cultural outsider, this time due to her socioeconomic status, which is lower than that of Camilla.

At this moment, viewers gain insight into one possible connection between the two narratives. As the one left behind, Diane, who hails from Deep River, Ontario, is cast in the role of La Llorona, a fact underscored not only by her association with a river, but with the colors red and black, the same colors La Llorona wears at Silencio. If this in fact is the case, we can interpret the first narrative as Diane's attempt to reinvent herself as Betty and to erase Camilla's strength and power. In her dream, Diane rewrites Camilla as Rita, a lost woman without self or memory who becomes wholly dependent on Diane. Moreover, Diane in her dream has reinvented herself as Betty for guidance, protection, and salvation, a Llorona of Diane's imagination. So while the patriarchy may not be able to control Camilla, Diane unwittingly becomes an agent of that order to do what it cannot. In spite of Diane's efforts, she is the one who remains lost, physically and morally, even going so far as to have Camilla murdered rather than be without her.

However, Camilla's power reaches beyond death and, like La Llorona, she returns to haunt Diane. Rather than allow herself to be tortured by her actions, Diane fantasizes about Camilla to save her from the death Diane orchestrated and to keep Camilla as a lover forever. Diane believes she can alter the outcome of the relationship by shifting the balance of power in her favor without realizing that Camilla, even in death, still holds all of the power. In an effort to dictate this game of seduction, Diane naively attempts to position Rita as La Llorona. Diane assumes the role of a patriarchal oppressor by relegating Rita to a position inferior to her own. As if to confirm that she has "successfully" written Rita into this role, throughout Diane's fantasy, Rita wears mostly red and black, the colors that in the later scene will link Betty and La Llorona de Los Angeles. Diane as Betty controls every aspect of Rita's life and does not allow the articulation of Rita's pain or horror. Indeed, as La Llorona's performance implies, Rita is not in command of her own narrative. When the two discover the dead body of "Diane Selwyn" in the first narrative, Rita's initial inclination is to scream, but as she opens her mouth to do so, Betty forces her hand over Rita's mouth to maintain silencio. In spite of the fact that Betty's reaction is apropos to narrative concerns about the duo avoiding detection for breaking into "Diane's" home,

Betty's behavior reveals an additional level of meaning: Diane gets to witness Camilla's despair over seeing the dead body, Diane's body, while Betty
contains Rita's grief, greedily keeping it only for herself.

When Diane writes the scene at Silencio with La Llorona into the Betty/
Rita narrative, she does so to acknowledge literally and symbolically that
women suffer. Diane, as Betty, empathizes so greatly with La Llorona's
Llorando that she openly weeps as the song virtually pours from del Rio's
mouth. What Diane does not acknowledge is that in her construction of
female anguish, it is the Chicana who suffers and swoons to give pleasure,
even in pain, to an audience, in this case, a white female. Furthermore, she
does not realize that she cannot control La Llorona. By including La Llorona
in her fantasy, she unwittingly provides Rita and Camilla a means of escape.
Diane, in her attempt to recreate Rita in her dreams, has given herself over to
seduction, unaware that it "seizes hold of all pleasures, affects and representations, and gets a hold of dreams themselves in order to reroute them from
their primary course, turning them into a sharper, more subtle game, whose
stakes have neither an end nor an origin, and concerns neither drives nor
desires."[13] Diane's fantasy or game has been rerouted from one in which she
is in control to one in which she is completely powerless; La Llorona's
appearance and song ensure this fact. Rita, who initially shares the same
reaction as Betty, ultimately changes her view when del Rio faints from the
sheer intensity of the song she mimes. A momentary look of recognition and
even anger washes over Rita to reflect a kind of cultural knowing, one that
makes her fully aware that she must not be the one left crying.

Even if Diane does control the first narrative, she can neither dictate nor
contain Camilla's ethnicity and cultural roots that come to the fore when
Camilla sleeps and asks for Silencio. Nor can she disengage the cultural
connection between La Llorona and Camilla. Even in the assigned guise of
Rita, Camilla seeks to silence Diane's narrative, and La Llorona makes this
possible by calling to Rita and warning her, by giving her back herself, her
identity as Camilla as represented by the box, and ultimately saving her for a
time. In the end, Diane loses control of the narrative and herself. Not even in
dreams will Camilla allow herself to be oppressed. Overwrought, Diane suc-
cumbs to guilt and takes her own life. In this scene, the room fills with
smoke, and a representation of the dark primal self slowly fades in and is
then replaced by the image of a blonde Rita and Betty superimposed over the
skyline of the city. This suggests that Diane's eternal punishment, her hell, is
to remember Camilla as Rita moments before Diane lost her forever. The
final scene of the film takes us back to Club Silencio, where a regally
dressed, blue-haired woman of obvious prominence sits in the balcony and
utters the word silencio. Her gilded dress and box seat imply that "silence is
golden" in women. Lynch seems keenly aware of the ways in which the

patriarchy silences women, but he also illustrates how women participate in the silencing of other women. Only La Llorona's voice endures to shatter both kinds of silencio.

SEARCHING FOR OURSELVES

The traditional and contemporary Lloronas in each of these films illustrate the expansion of the mythology to reflect a wide range of Chicana experiences within the cinematic landscape. Although these characters are often rendered in stereotypical if not racist terms, they cannot be wholly dismissed on this basis alone. For if we are to consume cinematic representations supposedly of ourselves as Chicana/os, we must look with better eyes to see beyond conventionalized constructions of race and ethnicity. Although, as film scholar Lester D. Friedman contends, production companies and filmmakers "should be held accountable for racist and sexist images, those visual representations which have important consequences beyond . . . the movie theater,"[14] we as viewers must also be held accountable for how we interpret these images. As Jason C. Johansen states, "as we acquire an understanding of the 'colonizing' process of 'First World' (Hollywood) cinema, we can begin to look for methods of 'decolonizing.'"[15] One of those decolonizing methods is the deconstruction of images within a Chicana/o cultural context. Chicana/o viewers can then speak from an informed position about the ways in which dominative filmmakers perpetuate discourses of dominance in Chicano-themed films. While characters such as Mercedes and Camilla represent complex and empowering images of Chicanas outside of the traditional stereotypes, filmmakers must continue to explore the difficulties of forming one's own cultural identity.

The characters in these films speak to Chicana and Chicano viewers in ways they may not to others. As cultural readers who have been exposed to aspects of La Llorona folklore since childhood, we possess the ability to read ourselves subversively, when necessary, across these texts. Through specific cultural lenses, disenfranchised people have the power to reclaim texts that are read by mainstream culture as palatable Otherness. Thus, using this analytical method, we can see how characters such as Isabel and Pilar can be allowed additional space beyond two-dimensional gender and cultural types. Cultural, racial and sexual hierarchies, when read through a culturally specific folkloric lens, become subversive. However, I am eager to see how a Chicana or Chicano filmmaker might consciously represent La Llorona in a mainstream film. As we take control of representing ourselves and no longer have to sift through refracted cultural materials to find favorable elements that speak to our experiences, we can create new textual encounters in which empowerment replaces subversion as the primary critical tool.

NOTES

1. According to Rebolledo, there are signs in New Mexico with La Llorona's image on them warning children not to play too closely to ditches, emphasizing her presence as an accepted and identifiable cultural and regional icon. See Tey Diana Rebolledo, *Women Singing in the Snow: A Cultural Analysis of Chicana Literature* (Tucson: University of Arizona Press, 1995), 65.

2. Rebolledo, *Women Singing in the Snow*, 77.

3. I do not wish to suggest that an "essential" La Llorona myth exists. In fact, Bess Lomax-Hawes, in "La Llorona in Juvenile Hall," *Western Folklore* 27 (1968): 153–70, suggests that because of variations in the weeping woman narrative, the only consistent element might be the name, La Llorona. I am, however, drawing upon traditional versions of the tale, which depend heavily on the seminal work done by Américo Paredes in *Folktales of Mexico* (Chicago: University of Chicago Press, 1970) and Thomas A. Janvier in *Legends of Mexico City* (New York and London: Harper and Brothers, 1910).

4. Jacqueline Bobo, *Black Women as Cultural Readers* (New York: Columbia University Press, 1995), 87.

5. bell hooks, *Black Looks: Race and Representation* (Boston: South End Press, 1992), 21–22.

6. I identify traditional tales as those that take place most frequently, but not exclusively, in a rural setting, near a body of water, and where a haunting is said to occur. The traditional stories also primarily focus on La Llorona as a threat due to the "loss" of her own children. Contemporary Llorona tales, in contrast, are defined by their movement toward urban settings, where traditional elements such as water or the weeping may not necessarily be included, though they often are in subtle ways. Generally, the emphasis in these stories is on the condition of being lost, whether that be politically, economically, socially, racially, or culturally.

7. José Limón, *American Encounters: Greater Mexico, the United States, and the Erotics of Culture* (Boston: Beacon Press, 1998), 152.

8. Limon, *American Encounters*, 154.

9. While Mercedes does emerge as a Malinche figure, particularly in her betrayal of the undocumented workers, I focus instead on what she represents as a Llorona figure and the legacy she hands down to her daughter.

10. These lines are from the song "Tres Dias" by Tomas Mendez, which is performed by Los Camperos de Nati Cano.

11. Anthony Lane, "Road Trips," *The New Yorker* (October 8, 2001): 88–89.

12. Trihn T. Minh-ha, *Woman, Native, Other: Writing Postcoloniality and Feminism* (Bloomington: Indiana University Press, 1989), 79.

13. Jean Baudrillard, *Seduction*, trans. Brian Singer (1979; New York: St Martin's, 1990), 124.

14. Lester J. Friedman, ed., *Unspeakable Images: Ethnicity and the American Cinema* (Chicago: University of Illinois Press, 1991), 9.

15. Jason C. Johansen, "Notes on Chicano Cinema," in *Chicanos and Film: Representation and Resistance*, ed. Chon A. Noriega (Minneapolis: University of Minnesota Press, 1992), 306.

Chapter Five

Chasing Fae

The Watermelon Woman *and Black Lesbian Possibility*

Laura L. Sullivan

Cheryl Dunye's 1996 film, *The Watermelon Woman*, is a groundbreaking and rulebreaking film. The first feature film made by a black lesbian film-maker (McAlister), the film employs both deconstructive and realist tech-niques to examine the way that identity in contemporary U.S. culture is shaped by multiple forces, primarily race, gender, and sexual orientation. Encouraging viewers to consider the unstable, complex, and often contradic-tory nature of identity, the film is humorous yet politically engaging. In this paper, I consider the ways that the film works simultaneously to represent and to decenter the identity and history of a figure most invisible in the textual production of the dominant culture—the black lesbian.

The Watermelon Woman, an independent film made on a shoestring bud-get, experimentally combines narrative and documentary forms. The film's storyline centers on the life and work of Cheryl, a black lesbian woman filmmaker living in Philadelphia. Cheryl works in a video store and in an independent video business with her acerbic friend Tamara, also black and lesbian. Cheryl is making a film about an African-American actress named Fae "The Watermelon Woman" Richards, who appeared in Hollywood films in the 1930s and 1940s. The central narrative's plot concerns Cheryl's rela-tionship with a white woman, Diana, and the parallels between Cheryl's experiences and the subject matter of her research: the life and work of Fae Richards, who was not only a black woman involved in film, but a lesbian who once had an affair with one of her white directors, a woman named Martha Page. Metafictionally, Cheryl often directly addresses the camera as she describes her progress in making the film within the film, and the film presents us with scenes of Cheryl creating her film, performing interviews, and undertaking archival research. The primary tension in the film occurs at the intersection of race and sexual orientation and addresses the feasibility—and politics—of black-white lesbian relationships.

The film also reworks filmic conventions, both traditional and postmodern, as it provokes the viewer's curiosity about this unknown "watermelon woman" actress. Many viewers find it "simply fascinating to follow along with Cheryl's detective work" as she searches for clues about this unknown black actress (McAlister). We participate in Cheryl's process of discovery as she learns about this historical figure with whom she increasingly identifies. The viewer does not discover until the film's end that the actress Fae "The Watermelon Woman" Richards never existed, and is, in fact, the creation of the film's writer and director, Dunye. I explore the implications of the way that the film draws upon and questions both fictional and documentary forms in more detail below. First, a consideration of how this film addresses the representation of members of marginalized groups.

DE/RECONSTRUCTING IMAGES OF BLACK WOMEN

In *Black Women as Cultural Readers*, Jacqueline Bobo asserts that "Black women are . . . knowledgeable recorders of their history and experiences and have a stake in faithfully telling their own stories" (36). In her first direct address of the viewer, Cheryl speaks to this imperative as she muses about what subject to use as the focus of her film: "I know it has to be about black women, because our stories have never been told." As this remark indicates, Cheryl Dunye recognizes that the voices of black women have been absent from the dominant cultural production of texts in this century; her film seeks to address this elision.

Recent cultural critics point out that the primary images of black women in film have been largely harmful and inaccurate stereotypes. Bobo explains that throughout the history of Hollywood cinema, we find "a venerable tradition of distorted and limited imagery" of representations of black women, who have been limitedly characterized "as sexually deviant, as the dominating matriarchal figure, as strident, eternally ill-tempered wenches, and as wretched victims" (33). Bobo specifies that within this last category, classical Hollywood portrayed black women as domestic servants, while more recent texts focus on black women as "'welfare' mothers" (33). In *The Watermelon Woman*, viewers are exposed to this history while they are also asked to critique it.

The film's central character, Cheryl, is fascinated by the unknown black actresses of early Hollywood cinema, while her friend Tamara chastises her for her interest in "all that niggamammy shit from the '30s." In her first monologue about her documentary, Cheryl tells viewers that she has been viewing tapes of 1930s and 1940s movies that have black actresses in them, exclaiming that she is "totally shocked" to discover that "in some of these films, the black actresses aren't even listed in the credits." In this way, Dunye the filmmaker comments on a real phenomenon, the historical invisibility of black women in film as well as the devaluation of their labor and identities, before she introduces us to the (fictitious) film that currently has her character Cheryl's attention. Cheryl relates that when she first watched this film, she "saw the most beautiful black mammy, named Elsie." Clearly intrigued by this actress, Cheryl insists that she show us a clip. Yet the "clip" from the video is typically racist and demeaning, containing a Civil War scene in which the mammy comforts a white woman, "Don't cry Missy, Massa Charles is coming back—I know he is!" This constructed excerpt is familiar to us, as heirs to a media culture that routinely assigned black actresses to such roles, not that many decades ago, as emblematized by Hattie McDaniel in *Gone with the Wind* (1939). While Cheryl is aware of the exploitation of black women in cinema, she is still seduced by these images. As she explains to the viewer, she is going to make a film about this actress, known as "The Watermelon Woman" because "something in her face, something in the way she looks and moves, is serious, is interesting."

Bobo notes that "Black female creative artists bring a different understanding of black women's lives and culture, seeking to eradicate the harmful and pervasive images haunting their history" (5). Dunye's film directly acknowledges the negative effects of the oppressive stereotypes with which black women have been imaged in the history of film. The title of the Fae Richards' film with which Cheryl is most fascinated is telling in this regard, *Plantation Memories*. Through mechanisms such as the naming of this (fictional) film, Dunye comments on the historical continuity of the oppression of black women. She reflects how the legacy of slavery affects the lives of black women in the twentieth century (and how this legacy also shapes the representations of such lives). She also reminds us that early stereotypical depictions of black women continue to impinge on the lived experiences of black women today and continue to delimit the options available for black women producers of contemporary cultural texts.

In the case of black lesbian women, however, what is "haunting their history," to use Bobo's phrase, is not so much a history of damaging and false images, but is instead a certain absence of participation in the representations of the mainstream media. Jewelle Gomez comments on the black lesbian's "invisibility in American society" and explains that black lesbians "are the least visible group not only in the fine arts, but also in the popular media, where the message conveyed about the Lesbian of color is that she does not even exist, let alone use soap, drive cars, drink Coke, go on vacations, or do much of anything else" (110). Thus, Dunye's film serves first to document the existence of black lesbians, in much the same way as Julie Dash's film *Daughters of the Dust* (1992) was unique in featuring a group that is not typically the visual or diegetic focus of most films—black women. As bell hooks comments in a dialogue with Julie Dash, "To de-center the white patriarchal gaze, we indeed have to focus on someone else for a change. And . . . the film takes up that group that is truly on the bottom of this society's race-sex hierarchy. Black women tend not to be seen, or to be seen solely as stereotype" (40). Dash and hooks discuss the discomfort of some viewers of *Daughters* in having to "spend . . . two hours as a black person, as a black woman" (40). While black women flocked to the film in droves (Bobo 9), black men and non-black viewers needed to connect with the film through mechanisms other than direct identification (Dash and hooks 40). Viewers from these subject positions were thus called upon to be more actively involved in the process of textual reception.

Dunye's film likewise calls upon an active viewer, but with the added dimension of sexual orientation. For if the black woman has been invisible or stereotyped in popular culture, the black lesbian woman has been even more invisible, and when present, this figure has caused even black women discomfort. (For example, Dash reports that the actress who played one of the black lesbian lovers in her film, Yellow Mary, later denied that her character was gay (Dash and hooks 66).) *The Watermelon Woman* foregrounds black lesbian identity throughout, but it does so in a way that invites the reader to connect the history of the black lesbian actress who rose to fame through a series of denigrating roles as servant and slave, with the present black lesbian filmmaker before us, Cheryl Dunye, who is playing a version of herself.

For example, in scenes filmed in Cheryl's home, the tape of *Plantation Memories* plays on the television, while Cheryl, a bandana tied around her head, lip syncs the mammy's part in the film's scene, exaggeratedly mimicking the fawning pretense of the black servant played by Fae Richards. Likewise, in another series of scenes in the film, Cheryl sits in front of her video camera, holding several postcards and pictures of the Watermelon Woman in her hands, hiding her face. The camera is tightly focused on the images of the Watermelon Woman that Cheryl leafs through, showing these pictures to the viewer, but Cheryl is visible in the background, an eye peering around these representations of the actress, a gesture of connection. Yet in the end what we have is a constructed history connected to a constructed but "real" figure, Cheryl the character standing in for Cheryl Dunye the filmmaker.

Commenting on the uniqueness of *Daughters of the Dust*, hooks notes that there are "very few other films where the camera really zooms in on black women's faces" (52). Dunye also employs this technique, and there are many scenes in which the faces and bodies of black women, in this case black lesbians, are prominent. These typically invisible bodies are rendered visible in a number of ways. First, there are many close-ups of Cheryl in the segments where she directly addresses her video camera. Second, there are explicit love scenes that break new ground. While viewers of alternative cinema have previously seen the naked bodies of white lesbians, such as Patricia Charbonneau and Helen Shaver in Donna Deitch's *Desert Hearts* (1985), and even including *The Watermelon Woman*'s Guin Turner who starred in the white lesbian film *Go Fish* (1994), love scenes that feature black lesbian women are rare. Patricia Rozema's *When Night Is Falling* (1995) is a notable exception in this regard, as it depicts a romance between a black lesbian woman and a previously straight white French woman. However, while that film's focus is on the white woman's "conversion" to lesbianism, *The Watermelon Woman* centrally engages the interracial dimension of its lesbian romances. The subjects of Cheryl's interviews about Fae Richards debate the nature of her relationship with Martha Page, and Fae's last lover, June Walker, refers to Page as "that white woman." More relevant to this discussion is the way that Dunye's film visually highlights the racial aspect of the lesbian relationship between Cheryl and Diana, in scenes technically reminiscent of Spike Lee's *Jungle Fever* (1991). Viewers are treated to tight close-ups of Cheryl and Diana's black and white bodies pressed together in explicit sex scenes. Their hands roam across each other's naked bodies as the women kiss. At one point, the camera zooms in on the interlocked black and white hands of the two characters in bed. In this way, the film not only requires that black lesbians be acknowledged; it also documents the existence of interracial lesbian romances.[1]

AVOIDING ESSENTIALISM

Queer female producers of cultural texts must wrestle with the nature of lesbian subjectivity. In the wake of the complete destabilizing of subject formation that has resulted from the theoretical insights provided by a postmodern perspective, such artists face the challenge of "reconstruct[ing] lesbian subject positions without reinstating essentialisms" (Dolan 42). Dunye has risen to this challenge, as the characters in *The Watermelon Woman* do not present a monolithic view of any featured group. As Dolan argues, "Lesbians disappear under the liberal humanist insistence that they are just like everyone else. Difference is effectively elided by readability" (44). In this film, there is no unified lesbian subject position, either black or white. Cheryl, Tamara, their white video store coworker Annie, Tamara's black girlfriend Stacy, and Diana are all very different types of lesbians. They have different styles of fashion, different race and gender politics, and distinctive personalities. For example, Cheryl and Tamara have short, close-shaven hair-

cuts, while Diana has long hair and wears lipstick. Stacy is a student finish-
ing her MBA degree at Wharton; Tamara is obsessed with sex; Cheryl is
passionate about filmmaking; and Diana wants to "figure out her life."

However, the film moves beyond merely presenting the wide variety of
lesbian subject positions. The film addresses what is required "to reconstruct
a tenable lesbian subject position . . . somewhere between deconstruction and
essentialism" (Dolan 53). Dolan specifies what this new representation of
lesbian subjectivity will entail:

> Reconstructing a variable lesbian subject position that will not rise like a
> phoenix in a blaze of essentialism from the ashes of deconstruction requires
> emptying lesbian references of imposed truths, whether those of the dominant
> culture or those of lesbian radical feminist communities which hold their own
> versions of truth. The remaining, complex, different referent, without truth,
> remains dependent on the materiality of actual lesbians who move in and out
> of dominant discourse in very different ways because of their positions within
> race, class, and variant expressions of their sexuality—dragging at the margins
> of structure and ideology. (53)

The Watermelon Woman answers Dolan's call, by refusing to accept the
heritage of racist and heterosexist Hollywood cinema, by interweaving questions of sexuality and race, and by presenting lesbians who have conflicted
relationships to dominant ideology. Additionally, the binary oppositions of
"good" and "bad" identities are similarly deconstructed, as the film avoids
simply reversing the dominant characterizations that attribute positive connotations to straight and/or white people and negative ones to gay and/or black
people.

Although black lesbians, real and imagined, present and historical, are the
focus in this text, the film presents a more complex view of lesbian subjectivity. The contrast between Cheryl and Tamara, for example, not only reflects
the variety of subject positions of black lesbians; it also reveals the way that
oppressions and their internalizations are layered and intertwined. Tamara
advocates black lesbian solidarity, yet she reveals her own sexism throughout
the film. Tamara frequently encourages the single Cheryl to "cruise" for
"cute girls" and declares that she hopes to "get some" from her girlfriend
Stacy on an upcoming date. When Tamara criticizes Cheryl at the video
store, telling her "All you do since you don't have a girlfriend is watch those
boring old films," Cheryl retorts, "I'd rather watch films than black porn like
you." In this way, the internalized sexism of some lesbian women is presented through the character of Tamara, who views women as sexual objects. As
always, this portrayal is presented with humor. For instance, one of the films
Tamara orders from the video store is called *Bad Black Ballbusters*; Tamara
justifies her film choice to Cheryl: "I was curious to see what they look like
without hair."

Cheryl is caught in the crossfire of the various vectors that pressure her identity. She is not a typical lesbian in Tamara's eyes because she is not obsessed with finding a girlfriend and because she does not visually objectify women. Tamara sees an inevitable connection between a lesbian identity and chasing women: "We're lesbians—remember, Cheryl? We're into female-to-female attraction. Anyway, you're the one who's supposed to be clocking all the girls—how long has it been since you've been with one, anyway?" Cheryl's lack of preoccupation with women is evidence to Tamara that Cheryl is not behaving authentically as a lesbian. Cheryl has other struggles as a lesbian. She feels "set up" by Diana, who invites her to dinner and then seduces her. After she sleeps with Diana, Cheryl tells us in a voiceover, "I'm still in shock over the whole having-sex-with-Diana thing. I've never done anything else like that before, let me assure you. The hip, swinging lesbian style isn't my forte . . . , I'm just an old-fashioned girl trying to keep up with the times." For many viewers, the idea that all lesbians are alike will be shattered by these depictions.

The film also reveals the instability of racial subjectivity. Bob, the owner of the video store, is a black man who oozes sexism—and heterosexism—in his mistreatment of the women who work for him, black and white. Lee Edwards, the black gay race film expert, knows nothing about the Watermelon Woman or Martha Page. He excuses his ignorance of these two women, telling Cheryl and Tamara, "Women are not my specialty." And black feminist essentialism is likewise critiqued in this film. Tamara, Cheryl, and Annie film a poetry reading by "Sistah Sound" at the local women's community center. With African drumming for background rhythm, a black woman performs a poem that repeats "I am black woman, black woman, yes," in a scene that both celebrates and pokes fun at such gatherings.

Racial politics also influence the relationship between Tamara and Cheryl, which becomes increasingly conflicted as the film's narrative progresses. Tamara's opinion of Diana is predicated on her wariness of white women. Tamara sees Diana as trying to usurp the black lesbian's place in the world, calling her Cheryl's "wannabe black girlfriend." Tamara questions Cheryl's alliance to black women once she begins dating Diana, telling Cheryl, "I see that once again you're going out with a white girl acting like she wants to be black, and you're being a black girl acting like she wants to be white. What's up with you, Cheryl? Don't you like the color of your skin?" While Cheryl defends herself to Tamara—defensively asking, "Who's to say that dating somebody white doesn't make me black?"—she is clearly uncomfortable when Diana reveals that she was born in Jamaica, and even more disturbed by Diana's revelations that she has had black boyfriends in the past and that her "father's sister's first husband was an ex-Panther" whose name was "Tyrone Washington."[2] Moreover, both the white lesbian archivist as well as the white sister of Martha Page, with whom Diana has arranged an interview, treat Cheryl condescendingly. When Diana does not stand up to Mrs. Page-Fletcher when she refers to "all those coloreds" that Martha Page employed and when she denies her sister's lesbianism, Cheryl has had enough. Thus, while Cheryl rejects Tamara's essentialist view of black lesbian identity, she struggles with race dynamics in her relationship nonetheless.

Likewise, Cheryl argues against June Walker's call for Cheryl to eliminate Martha Page from her film. In a letter to Cheryl, the woman who was Fae Richards' lover for the last twenty years of her life says,

> I was so mad that you mentioned the name of Martha Page. Why do you even want to include a white woman in a movie on Fae's life? Don't you know she had nothing to do with how people should remember Fae? I think it troubled her soul for the world to see her in those mammy pictures. . . . If you really are in "the family," you better understand that our family will only have each other.[3]

Cheryl responds to June's letter in her last monologue, insisting that there is no one black lesbian subject position, and declaring that she might make different choices about the meaning of this black actress's legacy. Cheryl tells June, "I know she meant the world to you, but she also meant the world to me, and those worlds are different." She refuses to erase the history of Fae's romance with the white woman director from her film: "The moments she shared with you—the life she had with Martha, on and off the screen—those are precious moments, and nobody can change that." She then points to the generational differences in operation in this debate, "But what she means to me—a twenty-five-year-old black woman, means something else," explaining how this figure inspires her as a black, lesbian filmmaker.

This film calls into question the idea of "difference" itself. The character Annie, the young white lesbian who works with Cheryl and Tamara in the video store, has blond streaks in her black hair and wears a dog collar. Cheryl and Annie get along well, but Tamara bristles at the girl's street style and sense of self-confidence. When Cheryl asks her why she so dislikes Annie, Tamara retorts, "She gets on my last black lesbian nerve with all that piercing and hair dye business. "When Cheryl reminds her that they also share a marginalized status—"Tamara, you know we're different, too"—Tamara reverts to segregationist and classist arguments to justify her denigration of Annie: "Yeah, but see we're not different amongst a group of ritzy black folk. I mean, we were there to get their business and to be professional. We weren't there to look like a bunch of hip-hop multicultural mess." She says that she is disgusted by Annie's way of dressing and by her dog collar. Later in the video store back room, Tamara tells Annie, "You're so helpful—you probably know a place to get a good clit piercing, don't you?" Annie responds, "Look Tamara, just because you and I are different doesn't mean you have to treat me like shit all the time." The conflict between these two women highlights the fragmentation and multiplicity in lesbian subject positions, as well as the way that different aspects of identity are sometimes at cross purposes with one another. This film undercuts the essentialist assumptions of both oppressive and liberatory positions, undermining a heterosexist view that lumps together all gay people, as well as an anti-racist view that would promote an essentialist view of all white people. In this way, the film moves beyond what hooks calls the "de-center[ing] of the white patriarchal gaze" (Dash and hooks 40) to question the racist heterosexist gaze, including the potentially homophobic gaze of non-white straight viewers, as well as the potentially racist gaze of white lesbian viewers. The film enacts this decentering both visually, as interracial lesbian romances are prominently pictured, and diegetically, through the conflicts of its characters. Revealing their racist and heterosexist agenda, the American Family Association labeled the film's depictions of lesbian sex "smut" (McAlister). However, the film forces even those viewers who are not on the "right wing" end of the political spectrum to confront their own prejudices.

The film also contains a complex presentation of class identity. The video store owner, Bob, wields power over his three female employees, incessantly berating them for not being familiar enough with what he calls "the Bob system," although they clearly know how to perform their jobs well. While Tamara and Cheryl barely make ends meet, and while Cheryl must work hard at two jobs in order to finance her film project, Diana is well-off financially, as indicated by the credit cards she flashes at the video store, by the spacious apartment she rents while she takes time off from school, and by the fact that she does not work during the time of the film, but volunteers with homeless children of color (a race dynamic that does not go unremarked upon by Tamara). In contrast to Diana's life of leisure, Cheryl and Tamara have had to resort to a "tape scam" at work in order to secure videos for themselves, films for Cheryl's research and porn movies for Tamara's enjoyment. They rent tapes under customers' names, preview them, and return them, as Cheryl explains to Diana. Finally, we learn that Annie is a Bryn Mawr college graduate, yet she needs the job at the video store, pointing to the way that college degrees no longer guarantee security in the work force. Even the parodied lesbian archives (in the film called C.L.I.T.—the Center for Lesbian Information and Technology) struggle financially, relying on volunteer help and not having a catalogued organization yet in place. The documentary portions similarly present class dimensions of the characters' experiences. Fae Richards, we learn, was a maid before she became an actress. Black cast films eventually became passé in part because even black audiences wanted to see Hollywood films instead, as Lee Edwards explains to Cheryl and Tamara. Although Tamara points to the real connection between race, power, and wealth when she refers to "the white folks at the bank" at the film's outset, in this film, there are no clear correlations between race, gender, sexual orientation, and class status. The film does not undertake an explicit class critique, but it does convey the oppressive elements of class and the way that class position meshes with and influences other types of identity formation.

(RE)WRITING HISTORY

The Watermelon Woman draws upon "pseudo-realism, borrowing heavily from the documentary format" (Turoff). The viewer's relationship to the film's presentation of "truth"—that is, whether or not the viewer is aware that "the Watermelon Woman" is a fictionalized construction—pivotally influences the viewing experience. For example, I first viewed this film at a local cinema in the spring of 1997. During the entire film, I was unaware that Fae "The Watermelon Woman" Richards is a fictional creation of Dunye's; I was shocked to read in the credits an acknowledgment of the fictionality of this character. At the time, I believed that Dunye's inclusion of this information in the credits revealed that the filmmaker did not anticipate that viewers would necessarily realize that the black actress named Fae Richards never existed. For while Dunye deconstructs and satirizes the documentary form throughout the film, she also replicates it in a way that leads viewers not to question its verisimilitude. In fact, the Internet Movie Database even goes so far as to list the film's genre as "Documentary."

Since the time of my initial viewing of the film, I have learned that when the film was first screened, it did not contain any reference to the fictional status of Fae Richards, so the film's first viewers were not aware of this dimension of the film (Jackson and Moore 500). Conversely, some viewers do not have the privilege of seeing the film and sorting through this issue of the actress's fictionality for themselves. I saw the film a second time while in London in August of 1998. Although I was thrilled that such a film was being shown on British television (as part of Channel 4's "Queer Street" series), and although I was prepared to watch the film again from a position of already knowing its "secret," I was dismayed to see that the British weekly magazine *Time Out* directly indicated that Fae Richards was not a real person in its description of the film. I knew that British first-time viewers would approach the film much differently because they already were aware that its documentary was staged.

Thus, there are three possible viewing positions of the film: never learning that the documentary portions record a fictional subject's life; realizing while viewing the film, or learning during the film's credits that Dunye created the character of Fae Richards; and knowing about the actress's fictional status at the film's outset, for example, after having read a review of the film. (I am aware that this article itself, ironically, reproduces this last dynamic for readers who have not yet seen the film.) Another irony is that while the issue of secrecy and confession are typically associated with gay identity, this film does not conceal homosexuality, but instead contains a "secret" about the fictional nature of the subject of the central character's documentary. Having now watched the film for a third time on video, I am convinced that much of its power comes from the ambiguity of the figure of Fae Richards. Dunye leads the viewer to ask herself why she is unfamiliar with this actress, a questioning that has significant implications for thinking through the relationship among media texts, politics, and history. Watching the film from the position of not knowing that the documentary subject is fictional enables viewers to appreciate fully the way that this film "create[s] a certain tension between the social formation, subjectivity, and representation" (Kaplan 138).

Bobo reminds us that "within the last several decades black women have effectively written themselves back into history; they have retrieved their collective past for sustenance and encouragement for present-day protest movements"' (36). In some ways, Dunye's film is situated within this tradition. However, Dunye's final remarks make clear that she was unable to retrieve this history she wanted to find; in the credits she tells viewers: "Sometimes you have to create your own history," explaining that "the Watermelon Woman is fiction." Yet although Dunye rewrites a history that is/ was not there, she does so with a firm grounding in historical realities for black people, particularly black women, in this century. For example, Cheryl's search for information on the Watermelon Woman leads her to interview her mother and others who were part of the vibrant black club scene in Philadelphia in the interwar decades. Cheryl learns that black films were played before the Hollywood features at the early twentieth-century black-owned cinemas from Lee Edwards, who tells her, "If they'd only played the black cast films, they would've gone out of business during the Depression. Black folks [in the 1920s and 1930s] wanted to see the Hollywood stuff with the stars, the costumes—all that junk." In such segments of the film, Dunye informs viewers about lost pieces of African-American history through her construction of Fae Richards' history and her fictional account of Cheryl's investigation of it.

The film liberally uses photographs in its documentary portions. The photograph is a textual form that supposedly signifies "this really happened" to the viewer; it testifies to the existence of people and events. Yet, in this case, the photographs have been created for this film, and the history they purportedly record is fabricated. In a further irony, these photographs are now objects of textual analysis themselves. A journal published in West Germany, *Parkett*, contains an article entitled, "Watermelon Woman: The Fae Richards Photo Archives." The abstract for this article specifies that it contains "A selection of photographs from a series created for use in Cheryl Dunye's film *The Watermelon Woman*." The abstract goes on to tell us, "Created in collaboration with Zoe Leonard, the photographs depict scenes from the life of a fictional character, Fae Richards." So the constructed figure of this black lesbian actress visually lives on, at least in the world of academic cultural criticism.

The feminist cultural critic Jeanie Forte, in the words of Jill Dolan, "suggests that because of its structural recognizability, or 'readability,' realism might be able to politicize spectators alienated by the more experimental conventions of non-realistic work" (43). This film draws upon this strategy of textual production. Both the film's narrative portions and the film's documentary segments contain realist aspects and are, as such, "readable" to the film's viewers. However, in the juxtaposition of these two "stories," the film enacts a postmodern deconstruction of both realist cinema and documentary forms. The film's metafictional elements, such as Cheryl's asides to the film's viewer, further serve to destabilize the film's realistic quality. And this critique of realism is also a critique of the racist politics often promoted by the mainstream mass media's realist presentations; as bell hooks explains, "one of the major problems facing black filmmakers is the way both spectators and, often, the dominant culture want to reduce us to some narrow notion of 'real' or 'accurate'" (Dash and hooks 31). *The Watermelon Woman* seduces viewers with realist elements, only to make us question our naïveté at the film's end, and in this way the film disrupts the naturalizing function of realist discourse.

This film's technical qualities, such as the use of montage, talking-head interviews, segments that appear to be from early film news spots, and film footage with an archival look, lead viewers to perceive the text initially as based upon reality. They see all the film's characters as "ethnographic subjects" and believe the film to be "Dunye's casually taped, autobiographical video journal" (Jackson and Moore 500). This reading of the film goes against what film critic E. Ann Kaplan recommends for a "counter-cinema" such as feminist cinema (131). She argues that filmmakers

> must confront within their films the accepted representations of reality so as to expose their falseness. Realism as a style is unable to change consciousness because it does not depart from the forms that embody the old consciousness. Thus, prevailing realist codes—of camera, lighting, sound, editing, mise-en-scène—must be abandoned and the cinematic apparatus used in a new way so as to challenge audiences' expectations and assumptions about life. (131)

The Watermelon Woman confronts realism not by presenting a film that radically breaks from realist form; rather, this film reworks Kaplan's formulation so that the challenge to viewers comes at the film's end, when we are often shocked to see that the documentary subject matter within the film has been constructed and when we thus must confront our own ideological investments that led us to misinterpret this aspect of the film.

In contrast, viewers who read about the film's fictional elements in reviews or who have previously seen the film with the final disclaimer included, are more able to appreciate the film's humor. In the words of Randy Turoff, the film is "savvy, wry, and self-consciously ironic." One way that the film employs humor is to enact a critique of what bell hooks calls "the Eurocentric biases that have informed our understanding of the African American experience" (Dash and hooks 39). Particularly through a scene featuring a mock interview of the white cultural scholar Camille Paglia, the film comments on the way that white scholars appropriate and treat condescendingly the work of non-white scholars. Paglia tells us,

> Well, actually, the mammy figure is a great favorite of mine, particularly Hattie McDaniels' brilliant performance in *Gone with the Wind*. I really am distressed with a lot of the tone of recent African American scholarship. [cut] It tries to say about the mammy that her largeness as a figure is de-sexualizing, degrading, and de-humanizing, and this seems to me utterly wrong. Where the large woman is a symbol of abundance and fertility, is a kind of goddess figure.

Demonstrating the way that white critics often falsely bring their own life histories and experiences to bear on those of the non-white objects of their investigations, Paglia continues:

> Even the presence of the mammy in the kitchen it seems to me has been misinterpreted: 'Oh the woman in the kitchen is a slave, a subordinate—'Well, my grandmas, my Italian grandmothers, never left the kitchen. In fact this is why I dedicated my first book to them. And Hattie McDaniel in *Gone with the Wind*, is the *spitting image* of my grandmother, in her style, in her attitude, in her ferocity. It brings tears to my eyes.

That I did not originally view this interview as a satire says a lot about my opinion of Camilla Paglia as a feminist critic, but the fact that almost all of the film's other initial viewers, college students and art house audiences, missed the irreverent and exaggerated portrayal here also speaks to the power of the film's precise simulation of the documentary form, right down to the title at the bottom of the screen at this interview's outset, "Camille Paglia, Cultural Critic." Alexandra Juhasz emphasizes that "many of the codes of documentary label, categorize, and imply understandings of authority," revealing that documentary images are not merely recording nor undermining traditional power relations, but rather, deepening them (98). Audiences have been taught to view the documentary's elements evidenced in *The Watermel-*

on Woman as indications of a person's credibility and expertise, and thus, initial audiences did not question this woman's authority. Additionally, because similar trends exist in academic criticism, where members of groups in power presume to speak for "marginalized" groups, Camille Paglia's monologue did not seem outside the realm of truth or possibility. As Bobo makes clear, there is "an unstated presumption that the only reliable information about [black women] is that collected by white observers" (11). Camille Paglia's character romanticizes representations of African-American women in her commentary; for instance, she completely elides the impact of slavery or issues of unequal power relations, yet viewers seduced by the realist coding of her presentation miss the film's implicit critique of racism in this section.

In the last point that Paglia makes in her "interview," the white scholar's actions are carried to their greatest point of exaggeration. As before, Paglia continues to speak rapidly, rarely pausing for breath, and to gesture frequently with her hands, in a parody of the ludicrous connections that some scholars often make in their work:

> The watermelon, it seems to me, is another image that has been misinterpreted by a lot of black commentary—the great extended family Italian get togethers that I remember as a child ended with the men bringing out a watermelon and ritualistically cutting it, distributing the pieces to everyone, almost like the communion service, [cut] And I really dislike these kinds of reductionism of a picture of, let's say, a small black boy with a watermelon, him smiling broadly over it, looking at that as negative. Why is that not, instead, a symbol of joy? and pleasure, and fruitfulness? After all, a piece of watermelon has the colors of the Italian flag—red, white, and green—so I'm biased to that extent. I think that if the watermelon symbolizes African American culture, then rightly so, because look what white, middle-class feminism stands for—anorexia and bulimia—

In this way, the film shows us not only how women of color must go up against white control of signifying practices, but also demonstrates the oppressiveness of the racist interpretation of signs (as well as the ridiculousness of much of the esoteric ideas of contemporary criticism).

The Watermelon Woman again parallels *Daughters of the Dust* in that "part of what [the film] does is construct for us an imaginative universe around the question of blackness and black identity" in an examination that the director does "situate historically," as bell hooks comments to Julie Dash about her film (28). Dunye takes this imaginative creation and historical situating a step further, however,because she has had to create a history of a lesbian black celebrity; these women, too, are invisible in our received history of popular culture. After the Paglia interview, we see Cheryl interviewing white (lesbian-looking) women on the street. One says that she has heard of

Martha Page, but does not know the Watermelon Woman. Another adds, "If she's in anything after the 1960s, don't ask us, we haven't covered women and blaxploitation yet," again parodically pointing to the way that the institutionalization of women's studies and African-American studies have yet to transcend gendered and racialized stereotypes in their curriculums. The film then segues back to Camille Paglia, who tells Cheryl, "I'm stunned to hear that the director was lesbian or bisexual" and that "any kind of interracial relationship at this time [is] mind-boggling," remarks that reveal how heterosexism and racism often underlie the romanticization of the celebrated white creators of popular culture's representations. When Paglia tells Cheryl, "This is an astounding discovery that you've made," she seems jealous of the young black woman, even though she then wishes her good luck. The competition amongst cultural scholars is invoked in this exchange.

At film's end, Cheryl addresses the viewer. She speaks to the concerns raised in June Walker's letter, explaining to Walker that they have different experiences of Fae Richards and thus she means different things to each of them, as described above. Cheryl then elaborates about what remembering this actress means to her:

> It means hope; it means inspiration; it means possibility. It means history. And most important what I understand is it means that I am gonna be the one who says, "I am a black, lesbian filmmaker," who's just beginning, but I'm gonna say a lot more and have a lot more work to do. Anyway—what you've all been waiting for—the biography of Fae Richards. Faith Richardson.

This monologue is followed by a series of images, including simulated film-stills and scenes from films, depicting the life of Fae Richards, in chronological order, narrated by Cheryl's voiceover. This "biography" is interspersed with titles giving the film's credits, and in the middle of this "documentary," the title that explains the fictionality of the character flashes by, rather quickly, I might add. Thus, we learn then that all of these "meanings" of Fae Richards to Cheryl—hope, inspiration, possibility, history—are, to some extent, illusions. Dunye had to make up a history of a black lesbian actress; in other words, she had to create her own hope, inspiration, and possibility through the creation of a history that was not, but could have been, in some ways should have been, there. However, this undoing of the power of the influence of Fae Richards is not total. For Cheryl's ending statement, while spoken by a fictional character about, we soon learn, another fictional character, documents a real black lesbian filmmaker, Cheryl Dunye, who has acted on hope, inspiration, and a sense of possibility through her (meta)fictional text. Thus Cheryl's declaration that she will be the one who says that she is a black, lesbian filmmaker is found to be true in Dunye, and in the end we are left to ponder just what effort it took for her to realize that proclamation, to reflect upon the invisibility of black lesbians in American popular culture.

NOTES

1. However, while the film breaks with convention in highlighting an interracial lesbian romance, its ultimate commentary on such relationships—especially between African-American and white women—is that they are unlikely to overcome the difficulties related to social dynamics that often plague such relationships. Class differences, including Diana's racist fetishization of the "Other," come between Cheryl and Diana in the end, and the film encourages us to speculate that racist social norms of the mid-century came between Fae Richards and Martha Page.

2. Scenes such as this only "work" in this film because they are exaggeratedly humorous and because they also ring true as well. It is likely that viewers are familiar with white women who fetishize people of color, and who date them in the spirit of this fetishization.

3. Here Walker invokes a phrase used throughout the film, "the family," slang for "homosexual," or, more specifically, "lesbian." In this passage, the character of June Walker makes it clear that "family" for her includes race and is limited to lesbians who are also women of color.

WORKS CITED

Bobo, Jacqueline. *Black Women as Cultural Readers*. New York: Columbia University Press, 1995.

Dash, Julie, and bell hooks. "Dialogue Between bell hooks and Julie Dash." *Daughters of the Dust: The Making of an African American Woman's Film*. New York: The New Press, 1992. 27–67.

Desert Hearts. Dir. Donna Deitch. Samuel Goldwyn, 1985.

Dolan, Jill. "'Lesbian' Subjectivity in Realism: Dragging at the Margins of Structure and Ideology." *Performing Feminisms: Feminist Critical Theory and Theatre*. Ed. Sue-Ellen Case. Baltimore: Johns Hopkins University Press, 1990. 40–53.

Go Fish. Dir. Rose Troche. Samuel Goldwyn, 1994.

Gomez, Jewelle. "A Cultural Legacy Denied and Discovered: Black Lesbians in Fiction by Women." *Home Girls: A Black Feminist Anthology*. Ed. Barbara Smith. New York: Kitchen Table: Women of Color Press, 1983. 110–23.

Gone with the Wind. Dir. Victor Fleming. MGM, 1939.

Jackson, Phyllis J., and Darrell Moore. "Fictional Seductions." (Film Review.) *GLQ* 4.3 (1998): 499–508.

Juhasz, Alexandra. *AIDS TV: Identity, Community, and Alternative Video*. Durham, NC: Duke University Press, 1995.

Jungle Fever. Dir. Spike Lee. Universal Pictures, 1991.

Kaplan, E. Ann. *Women and Film: Both Sides of the Camera*. New York: Routledge, 1983.

McAlister, Linda Lopez. "The Watermelon Woman." (28 June 1997). http://wwwinform.umd.edu.EdRes/Topic/WomensStudies/FilmReviews/watermelon. 1 February 1999.

Turoff, Randy. "Watermelon Woman." http://www.planetout.com/pno/popcornq/db/getfilm.html?2117&shop. 1 February 1999.

The Watermelon Woman (1996). The Internet Movie Database—http://us.imdb.com/Title?Watennelon+Woman,+The+(1996) 1 February 1999.

When Night Is Falling. Dir. Patricia Rozema. Crucial Pictures, 1995.

Part II

Beauty Images

Mirror, Mirror, On Whose Wall?

Chapter Six

Hey Girl, Am I More than My Hair?

African American Women and Their Struggles with
Beauty, Body Image, and Hair

Tracey Owens Patton

Throughout history and to present day, African American women have challenged white definitions of beauty. What or who is considered beautiful varies among cultures. What remains consistent is that many notions of beauty are rooted in hegemonically defined expectations. While definitions of beauty affect the identities of everyone, this article focuses on African American women and the intersection between beauty, body image, and hair. Specifically, this article looks historically at how differences in body image, skin color, and hair haunt the existence and psychology of black women, especially since one common U.S. societal stereotype is the belief that black women fail to measure up to the normative standard. Two theoretical frameworks guide my analysis of beauty standards: Afrocentric theory and standpoint theory. I argue that the continuance of hegemonically defined standards of beauty not only reify white European standards of beauty in the United States, but also that the marginalization of certain types of beauty that deviate from the "norm" are devastating to all women. Further, the unrealistic expectations of beauty and hairstyle reify the divisions that exist between African American and Euro American women.

First, in order to understand African American women and the intersection between beauty, body image, and hair, this article juxtaposes beauty standards of African American and Euro American women, reviewing them through historical and current lenses. Second, I consider the theoretical frameworks of standpoint theory and Afrocentric theory as a means to elucidate beauty issues. Third, aspects of body, image, and race are discussed. Finally, I explore the possibility of redefining standards of beauty and "normality" through black beauty liberation.

AN HISTORICAL REVIEW OF BEAUTY: BLACK BEAUTY VS. WHITE BEAUTY

> "I want to know my hair again, the way I knew it before I knew that my hair is me, before I lost the right to me, before I knew that the burden of beauty—or lack of it—for an entire race of people could be tied up with my hair and me."
> —Paulette Caldwell, "A Hair Piece" (2000, 275)

Beauty is subject to the hegemonic standards of the ruling class. Because of this, "beauty is an elusive commodity" (Saltzberg and Chrisler 1997, 135) and definitions of beauty vary among cultures and historical periods. Beauty issues and subjection to dominant standards are not the sole domain of black and white women. For example, while all cultures have had, and continue to have, various standards of beauty and body decoration, the Chinese practice of foot binding was one that forced women to conform to beauty ideals that reified patriarchal privilege and domination. "The Chinese may have been the first to develop the concept that the female body can and should be altered from its natural state. The practice of foot binding clearly illustrates the objectification of parts of the female body as well as the demands placed on women to conform to beauty ideals" (Saltzberg and Chrisler 1997, 135).

An example of other types of beauty being rendered "voiceless" is found in Fiji. After the export of American television shows to Fiji, the rates of anorexia and bulimia increased exponentially. Further, the women of Fiji, who tend to have larger, rounder body shapes and are brown-skinned, not only became very conscious of the fact that their body shape did not meet Euro American standards, but their skin did not as well (Lazarus and Wunderlich 2000). While this article focuses on beauty standards between black and white American women, this Fijian incident shows that adherence to white standards of beauty, as well as to American standards of beauty, can be exported to other countries with, in this case, devastating consequences. The following literature review historically chronicles some of the effects two co-cultures, black women and white women, have faced in relation to beauty issues and body image.

Black Beauty

Women of color looking for answers through an introspective gaze or through their communities in order to counter white hegemonically defined standards of beauty is not a new occurrence. Historically and into modern times, African American beauty has been disparaged. As much of the literature on African American women and beauty has pointed out, African American women have either been the subject of erasure in the various mediated forms or their beauty has been wrought with racist stereotypes. According to Michele Wallace,

> the black woman had not failed to be aware of America's standard of beauty nor the fact that she was not included in it; television and motion pictures had made this information very available to her. She watched as America expanded its ideal to include Irish, Italian, Jewish, even Oriental [sic] and Indian women. America had room among its beauty contestants for buxom Mae West, the bug eyes of Bette Davis, the masculinity of Joan Crawford, but the black woman was only allowed entry if her hair was straight, her skin light, and her features European, in other words, if she was as nearly indistinguishable from a white woman as possible. (1979, 157–58)

While mediated images of beauty have become more diverse (e.g., Tyra Banks, Naomi Campbell, Tomiko, Alex Wek, and Oprah Winfrey), "biases against Black women based on their physical appearance persist" (Jones and Shorter-Gooden 2003, 178) and many black women do not feel "free" from mediated beauty standards. Some historically popular yet recurring negative manifestations of African American beauty include the oversexed jezebel, the tragic mulatto, and the mammy figure.[1] Therefore, it is clear that the notions of black beauty and black inferiority are inextricably bound.

Given the racist past and present of the United States, there are several identity and beauty issues that African American women face. Since 1619, African American women and their beauty have been juxtaposed against white beauty standards, particularly pertaining to their skin color and hair. During slavery, black women who were lighter-skinned and had features that were associated with mixed progeny (e.g., wavy or straight hair, white/European facial features) tended to be house slaves and those black women with darker-skin hues, kinky hair, and broader facial features tended to be field slaves. This racist legacy and African American internalization of this white supremacist racial classification brought about what Jones and Shorter-Gooden have termed "The Lily Complex." This complex is defined as "altering, disguising, and covering up your physical self in order to assimilate, to be accepted as attractive. . . . As Black women deal with the constant pressure to meet a beauty standard that is inauthentic and often unattainable, the lily complex can set in" (2003, 177). The desire to change her outer appearance to meet a Eurocentric ideal may lead her to loathe her own physical appearance and believe that "Black is not beautiful . . . that she can only be lovely by impersonating someone else" (177).

According to Greene, "the United States idealizes the physical character-istics of white women and measures women of color against this arbitrary standard" (1994, 18). To challenge white beauty as the stereotypical de facto standard against which all women are measured, middle-class and lower middle-class black women formed Black Ladies societies to uplift the race to a level equal to or exceeding that of a white woman.

> To achieve this, it seemed necessary to make her more of a lady, more clean, more proper than any white woman could hope to be. As if to blot out the humiliation of working in the white woman's kitchen all day, of being virtual-ly defenseless before the sexual advances of white men, black women enacted a charade of teas, cotillions, and all the assorted paraphernalia and pretensions of society life. It was a desperate masquerade which seemed to increase in frenzy as time went on. . . . Black women began to turn their heads in Charlotte Forten's[2] direction, even if their economic circumstances prevented them from imitating her standard of living. Many fewer looked to the examples of Harriet Tubman and Sojourner Truth, whom no man in his right mind would want, except, perhaps, patient Uncle Tom. (Wallace 1979, 156–57)

Wallace challenges the concept of assimilation.[3] Creativity in hairstyling can be a challenge to assimilationist notions of beauty (regardless of style worn) because it can challenge perceived expectations. When hair must be straight-ened for employment or for social mobility, it can be seen as assimilation-ist—subscribing to dominant cultural standards of beauty. However, as Orbe and Harris noted, in an organizational situation an organizational member must balance her identity. "Just as [a] young woman must negotiate her identities, so must an organizational member who comes from an underrepre-sented racial/ethnic group. Some organizational members may feel their ra-cial/ethnic identities become less important as they climb the ladder of suc-cess" (2001, 192). However, engaging in organizational social mobility does not mean that one will automatically assimilate or substitute her cultural, racial, and ethnic identity for that of the majority culture. Rather, women can take creative measures in surviving the organization and being true to one's self. One way is with appearance. While individually not all African American women valorize white beauty standards, African American women have had to invent their own beauty measures. In utilizing the uniqueness of African hair textures, which range from the kinky curls of the Mandingos to the flowing locks of the Ashanti (Byrd and Tharps 2001, 1), blacks have been very creative in hairstyling. In the early fifteenth century hairstyle for the Wolof, Mende, Mandingo, and Yoruba signaled age, ethnic identity, marital status, rank within the community, religion, war, and wealth (2–4). Hairstyling sessions were a bonding time for women. A hairstylist always held a prominent position in these communities. "The complicated and time-consuming task of hair grooming included washing, combing, oiling, braiding, twisting, and/or decorating the hair with any number of adornments including cloth, beads, and shells. The process could last several hours, sometimes several days" (5–6). The most common hairstyles the Europeans encountered when they began exploring the western coast of Africa in the mid-1400s included "braids, plaits, patterns shaved into the scalp, and any combination of shells, flowers, beads, or strips of material woven into the hair" (9). During this time period hair was not only a cosmetic concern, but "its social, aesthetic, and spiritual significance has been intrinsic to their sense of self for thousands of years" (7). Realizing the prominence hair played in the lives of western Africans, the first thing enslavers did was shave their heads; this was an unspeakable crime for Africans, because the people were shorn of their identity (10).

Throughout the centuries of slavery, scarves became a practicable alternative to covering kinky, unstyled hair or hair that suffered from patchy baldness, breakage, or disease. For example, in the eighteenth and nineteenth centuries, because slaves did not have traditional styling tools and were not given combs, they developed new hair implements. One development was a "sheep fleece carding tool" (13), which was used to untangle their hair. Additional household hair care included "bacon grease and butter to condition and soften the hair, prepare it for straightening, and make it shine. Cornmeal and kerosene were used as scalp cleaners, and coffee became a natural dye for women" (17). Hairstyles were often determined by the kind of work a slave performed. If one was a field slave and lived in separate slave quarters, "the women wore head rags and the men took to shaving their heads, wearing straw hats, or using animal shears to cut their hair short" (13). If a slave worked directly with the white population, e.g., barbers, cooks, housekeepers, they often styled their hair similarly to those of whites. For example, house slaves were required to have a "neat and tidy appearance or risk the wrath of the master, so men and women wore tight braids, plaits, and cornrows" (13). Black male slaves, like upper class white males, chose to wear wigs in the eighteenth century or "styled their own hair to look like a wig" (13).

Emulating white hairstyles, particularly straight hair, signified many things in the black community. First, straighter hair was associated with free-person status. Light-skinned runaway slaves "tried to pass themselves off as free, hoping their European features would be enough to convince bounty hunters that they belonged to that privileged class" (17). Emulating whiteness offered a certain amount of protection. Second, lighter-skinned straighter-haired slaves "worked inside the plantation houses performing less backbreaking labor than the slaves relegated to the fields" (18). Because of this, these slaves had better access to clothes, education, food, and "the promise of freedom upon the master's death"(18). However, the "jealous mistress of the manor often shaved off the lustrous mane of hair, indicating that white women too understood the significance of long, kink-free hair" (19).

Thus, as has already been shown, adopting many white European traits was essential to survival; for example, free vs. slave; employed vs. unemployed; educated vs. uneducated; upper class vs. poor. Issues of hair straightening were hotly contested in the black community. The practice was viewed as "a pitiful attempt to emulate whites and equated hair straightening with self-hatred and shame" (37). The most vocal opponents of hair straightening were W. E. B. DuBois and Booker T. Washington (see Byrd and Tharps 2001, 37–40)—both men were light-skinned black males with wavy hair—and Marcus Garvey. All of these men had influence in the African American community. With regard to the issue of hair, Garvey proclaimed, "Don't remove the kinks from your hair! Remove them from your brain!" (38). However, most black women felt straightened hairstyles were not about emulating whites but having modern hairstylse. Madame C. J. Walker was one of the more popularly known hairstylists who helped African American women achieve modern hairstyles.

In the twentieth century, the 1905 invention of Madame C. J. Walker's hair softener, which accompanied a hair-straightening comb, was the rage.[4] Hair straightening was a way to challenge the predominant nineteenth-century belief that black beauty was ugly. According to Rooks, "African Americans had long struggled with issues of inferiority, beauty, and the meaning of particular beauty practices. . . . [Walker] attempted to shift the significance of hair away from concerns of disavowing African ancestry" (1996, 35). Walker's beauty empire, therefore, not only contributed to higher self-esteem among the black community, but also created a new job industry for those who attended her beauty schools.

Hair straightening has continued to be a controversial beauty move by some in the African American community, particularly after the 1960s' and 1970s' "Black is Beautiful" social movement. For example, Malcolm X spoke out against hair straightening due to the belief he had had that hair straightening caused black people to feel ashamed of their own unique beauty, as well as the belief that hair straightening emulated white standards of beauty. However, hair straightening, as Taylor challenged, "has taken on such racialized significance that participation in the practice can be a way of expressing black pride rather than a way of precluding it" (2000, 668). Additionally, straightening one's hair is not synonymous with racial shame or "acting white." Jones and Shorter-Gooden argued that "Not every woman who decides to straighten her hair or change the color of her eyes by wearing contacts believes that beauty is synonymous with whiteness. Trying on a new look, even one often associated with Europeans, does not automatically imply self-hatred. It is possible to dye your brown tresses platinum and still love your Blackness" (2003, 178). While blond straightened hair and colored contacts are still controversial and seen as assimilationist to many in the African American community, hair-straightening also may be an expression of creativity or for employment reasons. As Wallace noted, "White features were often a more reliable ticket into this society than professional status or higher education. Interestingly enough, this was more true for women than it was for men" (1979, 158). In addition to straightened hairstyles, other hairstyles that African American women use in order to define their own beauty include afros, braids, dreadlocks, and knots. All of the aforementioned hairstyles carry with it signs of beauty, boldness, rebellion, self-confidence, spiritual consciousness (Jones and Shorter-Gooden 2003, 187) and whether intended to or not, a challenge to white beauty standards.

African American and Latina women have adopted many strategies when confronting white standards of beauty from society in general, as well as from African American and Latino men in their communities: "Latino and African American men seem more often than white men to link long hair with attractiveness for women of all ages" (Weitz 2001, 672). The three most common standards of white beauty in the United States that women are subject to include: (1) women's hair should be long, curly or wavy—not kinky—and preferably blond; (2) women's hair should look hairstyled—this requires money and time; and (3) women's hair should look feminine and different from men's hair (Weitz 2001, 672). Due to the fact that beauty is subject to the social conditions of racism, sexism, and classism, few women are able to attain such nebulous standards. Through the development of strategies, African American women demonstrate Disch's claim that "Expectations for what constitutes femininity and masculinity are frequently affected by race, class, culture, and other factors. The freedom to be the kind of woman or man a person might like to be is greatly curtailed by sexism, poverty, racism, homophobia, and other cultural constraints and expectations" (1997, 20).

White Beauty

Saltzberg and Chrisler noted that "beauty cannot be quantified or objectively measured; it is the result of the judgements of others" (1997, 135). However, it is fair to say that in the United States, and in many countries that are influenced by the United States (largely through mediated forms), the current standard of beauty is a white, young, slim, tall, and upper class woman, and some take extraordinary measures in order to meet such standards.

> Constituting itself as the site of absolute presence, whiteness functions as an epistemological and ontological anchorage. As such, whiteness assumes the authority to marginalize other identities, discourses, perspectives, and voices.

By constituting itself as center, non-white voices are Othered, marginalized and rendered voiceless. Whiteness creates a binary relationship of self-Other, subject-object, dominator-dominated, center-margin, universal-particular. (Yancy 2000, 157)

Adherence to white beauty standards also can be traced throughout the centuries and since many of these beauty standards largely, but not exclusively, affected white women, the standards mentioned below can be juxtaposed against African American beauty standards. As Saltzberg and Chrisler illustrated, sixteenth-century European women "bound themselves into corsets of whalebone and hardened canvas. A piece of metal or wood ran down the front to flatten the breasts and abdomen. This made it impossible for women to bend at the waist and difficult to breathe" (1997, 136). In the seventeenth century, the waist was still cinched, but fashions were designed to enhance the breasts. "Ample breasts, hips, and buttocks became the beauty ideal, perhaps paralleling a generally warmer attitude toward family life" (136). In the eighteenth century, corsets were still worn; however, the introduction of large crinolines exaggerated the smallness of the waist and made movement difficult (The Victorian Era, n.d., n.p.). In the nineteenth century, wearing corsets and, paradoxically, dieting to gain weight, became popular in Europe and North America. Physicians and clergy spoke against the use of corsets because the tight lacing often led to "pulmonary disease, internal organ damage, fainting (also known as "the vapors"), and miscarriages" (Saltzberg and Chrisler 1997, 136).

In the twentieth century and twenty-first century, beauty trends continue to fluctuate. For example, in the 1920s slender legs, hips, and small breasts were popular. "Women removed the stuffing from their bodices and bound their breasts to appear young and boyish" (Saltzberg and Chrisler 1997, 136). In the 1940s and 1950s, the hourglass shape (e.g., Marilyn Monroe) was popular. In the 1960s, a youthful, thin body and long, straight hair were popular. In the 1970s, a thin, tanned physique and the "sensuous look was 'in'" (137). In the 1980s, the mesomorph body type was preferred (thin, but muscular and toned body) with large breasts. In the 1990s, two dichotomous beauty images prevailed: (1) the heroine-chic, gaunt, waiflike body with some breasts and (2) the very thin body with large breasts. "Small breasts [were] a disease that required surgical intervention" (137). In the beginning of the twenty-first century, youthful, slim body types with large breasts are still preferred.

There are several things learned from this brief history of body image. First, women were subjected to hegemonically defined standards of beauty. Second, history, and our knowledge of history and women, in general, privileges and largely traces Euro American body-image issues. Third, women currently continue to be held to hegemonically defined standards of beauty.

For example, modern beauty standards encompass tattoos, piercing (belly button, chin, ear, eyebrow, labia, nipples, nose, tongue), high-heeled shoes, tight jeans, curlers, perms, straighteners, diet aids, liposuction, plastic surgery, botox injections, skin lightening, and gastric bypass. All of the above are costly, but the physical costs of altering the body to attain hegemonic standards of beauty can range from breast cancer ["silicon leaks in some implants have resulted in breast cancer" (Saltzberg and Chrisler 1997, 137)], to anorexia, bulimia, and emotional stress.

Finally, it is clear from these beauty standards that not all types of whiteness are valued. Many Euro American women cannot measure up to the white normative standard of beauty promoted—beautiful, blondhaired, slim, tall, virginal, and upperclass. Because of this exclusionary standard of beauty, not all Euro American women emulate the stereotypical white woman; only a few women are privileged to be in this "beautiful" club. Those Euro American women who deviate from this standard of whiteness are displaced like ethnic minority women for their departure from "pure" white womanhood. In order to challenge the homogenized standards of beauty, standpoint theory and Afrocentric theory are appropriate theoretical frameworks to use.

STANDPOINT THEORY AND AFROCENTRIC THEORY

Standpoint Theory

In general, standpoint theory advocates the inclusion of all people and perspectives rather than reifying the status quo or inverting the current hegemonic order. Further, it focuses on how the circumstances and culture of one's life influence her or his perspective, values, beliefs. "Standpoint theory focuses on how gender, race, class and other social categories influence the circumstances of people's lives, especially the social positions they have and the kinds of experiences fostered within those social positions" (Wood 1994, 51). According to Allen, Orbe, and Olivas feminist standpoint theory "seeks to expose both acts of oppression and acts of resistance by asking disenfranchised persons to describe and discuss their experiences with hope that their knowledge will reveal otherwise unexposed aspects of the social order" (1999, 409). Standpoint theory can create cleavages in and assist in subverting the status quo because "To establish a woman's and ethnic minority woman's standpoint is to prepare to challenge hegemony" (Patton 2004, 198). To attempt to validate the self by resisting the oppositional binary system of either/or and embrace both/and (a dialectical perspective) is transformative and moves toward engaging in dialogue.

Standpoint theory coupled with Afrocentric theory is an extremely power-ful critical tool in which to examine body image, hair, and race. Afrocentric theory is another way to redefine and confront the marginalization and racist beauty standards felt by all women. Asante's Afrocentric theory has allowed for a centering of Africans and the African diaspora in research and practice. This move is important since African experiences in communication have often been analyzed through a European framework (Asante 1998). As Clif-ford illustrated, the black diaspora seems to be "complexly related to Africa and the Americas, to shared histories of enslavement, racist subordination, cultural survival, hybridization, resistance, and political rebellion" (1997, 252). Therefore, diaspora represents transnationality, political struggles, lo-cal community, and historical displacement (252). The aforementioned strug-gles contribute to the fluidity and fixity of diaspora and the diasporic con-sciousness, which ultimately impacts one's social and cultural inclusion or dislocation. Afrocentric theory "rejects the notions and practices of hege-monic or alleged universal tendencies and practices of a given paradigm" (Berkie 1994, 136–37). Additionally, Afrocentric theory seeks to develop agency through collective consciousness (Asante 1998). As Berkie stated, "Afrocentricity is an intellectual pursuit that endorses humanistic mission. This mission is pursued by first affirming our own humanity. It is pursued by defining and naming phenomena that emanate from our own experience. . . . It is about exercising one's agency. It is a theory that seeks to empower, free the mind, and ring the bell of harmony" (148).

Therefore, Afrocentricity is not to be placed above other perspectives but equally beside other cultural theories and historical contexts. Afrocentric theory challenges hegemony by moving the Euro standard from a hierarchi-cal norm to a horizontal equalizer. Afrocentricity also allows for a performa-tive nature of beauty. With its focus on humanity, the diversity one can find through Afrocentric theory is transformative. Afrocentric theory is important because it "embraces an alternative set of realities, experiences, and iden-tities" (Delgado 1998, 423). One need not necessarily be African or African American to embrace Afrocentricity and conduct Afrocentric research (Asante 1991). A woman cannot only exercise agency with her beauty choices, but Afrocentricity creates a performative space of creativity and acceptance that has room for all types of beauty because it is no longer in the context of a Euro-supremacist framework. There is not an adherence to any beauty standard but a celebration of the self. This celebration of self is challenged through Eurocentric beauty standards of body image, hair, and race.

BODY IMAGE AND RACE

"It rained and thundered just beautiful. I got soaked, but I love to walk and play in the rain, except my hair doesn't. I wish it would be alright for us Negro[e]s to wear our hair natural. I think it looks good but it's not [ac]cepted by society. Any way I got soaked anyway, hair & all and mommy nearly had a white child (Valerie Turner [Valerie Jean], June 12,1968, age fourteen)."
—Valerie Turner, "Part Two: Searching for Self" (1994, 77)

As the American standard of beauty continues to be stringent and marginalizing, "many women develop distorted body images and become frustrated with not being able to obtain the 'ideal figure'" (Molloy 1998, 1). Unlike Euro American women who are plagued by waif-like images they cannot attain, African American women are relatively positive about their body image. However, this is due to the fact that African American women tend to have different stereotypes to demythologize. A 1998 20/20 television broadcast questioned the different ways in which African American and Euro American women see themselves. The 20/20 broadcast found that Euro American women, as compared to African American women, tend to be more prone to anorexia and bulimia due to the mediated body images that tell women what they need to look like. Euro American women see their body image and beauty reified and accepted by mainstream society, as opposed to African American women whose body image has traditionally been defiled. Despite reification of Euro American images, a variety of reasons have been given concerning why Euro American women tend to be more prone to anorexia and bulimia, and why African American women deal with anorexia and bulimia to a lesser degree.

According to Molloy, there are four reasons. First, African American women "believe that African-American males prefer larger women, they have less need to lose weight, and therefore, feel more attractive." Whereas Euro American women "believe that white men prefer ultra-thin women" (1998, 2). Second, African American women are more likely to describe themselves using androgynous traits, whereas Euro American women use feminine traits. "Masculine and androgynous individuals exhibit higher levels of self-esteem, have more positive body image, and are more satisfied with their sexuality than those who are feminine or undifferentiated" (2). Third, ethnic identification may play a role. "To the extent that [African American women] interact mostly with other African-Americans, they may be 'protected' from white norms regarding body styles" (2). Fourth, socioeconomic class may impact body image. According to Allan, Mayo, and Michael (1993) as cited in Molloy, "lower socioeconomic African-American women were heavier and perceived heavier body styles as more attractive than did higher socioeconomic black women and white women of all socioeconomic groups" (1998, 2). Additionally, African American women who tended to be heavier were slower to identify themselves as overweight as compared to Euro American women, and tended not to "denigrate their weight as much as those who tend to interact with women who are thinner" (Molloy 1998, 3).

Finally, according to the study shown on the 20/20 broadcast, only 10 percent of Euro American women were happy with their bodies due to the pressure Euro American women feel about their bodies and beauty expectations. Conversely, 70 percent of African American women were happy with their bodies (1998). However, while research has shown that African American women tend to have a more positive attitude about their body image than white women, as Lester and Petrie noted, "the idea that all African American women are protected fails to take into account the reality of within group individual differences and the complexities associated with developing a self-image within an oppressive and racist society" (1998, 315). African American women, like all women, are constantly exposed to Eurocentric messages and images that question beauty standards outside the dominant realm. Some African American celebrities such as Halle Berry, Star Jones, and Oprah Winfrey have struggled with beauty image issues.

In addition, many African American women (younger and older generation), including those who grow up in predominantly Euro American areas, state that they are beginning to feel pressure to conform to the white standard of beauty. For example, while research about women of color and anorexia and bulimia is an under-researched area, Crago, Shisslak, and Estes found that eating disorders were more frequent among Hispanic and Native American females and less frequent among black and Asian American women (1996). However, they also found that risk factors associated with eating disorders were more common among ethnic minority women who were younger, heavier, better educated, and more identified with Euro American middle-class values.

In a 1999 University of Alabama survey of 3,700 black and white women and men, researchers found that "Black women were more invested in their physical appearance than White women and that Black and White women had similar levels of dissatisfaction with body and weight size ... heavy Black women were more satisfied with their weight than heavy White women" (Jones and Shorter-Gooden 2003, 180–81). However, this research does not belie the fact that black women, like their white counterparts, experience dissatisfaction with their body and feel pressure to conform to normative beauty standards. Sometimes this conformity can take dangerous and drastic measures in the form of anorexia and bulimia. For example, 7 million women have been diagnosed with eating disorders (National Association of Anorexia Nervosa and Associated Disorders n.d.). The cost of treating anorexia nervosa and/or bulimia often includes medical monitoring, treatment, and therapy often over a two-year period or longer. Treatment is expensive: $30,000 or more a month for outpatient treatment; $100,000 or more for inpatient treatment (n.d.). An eating disorder is something that women, regardless of race or ethnicity, as well as men, may face; the disease does not discriminate.

These hegemonically defined Euro American beauty standards are not only dangerous, they are "created and maintained by society's elite. Racism, class prejudice, and rejection of the disabled are clearly reflected in current American beauty standards" (Saltzberg and Chrisler 1997, 140). For example, the high cost of various beauty regimens such as cosmetics, tanning salons, perms, hair straighteners, gyms, diets, nice clothes, and plastic surgery eludes, excludes, and marginalizes poor women who cannot afford the high cost of fulfilling hegemonically defined beauty standards. Butler argued that gender is performative and is "produced as a ritualized repetition of convention" (1995, 31); beauty and hair are also performative. Haircare and styling become a performance in adherence to beauty standards. In listing the multiple ways in which women come to perform beauty, hairstyling for African American women not only becomes a performance or ritual in hegemonically defined beauty, but also hair is performed as a way for the marginalized to attempt to become centered in a world of beauty that tends not to value African American forms of beauty. African American beauty is the antithesis of white beauty, "white" hair, and "white" norms.

According to Wood, "appearance still counts. Women are still judged by their looks. They must be pretty, slim, and well-dressed to be desirable" (1994, 83). Lorde found that "institutionalized rejection of difference is an absolute necessity in a profit economy which needs outsiders as surplus people" (1997, 177). This quote aptly supports the ideology of racism and sexism; an ideology of gender relations that states one type of gender is superior to another, one type of woman superior to another, and one type of beauty is superior to another. As Wilson and Russell indicated, "if the two groups of women were better informed of each other's beauty issues, they would realize that their seemingly contradictory attitudes about tan skin were actually driven by the same underlying concern: improved social status" (1996, 75). Women who "fit" the social construction of the stereotypical woman may have a better chance of getting [the] jobs as opposed to those who do not fit the standardized model of beauty. "Those who were judged to be attractive were also more likely to be rated intelligent, kind, happy, flexible, interesting, confident, sexy, assertive, strong, outgoing, friendly, poised, modest, candid, and successful than those judged unattractive" (Saltzberg and Chrisler 1997,141). An ideology of race and gender relations that states that one racial group is superior to another is embedded in cultural symbols that support, justify, and maintain the current hegemonic order—a hegemonic order that supports race inequalities among women. Saltzberg and Chrisler summing up a study by Faludi (1991) noted that, "American women have the most negative body image of any culture studied by the Kinsey Institute" (1997, 138). Further, "Asian American and African American women have sought facial surgery in order to come closer to achieving the Euro-American beauty ideal" (Faludi 1991 in Saltzberg and Chrisler 1997, 140). As a result of "falling victim" to Euro American standards of beauty, hog lard (used during slavery), hot combs, curling irons, and formulas and solutions such as Madame C. J. Walker's hair softener were invented to help straighten curly hair. Assimilation into American society by changing hair is a very effective campaign. According to a 1997 American Health and Beauty Aids Institute (AHBAI) survey, "African Americans spend $225 million annually on hair weaving services and products" (Byrd and Tharps 2001, 177). In fact, although African Americans comprise about 12 to 13 percent of the U.S. population, "Black women spent three times as much as White women on their hair care" (Wilson and Russell 1996, 92). During the teen years the focus on assimilation to beauty standards, regardless of race, is prevalent.

As girls grow and mature and become women, one of the only items over which they have control is their hair. Perhaps the focus on beauty is to appear attractive to the opposite sex or play the role for which women are socialized—concern for beauty. Whatever the reason, "hair becomes such a major preoccupation for adolescent girls of both races that their self-esteem can actually rise and fall with every glance in the mirror" (Wilson and Russell 1996, 81). As Wilson and Russell also discovered, issues of hair can become politicized at this time: Euro American women needed constant feedback on their looks, whereas for African American teen girls, "hair decisions are subject to more critical feedback from friends, because hairstyles are laden with political overtones" (1996, 81). These political overtones can be seen when an African American woman wears a weave, or cuts her hair short, or wears a natural style, or when she dyes her hair blond which "smacks of White assimilationism to many in the Black community" (91). However, the range of beauty and hairstyles embraced by African American women can have an effect on employment opportunities.

Failure to work toward the Euro American beauty ideal can result in such consequences as the loss of a job. For example, some African American women have lost their jobs due to their hairstyle preference, which was deemed "too ethnic." The 1981 case of Rogers v. American Airlines, "upheld the right of employers to prohibit the wearing of braided hairstyles in the workplace" (Caldwell 2000, 276). In 1987, the Hyatt Regency, outside of Washington, D.C., using the 1981 precedent, forced Cheryl Tatum to resign after she came to work wearing cornrows and refused to have them taken out. She was told that she was in violation of the company policy (Caldwell 2000). According to Tatum, the Hyatt manager (a woman) stated, "I can't understand why you would want to wear your hair like that anyway. What would our guests think if we allowed you to all wear your hair like that?"

(Caldwell 2000, 284). In 1988, Pamela Mitchell was asked to leave her job at the Marriott Hotel in Washington, D.C., for refusing to remove her braids. Another case in 1988 concerned Renee Randall who was fired from her job with Morrison's Cafeteria because her multi-colored ponytail was "too extreme" (Wilson and Russell 1996, 88). In 2001, New York Federal Express and UPS offices were both facing religious discrimination lawsuits for firing employees with dreadlocks, which are a requirement of the Rastafarian religion (France 2001). Similar lawsuits pending around the country include claims against "police departments and prison authorities, schools and retailers, alleging that rules against knotted locks unfairly single out Rastafarians in particular and African Americans in general" (France 2001, n.p.). What these firings and ultimately lawsuits show is a lack of understanding by non-African Americans regarding hairstyle diversity and an enforcement of white standards of beauty. Subsequently, after the lawsuits many corporate grooming policies were changed to include braids and cornrows as an "acceptable hairstyle." Federal Express employees who seek a waiver against company appearance standards may "tuck their locks under uniform hats" (France 2001, n.p.). Despite this acceptance, "psychotherapists have noted increased reports from their black women clients of guilt, shame, anger, and resentment about skin color, hair texture, facial features, and body size and shape" (Saltzberg and Chrisler 1997, 140).

The fact remains that outside the African American community there is little appreciation and positive reification for African American beauty. This lack of appreciation can have a devastating effect on self-esteem. According to West, "this demythologizing of black sexuality [beauty] is crucial for black America because much of black self-hatred and self-contempt has to do with the refusal of many black Americans to love their own black bodies—especially their black noses, hips, lips, and hair" (1994, 122). However, physical and facial features equated with African Americans produce their own beautiful counter-narrative. For example fuller lips, tan skin, body curves, and curly hair are fashionable. Women who do not naturally have these beauty attributes pay to have what African Americans tend to have naturally by visiting their dermatologist, tanning salons, buying padded undergarments, or going to their hairstylist. In addition, the popularity of models such as Sudanese-born Alex Wek provides a visual and popular counter-narrative to white physical and facial beauty features. Unfortunately, the difficulty is finding this counter-narrative in the same abundance in which we find white beauty standards.

MEDIA STEREOTYPES: BODY IMAGE, HAIR, AND RACE

Historically, the relationship between African American women and their hair goes back to the days of slavery and is connected with the notion of the color caste system: the belief that the lighter one's skin color, the better one is and that straighter hair is better than kinky hair. This thinking creates a hierarchy of skin color and beauty that was promoted and supported by slave masters and slavery. The woman with the wavy hair was considered more attractive and had "good" hair, as opposed to the woman with the kinky hair who had "bad" hair. The notions of "good" hair and "bad" hair come from the social construction of beauty standards. According to Wallace, "the black community had for quite some time been plagued by color discrimination. The upper echelons of black society in particular tended to rate beauty and merit on the basis of the lightness of the skin and the straightness of the hair and features" (1979, 158). These notions are still maintained in some portions of the African American community and in the media.

In the media, many of the African American women who are glorified for their beauty tend to be lighter-skinned women who have long, wavy hair. However, this reification of the beauty standard does not come solely from the African American community but also from the Euro American community, which promotes the acceptable standard of beauty. All one has to do is pick up a hairstyle magazine for African American women and see that many of the models have very light skin (some models could be mistaken for Euro Americans), some have blue or green eyes, and most of them have long, straight or wavy hair. A few notable exceptions include Tyra Banks, Naomi Campbell, Tomiko, and Alex Wek. Despite these exceptions, it is important to note that while these models may have their own definition of beauty, the media may promote or single out a more Eurocentric-looking model because Euro American standards of beauty are paramount and mediated standards of beauty promote adherence to whiteness.

The performance of beauty comes to us through a variety of mediated images that we are bombarded with daily. These messages of beauty largely encompass ways in which women can make themselves look better, skin products that can tone, redefine, and take away age. Subsequently we learn that beauty is one of the defining characteristics of a woman. For example, among the numerous beauty products advertised on television are hair products. Most often the hair commercials show Euro American women tossing their bouncy, shiny, long, straight hair. Even humorist Erma Bombeck observed that,

> after watching supermodels Cindy Crawford and Christie Brinkley push what
> appear to be pounds of hair off their face over and over again there would be
> no time to do anything else. These people can't carry a package, eat hot dogs,

wave, or shake hands. Every second of their lives is consumed with raking their fingers through their hair and getting their sight back. (Wilson and Russell 1996, 82)

This image, while directed toward Euro American women, impacts African American women, because it is often not our image that becomes the vision and standard of beauty. We are socially constructed through language and mediated images to believe that what makes a woman beautiful is not her intelligence or her inner beauty but her outer beauty.

HISTORICAL RESISTANCE: BODY IMAGE, HAIR, AND RACE

As James Baldwin said, "The power to define the other seals one's definition of oneself" (n.d., n.p.). Whether intended or not, hair makes a political statement. To counter hegemonic Eurocentric standards of beauty black women in the past and present continue to create resistant strategies as their beauty was not and is not predominantly represented. The resistant strategy used by Africans and African Americans was in the counter-hegemonic creation of unique hairstyles that showcased both black beauty and creativity, whether it was through the use of curls, dreadlocks, plaits, scarves, waves, weaves, wigs, and ornamentation in the hair. Popular resistant strategies were most visibly seen during the Black Power movement that simultaneously promoted the "Black is Beautiful" campaign.

For example, as bell hooks indicated, the Black Power movement of the 1960s challenged white supremacy in many areas, and one area briefly challenged was hair. What this social movement did with slogans such as "Black is Beautiful" was work to "intervene in and alter those racist stereotypes that had always insisted black was ugly, monstrous, undesirable" (1995, 120). The Black Power movement raised and challenged the ingrained stereotypes of beauty that were and are perpetuated by Euro Americans. The movement also examined the psychological impact such beauty standards had on African American girls and women. First, the Black Power movement "sought to value and embrace the different complexions of blackness" (hooks 1995, 121). This meant that African Americans would examine the racist notions behind the divisive color caste system.

Second, the Black Power movement agenda allowed for an examination of children who suffered discrimination and who were "psychologically wounded in families and/or public school systems because they were not the right color" (122). This allowed for an examination of the effects of the color caste upon children. Third, African American women stopped straightening their hair. This means that there was a decade of acceptance for "natural" hairstyles. Fourth, many people who had stood passively by observing the mistreatment blacks received on the basis of skin color, "felt for the first time that it was politically appropriate to intervene" (122). Finally, in addressing issues of skin color and hair, African Americans could "militantly confront and change the devastating psychological consequences of internalized racism" (122). Hair, therefore, became one of the tools or mechanisms that African Americans could utilize in order to confront the damaging Eurocentric standards of beauty that African Americans were unable to attain. For a brief moment, African Americans were able to create and reify their own standards of beauty.

However, the progressive changes made during the Black Power movement eroded as assimilation became more dominant in the late 1970s and throughout the 1980s. As African Americans were told that the key to American success was through assimilation of hairstyle and dress, many African American women began to press or chemically straighten their hair again and "follow the latest fashions in Vogue and Mademoiselle, to rouge her cheeks furiously, and to speak, not infrequently, of what a disappointment the black man has been" (Wallace 1979, 172). Many women found that it was easier to don wigs, weaves, or undergo expensive chemical processes in order to replicate mainstream hairstyles rather than wear their hair in an afro, braids, or dreadlocks which may convey a political statement or socioeconomic status. According to hooks, "once again the fate of black folks rested with white power. If a black person wanted a job and found it easier to get it if he or she did not wear a natural hairstyle, etc. this was perceived by many to be a legitimate reason to change" (1995, 122).

Consequently, white standards of beauty became the norm and became further reified by both African Americans and Euro Americans in their communities and through mediated images. Assimilation, in essence, made African Americans more socially mobile. This assimilation also "meant that many black folks were rejecting the ethnic communalism that had been a crucial survival strategy when racial apartheid was the norm and were embracing liberal individualism. . . . Consequently, black folks could now feel that the way they wore their hair was not political but simply a matter of choice" (hooks 1995, 123). Not everyone saw African American hairstyles as a "freedom of choice." This can be seen from the Euro American reaction to braids and cornrows at work. In addition, the color caste system was back in place. This system pitted light-skinned African American women against dark-skinned African American women. African American men once again returned to valuing highly desirable white or lighter-skinned women who had long hair, as opposed to lighter-skinned or darker-skinned African American women who may have chosen to wear shorter or natural hairstyles. The return to the overt and internalized system of assimilation to the Euro

American standard of beauty not only created rifts between African American women but also pitted African American and other women against one another.

In the 1990s through the present, African Americans have begun to use a resistive strategy of acceptance. In this counter-hegemonic turn, beauty differences within the black community are considered good, because one is being creative in their own individual beauty standard, rather than looking for outside acceptance. According to Susan Taylor (20/20 1998), editorial director of Essence magazine, African American women, have not traditionally seen themselves represented positively in any mediated form, so African American women create their own standard of beauty. Because of this counter-hegemonic creation, there is a wider range of beauty norms among African American women and more acceptance of different body types and weights. Some of the African American women interviewed for the 20/20 segment said that they do not concern themselves with weight, but rather they look at the whole package: hair, disposition, dress, style, and the way a person carries herself (1998). With this counter-hegemonic strategy in place, this approach begs the questions: who determines difference? and who determines which differences matter? These questions are best answered using standpoint theory and Afrocentric theory because they allow for a cultural critique of hegemony and beauty.

BLACK BEAUTY LIBERATION: CHALLENGING HEGEMONICALLY DEFINED BEAUTY NORMS

Signified meanings over time by people, groups, and politics become fixed to a group and can impact identity. Rather than being fluid, identities become trapped in the marginalizing rhetoric that initially erected the boundary. Boundaries not only define the borders of nations, territories, communities, and imaginations of the mind, but also they define the limits of space, place, and territory (Cottle 2000). One marginalized demarcation point is understanding and appreciation of difference—appreciation of African American beauty. The boundaries of beauty become deeply entrenched and thus are accepted as "common sense." The fictions and narratives about African American women exist, but without thoughtful understanding and knowledge, the dialectical tension between body image, hair, and race will continue to exist and contribute to oppression and marginalization. In order for bridges of understanding to be built, the boundaries of beauty need to be redefined and the borderland of marginalized beauty needs to be centered.

How do we transcend the interlocking system of domination that reifies the hegemonic order to the detriment of all women? Marable found that "the challenge begins by constructing new cultural and political identities, based on the realities of America's changing multicultural, democratic milieu" (2000, 448). According to Moon, "it might be more useful to think of identity as a habit rather than an essence. Identity-as-habit is an idea that allows both for the ingrainedness of habits (as anyone who has attempted to break a long-term habit can attest) and for the possibility of movement away from such habits" (1998, 324). One way to enact "identity as habit" is to think of African American women and the intersections between beauty, body image, and hair through the lens of womanism and black beauty liberation.

Standpoint theory and Afrocentric theory support a womanist critique of beauty, body image, and hair. Both theoretical perspectives are important in allowing for a critique of marginalizing Eurocentric beauty standards. First, standpoint theory allows for a centering of individual experience and allows for a space for that story to be told. This space for alternative narratives and experiences allows room for acts of oppression and resistance to be exposed. Standpoint theory also considers how social categories, like gender, race, sexuality, and socioeconomic class influence our lives. Finally, standpoint theory allows one the ability to validate the self by resisting participation in the continuance of the hegemonic order.

Second, Afrocentric theory is complementary to standpoint theory because it allows for a centering of black people and black experiences. Just like in standpoint theory, Afrocentric theory allows room for acts of oppression and resistance to be exposed. In this case, it allows the centering of black beauty and counter-hegemonic experiences to be exposed. Afrocentric theory also allows room for the possibility of diversity in beauty and diversity in beauty standards among this group. Rather than this theory being rigid, Afrocentric theory is used in a dynamic way that allows one to be able to look at the beauty diversity within black women, instead of treating all black women as a monolithic group. Just like in standpoint theory, Afrocentric theory allows one the ability to validate the self by resisting the continuance of hegemony. Finally, Afrocentric theory allows one to see the diversity among black women in terms of body image, body size, hair, and skin color because of the focus on valuing the personal experience, allowing one to name and define her own experience(s). As Delgado aptly stated, Afrocentric theory, "embraces an alternative set of realities, experiences, and identities" (1998, 423). Through embracing alternatives, Afrocentric theory shatters the myth that black women constitute a monolithic group because one is allowed to be considered intragroup diversity

In using the standpoint/Afrocentric theoretical matrix, the ideas behind Alice Walker's womanism are complementary because womanism also advocates the inclusion of the traditionally oppressed and marginalized, as well as promotes consciousness raising for both the oppressor and oppressed. Womanism recognizes that society is stratified by class, gender, ethnicity, race, and sexuality, however, the placement of race, the importance of race, and the experiences ethnic minority women have had to deal with regarding race and racism are central and key points in womanism. (Patton 2001, 242–43)[5]

It is through this framework that I offer a womanist liberatory Black Beauty Liberation campaign. Much like the "Black is Beautiful" campaigns of the 1970s, African American women need to be liberated from the confines of white-dominated standards of beauty. A womanist Black Beauty Liberation campaign would encompass a black or woman of color whose beauty issues (e.g., body image, hair, and race) are brought in from the margin to the center in an attempt to honor the beauty in her that has been reviled, rebuffed, and ignored. To be a black beauty liberationist means that you are not identified with the powers that be, but rather directly challenge the white supremacist hegemony that has kept your beauty and your body invisible, marginalized, and stereotyped.

To create a revolution of beauty it is not enough that "creative" style challenges to white beautification be accepted only by celebrities or by "radical" professors. The acceptance of these marginal groups still means that the majority of women are marginalized based on white supremacist beauty standards. In the standpoint/Afrocentric theoretical matrix, the visible invisible center is decentralized. A direct challenge to hegemonic beauty standards comes under critique as black women define their beauty standards—not the white center defining it for them.

For example, in a commodification of the Other through whites setting the beauty norms then coveting aspects of otherized beauty, while at the same time rejecting the Other, we find that many white women are incorporating black beauty standards into their regime. For example, injecting collagen into their lips to get the full effect that African American women have naturally, tanning in order to achieve the natural brown skin of African Americans, and padding the derriere in order to have a fuller backside. What these few differences show is that beauty concerns and the expectations of living up to and fulfilling the stereotypical socialized role of "woman" is something that unites women since we all have to endure the scrutiny. Without understanding and respecting beauty differences in general, women face alienating and stereotyping one another, rather than becoming a united force. As Wallace noted "white men, white women, black men, and black women are just an accumulation of waste—wasted hope and wasted cockiness, born of insecurity and anxiety, which help to keep us all in our respective places" (1979, 130). We need to understand the implications and history behind the standards of beauty. "Being a Black woman in the United States is necessarily different from being a White woman because of the different histories that lie behind each social identity or point of intersection, but alliances can be formed across these differences if both parties consent to the repression of difference involved" (Fiske 1996, 93). By resisting ascribed identities, we may begin to challenge the notion of beauty as it is currently defined because we are critically and actively challenging hegemony. Through the standpoint/ Afrocentric matrix we are able to challenge the hegemonic narratives that confine beauty into binaries of white-beautiful, black-ugly.

Such libratory stances against white supremacist beauty have taken place; however, it is now time to directly challenge the assimilated beauty standards that are continually promoted through the media. Reality TV shows like *Extreme Makeover* and *The Swan* attempt to produce the same type of woman—one who maintains hegemonic beauty standards—that no woman can naturally attain. Through an oppositional beauty gaze an appreciation of black beauty has flourished in children's books [e.g., *Happy to be Nappy* (*Jump at the Sun*), by bell hooks; *Nappy Hair* by Carolivia Herron] and in hairstyles beyond straightened styles (e.g., afros, dreadlocks, and twists are again considered stylish for black musical artists, athletes, and on college campuses). However, these venues are not enough to promote the feeling of beauty acceptance on a large scale. With liberation comes a critical transformation. "Liberation means challenging systemic assumptions, structures, rules, or roles that are flawed" (Harro 2000, 463). Through liberation and challenging the systems of domination that exist in regard to body image, hair, and race, a recentering of marginalized beauty can begin. For example, black communities have already taken smaller steps that have led to some success in redefining beauty whether through lawsuits or in their own practices. In order to be a liberated self, white hegemonic beauty needs to be challenged. Instead of succumbing to the white supremacist status quo, African American women need to continue to challenge the norm. We need to demand the same recognition of diversified black beauty. As Spellers noted, "Silencing the stories of marginalized groups aids in the creation of a dominant discourse. By studying personal stories, the tendency to naturalize one's experiences of reality as a universal experience of reality becomes minimized and we come to understand that there are different ways of knowing" (1998, 72). Through acknowledging and recognizing that other forms of beauty exist in the world beyond white supremacist definitions, we come to understand that there are different types of beauty in the world. One of the more immediate effects of beauty challenges can be seen in mediated diversity largely on "black" television shows on UPN: *Girlfriends* and *Kevin Hill* both showcase a variety of hairstyles and skin colors. And *Ally McBeal* was the first "white" show that featured an African American female main character with naturally curly, non-straightened hair.

BEAUTY IDENTITY: TO BEGIN AGAIN

Challenging and redefining the self, ingrained identities, and white hegemony is very difficult. "These stereotypes and the culture that sustains them exist to define the social position of black women as subordinate on the basis of gender to all men, regardless of color, and on the basis of race to all other women. These negative images also are indispensable to the maintenance of an interlocking system of oppression based on race and gender that operates to the detriment of all women and all blacks" (Caldwell 2000, 280). Debunking the myth of what is beauty would require Euro American women to say "the hell with what men think" and African American women would have to say "the heck with what all of White culture thinks" (Wilson and Russell 1996, 85). This is quite a difficult position for all women and even more so for African American women because African American women have to challenge an entire race of people and system of thought. As a society, we seem to forget our rhizomatic past (Gilroy 1993), a past that is impacted by the diasporic connections between people and cultures. For example, much of what once was African or African American culture is now mainstream and worldwide: pierced ears, nose, nipples, and other body parts come from the twelfth century and were introduced to Euro Americans once Africans were enslaved; music (spirituals, gospels, jazz, rock, blue grass, country, rap, and hip hop) all have origins or have been influenced by African or African American culture. "No matter what a woman does or doesn't do with her hair—dyeing or not dyeing, curling or not curling, covering with a bandana or leaving uncovered—her hair will affect how others respond to her, and her power will increase or decrease accordingly" (Weitz 2001, 683). Until we critique the message of stereotypical standardizations of beauty, African American women, and all women in general, and the disparagement of their beauty, we will never get past the wall of misunderstanding, sexism, and racism. As hooks stated, "Everyone must break through the wall of denial that would have us believe hatred of blackness emerges from troubled individual psyches and acknowledge that it is systematically taught through processes of socialization in white supremacist society" (1995, 131). We will not only continue to cause self-esteem and psychological damage to women and to African American women specifically, but we will continue to pass on our sexist and racist ways to generations of young people. We have all seen the devastation that societal standards of beauty wreak upon women: psychological damage, loss of self-esteem, anorexia, bulimia, sexism, racism, ignorance, and lack of communication. The language, verbal and nonverbal, as well as the reification of white standards of beauty needs to be challenged and will continue to be challenged as women create their own standards of beauty.

NOTES

1. For a thorough analysis of stereotypes, see Donald Bogle's (2001) seminal book, *Toms, Coons, Mulattoes, Mammies, and Bucks: An Interpretative History of Blacks in American Films*.

2. Charlotte Forten of Philadelphia was "one of the tiny minority of free, educated black women of the nineteenth century." She came from a middle-class abolitionist family "who did not differ appreciably from their well-off white neighbors in demeanor and values." She was a teacher at an integrated grammar school in Salem "charged with teaching the Negroes all the necessary rudiments of civilization . . . until they be [sic] sufficiently enlightened to think and provide for themselves." Despite her status, she suffered racist incidents from whites and berates herself for not being worthy enough or intelligent enough. Although her "contemporaries described her as a handsome girl, delicate, slender, attractive, whereas she saw herself as hopelessly ugly" (Wallace 145, 147–49).

3. Yep defines assimilation as a "view [that] directs the marginalized person to try harder and harder to adhere, obey, and follow the rules of the dominant group—rules that he or she can never fully and completely participate in creating" (80). Martin and Nakayama (2000) state that "In an assimilation mode, the individual does not want to maintain an isolated cultural identity but wants to maintain relationships with other groups in the new culture. And the migrant is more or less welcomed by the new cultural hosts. . . . When the dominant group forces assimilation, especially on immigrants [or U.S. ethnic minority groups] whose customs are different from the predominant customs of the host society, it creates a 'pressure cooker'" (1998, 207).

4. Madame C. J. Walker did not invent the hot comb. Marcel Grateau, a Parisian, used "heated metal hair care implements as early as 1872, and hot combs were available in sears and Bloomingdale's catalogues in the 1890s, presumably designed for white women" (Princeton n.d.).

5. Alice Walker created the term "womanism." Walker's definition of womanism found in Smith, states that "womanist comes from the word 'womanish': Opposite of 'girlish,' i.e., frivolous, irresponsible, not serious. A black feminist or feminist of color. From the colloquial expression of mothers to daughters. 'You're acting womanish,' i.e. like a woman. Usually referring to outrageous, audacious, courageous, or willful behavior. Wanting to know more and in greater depth than is considered 'good' for one. Interested in grown-up doings. Acting grown-up, being grown-up. Interchangeable with other colloquial expression: 'You're trying to be grown.' Responsible. In charge. Serious" (1983, xxii). A womanist or black feminist critique makes one aware of the exclusive nature of feminism as it has been popularly articulated by white, educated, middle-class women (Wood 1994). Womanists believe that challenging patriarchal oppression and sexism is equally important with fighting against racism. Therefore, articulating a type of feminism that shows how the twin oppressions of racism and sexism are interrelated is paramount, as both are necessary in fighting against a system built on oppression.

REFERENCES

20/20. 1998. "Black Women, White Women and Weight." Television Broadcast, May. New York: American Broadcast Corporation.

Allan, Janet D, Kelly Mayo, and Yvonne Michael. 1993. "Body Size Values of White and Black Women." *Research in Nursing & Health* 16: 323–33.

Allen, Brenda J., Mark P. Orbe, and Margarita Refugia Olivas. 1999. "The Complexity of Our Tears: Dis/enchantment and (In)Difference in the Academy." *Communication Theory* 9(4): 402–29.

Asante, Molefi K. 1998. *Afrocentricity.* Trenton, NJ: Africa World Press.

Asante, Molefi K. 1991. "The Afrocentric Idea in Education." *Journal of Negro Education* 60(2): 170–80.

Baldwin, James. n.d. Just Above My Head, quoted in Tijuana Murray, "Differences and Blurred Vision." In *Life Notes: Personal Writings by Contemporary Black Women*, ed. P. Bell-Scott 1994, 396. New York: W. W. Norton & Company.

Berkie, Ayele. 1994. "The Four Corners of a Circle: Afrocentricity as a Model of Synthesis." *Journal of Black Studies* 25: 131–49.

Bogle, Donald. 2001. *Toms, Coons, Mulattoes, Mammies, and Bucks: An Interpretative History of Blacks in American Films*. New York: Continuum International Publishing Group.

Butler, Judith. 1995. "Melancholy Gender/Refused Identification." In *Constructing Masculinity*, eds. Maurice Berger, Brain Wallis, and Simon Watson, 21–36. New York: Routledge.

Byrd, Ayana D., and Lori L. Tharps. 2001. *Hair Story: Untangling the Roots of Black Hair in America*. New York: St. Martin's Griffin.

Caldwell, Paulette M. 2000. "A Hair Piece: Perspectives on the Intersection of Race and Gender." In *Critical Race Theory: The Cutting Edge*, eds. Richard Delgado and Jean Stefancic, 275–85. Philadelphia: Temple University Press.

Clifford, James. 1997. *Routes: Travel and Translation in the Late Twentieth Century*. Cambridge: Harvard University Press.

Cottle, Simon. 2000. "Introduction Media Research and Ethnic Minorities: Mapping the Field." In *Ethnic Minorities and the Media: Changing Cultural Boundaries*, ed. Simon Cottle, 2–30. Philadelphia: Open University Press.

Crago, Marjorie, Catherine M. Shisslak, and Linda S. Estes. 1996. "Eating Disturbances Among American Minority Groups: A Review." [Electronic version] *International Journal for Eating Disorders* 19(3): 239–48.

Delgado, Fernando P. 1998. "When the Silenced Speak: The Textualization and Complications of Latino/a Identity." *Western Journal of Communication* 62(4): 420–38.

Disch, Estelle. 1997. "Social Contexts of Gender." In *Reconstructing Gender: A Multicultural Anthology*, ed. Estelle Disch, 19–20. Mountain View, CA: Mayfield Publishing.

Faludi, Susan. 1991. *Backlash: The Undeclared War Against American Women*. New York: Crown Publishers.

Fiske, John. 1996. *Media Matters: Race and Gender in U.S. Politics*. Minneapolis: University of Minnesota Press.

France, David. 2001. "Law: The Dreadlock Deadlock." *Newsweek*. September 5. Retrieved from http://www.msnbc.com/news/622786.asp (accessed September 5, 2001; site now discontinued).

Gilroy, Paul. 1993. *The Black Atlantic: Modernity and Double Consciousness*. Cambridge: Harvard University Press.

Greene, Beverly. 1994. "African American Women." In *Women of Color: Integrating Ethnic and Gender Identities in Psychotherapy*, eds. Lillian Comas-Díaz and Beverly Greene, 10–29. New York: Guilford Press.

Harro, Bobbie. 2000. "The Cycle of Liberation." In *Readings for Diversity and Social Justice: An Anthology on Racism, Anti-Semitism, Sexism, Heterosexism, Abelism, and Classism*, eds. Maurianne Adams, Warren J. Blumenfeld, Rosie Castaneda, Heather W. Hackman, Madeline L. Peters, and Ximena Zuniga, 463–69. New York: Routledge.

hooks, bell. 1995. *Killing Rage*. New York: H. Holt & Company.

Jones, Charisse, and Kumea Shorter-Gooden. 2003. *Shifting: The Double Lives of Black Women in America*. New York: HarperCollins Publishers.

Lazarus, Margaret, and Renner Wunderlich. 2000. *Beyond Killing Us Softly: The Impact of Media Images on Women and Girls*. Motion picture. Dirs. Margaret Lazarus and Renner Wunderlich. Cambridge, MA: Cambridge Documentary Films.

Lester, Regan, and Trent A. Petrie. 1998. "Physical, Psychological, and Societal Correlates of Bulimic Symptomatology among African American College Women." *Journal of Counseling Psychology* 45(3): 315–21.

Lorde, Audrey. 1997. "Age, Race, Class, and Sex: Women Redefining Difference." In *Race, Class, and Gender: An Anthology*, eds. Margaret Andersen and Patricia Hill Collins, 177–84. Belmont, CA: Wadsworth Publishing.

Marable, Manning. 2000. "Beyond Racial Identity Politics: Towards a Liberation Theory for Multicultural Democracy." In *Critical Race Theory: The Cutting Edge*, eds. Richard Delgado and Jean Stefancic, 448–54. Philadelphia: Temple University Press.

Martin, Judith N., and Thomas K. Nakayama. 2000. *Intercultural Communication in Contexts*. Mountain View, CA: Mayfield Publishing Company.

Molloy, Beth L. 1998. "Body Image and Self-Esteem: A Comparison of African-American and Caucasian Women." *Sex Roles: A Journal of Research*, 111. Retrieved from http://www.findarticles.com/cf_0/m2294/n7-8_v38/20914081/print.jhtml.

Moon, Dreama. 1998. "Performed Identities: "Passing" as an Inter/cultural Discourse." In *Readings in Cultural Contexts*, eds. Judith N. Martin, Thomas K. Nakayama, and Lisa A. Flores, 322–30. Mountain View, CA: Mayfield Publishing.

National Association of Anorexia Nervosa and Associated Disorders (n.d.). Retrieved from http://www.anad.org/facts.htm (accessed December 5, 2003; site now discontinued).

Orbe, Mark P., and Tina M. Harris. 2001. *Interracial Communication: Theory into Practice*. Belmont, CA: Wadsworth/Thompson Learning.

Patton, Tracey O. 2001. "Ally McBeal and Her Homies: The Reification of White Stereotypes of the Other." *Journal of Black Studies* 32(2): 229–60.

Patton, Tracey O. 2004. "Reflections of a Black Woman Professor: Racism and Sexism in Academia." *Howard Journal of Communications* 15(3): 185–200.

Princeton, n.d. "Walker Display." Retrieved from http://www.princeton.edu/~mcbrown/display/walker.html (accessed February 22, 2002; site now discontinued).

Rooks, Noliwe. 1996. *Hair Raising*. New Jersey: Rutgers University Press.

Saltzberg, Elayne A., and Joan C. Chrisler. 1997. "Beauty Is the Beast: Psychological Effects of the Pursuit of the Perfect Female Body." In *Reconstructing Gender: A Multicultural Anthology*, ed. Estelle Disch, 134–45. Mountain View, CA: Mayfield Publishing.

Smith, Barbara. 1983. "Introduction." In *Home Girls: A Black Feminist Anthology*, ed. Barbara Smith, xxii. New York: Kitchen Table: Women of Color Press.

Spellers, Regina E. 1998. "Happy to Be Nappy!: Embracing an Afrocentric Aesthetic for Beauty." In *Readings in Cultural Contexts*, eds. Judith N. Martin, Thomas K. Nakayama, and Lisa A. Flores, 70–78. Mountain View, CA: Mayfield Publishing.

Taylor, Paul C. 2000. "Malcolm's Conk and Danto's Colors; or Four Logical Petitions Concerning Race, Beauty, and Aesthetics." In *African American Literary Theory: A Reader*, ed. Winston Napier, 665–71. New York: New York University Press.

Turner, Valerie. 1994. "Part Two: Searching for Self." In *Life Notes: Personal Writings by Contemporary Black Women*, ed. Patricia Bell-Scott, 77. New York: Norton.

Victorian Era, The (n.d.). "The Victorian Era," Retrieved from http://www.media-awareness.ca/eng/med/class/teamedia/body/lookll.htm (accessed 22 February 2002; site now discontinued).

Wallace, Michele. 1979. *Black Macho and the Myth of the Superwoman*. New York: Dial Press.

Weitz, Rose. 2001. "Women and Their Hair: Seeking Power through Resistance and Accommodation." *Gender & Society* 15(5): 667–86.

West, Cornel. 1994. *Race Matters*. New York: Vintage Books.

Wilson, Midge, and Kathy Russell. 1996. *Divided Sisters: Bridging the Gap between Black Women and White Women*. New York: Anchor Books.

Wood, Julia T. 1994. *Gendered Lives: Communication, Gender, and Culture*. Belmont, CA: Wadsworth Publishing.

Yancy, George. 2000. "Feminism and the Subtext of Whiteness: Black Women's Experiences as a Site of Identity Formation and Contestation of Whiteness." *Western Journal of Black Studies* 24(3): 156–66.

Yep, Gust A. 1998. "My Three Cultures: Navigating the Multicultural Identity Landscape." In *Reading in Cultural Contexts*, eds. Judith N. Martin, Thomas K. Nakayama, and Lisa A. Flores, 79–85. Mountain View, CA: Mayfield Publishing.

Chapter Seven

Barbie's Hair

Selling Out Puerto Rican Identity in the Global Market

Frances Negrón-Muntaner

A year before the life-size Puerto Rican "Ken" doll—Ricky Martin—jolted a jaded Grammy Awards audience to their feet with Latin pop,[1] Puerto Ricans from both the Island and the United States had been tearing their hair out over the impact of another "plastic" globalized commodity bearing the sign of *boricuaness*: the Puerto Rican Barbie. Mattel seemed genuinely surprised at the unforeseen entanglement. After all, the company had already manufactured dozens of dolls representing countries from the world over without any complaints, including such close cousins in the ethnic and colonial divide as Hispanic Barbie, American Indian Barbie, and Hawaiian Barbie.[2] As with many other objects of *boricua* wrath or affection, however, this Puerto Rican doll is unique if only because it comes with anticipated political baggage. No assembly required.

The notorious "PR" Barbie was introduced to eager Island consumers with some fanfare at a ceremony held in the capital city of San Juan in February 1997. The first doll, in what many saw as a biased political performance, was presented to Irma Margarita Rosselló, the wife of Pedro Rosselló, pro-statehood governor who at the time was investing considerable energy to obtain binding congressional legislation on the Island's political status.[3] The convergence of capital's ingratiating gaze at Island consumers and a congressional wink toward a process of decolonization, which some feared favored statehood as the "final solution," prompted an anxious response, particularly on the mainland: "This toy can be seen as something of a pro-statehood move, and certainly a tricky issue when it comes to the question of identity," stated Concordia University professor Víctor Rodríguez, with apparent seriousness.[4]

137

Rodríguez's take was, however, far from universal, and instead became part of one of the most furious debates on Puerto Ricans and pop culture since *West Side Story*.[5] While most U.S.-based *boricuas*—who already live in a state of the Union but still consider themselves Puerto Ricans—feared Barbie as a Trojan horse of identity destruction, Island intellectuals and consumers—who often denounce the eroding effects of Americanization on Puerto Rican culture—gleefully embraced the doll and their right to enjoy it. Evidently both communities wrapped a different narrative around the plastic and made the Barbie a desirable playmate—silent, but endowed—to engage in the increasingly high-stakes game of interests and intrigue called "Puerto Rican identity."

Barbie is one of the most globalized toys in history—"every second, somewhere in the world, two Barbies are sold"[6]—as well as the most transnational of American icons. Barbie play constitutes a privileged site to convey discontent and to negotiate conflicts in (and with) the United States, particularly around race, ethnicity, and gender. Indeed, one of the aspects that made this contest exceptional is that it took place on the pages of mainstream American and Puerto Rican newspapers, rather than in the usually more rarefied halls of academia and organizational newsletters. Furthermore, the Barbie skirmish reiterated for all to see that key sites of cultural rearticulations of Puerto Rican identification are increasingly sponsored by American-made and/or –distributed commodities—even when they feature "plastic" Puerto Ricans.

The few weeks that intellectuals debated the dangers and charms of the Puerto Rican Barbie can also be revisited as a virtual play-therapy session through which each community used Barbie to tease out its location regarding its disenfranchised colonial status, both avowed (most U.S. Puerto Ricans) and disavowed (most Islanders), on the same playing field of (national) cultures, albeit with different resources and from varying capital(s). Significantly, although both groups used the tools of globalization to tell their story, Islanders engaged in a game of make-believe—we are Barbie—as U.S. Puerto Ricans focused on the violence and pain of intercultural exchange. They positioned themselves as "masters" of another game—the political domain—and pointed out that Barbie was an inappropriate plaything for Puerto Ricans. Angelo Falcón, director of the Puerto Rican Policy Institute based in New York, defended this oppositional stance in urgent terms: "Over here, there's a real question of how we're presented because the negative stereotypes hit us hard."[7]

That one of the most public disputes between Puerto Ricans in recent years took place around a toy rather than more worldly matters stresses that "play" allowed specific subjects and groups to "model and experiment with personhood, [and] different contexts in which we may be selves" without the risk associated with binding political action.[8] This is precisely what Rosselló was after in seeking a congressionally sanctioned plebiscite to determine Puerto Rico's ultimate status. Play became politics as a way to negotiate inclusion—and exclusion—within several national imaginaries, not coincidentally through a feminized object that all aimed to control, but ultimately no one could quite pin down.

The striking divergence among pro-and anti-Barbie camps quickly became evident in the field of vision itself as highly educated and hence arguably good observers could not agree on what the doll actually looked like. Writer Aurora Levins Morales—who is of Puerto Rican and Jewish descent, was raised in Puerto Rico's countryside and New York City, and currently resides in California—claimed that the Puerto Rican Barbie was "an Anglicized image of what we're supposed to be."[9] On the other side of the Dream House, however, light-skinned, Island-based, and pro-associated republic advocate Juan Manuel García Passalacqua saw quite the opposite, a doll that resembles who "we are" as Puerto Ricans: "mulatto complexion . . . almond eyes . . . thick nose . . . plump lips . . . raven hair."[10] As in most lengthy conversations about Barbie, through which "one usually learns more about the speaker than about the doll,"[11] a distinct pattern emerged from the fray. Those who identified as Island Puerto Ricans saw the doll as a wavy-haired mulatta, while most U.S. Puerto Ricans disagreed: the doll was straight-haired and white.

The most documented exception to the U.S. trend—Puerto Ricans in Florida—poignantly establishes, however, that less than a dichotomy between Puerto Rico and the United States, at issue was the real and perceived power of different Puerto Rican communities to invent, control, and deploy their cultural specificity within hostile or relatively auspicious contexts. Puerto Ricans in Florida, who in the last decade have migrated directly from the Island and/or come from upwardly mobile backgrounds, tended to view themselves as either part of a Hispanic cultural majority in Miami or as a dominant (largely middle-class) Hispanic group in Orlando and, thus, less likely to mobilize around racial disenfranchisement. Although inter-Latino conflicts exist—particularly with the more influential Cuban Americans—Florida Ricans can live in environments where bilingualism is an appreciable commodity and can also enjoy a significant presence in politics and the media. In fact, Florida is currently the home of many prominent Puerto Ricans, including singers Ricky Martin and Chayanne; television personalities María Celeste Arrarás and Rafael José, former Miami mayor Maurice Ferré, and even astrologer Walter Mercado.

Curtly excluded from the imaginary created by the Puerto Rican Barbie, U.S. Puerto Ricans outside Florida (and to some extent Washington, D.C.) refused to play with it in the way that it was intended and proceeded to "remove the sting," to quote Walter Benjamin,[12] by validating their own brand of (neo)Puerto Rican experience, using the weapons stored up by decades of civil rights struggles in the United States. That so many men felt compelled to play with the Barbie as a way publicly to express themselves politically also recalls what José Quiroga has argued in relation to the increasing popularity of gay dolls. As for some gay men who long to caress queer plastic, for some Puerto Ricans who faced Barbie glaring from its box at Toys R' Us, "childhood is not necessarily something that is looked back on with affection, but hostility. They remind the subject of all those dolls that were never given and never received, all those prohibitions."[13] The irony of this strategy, however, is not only that they were aiming all their guns at the wrong enemy (as I will explore later), but also that the U.S.-based intelligentsia hurled at Puerto Rican Barbie the one charge that Islanders had traditionally—and painfully—thrown at them: inauthenticity. As a *Miami Herald* journalist put it, "Le imputan [a Barbie] que su 'puertorriqueñidad' no es genuina."[14] And this had hairy consequences.

RAISING HAIR! BARBIE'S LOCKS AND PUERTO RICAN–AMERICAN IDENTITY

The cultural knowledge that Barbies are "essentially" white, despite their outward appearance, constitutes the first clue to the seemingly untenable color blindness. As Erica Rand has observed, "Although some 'ethnic' dolls now get the name Barbie, a 'nonethnic' Barbie still occupies the center stage."[15] Most consumers seem to be able to accept an ethnic Barbie doll simultaneously as both culturally specific and "white" at heart, since the essential Barbie is unarguably light-skinned, blonde, and blue-eyed. The lingering impression that the Puerto Rican Barbie was essentially white and that its "mulattoness" was a cultural masquerade was reinforced by the box's ethnic "origin" story for Puerto Ricans: "My country was discovered in 1493 by Christopher Columbus who claimed it for Spain." In only mentioning that the island was discovered by Columbus, Mattel and its allies connote that all Puerto Ricans are fundamentally Europeans and banish the influence of Natives and Africans to the back of the bus. Due to the category of race's preeminence in the regulation and management of minorities, Puerto Rican struggles over representation tend to demand "realistic" depictions (epidermal and demographic) as a measure of democratic inclusion. If Puerto Ricans in the United States have traditionally visualized themselves as "of color" in the struggle for enfranchisement, the Barbie could be authentic only if it were "brown."

Remarkably, Puerto Rican Barbie's perceived skin color was not the doll's most controversial physical aspect for *boricuas* in the United States, particularly women. Although in Puerto Rico and Florida the doll's racial makeup was deemed acceptable, representative, and even beautiful, much of the U.S. discussion focused on a specific Barbie feature: its hair, or more specifically, *the texture* of the doll's hair, not color (black) or length (long). Lourdes Pérez, a Puerto Rican Chicago-based, San Juan-raised interior decorator, was horrified at what she saw: "I don't care that she's white. Puerto Ricans come in all colors. But when I saw that hair, I thought 'Dios mío' ('my God'), we just passed a terrible legacy to the next generation."[16] Despite exasperated responses from some Puerto Rico-based (white) men— "[t]his woman is saying that the prevalent lack of respect, the lawlessness, drugs, driving conditions, domestic and child abuse aren't as terrible a legacy as a straight-haired Barbie"—the charges stuck.[17] Journalist Louis Aguilar, who wrote several stories on the topic, pointed out that Lourdes' response was not isolated: "For some Puerto Rican women who have spent countless hours ironing the curl out of their hair before going to the office or school, it's Barbie's hair that makes them cringe."[18]

Playing with the doll's hair is reportedly the most popular activity that children engage in with Barbie, and the grown-up argument over the doll's locks raged on for weeks in print and on the Internet. Hair became, as anthropologist Patrick Olivelle has theorized, a "condensed symbol": "so powerful that it encapsulates all the diverse aspects of the symbolized, which under normal circumstances would require separate symbolic expressions."[19] That the dead weight of Puerto Rican identity fell on Barbie's weave should not be surprising on at least three counts. The ways hair is coiffured are universally used to signify cultural identity, social status, age, and gender. "Hair worn in a polarized manner has served to indicate the masculine and the feminine, the slave and the ruler, the young, the old, the virgin, the married, the widowed, the mourners."[20] Across many cultures and historical periods, hair is also linked to the power of women to destroy, kill, and seduce their own and others, hence its care and representation are not trivial matters. Most important in this case, the Barbie's Puerto Rican roots could only really show up in its intractable hair.

In Puerto Rico, unlike the United States, a person's race is not solely dictated by a single African ancestor. "El color y las facciones," writes the appropriately surnamed Tomás Blanco, "valen más que la sangre."[21] Whereas one drop of "black blood" makes you African American in the United States, one of "white" can have the opposite effect on the Island, where a person does not need to claim exclusively European lineage to access the benefits of whiteness. The greater value attributed to white blood in the Puerto Rican scheme allows for a larger number of mixed-race people to qualify as *blancos*, yet this does not diminish the fact that Puerto Ricans of African descent are socially encouraged to seek upward mobility by flushing out the inauspicious "black" blood in each subsequent generation, as the infamous "mejorar la raza" mantra implies. Given the possibility of *becom-*

ing white—which is denied in the United States—"racial" identification (and attribution) in Puerto Rico is partly determined by a combination of phenotypical factors, including thickness of lips, skin tone, broadness of nose, eye color, cheekbones, and—most important—hair texture, which is physically coterminous with the skin and hence often symbolizes the entire body's "race."

The lavish attention given to "black hair" in Puerto Rican racial discourse—it has considerably more (mostly demeaning) names than any other racialized corporal matter—prompted anthropologist Sidney Mintz to claim that "Puerto Rican cultural standards for racial identity appear to place the most weight on hair type, less on skin color."[22] However, it is not so much that hair is more important than color, but that once hair is called upon to stand up for (the) race, it is not necessary to also mention the skin's hue. Mulatta poet Julia de Burgos, for example, identifies hair first in defining blackness in "Ay ay ay de la grifa negra" (not the negra grifa),[23] while Francisco Arrivís's mulatta character Cambucha describes herself as "Pasúa, hocicúa y bembúa"—not dark-skinned—in his "liberal" play on racial relations, *Sirena*,[24] Consequently, Luis Palés Matos's foundational opera magna celebrating Caribbean syncretism and black (mythic) sensuality could only be aptly titled Tuntún de pasa y grifería —tuntún of kinky and mulatto hair.[25]

Despite the deceiving laxness (from a U.S. standpoint) in determining race among Puerto Ricans, the emphasis on hair remits to biologically based understandings of difference that are shared with Americans. Anthropologist Franz Boas, who once testified in a 1914 case in which a white man sued for divorce on the grounds that his wife was not really white, argues for both sides when he claims that "You can tell by a microscopic examination of a cross section of hair to what race that person belongs."[26] In fact, because it can be altered or hidden, hair is the object of much scrutiny in liminal social situations, particularly if background information is not self-evident or forthcoming. As Renzo Sereno bluntly phrased it, "la contextura del pelo—bueno o malo—puede de-cidir el matrimonio mixto."[27] Advocate Isabelo Zenón confirms the crucial role of hair when he recalls a "test" through which "whites" can detect whether someone is a "grifo" (racially mixed) or simply an "olive-skinned" white, by placing him in front of a fan to see if the hair follows the wind: "Si no se despeina, queda fuera del grupo de privilegiados."[28] Hair is, undoubtedly, the thin wavy line that separates the "authentic" whites from the deceiving upwardly mobile mulattos.

At the same time, although U.S. Puerto Ricans repudiated Barbie's straight hair, these discriminating—and discriminated—consumers were not demanding that the doll have "bad" hair, as if a Black Puerto Rican Barbie could not be representative of all Puerto Ricans. Ironically, a Black Puerto Rican Barbie, particularly one who wears contemporary clothes, could not have looked much different from Black (African American) Barbie, thus undermining the notion of essential differences between both groups, and any modest racial capital that light-skinned Puerto Ricans may wish to claim in the colonial metropolis.

Due to the many cultural convergences between Puerto Ricans and African Americans in cities such as New York, a black Puerto Rican Barbie could have ended up legitimizing poet Willie Perdomo's motto that an Afro-Puerto Rican is just a black man—or woman—with an accent.[29] As Rodríguez affirmed, "to introduce a doll . . . that looks like it has no *trace* of African ancestry, to a group of young Puerto Rican females who are at a crucial age in the formation of their identity, this becomes a very serious issue" (my emphasis).[30] What U.S. critics were after, then, was the "correct" ethnic representational formula that could prevent Puerto Ricans from being confused with *either* African Americans or Anglos. In this, they converged—perhaps inadvertently—with the Island elites, who would likely agree that it's tough to play at being *boricua* with the "wrong" kind of hair, because as Elsie Crumb McCaeb and Anne H. Stark agree, "[Y]ou don't feel good until your hair looks good."[31]

Considering that Puerto Rican ethnic identity in the United States has often been produced within racial discourses, and upward mobility in Puerto Rico implies a willed loss of racialized identity, the mainland's response to Puerto Rican Barbie's hair evokes a social distress over losing control of an important identity sign. The fears of cultural consumption and political dissolution triggered by Puerto Rico becoming the fifty-first state of the Union—and Puerto Ricans morphing into "Americans"—were hence curled around tropes of de-ethnification such as "straight hair." The organizing assumption was that the Barbie's hair could only have been straight because it had been "straightened," an act of self-hatred or conformity that would also be judged by American whites derisively. Critics focused on the wavy hair to protect the specificity of the group against changes already taking place in the United States, such as language dominance (to English), territorial residence, intermarriage, and hyphenated children. Ultimately, pulling Barbie's hair was a way to manage anxieties about the transculturation of future Puerto Rican generations, for as Walter Benjamin has written, "toys are a site of conflict, less of the child with the adult than of the adult with the child."[32]

The fears of giving up your hair (to Mattel) also recall the importance that many cultures assign to the custody of hair. In Africa, for instance, only trusted friends and relatives may touch or have access to your hair since "in the hands of the enemy, it could become an ingredient in the production of a dangerous charm or 'medicine' that would injure the owner."[33] The relationship between hair and potential harm is not confined to actual people's hair, but also to hair found in sculptures—which the Barbie arguably is. Puerto Rican popular sayings also stress the importance of keeping hair in its proper place—*cuídate los pelos*—but also of getting rid of it if you need to defend yourself: *sin pelos en la lengua.* To allow the Puerto Rican Barbie to have the wrong hair and to put it into the wrong hands can then be quite dangerous to a group: it signifies social submission, can bring about shame, and even lead to (cultural) death—the "terrible legacy" alluded to by the Chicago decorator. But as some observers noticed (though they preferred to stay at least a hair away) one community's bristly nightmare was another's synthetic fantasy.

PLAYING WITH YOUR SELF: WHY ISLANDERS LOVED BARBIE

Barbie was a reliable—if frustrating—toy used by U.S. *boricuas* to imagine Puerto Ricanness as a distinct ethnic identity, and to make demands on American public culture as a politically disenfranchised minority. The doll's wild success with Islanders—by December 31, 1997, one Carolina store alone had sold over five thousand dolls[34] —asserts, however, that for many Islanders, the Puerto Rican Barbie was the perfect doll for playing with the "self." In playing with Barbie, these consumers not only "enjoyed" themselves, but also enacted the material and symbolic conditions that make their (limited) identity play intelligible.

Significantly, although Island intellectuals and cultural institutions often make use of cultural differences as part of a struggle to expand or protect local political control within camouflaged colonial parameters, the Puerto Rican Barbie was not perceived as threatening to the main pillars of national identity as defined by the state apparatus and the elites: Spanish language (Barbie does not speak), symbols such as *el jíbaro* (which it is), and sports sovereignty (which does not apply).[35] While a rampantly "commercial" product made by an American multinational (as opposed to the "purely" folkloric art dear to the intelligentsia), the Puerto Rican Barbie is more consistent with dominant discourses of *puertorriqueñidad* on the Island than many "real" Puerto Rican-produced art forms that have undergone different degrees of commodification, such as salsa or hip hop. In this sense, the Puerto Rican Barbie is the consummate nationalist elite product bred by the contradictions of the commonwealth: a modern packaging (plastic) of a premodern essence (rural Puerto Rico), for postmodern nationalists (colonial survivors).

The emphasis on Barbie's hair and the attack on Mattel as a symbol of corporate whiteness facilitated a dialogue on race but overlooked Puerto Rican agency in the doll's production as a symbolic good (or evil). As Néstor García Canclini writes, "David did not really know where Goliath was."[36] Most notably, these critics did not engage with the significant fact that the doll was fashioned as a *jíbara* —the mythical nineteenth-century, mountain-dwelling, white Spanish creolized peasant—with all that this implies within hegemonic elite discourses. U.S. critics did not address how *jibarismo* excludes them as much as—and perhaps more than—Mattel with its dreadlocked Hispanic Barbie and the broad-nosed Quinceañera Teresa. This critical slip can be partly attributed to the acceptance and reworkings of the *jíbaro* myth in the United States, and the popularity of this icon to the virtual tribe in multiple contexts, including Internet sites such as jíbaro.com, ("el lugar Boricua más jíbaro del Interné"). In hindsight, Mattel's contribution was relatively minimal, albeit practically indestructible: it commercialized the already officialized *jíbaro* myth by casting it in plastic and giving it worldwide commodity status.

As has been noted with a mixture of scorn and disbelief, the Institute of Puerto Rican Culture—the official voice of government-sanctioned Puerto Ricanness created by the commonwealth—was the corporation's chief advisor in designing the doll's accessories and writing the box's copy (which, nevertheless, contains several mistakes and typos). Interestingly, the pro-statehood administration seemed to have supported the doll, underlining the success of *jibarista* discourse among all ideological sectors. The hold of *jibarismo* is, in fact, so strong that statehooders refer to their brand of federalism as *estadidad jíbara*, a specifically Puerto Rican "way" of becoming a state of the Union; and the supporters of commonwealth still use a silhouetted *jíbaro* as a beacon, even when their party's economic policies were largely responsible for the obliteration of the peasants' way of life. The obviousness of why Barbie had to be a *jíbara*—and not a "Return Nuyorican Barbie" or a "Sugar Cane Babe Barbie"—begins to untangle the question of who belongs (and who calls the shots) in *jíbaro* country.

From the nineteenth century the mostly male, white, affluent intellectual elites have been elaborating the myth of the *jíbaro* as the repository of the Puerto Rican people's true (white) soul. "El 'denso contenido espiritual,'" writes Luis Zayas, "es legado del alma hispana."[37] As Francisco Scarano argues, early identification with the *jíbaros* by the elites can reasonably be interpreted as a progressive gesture to include the peasants into a proto-national imaginary in the face of a retrograde colonial regime.[38] After the Spanish-American War, however, this investment became increasingly problematic as a sign of national democratic inclusion. Despite the fact that the term *jíbaro* was generally used to refer to a (mixed) racial category in several regions of the Americas (a usage not unknown in Puerto Rico), this knowledge was conveniently disregarded as living peasants became paper icons in the hands of nationalist writers.

The *jíbaro* was the symbol of choice for a wide range of reasons, including the peasants' alleged "whiteness" as the presumed (pure) descendants of the Spanish. The insistence on the *jíbaro*'s uncorrupted Europeanness suggests that the *jíbaro* became the "great white hope" for the elites in defending a separate and unique national identity from the United States. "En él vinculamos nuestros júbilos," wrote one of Puerto Rico's (still) most influential intellectuals, Antonio S. Pedreira, "nuestros favores y nuestras aspiraciones."[39] Investing in the *jíbaro*'s whiteness served (and continues to serve) at least two contradictory political impulses. On the one hand, it affirmed that Puerto Ricans shared an equally civilized (European) culture as that of the new colonial ruler, who branded them racially inferior. On the other, it allowed elites to ward off uncomfortable associations with the emerging working class, whose members, despite increased capitalist exploitation, were savoring previously unavailable political rights and challenging their subordinate class status.

Drastically different from the passive *jíbaro* of the elite's imagination, the working class was combative in its demand for a decent wage and material comfort, had little trouble openly collaborating with Americans to achieve political objectives, and possessed its own intellectual traditions and modes of expression. Some of its leadership even rejected "nationalism" as an ideology. In other words, these flesh-and-blood proletarians resembled the elites in threatening ways. As Pedreira would say, the *jíbaro*—as the elite—had to protect himself "del atropello de la zona urbana y de la negra competencia de la costa."[40]

The more Puerto Ricans resembled Americans—in this *boricuas* share some terrain with Canadians—the more imperative it was for cultural discourse to create and police distance. As Lillian Guerra suggests, "[T]he elite needed the *jíbaro* in order to remind them of who they truly were—Spanish and Puerto Rican—rather than who their own actions told them they were trying to become—North Americans."[41] Despite appearances to the contrary—such as the growing statehood movement, the critical dependence on federal transfers, demographic shifts, and transculturation—the *jíbaro*, and with him the nation, remains intact, authentic, and unchanging. This is why Pedreira contributed to creating the equivalent of a national holy ghost that protects Puerto Ricans from themselves and their "suicidal" tendencies: "en cada *puertorriqueno* hay *escondido* un jíbaro" (my emphasis).[42] We may often "look" American, but Puerto Ricanness comes from the soul, not the body; it can only be heartfelt. Or collected.

Conveniently, twentieth-century elites called upon the *jíbaro*'s specter to serve their spiritual and political needs at a time when peasants were undergoing a rapid process of proletarianization. The vanishing *jíbaro* became the emblem of another time, in which the currently displaced elites faced less competition for control over bodies and resources. The *jíbaro*'s intimate relationship to the land is also crucial to this formulation, as not only did the soil change hands during this period (from Spanish and creole *hacendados* to American corporations), but also Puerto Rico was reduced to being a property of the United States: it legally belongs to, but is not part of, the metropolis.

By exalting the *jíbaro*, the elites aimed symbolically to repossess the land and regain its control. The main irony of this identification, particularly for future generations, is that the elites fashioned identity as a simulacra—technically dead but symbolically alive—like a doll.

Although never a static discourse, *jibarismo*, however, has been primarily concerned with the *jíbaro*, not the *jíbara*. As Arlene Dávila observes, "An African contribution to the *jíbaro* is never acknowledged or emphasized, as neither is a female gender identity."[43] The (male) engendering of the national myth is, of course, not surprising, particularly when control over the *jíbaras* was taken for granted by men of all classes and the female proletarian represented doubly transgressive possibilities. As was not lost on most observers, women took advantage of American-sponsored modernity in ways that challenged social and reproductive structures, including labor, politics, and the patriarchal family. After 1898 *jíbaras* joined the workforce and then the unions in substantial numbers, sought divorces, used birth control, publicly challenged male authority, and gladly incorporated technology into their lives. If the *jíbaro* constituted a space/time of longing for the old labor regime, the *jíbara*'s proper place could only be safely evoked as passively below the belt.

As might be expected, dominant discourse about *jíbaras* tends to highlight their seductiveness, even amid the squalor. According to poet Virgilio Dávila, the *jíbara* is anemic and sad, "como una flor escuálida de malogrado abril," and her dress is "un harapo / que cubre a duras penas un cuerpo virginal."[44] Sociologist Salvador Brau describes the peasant woman who inspired him to write one of the first sociological texts on the *jíbara* as "pobre mujer indolente y sensual."[45] Writer Abelardo Díaz Alfaro also contributes his pity when he says that *jíbaras* are "Mujeres gastadas por la maternidad y el trabajo excesivo."[46] Yet, in welding the Barbie and the mythical *jíbara*, the contemporary elites modernized and let go of the crudest discourses of female subordination in the interest of a globally recognized hegemony. As Mattel has made it clear, Barbie lives in a sanitized world of glamour and autonomy, in which men are just one more accessory.

Given the meager, but fairly consistent, discourse on *jíbaras* and the hegemony of the male *jíbaro* myth, the Puerto Rican Barbie has rewritten parts of the *jibarista* script for generations to come, giving it even more currency. If early *jibarista* discourse was concerned with the *jíbaro*'s grave sociological, political, and economic problems, the Puerto Rican Barbie is fantastically free from want and openly transnational. Furthermore, it is American-financed and Malaysian-made, and it's definitely not going back to picking coffee. The doll's main concern is for you to "like the special white dress I am wearing. It is very typical of a dress I might wear to a festival or party." The use of the *jíbara* as a spectacle, however, is not new. As Guerra has argued, the *jíbara*'s imagined "natural inclination toward promiscuity made her fair game for these intellectuals to put her body on display for their own amusement and to invade her gynecology for the sake of the public interest."[47] In fact, the back of the box is clear about the intent of urging the Barbie to put out a *jíbara* show: "Tourism is a very significant part of our economy. . . . Today, people from all over the world come to enjoy our beautiful country, delicious food and friendly people. I hope you can come and visit us soon."

The Puerto Rican Barbie's divorce from the realm of agricultural want is specifically signified by its accessories—a disproportionately large hairbrush, a pair of high heels, earrings, and a ring—and, above all, its "magnificently simple but gorgeous local folkloric dress."[48] The dress worn by the Barbie was criticized by some Puerto Ricans as forcing women to be "stuck in the feminine stereotype of the nineteenth century,"[49] but no one questioned its contribution to whitening Barbie or its status as an invented tradition from above. A Mattel spokeswoman defended it by affirming that "Barbie's dress is a traditional costume not meant to offend, and not meant to depict the clothes of today's women."[50] Still, the doll's elaborate costume does not conform to any dress worn by a peasant in the visual record. In an essay criticizing a 1953 competition to reward the best entry depicting a Puerto Rican "regional dress," writer Nilita Vientós Gastón categorically denied its existence and chastised those who seek this form of national validation by labeling it "un alarde de la fantasía, una invención. . . . Imagino que su destino será convertirse en disfraz."[51] Indeed, the dress definitely makes the Barbie a plastic *jíbara*, in the slang implication of the term: superficial, fake, and materialistic.

Barbie's dress is also an important part of the elaboration of a postmortem *jíbaro* myth as it incorporates a wide array of influences and patriarchal nationalist desires. For instance, the dress is low-cut (quite rare before the 1940s but emphasizing the *jíbara*'s femininity), and has five pieces of *encaje*, a very expensive material that only wealthy women could purchase during the first part of the century. By using *encaje*, the dress is fit to signify the Barbie as a "country" girl, but imagines it with the same affluence of the *hacendada*, the landowner or his wife. The extensive use of the *encaje* also brings the Barbie closer to Spain, as folkloric Spanish costumes usually exhibit large quantities of this fabric, including in the Mattel versions of Spanish Barbie. Furthermore, the dress's finery and elaborateness connote access to the city, not the mythic isolation of the countryside. The general acceptance of the doll's dress as historically accurate spells yet another victory for the elites by avoiding questions about the "authenticity" of the *jíbaro* myth, and affirming that "culture" is not a struggle over representation or participation but a collection of essential accessories. Once more, corporate America and Puerto Rican colonial institutions see eye to eye: It's the dress that makes the *jíbara*.

The fact that Puerto Rican Barbie is a "collectible" doll further reinforces its colonial cast as well as certain *jíbara* imagined characteristics. In Mattel's universe, to be a "collectible" is to live as a folkloric object with limited agency (i.e., accessories). The doll's transformation into an aesthetic commodity also takes *jibarista* discourse further than even Pedreira intended when he wrote, "Por encima de su angustia económica pondremos su valor humano, su bella calidad representativa."[52] Puerto Rican Barbie confirms the *jíbara* as the symbol of a Puerto Rican essence, not a historically specific product of colonial relations and economic exploitation. Different from other black and white Barbies, but similar to most other Latin American ones, the Puerto Rican Barbie does not achieve anything but being itself, eternally and tirelessly "national." In culminating the *jíbaro* myth as an aesthetic commodity, Mattel rejects the economy of lack associated with the *jíbaro*, and actualizes an orgy of plenty in which the consumer in need of national affirmation is "free" to buy his-or herself some pleasure—and own it (if not own up to it).

This pleasure is further enhanced by the fact that the doll is perceived as a light-skinned mulatta, a departure from most historical accounts of the *jíbara*, who is often represented as sickly pale. Puerto Rican Barbie is, however, the kind of mulatta "that won't tap her feet" when it hears the drum, but instead, dances the *seis chorreao* wearing a very virginal white dress. The passion for the whitewashed mulatta among the middle-class elites, however, should not be confused with the questioning of racism as an ideology of exclusion. As Tomás Blanco remarks without a trace of irony, the mulatta "parece tener valor estético o de selección erótica" for creole men.[53] Not coincidentally, the embracing of a mulatto aesthetics comes at a time when the elites—more American and "modern" than ever—wish to distinguish themselves from (other) Americans by establishing that they are not racists. In fact, the educated elites, as Eduardo Seda Bonilla has written, tend to produce the most inclusive democratic public discourse, while exhibiting equally segregationist behavior in their familial lives, with the possible exception of (out-of-wedlock) sexuality.[54]

Simultaneously, the Puerto Rican Barbie established several lines of continuity with certain *jíbaro* texts, as the doll is sexually desirable, eager to do the work of the nation, and willing to serve as a (non)maternal reproductive machine.[55] The fact that the Barbie is gendered feminine also wards off associations with threatening mulatto sexuality (urban, male, and possibly homosexual). While never vulnerable within Mattel's gripping narrative, the Puerto Rican Barbie can be imagined as the seductive body—*sabrosamente femenina*—dreamed most forcefully by twentieth-century poet Luis Lloréns Torres. The Barbie fuses the passive (yet sensual) *jíbara* with the social climbing hot mulatta, transforming it into the ultimate user-friendly object of national excitement and interracial desires, queerly recalling the doll's historical predecessor, the post-World War II German novelty toy for men, Lilli. [56] In the elite's collaboration with Mattel, you could say that they had their way with the Barbie thrice: as a *gringa*, a *jíbara*, and a mulatta. Not surprisingly, many indignities projected onto the *jíbara* have been forced upon Barbie dolls by their (ab)users with a vengeance. Both bodies have been known to suffer the erotic urges (hard-ons, breast fondling), paranoia, racist rage, misogyny, amputated limbs, and decapitations of their owners—with a pasted-on smile. Ultimately, if as Lillian Guerra suggests, the elites have historically perceived the *jíbaro*'s alleged passivity as a "deep reservoir of nationalism,"[57] the Puerto Rican Barbie is the most anticolonial object ever invented for the cause.

Furthermore, whereas Barbie's corporate "parents" do not encourage consumers to imagine it as a mother, the elites were able to transfigure the doll into a reproductive vessel—of *jibarismo*. Political analyst García Passalacqua, in fact, specifically praised the doll because it would help Puerto Ricans "explain ourselves, as we are, to all Americans."[58] In becoming a *jíbara* commodity, the Puerto Rican Barbie is unable physically to give birth to the *jíbarito* of tomorrow, but does reproduce its myth to new generations, rephrasing the popular nationalist aphorism: *la patria es valor (en el mercado) y sacrificio (para el intelectual)*. Characteristically for the Island's elite, although the Puerto Rican Barbie is doing their symbolic work, it is mostly benefiting American capital and the colonial status quo.

TRAÍDO POR LOS PELOS: SELLING OUT PUERTO RICANNESS

A Puerto Rican Barbie dressed as a *jíbara*, however, would not have been enough to draw thousands of adults to Island stores. To sell Puerto Ricanness out, the *jíbara* had to stand in the "right" political pose; it needed to affirm hegemonic ideas about Puerto Rico's (central) place in the world, not only local racial hierarchies. Luckily, Mattel was again able to capitalize on the winning formula. By including the Puerto Rican Barbie as part of the "Dolls-of-the-World" series, Mattel recognized Islanders' specificity as a distinct Spanish(only)-speaking, white, Latin American nation, with merely bureaucratic ties to the United States, and without a sizable diaspora, politically subaltern status, or financial dependency. Ironically, the series' main objective is to introduce "children in the United States to other cultures,"[59] as if there were not already three million Puerto Ricans in the United States, and the Puerto Rican doll was not based on the "Hispanic" one. In this, the elite's culturalist strategy of difference—manipulated for over one hundred years to obtain political concessions—coalesced with Mattel's marketing department to deny U.S. Puerto Ricans their market worth. But as we know, the Barbie aims to please—for a profit.

Mattel has always been aware of its Latin market, not only because one of its plants is located in Mexico, but also because it was born in a state that is home to millions of Hispanics: California. As early as 1968, the company came out with "Spanish Talker," a Hispanic Barbie with a Mexican accent. The first "Hispanic Barbie," launched in 1980, was dressed in a pseudo-Spanish costume called "fiesta-style."[60] Ironically, the Barbies' colorful wardrobes and risqué poses have been partially attributed to the dress codes of working-class Hispanics: "Whatever the fashion, the California version will be more extreme . . . much more colorful. . . . Clothes tend to fit more tightly than is considered elsewhere, and to expose more flesh."[61] No wonder Ken Handler, the son of two of Barbie's "inventors" and the reason the doll's male companion's name is Ken, calls Barbie a "bimba," not a bimbo.[62]

In 1996—a year before the introduction of the Puerto Rican Barbie—Latin America had been experiencing a higher rate of growth (47 percent) than the United States (32 percent),[63] consolidating itself as the doll's third largest market.[64] Puerto Rico's four million consumers do not constitute in themselves a substantial market—there are almost as many *boricuas* in the United States. Islanders, however, have the highest per capita number of Barbies in Latin America, the context in which Mattel and most of the Island's elites locate Puerto Rico. A whopping 72 percent of Puerto Rican children own at least one Barbie, as compared to the second highest, Chile, with 49 percent. Eight-year-old Amanda from Bayamón alone owns forty-three Barbies, but the Puerto Rican Barbie reigns "supreme in her collection."[65] The difference in Barbie penetration can be linked to closer economic and cultural ties to the United States, a higher per capita income than most Latin American nations (at twenty dollars, Barbie is considered an expensive children's toy), and higher consumption rates.

Since the changes Mattel makes to each doll are minimal—pure genius from a Warholian ethos—the company is able to change hair color, pigmentation, and costume and appeal to dozens of markets in their best (white) light, which tends to be appealing to the country's most affluent sectors. Puerto Rican Barbie may be a globalized product, but it is ably designed to cash in on the needs of many to affirm their national pride and prominence in the family of nations. "Globalization," in fact, tends to encourage a hunger for what is unique, local, regional, and national among certain social sectors. In many parts of the world, and notoriously in Puerto Rico,[66] advertising a product as if it was native or with native characteristics can spell impressive profits, even if changes to the product are nil. A disgruntled Nuyorican consumer, Andrés Quiñones, criticized the doll precisely on those grounds: "lo que hizo Mattel fue hacerle la nariz más grande y oscurecerle los ojos. Ahora nos quieren vender como boricua la misma muñeca de siempre."[67]

Although Andrés was not impressed, Mattel managed to do what Bacardí, Budweiser, and Winston had already achieved on the Island: sell Puerto Ricans an "American" product while affirming Puerto Rico's unassimilable difference and specificity (nationality) in sameness (capital). True to form, Mattel's boxed history makes it clear that the Island is separate and different from the United States, in every exoticizing way, including culinary traditions (*plátanos, arroz con gandules*) and wildlife (*coquí*). The doll was a triumph for Island elites: corporate America gave them what reality denies them—a purely plastic Puerto Rican identity—and they enjoyed it without financial or political responsibility. Unlike other, more impoverished markets, the Puerto Rican consumer is proud to verify his worth as a commodity, even if he doesn't financially benefit. Purchasing also highlights how hegemonic identity constructs—even if culled from elite culture—are today manufactured for mass consumption, and largely understood as an accessory: T-shirt, *coquí* souvenir, and CD car flag.

The tendency to construct identity as an accessory, however, points to the increasing complexity of the current cultural terrain for Puerto Ricans. The same year that the Puerto Rican Barbie was introduced to the world, a second *boricua* doll made an entrance fit for royalty. As *Latina* magazine tells it, "Now there's more to complain about with the debut of a Puerto Rican doll named Carlos: If Barbie wants to date this plastic papi, she can forget about it. He's gay. Carlos is the boyfriend of Billy."[68] Although *Latina*'s complaint suggests a lack of imagination, it also fails to take into account to what extent playing with Barbie, Ken, and G.I. Joe is always, already, a queer experience for most. Although this debate lasted less than the Barbie's and was not aired out in the *New York Times*, Carlos's existence makes seeing the Puerto Rican Barbie straight a difficult endeavor. As *Latina*'s campy prose put it, "[T]he *fashionistas* outraged over Barbie's clichéd vestido criollo should find solace. At least he's not wearing a straw hat."[69]

Queerly, the same year that the Puerto Rican Barbie came out, it occurred to Island-based drag performer Vanessa Fox to refashion the Puerto Rican Barbie's wardrobe to her own as a strategy to raise money for charity. After the introduction of Fox's personalized Puerto Rican Barbie, she was able to raise hundreds of dollars to purchase dolls for disadvantaged girls and boys: "O sea, que con una Barbie hemos podido hacer felices a muchos niños."[70] With Fox, the Puerto Rican Barbie brought about a miraculous state of affairs, akin to the biblical miracles of the loaves and fishes. Fox not only managed to make more children happy, she also created value for a doll that has not experienced any appreciation among Barbie collectors. Mattel may have made the doll for corporate profit, but it has ultimately been Puerto Ricans who have infused it with alternative values and made it theirs.

At the same time, Barbie's Aryan origins and "white" corporate parents certainly limit its capacity to stake new ground in decolonizing politics. But when Mattel put Puerto Rican Barbie within our mature reach, it forced us to relive our childhood as colonial survivors, racialized migrants, and/or queer kids, and to enact our frustrations toward whoever made us feel subordinate, ugly, and vulnerable. Symbolically teasing Barbie's hair let some blow off steam; lovingly combing it held fantastic pleasures for others. As a fairly well-adjusted child, I do not remember ever giving much thought to my Barbie, Ken, and G.I. Joe. I do vividly recall, however, the day when I stopped in the Barbie aisle in a Miami toy store and could not believe my wondering eyes, hurt in so many colonial battles for dignity. The big, corny, white and pink letters spelling Puerto rican barbie drew me in, for they seemed to confirm what as a child I always knew, but as a migrant adult, had been denied: Barbie has always been Puerto Rican. Even as I delighted in the recognition of this archaic and secret code, I was mostly savoring the bitter-sweet constraints of my own political agency.

NOTES

1. Frances Negrón-Muntaner, "Ricky's Hips," in *Passing Memories* (New York: New York University Press, forthcoming).

2. Mireya Navarro, "A New Barbie in Puerto Rico Divides Island and Mainland," *New York Times*, 27 December 1997, A1.

3. Louis Aguilar, "Barbie Stirs Debate in Puerto Rico," *Miami Herald*, 14 November 1997, 25A.

4. Ibid., 25A.

5. Frances Negrón-Muntaner, "Feeling Pretty: West Side Story and Puerto Rican-American Identity," *Social Text* 63 (summer 2000): 83–106.

6. M. G. Lord, Forever Barbie: The Unauthorized Biography of a Real Doll (New York: Morrow, 1994), 7.

7. Navarro, A9.

8. Margaret Carlisle Duncan, Garry Chick, and Alan Aycock, eds., *Play and Culture Studies*, vol. 1 (Greenwich, CT: Ablex, 1998), 4.

9. Froma Harrop, "Ask Real Barbie Experts," *Miami Herald*, 6 January 1998, 7A.

10. Navarro, A9, A10.

11. Lord, 298.

12. Walter Benjamin, "The Cultural History of Toys," in *Selected Writings*, vol. 2 (Cambridge: Harvard University Press, 1999), 100.

13. José Quiroga, *Tropics of Desire: Interventions from Queer Latino America* (New York: New York University Press, 2000).

14. Jeannette Rivera-Lyles, "Boricuas divididos con la Barbie puertor-riqueña," *El Nuevo Herald*, 31 December 1997, sec. 1, 16A.

15. Erica Rand, *Barbie's Queer Accessories* (Durham, NC: Duke University Press, 1995).

16. Louis Aguilar, "Barbie Has Serious Implications for Puerto Ricans," *Miami Herald*, 9 November 1997, 127.

17. Adrian Febles, "Coming Soon: Political Activist Barbie," *San Juan Star*, 14 November 1997, 76.
18. Aguilar, "Barbie Stirs Debate," 25A.
19. Patrick Olivelle, "Hair and Society: Social Significance of Hair in South Asian Traditions," in *Hair: Its Power and Meaning in Asian Cultures*, ed. Alf Hilte-beitel and Barbara D. Miller, 40–41 (Albany: State University of New York Press, 1998).
20. Susan Brownmiller, *Femininity* (New York: Linden Press, Simon and Schuster, 1984), 57.
21. Tomás Blanco, *El prejuicio racial en Puerto Rico* (Río Piedras: Ediciones Huracán, 1985), 138.
22. Sidney Mintz, "Cañamelas: The Subculture of a Rural Sugar Plantation Proletariat," in *The People of Puerto Rico: A Study in Social Anthropology*, ed. Julián H. Steward et al. (Urbana: University of Illinois, 1956), 410.
23. Julia de Burgos, "Ay ay ay de la grifa negra," in *Poema en veinte surcos* (Río Piedras: Editorial Huracán, 1997), 52.
24. Francisco Arriví, Sirena (Río Piedras: Editorial Cultural, 1971), 45.
25. Luis Palés Matos, *Tuntún de pasa y grifería* (San Juan: Biblioteca de Autores Puertorriqueños, 1974).
26. Quoted in Noliwe M. Rooks, *Hair Raising: Beauty, Culture, and African-American Women* (New Brunswick: Rutgers University Press, 1996), 14.
27. Quoted in Isabelo Zenon, *Narciso descubre su trasero: El negro en la cultura puertorriqueña*, vol. 2 (Humacao, Puerto Rico: Editorial Furidi, 1975), 79.
28. Zenón, vol. 1, 84.
29. Willie Perdomo, "Nigger Reecan Blues," in *Aloud: Voices from the Nuyorican Poets Café*, ed. Miguel Algarín and Bob Holzan (New York: Henry Holt, 1994), 111–13.
30. Aguilar, "Barbie Stirs Debate," 25A.
31. Elsie Crumb McCaeb and Anne H. Stark, preface to *Hair in African Art and Culture*, ed. Roy Sieber, and Frank Herreman (New York: Museum for African Art, 2000), 8.
32. Walter Benjamin, "Toys and Play," in *Selected Writings*, vol. 2 (Cambridge: Harvard University Press, 1999), 117–21, 118.
33. McCaeb and Stark, 11.
34. Rivera-Lyles, 16A.
35. Francisco A. Scarano, "The Jibaro Masquerade and the Subaltern Politics of Creole Identity Formation in Puerto Rico, 1745-1823," *American Historical Review* 101, no. 5 (December 1996): 1398–431.
36. Néstor García Canclini, *La globalizatión* (Buenos Aires: Paidós, 2000), 11.
37. Luis O. Zayas Micheli, "La trascendencia como Coyuntura del jíbaro," in *El jíbaro*, ed. Manuel Alonso (Río Piedras: Edil, 1992), 16.
38. Scarano, 1398–431.
39. Antonio S. Pedreira, "La actualidad del jíbaro," in *El jíbaro de Puerto Rico: Símbolo y figura*, ed. Enrique Laguerre and Esther Mel ó n (Sharon, CT: Troutman Press, 1968), 14.
40. Pedreira, 23.
41. Lillian Guerra, *Popular Expression and National Identity in Puerto Rico: The Struggle for Self, Community, and Nation* (Gainesville: University Press of Florida, 1998).
42. Pedreira, 20.
43. Virgilio Dávila, "La jibarita," in *El jíbaro de Puerto Rico: Símbolo y figura*, ed. Laguerre and Melón, 72.
44. Dávila, 100–101.
45. Salvador Brau, "La campesina," in *El jíbaro de Puerto Rico: Símbolo y figura*, ed. Enrique Laguerre and Esther Melón, 27.
46. Abelardo Díaz Alfaro, "El boliche," in *El jíbaro de Puerto Rico: Símbolo y figura*, ed. Laguerre and Melón, 206.
47. Guerra, 117.
48. Navarro, Al.
49. Rivera-Lyles, 16A.

50. Shelley Emling, "Barbie Creates Brouhaha, This Time among Puerto Ricans," *Charlotte Observer*, 30 December 1997, available www.charlotte .com/barbiel.htm.

51. Nilita Vientós Gastón, "El 'traje típico' puertorriqueno," in *Indice cultural*, vol. 1 (Río Piedras: Ediciones de la Universidad de Puerto Rico, 1962), 204.

52. Pedreira, 8.

53. Blanco, 130.

54. Eduardo Seda Bonilla, *Los derechos civiles en la cultura puertorriqueña* (Río Piedras: Ediciones de Bayoán, 1973), 189.

55. Guerra, 111.

56. Lord, 8.

57. Guerra, 102.

58. Navarro, A9.

59. Emling, www.charlotte.com/barbiel.htm.

60. Lord, 108.

61. Ibid., 190.

62. Ibid., 190.

63. "Mattel populariz ó a Barbie mediante productos con licencias," *El Universal*, 13 Dec 2000, available at http://noticias.eluniversal.com/1998/06/28/28502AA.shtml.

64. Ibid.

65. Navarro, A9.

66. Arlene Dávila, *Sponsored Identities: Cultural Politics in Puerto Rico* (Philadelphia: Temple University Press, 1997).

67. Rivera-Lyles, 16A.

68. "Boy Toy," *Latina*, July 1998, 20.

69. Ibid., 20.

70. Patricia Vargas, "Por la felicidad de un niño," *El Nuevo Día*, 23 December 1997, 77.

Chapter Eight

The Pocahontas Perplex

The Image of Indian Women in American Culture

Rayna Green

In one of the best known old Scottish ballads, "Young Beichan" or "Lord Bateman and the Turkish King's Daughter," as it is often known in America, a young English adventurer travels to a strange, foreign land. The natives are of a darker color than he, and they practice a pagan religion. The man is captured by the king (Pasha, Moor, Sultan) and thrown in a dungeon to await death. Before he is executed, however, the pasha's beautiful daughter—smitten with the elegant and wealthy visitor—rescues him and sends him homeward. But she pines away for love of the now remote stranger who has gone home, apparently forgotten her, and contracted a marriage with a "noble" "lady" of his own kind. In all the versions, she follows him to his own land, and in most, she arrives on his wedding day whereupon he throws over his bride-to-be for the darker but more beautiful princess. In most versions, she becomes a Christian, and she and Lord Beichan live happily ever after.

In an article called "The Mother of Us All," Philip Young suggests the parallel between the ballad story and the Pocohantas-John Smith rescue tale.[1] With the exception of Pocohantas' marriage to John Rolfe (still, after all, a Christian stranger), the tale should indeed sound familiar to most Americans nurtured on Smiths' salvation by the Indian Princess. Actually, Europeans were familiar with the motif before John Smith offered his particular variant in the *Generall Historie of Virginie* (1624).

Francis James Child, the famous ballad collector, tells us in his *English and Scottish Popular Ballads* that "Young Beichan" (Child #40) matches the tale of Gilbert Beket, St. Thomas Aquinas' father, as well as a legend recounted in the *Gesta Romanorum,* one of the oldest collections of popular tales. So the frame story was printed before 1300 and was, no doubt, well distributed in oral tradition before then. Whether or not our rakish adventur-er-hero, John Smith, had heard the stories or the ballad, we cannot say, but we must admire how life mirrors art since his story follows the outlines of the traditional tale most admirably. What we do know is that the elements of the tale appealed to Europeans long before Americans had the opportunity to attach their affection for it onto Pocahontas. Whether or not we believe Smith's tale—and there are many reasons not to—we cannot ignore the impact the story has had on the American imagination.

"The Mother of Us All" became our first aristocrat, and perhaps our first saint, as Young implies. Certainly, the image of her body flung over the endangered head of our hero constitutes a major scene in national myth. Many paintings and drawings of this scene exist, and it appears in popular art on everything from wooden fire engine side panels to calendars. Some ren-derings betray such ignorance about the Powhatan Indians of Virginia—often portraying them in Plains dress—that one quickly comes to understand that it is the mythical scene, not the accuracy of detail that moved artists. The most famous portrait of Pocahontas, the only one said to be done from life (at John Rolfe's request), shows the Princess in Elizabethan dress, complete with ruff and velvet hat—the Christian, English lady the ballad expects her to become and the lady she indeed became for her English husband and her faithful audience for all time. The earliest literary efforts in America, intended to give us American rather that European topics, featured Pocahontas in plenty. Poems and plays—like James Nelson Barber's *The Indian Princess; or, La Bell Sauvage* (1808) and George Washington Custis's *The Settlers of Virgin-ia* (1827), as well as contemporary American novels, discussed by Leslie Fiedler in *The Return of the Vanishing American*—dealt with her presence, or sang her praises from the pages of literary magazines and from the stages of popular playhouses throughout the east.[2] Traditional American ballads like "Jonathan Smith" retold the thrilling story; schoolbook histories in-cluded it in the first pages of every text; nineteenth century commercial products like cigars, perfume, and even flour used Pocahontas's name as come-on; and she appeared as the figurehead for American warships and clippers. Whether or not she saved John Smith, her actions as recounted by Smith set up one kind of model for Indian-White relations that persists—long after most Indians and Anglos ceased to have face-to-face relationships. Moreover, as a model for the national understanding of Indian women, her significance is undeniable. With her darker, negatively viewed sister, the Squaw—or, the anti-Pocahontas, as Fiedler call her—the Princess intrudes on the national consciousness, and a potential cult waits to be resurrected when our anxieties about who we are make us recall her from her woodland retreat.[3]

Americans had a Pocahontas Perplex even before the teenage Princess offered us a real figure to hang the iconography on. The powerfully symbolic Indian woman, as Queen and Princess, has been with us since 1575 when she appeared to stand for the New World. Artists, explorers, writers and political leaders found the Indian as they cast about for some symbol with which to identify this earthly, frightening, and beautiful paradise; E. McClung Fleming has given one of the most complete explications of these images.[4] The misnamed Indian was the native dweller, who fit conveniently into the various traditional folkloric, philosophical and literary patterns characteristic of European thought at the time.[5] Europeans easily adopted the Indians as the iconographic representative of the Americas. At first, Caribbean and Brazilian (Tupinamba) Indians, portrayed amidst exotic flora and fauna, stood for the New World's promises and dangers. The famous and much-reproduced "Four Continents" illustrations (circa, early sixteenth century) executed by artists who had seen Indians and ones who had not, ordinarily pictured a male and female pair in America's place.[6] But the paired symbol apparently did not satisfy the need for a personified figure, and the Indian Queen began to appear as the sole representation for the Americas in 1575. And until 1765 or thereabouts, the bare-breasted, Amazonian Native American Queen reigned. Draped in leaves, feathers, and animal skins as well as in heavy Caribbean jewelry, she appeared aggressive, militant, and armed with spears and arrows. Often, she rode on an armadillo, and stood with her foot on the slain body of an animal or human enemy. She was the familiar Mother-Goddess figure—full-bodied, powerful, nurturing but dangerous—embodying the opulence and peril of the New World. Her environment was rich and colorful, and that, with the allusions to Classical Europe through the Renaissance portrayal of her large, naked body, attached her to Old World History as well as to New World virtue.

Her daughter, the Princess, enters the scene when the colonies begin to move toward independence, and she becomes more "American" and less Latin than her mother. She seems less barbarous than the Queen; the rattlesnake (Jones' "Don't Tread on Me" sign) defends her, and her enemies are defeated by male warriors rather than by her own armed hand. She is Britannia's daughter as well as that of the Carib Queen, and she wears the triangular Phrygian cap and holds the liberty pole of her later, metamorphosed sister, Miss Liberty (the figure on the Statue of Liberty and the Liberty dime). She is young, leaner in the Romanesque rather than Greek mode, and distinctly Caucasian, though her skin remains slightly tinted in some renderings. She wears the loose, flowing gowns of classical statuary rather than animal skins, and Roman sandals grace her feet. She is armed, usually with a spear, but she also carries a peace pipe, a flag, or the starred and striped shield of Colonial America. She often stands with the Sons of Liberty, or later, with George Washington.

Thus, the Indian woman began her symbolic, many-faceted life as a Mother figure—exotic, powerful, dangerous, and beautiful—and as a representative of American liberty and European classical virtue translated into New World terms. She represented, even defended America. But when real Indian women—Pocahontas and her sisters—intruded into the needs bound up in symbols and the desires inherent in daily life, the responses to the symbol became more complex, and the Pocahontas perplex emerged as a controlling metaphor in the American experience. The Indian woman, along with her male counterparts, continued to stand for the New World and for rude native nobility, but the image of the savage remained as well. The dark side of the Mother-Queen figure is the savage Squaw, and even Pocahontas, as John Barth suggests in *The Sotweed Factor*, is motivated by lust.

Both her nobility as a Princess and her savagery as a Squaw are defined in terms of her relationships with male figures. If she wishes to be called a Princess, she must save or give aid to white men. The only good Indian—male or female, Squanto, Pocahontas, Sacagawea, Cochise, the Little Mohee or the Indian Doctor—rescues and helps white men. But the Indian woman is even more burdened by this narrow definition of a "good Indian," for it is she, not the males, whom white men desire sexually. Because her image is so tied up with abstract virtue—indeed, with America—she must remain the Mother Goddess-Queen. But acting as a real female, she must be a partner and lover of Indian men, a mother to Indian children, and an object of lust for white men. To be Mother, Queen, and lover is, as Oedipus' mother, Jocasta, discovered, difficult and perhaps impossible. The paradox so often noted in Latin/Catholic countries where men revere their mothers and sisters, but use prostitutes so that their "good" women can stay pure is to the point here. Both race conflict and national identity, however, make this particular Virgin-Whore paradox more complicated than others. The Indian woman finds herself burdened with an image that can only be understood as dysfunctional, even though the Pocahontas perplex affects us all. Some examination of the complicated dimensions of that image might help us move toward change.

In songs like "Jonathan Smith," "Chipeta's Ride" and others sung in oral tradition, the Indian woman saves white men.[7] In "Chipeta's Ride," she even saves a white woman from lust-enraged Indian males. Ordinarily, however, she rescues her white lover or an anonymous male captive. Always called a Princess (or Chieftain's Daughter), she, like Pocahontas, has to violate the wishes and customs of her own "barbarous" people to make good the rescue, saving the man out of love and often out of "Christian sympathy." Nearly all the "good" Princess figures are converts, and they cannot bear to see their fellow Christian slain by "savages." The Princess is "civilized"; to illustrate her native nobility, most pictures portray her as white, darker than the Europeans, but more Caucasian than her fellow natives.

If unable to make the grand gesture of saving her captive lover or if thwarted from marrying him by her cruel father, the Chieftain, the Princess is allowed the even grander gesture of committing suicide when her lover is slain or fails to return to her after she rescues him. In the hundreds of "Lover's Leap" legends which abound throughout the country, and in traditional songs like "The Indian Bride's Lament," our heroine leaps over a precipice, unable to live without her loved one. In this movement from political symbolism (where the Indian woman defends America) to psychosexual symbolism (where she defends or dies for white lovers), we can see part of the Indian woman's dilemma. To be "good," she must defy her own people, exile herself from them, become white, and perhaps suffer death.

Those who did not leap for love continued to fall in love with white men by the scores, and here the sacrifices are several. The women in songs like "The Little Mohee," "Little Red Wing," and "Juanita, the Sachem's Daughter" fall in love with white travellers, often inviting them to share their blissful, idyllic, woodland paradise. If their lovers leave them, they often pine away, die of grief, or leap off a cliff, but in a number of songs, the white man remains with the maiden, preferring her life to his own, "civilized" way. "The Little Mohee" is a prime example of such a song.

> As I went out walking for pleasure one day,
> In the sweet recollection, to dwell time away.
> As I sat amusing myself on the grass,
> Oh, who should I spy but a fair Indian lass.
>
> She walked up' behind me, taking hold of my hand,
> She said, "You are a stranger and in a strange land,
> But if you will follow, you're welcome to come
> And dwell in my cottage that I call my home."
>
> My Mohea was gentle, my Mohea was kind.
> She took me when a stranger and clothed me when cold.
> She learned me the language of the lass of Mohea.
>
> "I'm going to leave you, so farewell my dear.
> The ship's sails are spreading and home I must steer."
> The last time I saw her she was standing on the strand,
> And as my boat passed her she waved me her hand.
>
> Saying "when you have landed and with the one you love,
> Think of pretty Mohea in the coconut grove."
> I am home but no one comes near me nor none do I see,
> That would equal compare with the lass of Mohea.
>
> Oh, the girl that I loved proved untrue to me.
> I'll turn my course backward far over the sea.

I'll turn my course backward, from this land I'll go free,
And go spend my days with the little Mohea.

Such songs add to the exotic and sexual, yet maternal and contradictorily virginal image of the Indian Princess, and are reminiscent of the contemporary white soldier's attachments to "submissive," "sacrificial," "exotic" Asian women.

As long as Indian women keep their exotic distance or die (even occasionally for love of Indian men), they are permitted to remain on the positive side of the image. They can help, stand by, sacrifice for, and aid white men. They can, like their native brothers, heal white men, and the Indian reputation as healer dominated the nineteenth century patent medicine business: In the ads for such medicines, the Indian woman appears either as a helpmate to her "doctor" husband or partner or as a healer herself. In several ads (and the little dime novels often accompanying the patent medicine products), she is the mysterious witch-healer. Thus, she shares in the Caucasian or European female's reputation for potential evil. The references here to power, knowledge, and sexuality remain on the good side of the image. In this incarnation, the Princess offers help in the form of medicine rather than love.

The tobacco industry also capitalized on the Princess image, and the cigar-store figures and ads associated with the tobacco business replicate the Princess figures to sell its products. Cigar-store Princesses smile and beckon men into tobacco shops. They hold a rose, a bundle of cigars, or some tobacco leaves (a sign of welcome in the colonial days), and they smile invitingly with their Caucasian lips. They also sell the product from tobacco packages, and here, like some of the figures in front of the shops, Diana-like or more militant Minerva (Wonder Woman)-like heroines offer the comforts of the "Indian weed." They have either the rounded, infantile, semi-naked (indicating innocence) bodies of Renaissance angels or the bodies and clothes of classical heroines. The Mother Goddess and Miss Liberty peddle their more abstract wares, as Indian Princesses, along with those of the manufacturer. Once again, the Princess comforts white men, and while she promises much, she remains aloof.

But who becomes the white man's sexual partner? Who forms liaisons with him? It cannot be the Princess, for she is sacrosanct. Her sexuality can be hinted at but never realized. The Princess' darker twin, the Squaw, must serve this side of the image, and again, relationships with males determine what the image will be. In the case of the Squaw, the presence of overt and realized sexuality converts the image from positive to negative. White men cannot share sex with the Princess, but once they do so with a real Indian woman, she cannot follow the required love-and-rescue pattern. She does what white men want for money and lust. In the traditional songs, stories, obscene jokes, contemporary literary works and popular pictorializations of the Squaw, no heroines are allowed. Squaws share in the same vices attributed to Indian men—drunkenness, stupidity, thievery', venality of every kind—and they live in shacks on the edge of town rather than in a woodland paradise.

Here, Squaws are shamed for their relationships with white men, and the males who share their beds—the "squaw men"—or "bucks," if they are Indian—share their shame. When they live with Indian males, Squaws work for their lazy bucks and bear large numbers of fat "papooses." In one joke, a white visitor to a reservation sees an overburdened squaw with ten children hanging on her skirts. "Where's your husband?" the visitor demands. "He ought to be hung!" "Ugh," says the squaw, "pretty well-hung!" They too are fat, and unlike their Princess sisters, dark and possessed of cruder, more "Indian" features. When stories and songs describe relationships with white men, Squaws are understood as mere economic and sexual conveniences for the men who—unlike John Smith or a "brave"—are tainted by association with her. Tale after tale describes the Indian whores, their alcoholic and sexual excesses with white trappers and hunters. A parody of the beautiful-maiden song, "Little Red Wing," speaks of her lewd sister who "lays on her back in a cowboy shack, and lets cowboys poke her in the crack." The result of this cowboy-squaw liaison is a "brat in a cowboy hat with his asshole between his eyes." This Squaw is dark, and squat, and even the cigar-store Indians show the changes in conception. No Roman sandals grace their feet, and their features are more "Indian" and "primitive" than even their male counterparts. The cigar-store squaws often had papooses on their backs, and some had corrugated places on their hips to light the store patrons' matches. When realities intrude on mythos, even Princesses can become Squaws as the text of the ragtime song, "On An Indian Reservation," illustrates:

> On an Indian reservation, far from home and civilization,
> Where the foot of Whiteman seldom trod.
> Whiteman went to fish one summer,
> Met an Indian maid—a hummer,
> Daughter of Big-Chief-Spare-the-Rod.
> Whiteman threw some loving glances, took this maid to Indian dances,
> Smoked his pipe of peace, took chances living in a teepee made of fur.
> Rode with her on Indian ponies, bought her diamond rings, all phonies,
> And he sang these loving words to her:
>
> Chorus:
>> You're my pretty little Indian Napanee.
>> Won't you take a chance and marry me.
>> Your Daddy Chief, 'tis my belief,
>> To a very merry wedding will agree.
>> True, you're a dark little Indian maid,
>> But I'll sunburn to a darker shade,

I'll wear feathers on my head,
Paint my skin an Indian red,
If you will be my Napanee.

With his contact soon he caught her,
Soon he married this big chiefs daughter,
Happiest couple that you ever saw.
But his dreams of love soon faded,
Napanee looked old and jaded,
Just about like any other squaw.
Soon there came papoose in numbers, redskin yells disturbed his slumbers,
Whiteman wonders at his blunders—now the feathers drop upon his head.
Sorry to say it, but he's a-wishing, that he'd never gone a-fishing,
Or had met this Indian maid and said:

Chorus

The Indian woman is between a rock and a hard place. Like that of her male counterpart, her image is freighted with such ambivalence that she has little room to move. He, however, has many more modes in which to participate though he is still severely handicapped by the prevailing stereotypes. They are both tied to definition by relationships with white men, but she is especially burdened by the narrowness of that definition. Obviously, her image is one that is troublesome to all women, but, tied as it is to a national mythos, its complexity has a special piquance. As Vine Deloria points out in *Custer Died for Your Sins*, many whites claim kinship with some distant Indian Princess grandmother, and thus try to resolve their "Indian problem" with such sincere affirmation of relationship.[8]

Such claims make it impossible for the Indian woman to be seen as real. She does not have the power to evoke feeling as a real mother figure, like the black woman, even though *that* image has a burdensome negative side. American children play with no red mammy dolls. She cannot even evoke the terror the "castrating (white) bitch" inspires. Only the male, with upraised tomahawk, does that. The many expressions which treat of her image remove her from consideration as more than an image. As some abstract, noble Princess tied to "America" and to sacrificial zeal, she has power as a symbol. As the Squaw, a depersonalized object of scornful convenience, she is powerless. Like her male relatives she may be easily destroyed without reference to her humanity. (When asked why he killed women and children at Sand Creek, the commanding general of the U. S. Cavalry was said to have replied, "nits make lice.") As the Squaw, her physical removal or destruction can be understood as necessary to the progress of civilization even though her abstracted sister, the Princess, stands for that very civilization. Perhaps the Princess had to be removed from her powerful symbolic place, and replaced with the male Uncle Sam because she confronted America with too many contradictions. As symbol and reality, the Indian woman suffers from our needs, and by both race and sex stands damned.

Since the Indian so much represents America's attachment to a romantic past and to a far distant nobility, it is predictable but horrible that the Indian woman should symbolize the paradoxical entity once embodied for the European in the Princess in the tower and the old crone in the cave. It is time that the Princess herself is rescued and the Squaw relieved of her obligatory service. The Native American woman, like all women, needs a definition that stands apart from that of males, red or white. Certainly, the Native woman needs to be defined as Indian, in Indian terms. Delightful and interesting as Pocahontas' story may be, she offers an intolerable metaphor for the Indian-White experience. She and the Squaw offer unendurable metaphors for the lives of Indian women. Perhaps if we give up the need for John Smith's fantasy and the trappers' harsher realities, we will find, for each of us, an image that does not haunt and perplex us. Perhaps if we explore the meaning of Native American lives outside the boundaries of the stories, songs, and pictures given us in tradition, we will find a more humane truth.

NOTES

1. "The Mother of Us All," *Kenyon Review* 24 (Summer 1962), 391–441.

2. See Jay B. Hubbell, "The Smith-Pocahontas Story in Literature," *The Virginia Magazine of History and Biography* 65 (July 1957), 275–300.

3. The many models, stereotypes, and images operative for the Indian in Anglo-American vernacular culture are discussed in my dissertation, "The Only Good Indian: The Image of the Indian in Vernacular American Culture," Indiana University, 1973.

4. E. McClung Fleming, "Symbols of the United States; From Indian Queen to Uncle Sam," in Ray B. Browne el al., eds. *The Frontiers of American Culture* (Lafayette, Indiana: Purdue University Press, 1967), 1–24; "The American Image as Indian Princess, 1765–1783," *Winderthur Portfolio* 2 (1968), 65–81.

5. For a summary of the philosophical backgrounds of the "Noble Savage" complex of beliefs and ideas, see Roy Harvey Pearce, *Savagism and Civilization: A Study of the Indian and the American Mind* (1953 rpt., Baltimore: Johns Hopkins University Press, 1967). For references to folk motifs in Indo-European tradition, see Stith Thompson. *The Motif Index of Folk Literature*, 6 vols. (rpt. 1932–1936, Bloomington: Indiana University Press, 1955–1958).

6. See Clare de Corbellier, "Miss America and Her Sisters: Personification of the Four Pans of the World," *Bulletin of the Metropolitan Museum of Art* 19 (1961), 209–23; James Hazen Hyde *L'Iconographic des quatre parties du monde dans les tapisseries de Gazette des Beaux Arts* (Paris: Beaux Arts, 1924).

7. Austin Fife and Francesca Redden. "The Pseudo-Indian Folksongs of the Anglo-Americans and French-Canadians," *Journal of American Folklore* 67, no. 266 (1954), 381; Olive Wooley Burt. *American Murder Ballads and Their Stories* (1958 rpt., New York: Citadel Press, 1964), 146–49.

8. Vine Deloria, *Custer Died For Your Sins* (New York: Avon Books, 1968), 11.

Chapter Nine

Yearning for Lightness

Transnational Circuits in the Marketing and Consumption of Skin Lighteners

Evelyn Nakano Glenn

With the breakdown of traditional racial categories in many areas of the world, colorism, by which I mean the preference for and privileging of lighter skin and discrimination against those with darker skin, remains a persisting frontier of intergroup and intragroup relations in the twenty-first century. Sociologists and anthropologists have documented discrimination against darker-skinned persons and correlations between skin tone and socioeconomic status and achievement in Brazil and the United States (Hunter 2005; Sheriff 2001; Telles 2004). Other researchers have revealed that people's judgments about other people are literally colored by skin tone, so that darker-skinned individuals are viewed as less intelligent, trustworthy, and attractive than their lighter-skinned counter-parts (Herring, Keith, and Horton 2003; Hunter 2005; Maddox 2004).

One way of conceptualizing skin color, then, is as a form of symbolic capital that affects, if not determines, one's life chances. The relation between skin color and judgments about attractiveness affect women most acutely, since women's worth is judged heavily on the basis of appearance. For example, men who have wealth, education, and other forms of human capital are considered "good catches," while women who are physically attractive may be considered desirable despite the lack of other capital. Although skin tone is usually seen as a form of fixed or unchangeable capital, in fact, men and women may attempt to acquire light-skinned privilege. Sometimes this search takes the form of seeking light-skinned marital partners to raise one's status and to achieve intergenerational mobility by increasing the likelihood of having light-skinned children. Often, especially for women, this search takes the form of using cosmetics or other treatments to change the appearance of one's skin to make it look lighter.

This article focuses on the practice of skin lightening, the marketing of skin lighteners in various societies around the world, and the multinational corporations that are involved in the global skin-lightening trade. An analysis of this complex topic calls for a multilevel approach. First, we need to place the production, marketing, and consumption of skin lighteners into a global political-economic context. I ask, How is skin lightening interwoven into the world economic system and its transnational circuits of products, capital, culture, and people? Second, we need to examine the mediating entities and processes by which skin lighteners teach specific national/ethnic/racial/class consumers. I ask, What are the media and messages, cultural themes and symbols, used to create the desire for skin-lightening products among partic-ular groups? Finally, we need to examine the meaning and significance of skin color for consumers of skin lighteners. I ask, How do consumers learn about, test, and compare skin-lightening products, and what do they seek to achieve through their use?

The issue of skin lightening may seem trivial at first glance. However, it is my contention that a close examination of the global circuits of skin lightening provides a unique lens through which to view the workings of the Western-dominated global system as it simultaneously promulgates a "white is right" ideology while also promoting the desire for and consumption of Western culture and products.

SKIN LIGHTENING AND GLOBAL CAPITAL

Skin lightening has long been practiced in many parts of the world. Women concocted their own treatments or purchased products from self-styled beau-ty experts offering special creams, soaps, or lotions, which were either inef-fective sham products or else effective but containing highly toxic materials such as mercury or lead. From the perspective of the supposedly enlightened present, skin lightening might be viewed as a form of vanity or a misguided and dangerous relic of the past.

However, at the beginning of the twenty-first century, the search for light skin, free of imperfections such as freckles and age spots, has actually accel-erated, and the market for skin-lightening products has mushroomed in all parts of the world. The production and marketing of products that offer the prospect of lighter, brighter, whiter skin has become a multi-billion-dollar global industry. Skin lightening has been incorporated into transnational flows of capital, goods, people, and culture. It is implicated in both the formal global economy and various informal economies. It is integrated into both legal and extralegal transnational circuits of goods. Certain large multi-national corporations have become major players, spending vast sums on research and development and on advertising and marketing to reach both mass and specialized markets. Simultaneously, actors in informal or under-ground economies, including smugglers, transnational migrants, and petty traders, are finding unprecedented opportunities in producing, transporting, and selling unregulated lightening products.

One reason for this complex multifaceted structure is that the market for skin lighteners, although global in scope, is also highly decentralized and segmented along socioeconomic, age, national, ethnic, racial, and cultural lines. Whether the manufacturers are multi-billion-dollar corporations or small entrepreneurs, they make separate product lines and use distinct mar-keting strategies to reach specific segments of consumers. Ethnic companies and entrepreneurs may be best positioned to draw on local cultural themes, but large multinationals can draw on local experts to tailor advertising im-ages and messages to appeal to particular audiences.

The Internet has become a major tool/highway/engine for the globalized, segmented, lightening market. It is the site where all of the players in the global lightening market meet. Large multinationals, small local firms, indi-vidual entrepreneurs, skin doctors, direct sales merchants, and even eBay sellers use the Internet to disseminate the ideal of light skin and to advertise and sell their products. Consumers go on the Internet to do research on products and shop. Some also participate in Internet message boards and forums to seek advice and to discuss, debate, and rate skin lighteners. There are many such forums, often as part of transnational ethnic Web sites. For example, IndiaParenting.com and sukh-dukh.com, designed for South Asians in India and other parts of the world, have chat rooms on skin care and lightening, and Rexinteractive.com, a Filipino site, and Candymag.com, a site sponsored by a magazine for Filipina teens, have extensive forums on skin lightening. The discussions on these forums provide a window through which to view the meaning of skin color to consumers, their desires and anxieties, doubts and aspirations. The Internet is thus an important site from which one can gain a multilevel perspective on skin lightening.

COMSUMER GROUPS AND MARKET NICHES

Africa and African Diaspora

In Southern Africa, colorism is just one of the negative inheritances of Euro-pean colonialism. The ideology of white supremacy that European colonists brought included the association of Blackness with primitiveness, lack of civilization, unrestrained sexuality, pollution, and dirt. The association of Blackness with dirt can be seen in a 1930 French advertising poster for Dirtoff. The poster shows a drawing of a dark African man washing his hands, which have become white, as he declares, "Le Savon Dirtoff me blanchit!" The soap was designed not for use by Africans but, as the poster notes, *pour mechanciens automobilises et menagers* —French auto mechanics and housewives. Such images showing Black people "dramatically losing their pigmentation as a result of the cleansing process," were common in late nineteenth- and early twentieth-century soap advertisements, according to art historian Jean Michel Massing (1995, 180).

Some historians and anthropologists have argued that precolonial African conceptions of female beauty favored women with light brown, yellow, or reddish tints. If so, the racial hierarchies established in areas colonized by Europeans cemented and generalized the privilege attached to light skin (Burke 1996; Ribane 2006, 12). In both South Africa and Rhodesia/Zimbabwe, an intermediate category of those considered to be racially mixed was classified as "coloured" and subjected to fewer legislative restrictions than those classified as "native." Assignment to the coloured category was based on ill-defined criteria, and on arrival in urban areas, people found themselves classified as native or coloured on the basis of skin tone and other phenotypic characteristics. Indians arriving in Rhodesia from Goa, for example, were variously classified as "Portuguese Mulatto" or coloured. The multiplication of discriminatory laws targeting natives led to a growing number of Blacks claiming to be coloured in both societies (Muzondidya 2005, 23–24).

The use of skin lighteners has a long history in Southern Africa, which is described by Lynn Thomas and which I will not recount here (in press). Rather, I will discuss the current picture, which shows both a rise in the consumption of skin-lightening products and concerted efforts to curtail the trade of such products. Despite bans on the importation of skin lighteners, the widespread use of these products currently constitutes a serious health issue in Southern Africa because the products often contain mercury, corticosteroids, or high doses of hydroquinone. Mercury of course is highly toxic, and sustained exposure can lead to neurological damage and kidney disease. Hydroquinone (originally an industrial chemical) is effective in suppressing melanin production, but exposure to the sun—hard to avoid in Africa— damages skin that has been treated. Furthermore, in dark-skinned people, long-term hydroquinone use can lead to ochronosis, a disfiguring condition involving gray and blue-black discoloration of the skin (Mahe, Ly, and Dangou 2003). The overuse of topical steroids can lead to contact eczema, bacterial and fungal infection, Cushing's syndrome, and skin atrophy (Margulies n.d.; Ntambwe 2004).

Perhaps the most disturbing fact is that mercury soaps used by Africans are manufactured in the European Union (EU), with Ireland and Italy leading in the production of mercury soap. One company that has been the target of activists is Killarney Enterprises, Ltd., in County Wicklow, Ireland. Formerly known as W&E Products and located in Lancashire, England, the company was forced to close following out-of-court settlements of suits filed by two former employers who had given birth to stillborn or severely malformed infants due to exposure to mercury. However, W&E Products then secured a 750,000-pound grant from the Irish Industrial Development Authority to relocate to Ireland, where it changed its name to Killarney Enterprises, Ltd. The company remained in business until April 17, 2007, producing soaps under the popular names Tura, Arut, Swan, Sukisa Bango, Meriko, and Jeraboo (which contained up to 3 percent mercuric iodide). Distribution of mercury soap has been illegal in the EU since 1989, but its manufacture has remained legal as long as the product is exported (Chadwick 2001; Earth Summit 2002, 13–14). These soaps are labeled for use as antiseptics and to prevent body odor; however, they are understood to be and are used as skin bleaches. To complete the circuit, EU-manufactured mercury soaps are smuggled back into the EU to sell in shops catering to African immigrant communities. An Irish journalist noted that the very same brands made by Killarney Enterprises, including Meriko and Tura (banned in both the EU and South Africa) could easily be found in African shops in Dublin (De Faoite 2001; O'Farrell 2002).

As a result of the serious health effects, medical researchers have conducted interview studies to determine how prevalent the practice of skin lightening is among African women. They estimate that 25 percent of women in Bamaki, Mali; 35 percent in Pretoria, South Africa; and 52 percent in Dakar, Senegal, use skin lighteners, as do an astonishing 77 percent of women traders in Lagos, Nigeria (Adebajo 2002; del Guidice and Yves 2002; Mahe, Ly, and Dangou 2003; Malangu and Ogubanjo 2006).

There have been local and transnational campaigns to stop the manufacture of products containing mercury in the EU and efforts to inform African consumers of the dangers of their use and to foster the idea of Black pride. Governments in South Africa, Zimbabwe, Nigeria, and Kenya have banned the import and sale of mercury and hydroquinone products, but they continue to be smuggled in from other African nations (Dooley 2001; Thomas 2004).

Despite these efforts, the use of skin lighteners has been increasing among modernized and cosmopolitan African women. A South African newspaper reported that whereas in the 1970s, typical skin lightener users in South Africa were rural and poor, currently, it is upwardly mobile Black women, those with technical diplomas or university degrees and well-paid jobs, who are driving the market in skin lighteners. A recent study by Mictert Marketing Research found that 1 in 13 upwardly mobile Black women aged

25 to 35 used skin lighteners. It is possible that this is an underestimation, since there is some shame attached to admitting to using skin lighteners (Ntshingila 2005).

These upwardly mobile women turn to expensive imported products from India and Europe rather than cheaper, locally made products. They also go to doctors to get prescriptions for imported lighteners containing corticosteroids, which are intended for short-term use to treat blemishes. They continue using them for long periods beyond the prescribed duration, thus risking damage (Ntshingila 2005). This recent rise in the use of skin lighteners cannot be seen as simply a legacy of colonialism but rather is a consequence of the penetration of multinational capital and Western consumer culture. The practice therefore is likely to continue to increase as the influence of these forces grows.

African America

Color consciousness in the African American community has generally been viewed as a legacy of slavery, under which mulattos, the offspring of white men and slave women, were accorded better treatment than "pure" Africans. While slave owners considered dark-skinned Africans suited to fieldwork, lighter-skinned mulattos were thought to be more intelligent and better suited for indoor work as servants and artisans. Mulattos were also more likely to receive at least rudimentary education and to be manumitted. They went on to form the nucleus of many nineteenth-century free Black communities. After the civil war, light-skinned mulattos tried to distance themselves from their darker-skinned brothers and sisters, forming exclusive civic and cultural organizations, fraternities, sororities, schools, and universities (Russell, Wilson, and Hall 1992, 24-40). According to Audrey Elisa Kerr, common folklore in the African American community holds that elite African Americans used a "paper bag" test to screen guests at social events and to determine eligibility for membership in their organizations: anyone whose skin was darker than the color of the bag was excluded. Although perhaps apocryphal, the widespread acceptance of the story as historical fact is significant. It has been credible to African Americans because it was consonant with their observations of the skin tone of elite African American society (Kerr 2005).

The preference and desire for light skin can also be detected in the long-time practice of skin lightening. References to African American women using powders and skin bleaches appeared in the Black press as early as the 1850s, according to historian Kathy Peiss. She notes that *American Magazine* criticized African Americans who tried to emulate white beauty standards: "Beautiful black and brown faces by application of rouge and lily white are made to assume unnatural tints, like the vivid hue of painted corpses" (Peiss 1998, 41). How common such practices were is unknown. However, by the

1880s and 1890s, dealers in skin bleaches were widely advertising their wares in the African American press. A Crane and Company ad in the *Colored American Magazine* (1903) promised that use of the company's "wonderful Face Bleach" would result in a "peach-like complexion" and "turn the skin of a black or brown person five or six shades lighter and of a mulatto person perfectly white" (Peiss 1998, 41, 42).

Throughout the twentieth century, many African American leaders spoke out against skin bleaching, as well as hair straightening, and the African American press published articles decrying these practices. However, such articles were far outnumbered by advertisements for skin bleaches in prominent outlets such as the *Crusader*, *Negro World*, and the *Chicago Defender*. An estimated 30 to 40 percent of advertisements in these outlets were for cosmetics and toiletries including skin bleaches. Many of the advertised lighteners were produced by white manufacturers; for example, Black and White Cream was made by Plough Chemicals (which later became Plough-Shearing), and Nadolina was made by the National Toilet Company. A chemical analysis of Nadolina Bleach conducted in 1930 found it contained 10 percent ammoniated mercury, a concentration high enough to pose a serious health risk. Both brands are still marketed in African American outlets, although with changed ingredients (Peiss 1998, 210, 212).[1]

The manufacture and marketing of Black beauty products, including skin lighteners, provided opportunities for Black entrepreneurs. Annie Turnbo Malone, who founded the Poro brand, and Sara Breedlove, later known as Madam C. J. Walker, who formulated and marketed the Wonder Hair Grower, were two of the most successful Black entrepreneurs of the late nineteenth and early twentieth centuries. Malone and Walker championed African American causes and were benefactors of various institutions (Peiss 1998, 67–70; see also Bundles 2001). Significantly, both refused to sell skin bleaches or to describe their hair care products as hair straighteners. After Walker died in 1919, her successor, F. B. Ransom, introduced Tan-Off, which became one of the company's best sellers in the 1920s and 1930s. Other Black-owned companies, such as Kashmir (which produced Nile Queen), Poro, Overton, and Dr. Palmer, advertised and sold skin lighteners. Unlike some white-produced products, they did not contain mercury but relied on such ingredients as borax and hydrogen peroxide (Peiss 1998, 205, 212, 213).

Currently, a plethora of brands is marketed especially to African Americans, including Black and White Cream, Nadolina (sans mercury), Ambi, Palmer's, DR Daggett and Remsdell (fade cream and facial brightening cream), Swiss Whitening Pills, Ultra Glow, Skin Success, Avre (which produces the Pallid Skin Lightening System and B-Lite Fade Cream), and Clear Essence (which targets women of color more generally). Some of these products contain hydroquinone, while others claim to use natural ingredients.

Discussions of skin lightening on African American Internet forums indicate that the participants seek not white skin but "light" skin like that of African American celebrities such as film actress Halle Berry and singer Beyonce Knowles. Most women say they want to be two or three shades lighter or to get rid of dark spots and freckles to even out their skin tones, something that many skin lighteners claim to do. Some of the writers believe that Halle Berry and other African American celebrities have achieved their luminescent appearance through skin bleaching, skillful use of cosmetics, and artful lighting. Thus, some skin-lightening products, such as the Pallid Skin Lightening System, purport to offer the "secret" of the stars. A Web site for Swiss Lightening Pills claims that "for many years Hollywood has been keeping the secret of whitening pills" and asks, rhetorically, "Have you wondered why early childhood photos of many top celebs show a much darker skin colour than they have now?"[2]

India and Indian Diaspora

As in the case of Africa, the origins of colorism in India are obscure, and the issue of whether there was a privileging of light skin in precolonial Indian societies is far from settled. Colonial-era and postcolonial Indian writings on the issue may themselves have been influenced by European notions of caste, culture, and race. Many of these writings expound on a racial distinction between lighter-skinned Aryans, who migrated into India from the North and darker-skinned "indigenous" Dravidians of the South. The wide range of skin color from North to South and the variation in skin tone within castes make it hard to correlate light skin with high caste. The most direct connection between skin color and social status could be found in the paler hue of those whose position and wealth enabled them to spend their lives sheltered indoors, compared to the darker hue of those who toiled outdoors in the sun (Khan 2008).

British racial concepts evolved over the course of its colonial history as colonial administrators and settlers attempted to make sense of the variety of cultural and language groups and to justify British rule in India. British observers attributed group differences variously to culture, language, climate, or biological race. However, they viewed the English as representing the highest culture and embodying the optimum physical type; they made invidious comparisons between lighter-skinned groups, whose men they viewed as more intelligent and marital and whose women they considered more attractive, and darker-skinned groups, whose men they viewed as lacking intelligence and masculinity, and whose women they considered to be lacking in beauty (Arnold 2004).

Regardless of the origins of color consciousness in India, the preference for light skin seems almost universal today, and in terms of sheer numbers, India and Indian diasporic communities around the world constitute the largest market for skin lighteners. The major consumers of these products in South Asian communities are women between the ages of 16 and 35. On transnational South Asian blog sites, women describing themselves as "dark" or "wheatish" in color state a desire to be "fair." Somewhat older women seek to reclaim their youthful skin color, describing themselves as having gotten darker over time. Younger women tend to be concerned about looking light to make a good marital match or to appear lighter for large family events, including their own weddings. These women recognize the reality that light skin constitutes valuable symbolic capital in the marriage market (Views on Article n.d.).

Contemporary notions of feminine beauty are shaped by the Indian mass media. Since the 1970s, beauty pageants such as Miss World-India have been exceedingly popular viewer spectacles; they are a source of nationalist pride since India has been highly successful in international pageants such as Miss World. As might be expected, the competitors, although varying in skin tone, tend to be lighter than average. The other main avatars of feminine allure are Bollywood actresses, such as Isha Koopikari and Aiswarya Rai, who also tend to be light skinned or, if slightly darker, green eyed (see http://www.indianindustry.com/herbalcosmetics/10275.htm).

Many Indian women use traditional homemade preparations made of plant and fruit products. On various blog sites for Indians both in South Asia and diasporic communities in North America, the Caribbean, and the United Kingdom, women seek advice about "natural" preparations and trade recipes. Many commercial products are made by Indian companies and marketed to Indians around the globe under such names as "fairness cream," "herbal bleach cream," "whitening cream," and "fairness cold cream." Many of these products claim to be based on ayurvedic medicine and contain herbal and fruit extracts such as saffron, papaya, almonds, and lentils (Runkle 2004).

With economic liberalization in 1991, the number of products available on the Indian market, including cosmetics and skin care products, has mushroomed. Whereas prior to 1991, Indian consumers had the choice of two brands of cold cream and moisturizers, today, they have scores of products from which to select. With deregulation of imports, the rise of the Indian economy, and growth of the urban middle class, multinational companies see India as a prime target for expansion, especially in the area of personal care products. The multinationals, through regional subsidiaries, have developed many whitening product lines in various price ranges that target markets ranging from rural villagers to white-collar urban dwellers and affluent professionals and managers (Runkle 2005).

Southeast Asia: The Philippines

Because of its history as a colonial dependency first of Spain and then of the United States, the Philippines has been particularly affected by Western ideology and culture, both of which valorize whiteness. Moreover, frequent intermarriage among indigenous populations, Spanish colonists, and Chinese settlers has resulted in a substantially mestizo population that ranges widely on the skin color spectrum. The business and political elites have tended to be disproportionately light skinned with visible Hispanic and/or Chinese appearance. In the contemporary period, economic integration has led to the collapse of traditional means of livelihood, resulting in large-scale emigration by both working-class and middle-class Filipinos to seek better-paying jobs in the Middle East, Asia, Europe, and North America. An estimated 10 million Filipinos were working abroad as of 2004, with more than a million departing each year. Because of the demand for domestic workers, nannies, and care workers in the global North, women make up more than half of those working abroad (Tabbada 2006). Many, if not most, of these migrants remit money and send Western consumer goods to their families in the Philippines. They also maintain transnational ties with their families at home and across the diaspora through print media, phone, and the Internet. All of these factors contribute to an interest in and fascination with Western consumer culture, including fashion and cosmetics in the Philippines and in Filipino diasporic communities (Parrenas 2001).

Perhaps not surprising, interest in skin lightening seems to be huge and growing in the Philippines, especially among younger urban women. Synovate, a market research firm, reported that in 2004, 50 percent of respondents in the Philippines reported currently using skin lightener (Synovate 2004). Young Filipinas participate in several Internet sites seeking advice on lightening products. They seek not only to lighten their skin overall but also to deal with dark underarms, elbows, and knees. Judging by their entries in Internet discussion sites, many teens are quite obsessed with finding "the secret" to lighter skin and have purchased and tried scores of different brands of creams and pills. They are disappointed to find that these products may have some temporary effects but do not lead to permanent change. They discuss products made in the Philippines but are most interested in products made by large European and American multinational cosmetic firms and Japanese and Korean companies. Clearly, these young Filipinas associate light skin with modernity and social mobility. Interesting to note, the young Filipinas do not refer to Americans or Europeans as having the most desirable skin color. They are more apt to look to Japanese and Koreans or to Spanish- or Chinese- appearing (and light-skinned) Filipina celebrities, such as Michelle Reis, Sharon Kuneta, or Claudine Baretto, as their ideals.[3]

The notion that Japanese and Korean women represent ideal Asian beauty has fostered a brisk market in skin lighteners that are formulated by Korean and Japanese companies. Asian White Skin and its sister company Yumei Misei, headquartered in Korea, sell Japanese and Korean skin care products in the Philippines both in retail outlets and online. Products include Asian-whiteskin Underarm Whitening Kit, Japanese Whitening Cream Enzyme Q-10, Japan Whitening Fruit Cream, Kang Han Sheep Placenta Whitening Capsules, and Kyusoku Bhaku Lightening Pills (see http://yumeimise.com/store/index).

East Asia: Japan, China, and Korea

East Asian societies have historically idealized light or even white skin for women. Intage (2001), a market research firm in Japan, puts it, "Japan has long idolized ivory-like skin that is 'like a boiled egg'—soft, white and smooth on the surface." Indeed, prior to the Meiji Period (starting in the 1860s), men and women of the higher classes wore white-lead powder make-up (along with blackened teeth and shaved eyebrows). With modernization, according to Mikiko Ashikari, men completely abandoned makeup, but middle- and upper-class women continued to wear traditional white-lead powder when dressed in formal kimonos for ceremonial occasion such as marriages, and adopted light-colored modern face powder to wear with Western clothes. Ashikari finds through observations of 777 women at several sites in Osaka during 1996–1997 that 97.4 percent of women in public wore what she calls "white face," that is, makeup that "makes their faces look whiter than they really are" (2003, 3).

Intage (2001) reports that skin care products, moisturizers, face masks, and skin lighteners account for 66 percent of the cosmetics market in Japan. A perusal of displays of Japanese cosmetics and skin care products shows that most, even those not explicitly stated to be whitening products, carry names that contain the word "white," for example, facial masks labeled "Clear Turn White" or "Pure White." In addition, numerous products are marketed specifically as whiteners. All of the leading Japanese firms in the cosmetics field, Shiseido, Kosa, Kanebo, and Pola, offer multiproduct skin-whitening lines, with names such as "White Lucent" and "Whitissimo." Fytokem, a Canadian company that produces ingredients used in skin-whitening products, reports that Japan's market in skin lighteners topped $5 billion in 1999 (Saskatchewan Business Unlimited 2005). With deregulation of imports, leading multinational firms, such as L'Oreal, have also made large inroads in the Japanese market. French products have a special cachet (Exhibitor Info 2006).

While the Japanese market has been the largest, its growth rate is much lower than those of Korea and China. Korea's cosmetic market has been growing at a 10 percent rate per year while that of China has been growing by 20 percent. Fytokem estimates that the market for skin whiteners in China was worth $1 billion in 2002 and was projected to grow tremendously. A 2007 Nielsen global survey found that 46 percent of Chinese, 47 percent of people in Hong Kong, 46 percent of Taiwanese, 29 percent of Koreans, and 24 percent of Japanese had used a skin lightener in the past year. As to regular users, 30 percent of Chinese, 20 percent of Taiwanese, 18 percent of Japanese and Hong Kongers, and 8 percent of Koreans used them weekly or daily. However, if money were no object, 52 percent of Koreans said they would spend more on skin lightening, compared to 26 percent of Chinese, 23 percent of Hong Kongers and Taiwanese, and 21 percent of Japanese (Nielsen 2007).

Latin America: Mexico and the Mexican Diaspora

Throughout Latin America, skin tone is a major marker of status and a form of symbolic capital, despite national ideologies of racial democracy. In some countries, such as Brazil, where there was African chattel slavery and extensive miscegenation, there is considerable color consciousness along with an elaborate vocabulary to refer to varying shades of skin. In other countries, such as Mexico, the main intermixture was between Spanish colonists and indigenous peoples, along with an unacknowledged admixture with African slaves. *Mestizaje* is the official national ideal. The Mexican concept of mestizaje meant that through racial and ethnic mix, Mexico would gradually be peopled by a whiter "cosmic race" that surpassed its initial ingredients. Nonetheless, skin tone, along with other phenotypical traits, is a significant marker of social status, with lightness signifying purity and beauty and darkness signifying contamination and ugliness (Stepan 1991, 135). The elite has remained overwhelmingly light skinned and European appearing while rural poor are predominantly dark skinned and Indigenous appearing.

Ethnographic studies of Mexican communities in Mexico City and Michoacan found residents to be highly color conscious, with darker-skinned family members likely to be ridiculed or teased. The first question that a relative often poses about a newborn is about his or her color (Farr 2006, chap. 5; Guttman 1996, 40; Martinez 2001). Thus, it should not be a surprise that individuals pursue various strategies to attain light-skinned identity and privilege. Migration from rural areas to the city or to the United States has been one route to transformation from an Indian to a mestizo identity or from a mestizo to a more cosmopolitan urban identity; another strategy has been lightening one's family line through marriage with a lighter-skinned partner. A third strategy has been to use lighteners to change the appearance of one's skin (Winders, Jones, and Higgins 2005, 77–78).

In one of the few references to skin whitening in Mexico, Alan Knight claims that it was "an ancient practice . . . reinforced by film, television, and advertising stereotypes" (1990, 100). As in Africa, consumers seeking low-cost lighteners can easily purchase mercury-laden creams that are still manufactured and used in parts of Latin America (e.g., Recetas de la Farmacia-Crema Blanqueadora, manufactured in the Dominican Republic, contains 6000 ppm of mercury) (NYC Health Dept 2005). The use of these products has come to public attention because of their use by Latino immigrants in the United States. Outbreaks of mercury poisoning have been reported in Texas, New Mexico, Arizona, and California among immigrants who used Mexican-manufactured creams such as Crema de Belleza-Manning. The cream is manufactured in Mexico by Laboratories Vide Natural S A de CV., Tampico, Tamaulipas, and is distributed primarily in Mexico. However, it has been found for sale in shops and flea markets in the United States in areas located along the U.S.-Mexican border in Arizona, California, New Mexico, and Texas. The label lists the ingredient calomel, which is mercurous chloride (a salt of mercury). Product samples have been found to contain 6 to 10 percent mercury by weight (Centers for Disease Control 1996; U.S. Food and Drug Administration 1996).

For high-end products, hydroquinone is the chemical of choice. White Secret is one of the most visible products since it is advertised in a 30-minute, late-night television infomercial that is broadcast nationally almost nightly.[4] Jamie Winders and colleagues (2005), who analyze the commercial, note that the commercial continually stresses that White Secret is "una formula Americana." According to Winders, Jones, and Higgins, the American pedigree and English-language name endow White Secret with a cosmopolitan cachet and "a first worldliness." The infomercial follows the daily lives of several young urban women, one of whom narrates and explains how White Secret cream forms a barrier against the darkening rays of the sun while a sister product transforms the color of the skin itself. The infomercial conjures the power of science, showing cross sections of skin cells. By showing women applying White Secret in modem, well-lit bathrooms, relaxing in well-appointed apartments, and protected from damaging effects of the sun while walking around the city, the program connects skin lightening with cleanliness, modernity, and mobility (Winders, Jones, and Higgins 2005, 80–84).

Large multinational firms are expanding the marketing of skin care products, including skin lighteners, in Mexico and other parts of Latin America. For example, Stiefel Laboratories, the world's largest privately held pharmaceutical company, which specializes in dermatology products, targets Latin

America for skin-lightening products. Six of its twenty-eight wholly owned subsidiaries are located in Latin America. It offers Clariderm, an over-the-counter hydroquinone cream and gel (2 percent), in Brazil, as well as Clasifel, a prescription-strength hydroquinone cream (4 percent), in Mexico, Peru, Bolivia, Venezuela, and other Latin American countries. It also sells Claripel, a 4 percent hydroquinone cream, in the United States.[5]

Middle-Aged and Older White Women in North America and Europe

Historically, at least in the United States, the vast majority of skin lightener users have been so-called white women. Throughout the nineteenth and early twentieth centuries, European American women, especially those of Southern and Eastern European origins, sought to achieve whiter and brighter skin through use of the many whitening powders and bleaches on the market. In 1930, J. Walter Thomson conducted a survey and found 232 brands of skin lighteners and bleaches for sale. Advertisements for these products appealed to the association of white skin with gentility, social mobility, Anglo-Saxon superiority, and youth. In large cities, such as New York and Chicago, some Jewish women used skin lighteners and hair straighteners produced by Black companies and frequented Black beauty parlors (Peiss 1998, 85, 149, 224).

By the mid-1920s, tanning became acceptable for white women, and in the 1930s and 1940s, it became a craze. A year-round tan came to symbolize high social status since it indicated that a person could afford to travel and spend time at tropical resorts and beaches. In addition, there was a fad for "exotic" Mediterranean and Latin types, with cosmetics designed to enhance "olive" complexions and brunette hair (Peiss 1998, 150–51, 148–49).

However, in the 1980s, as the damaging effects of overexposure to sun rays became known, skin lightening among whites reemerged as a major growth market. Part of this growth was fueled by the aging baby boom generation determined to stave off signs of aging. Many sought not only toned bodies and uplifted faces but also youthful skin—that is, smooth, unblemished, glowing skin without telltale age spots. Age spots are a form of hyperpigmentation that results from exposure to the sun over many years. The treatment is the same as that for overall dark skin: hydroquinone, along with skin peeling, exfoliants, and sunscreen.[6]

MULTINATIONAL COSMETIC AND PHARMACEUTICAL FIRMS AND THEIR TARGETING STRATEGIES

Although there are many small local manufacturers and merchants involved in the skin-lightening game, I want to focus on the giant multinationals, which are fueling the desire for light skin through their advertisement and marketing strategies. The accounts of the skin-lightening markets have shown that the desire for lighter skin and the use of skin bleaches is accelerating in places where modernization and the influence of Western capitalism and culture are most prominent. Multinational biotechnology, cosmetic, and pharmaceutical corporations have coalesced through mergers and acquisitions to create and market personal care products that blur the lines between cosmetics and pharmaceuticals. They have jumped into the field of skin lighteners and correctors, developing many product lines to advertise and sell in Europe, North America, South Asia, East and Southeast Asia, and the Middle East (Wong 2004).

Three of the largest corporations involved in developing the skin-light market are L'Oreal, Shiseido, and Unilever. The French-based L'Oreal, with €15.8 billion in sales in 2006, is the largest cosmetics company in the world. It consists of twenty-one major subsidiaries including Lancome; Vichy Laboratories; La Roche-Posay Laboratoire Pharmaceutique; Biotherm; Garnier, Giorgio Armani Perfumes; Maybelline, New York; Ralph Lauren Fragrances; Skinceuticals, Shu Uemura; Matrix; Redken; and SoftSheen Carlson. L'Oreal is also a 20 percent shareholder of SanofiSynthelabo, a major France-based pharmaceutical firm. Three L'Oreal subsidiaries produce the best-known skin-lightening lines marketed around the world (which are especially big in Asia): Lancome Blanc Expert with Melo-No Complex, La-Roche-Posay Mela-D White skin lightening daily lotion with a triple-action formula, and Vichy Biwhite, containing procystein and vitamin C.

A second major player in the skin-lightening market is Shiseido, the largest and best-known Japanese cosmetics firm, with net sales of $5.7 billion. Shiseido cosmetics are marketed in sixty-five countries and regions, and it operates factories in Europe, the Americas, and other Asian countries. The Shiseido Group, including affiliates, employs approximately 25,200 people around the globe. Its two main luxury lightening lines are White Lucent (for whitening) and White Lucency (for spots/aging). Each product line consists of seven or eight components, which the consumer is supposed to use as part of a complicated regimen involving applications of specific products several times a day.[7]

The third multinational corporation is Unilever, a diversified Anglo-Dutch company with an annual turnover of more than €40 billion and net profits of €5 billion in 2006 (Unilever 2006). It specializes in so-called fast-moving consumer goods in three areas: food (many familiar brands, including Hellman's Mayonnaise and Lipton Tea), home care (laundry detergents, etc.), and personal care, including deodorants, hair care, oral care, and skin care. Its most famous brand in the skin care line is Ponds, which sells cold creams in Europe and North America and whitening creams in Asia, the Middle East, and Latin America.

Through its Indian subsidiary, Hindustan Lever Limited, Unilever patented Fair & Lovely in 1971 following the patenting of niacinamide, a melanin suppressor, which is its main active ingredient. Test marketed in South India in 1975, it became available throughout India in 1978. Fair & Lovely has become the largest-selling skin cream in India, accounting for 80 percent of the fairness cream market. According to anthropologist Susan Runkle (2005), "Fair and Lovely has an estimated sixty million consumers throughout the Indian subcontinent and exports to thirty four countries in Southeast and Central Asia as well as the Middle East."

Fair & Lovely ads claim that "with regular daily use, you will be able to unveil your natural radiant fairness in just 6 weeks!" As with other successful brands, Fair & Lovely has periodically added new lines to appeal to special markets. In 2003, it introduced Fair & Lovely, Ayurvedic, which claims to be formulated according to a 4,500-year-old Indian medical system. In 2004, it introduced Fair & Lovely Oil-Control Gel and Fair & Lovely Anti-Marks. In 2004, Fair & Lovely also announced the "unveiling" of a premium line, Perfect Radiance, "a complete range of 12 premium skin care solutions" containing "international formulations from Unilever's Global Skin Technology Center, combined with ingredients best suited for Indian skin types and climates." Its ads say "Experience Perfect Radiance from Fair & Lovely. Unveil Perfect Skin." Intended to compete with expensive European brands, Perfect Radiance is sold only in select stores in major cities, including Delhi, Mumbai, Chennai, and Bangalore.[8]

Unilever is known for promoting its brands by being active and visible in the locales where they are marketed. In India, Ponds sponsors the Femina Miss India pageant, in which aspiring contestants are urged to "be as beautiful as you can be." Judging by photos of past winners, being as beautiful as you can be means being as light as you can be. In 2003, partly in response to criticism by the All India Democratic Women's Association of "racist" advertisement of fairness products, Hindustani Lever launched the Fair and Lovely Foundation, whose mission is to "encourage economic empowerment of women across India" through educational and guidance programs, training courses, and scholarships.[9]

Unilever heavily promotes both Ponds and Fair & Lovely with television and print ads tailored to local cultures. In one commercial shown in India, a young, dark-skinned woman's father laments that he has no son to provide for him and his daughter's salary is not high enough. The suggestion is that she could neither get a better job nor marry because of her dark skin. The young woman then uses Fair & Lovely, becomes fairer, and lands a job as an airline hostess, making her father happy. A Malaysian television spot shows a college student who is dejected because she cannot get the attention of a classmate at the next desk. After using Pond's lightening moisturizer, she appears in class brightly lit and several shades lighter, and the boy says, "Why didn't I notice her before?" (BBC 2003).

Such advertisements can be seen as not simply responding to a preexisting need but actually creating a need by depicting having dark skin as a painful and depressing experience. Before "unveiling" their fairness, dark-skinned women are shown as unhappy, suffering from low self-esteem, ignored by young men, and denigrated by their parents. By using Fair & Lovely or Ponds, a woman undergoes a transformation of not only her complexion but also her personality and her fate. In short, dark skin becomes a burden and handicap that can be overcome only by using the product being advertised.

CONCLUSION

The yearning for lightness evident in the widespread and growing use of skin bleaching around the globe can rightfully be seen as a legacy of colonialism, a manifestation of "false consciousness," and the internalization of "white is right" values by people of color, especially women. Thus, one often-proposed solution to the problem is reeducation that stresses the diversity of types of beauty and desirability and that valorizes darker skin shades, so that lightness/whiteness is dislodged as the dominant standard.

While such efforts are needed, focusing only on individual consciousness and motives distracts attention from the very powerful economic forces that help to create the yearning for lightness and that offer to fulfill the yearning at a steep price. The manufacturing, advertising, and selling of skin lightening is no longer a marginal, underground economic activity. It has become a major growth market for giant multinational corporations with their sophisticated means of creating and manipulating needs.

The multinationals produce separate product lines that appeal to different target audiences. For some lines of products, the corporations harness the prestige of science by showing cross-sectional diagrams of skin cells and by displaying images of doctors in white coats. Dark skin or dark spots become a disease for which skin lighteners offer a cure. For other lines, designed to appeal to those who respond to appeals to naturalness, corporations call up nature by emphasizing the use of plant extracts and by displaying images of light-skinned women against a background of blue skies and fields of flowers. Dark skin becomes a veil that hides one's natural luminescence, which natural skin lighteners will uncover. For all products, dark skin is associated with pain, rejection, and limited options; achieving light skin is seen as necessary to being youthful, attractive, modern, and affluent—in short, to being "all that you can be."

NOTES

1. Under pressure from African American critics, Nadolina reduced the content to 6 percent in 1937 and 1.5 percent in 1941.
2. Discussions on Bright Skin Forum, Skin Lightening Board, are at http://excoboard.com/exco/forum.php?forumid=65288. Pallid Skin Lightening system information is at http://www.avreskincare.com/skin/pallid/index.html. Advertisement for Swiss Whitening Pills is at http://www.skinbleaching.net.
3. Skin whitening forums are at http://www.candymag.com/teentalk/index.php/topic,131753.0.html and http://www.rexinteractive.com/forum/topic.asp7TOPIC_ID=41.
4. Discussion of the ingredients in White Secret is found at http://www.vsantivirus.com/hoax-white-secret.htm.
5. I say that Stiefel targets Latin America because it markets other dermatology products, but not skin lighteners, in the competitive Asian, Middle Eastern, African, and European countries. Information about Stiefel products is at its corporate Web site, http://www.stiefel.coin/why/about.aspx (accessed May 1, 2007).
6. Many of the products used by older white and Asian women to deal with age spots are physician-prescribed pharmaceuticals, including prescription-strength hydroquinone formulas. See information on one widely used system, Obagi, at http://www.obagi.com/article/homepage.html (accessed December 13, 2006).
7. *Shiseido Annual Report 2006*, 34, was downloaded from http://www.shiseido.co.jp/e/annual/html/index.htm. Data on European, American, and Japanese markets are at http://www.shiseido.co.jp/e/story/html/sto40200.htm. World employment figures are at http://www.shiseido.co.jp/e/story/html/sto40200.htm. White Lucent information is at http://www.shiseido.co.jp/eAvhitelucent_us/products/product5.htm. White Lucency information is at http://www.shiseido.co.jp/e/whitelucency/(all accessed May 6, 2007).
8. "Fair & Lovely Launches Oil-Control Fairness Gel" (Press Release, April 27, 2004) is found at http://www.hll.com/mediacentre/release.asp?fl=2004/PR_HLL_042704.htm (accessed May 6, 2007). "Fair & Lovely Unveils Premium Range" (Press Release, May 25, 2004) is available at http://www.hU.com/mediacentre/release.asp?fl=2004/PR_HLL_052104_2Jitm (accessed on May 6, 2007).
9. The Pond's Femina Miss World ad is at http://feminamissindia.iiKlialimes.com/articleshow/1375041.cms. The All India Democratic Women's Association objects to skin lightening ad is at http://www.aidwa.org/content/issues_of_concern/women_and_media.php. Reference to Fair & Lovely campaign is at http://www.aidwa.org/content/issues_of_concern/women_and_media.php. "Fair & Lovely Launches Foundation to Promote Economic Empowerment of Women" (Press Release, March 11, 2003) is found at http://www.hlLcom/mediacentre/release.asp?fl=2003/PR_HLL_031103.htm (all accessed December 2, 2006).

REFERENCES

Adebajo, S. B. 2002. An epidemiological survey of the use of cosmetic skin lightening cosmetics among traders in Lagos, Nigeria. *West African Journal of Medicine* 21 (1): 51–55.

Arnold, David. 2004. Race, place and bodily difference in early nineteenth century India. *Historical Research* 77:162.

Ashikari, Makiko. 2003. Urban middle-class Japanese women and their white faces: Gender, ideology, and representation. *Ethos* 31 (1): 3, 3–4, 9–11.

BBC. 2003. India debates "racist" skin cream ads. *BBC News World Edition*, July 24. http://news.bbc.co.Uk/l/hi/world/south_asia/3089495.stm (accessed May 8, 2007).

Bundles, A'Lelia. 2001. *On her own ground: The life and times of Madam C. J. Walker*. New York: Scribner.

Burke, Timothy. 1996. *Lifebuoy men, lux women: Commodification, consumption, and cleanliness in modem Zimbabwe*. Durham, NC: Duke University Press.

Centers for Disease Control and Prevention. 1996. *FDA warns consumers not to use Crema De Belleza*. FDA statement. Rockville, MD: U.S. Food and Drug Administration.

Chadwick, Julia. 2001. Arklow's toxic soap factory. *Wicklow Today*, June. http://www.wicklowtoday.com/fealures/mercurysoap.htm (accessed April 18, 2007).

De Faoite, Dara. 2001. Investigation into the sale of dangerous mercury soaps in ethnic shops. *The Observer*, May 27. http://observer.guardian.co.uk/uk_news/story/0,6903,497227,00.html (accessed May 1, 2007).

del Guidice, P., and P Yves. 2002. The widespread use of skin lightening creams in Senegal: A persistent public health problem in West Africa. *International Journal of Dermatology* 41:69–72.

Dooley, Erin. 2001. Sickening soap trade. *Environmental Health Perspectives*, October.

Earth Summit. 2002. *Telling it like it is: 10 years of unsustainable development in Ireland*. Dublin, Ireland: Earth Summit.

Exhibitor Info. 2006. http://www.beautyworldjapan.com/en/efirst.html (accessed May 8, 2007).

Farr, Marcia. 2006. *Rancheros in Chicagocan: Language and identity in a transnational community*. Austin: University of Texas Press.

Guttman, Matthew C. 1996. *The meanings of macho: Being a man in Mexico City*. Berkeley: University of California Press.

Herring, Cedric, Verna M. Keith, and Hayward Derrick Horton, eds. 2003. *Skin deep: How race and complexion matter in the "color blind" era*. Chicago: Institute for Research on Race and Public Policy.

Hunter, Margaret 2005. *Race, gender, and the politics of skin tone*. New York: Routledge.

Intage. 2001. Intelligence on the cosmetic market in Japan, http://www.intage.co.jp/expess/01_08/market/index1.html (accessed November 2005).

Kerr, Audrey Elisa. 2005. The paper bag principle: The myth and the motion of colorism. *Journal of American Folklore* 118: 271–89.

Khan, Aisha. 2008. "Caucasian," "coolie," "Black," or "white"? Color and race in the Indo-Caribbean Diaspora. Unpublished paper.

Knight, Alan. 1990. Racism, revolution, and indigenismo: Mexico, 1910–1940. In *The idea of race in Latin America, 1870–1940*, edited by Richard Graham. Austin: University of Texas Press.

Maddox, Keith B. 2004. Perspectives on racial phenotypicality bias. *Personality and Social Psychology Review* 8:383–401.

Mahe, Antoine, Fatimata Ly, and Jean-Marie Dangou. 2003. Skin diseases associated with the cosmetic use of bleaching products in women from Dakar, Senegal. *British Journal of Dermatology* 148 (3): 493–500.

Malangu, N., and G. A. Ogubanjo. 2006. Predictors of tropical steroid misuse among patrons of pharmacies in Pretoria. *South African Family Practices* 48 (1): 14.

Margulies, Paul. n.d. Cushing's syndrome: The facts you need to know. http://www.nadf.us/diseases/cushingsmedhelp.org/www/nadf4.htm (accessed May 1, 2007).

Martinez, Ruben. 2001. *Crossing over: A Mexican family on the migrant trail*. New York: Henry Holt.

Massing, Jean Michel. 1995. From Greek proverb to soap advert: Washing the Ethiopian. *Journal of the Warburg and Courtauld Institutes* 58:180.

Muzondidya, James. 2005. *Walking a tightrope, towards a social history of the coloured community of Zimbabwe.* Trenton, NJ: Africa World Press.

Nielsen. 2007. Prairie plants take root In *Health, beauty & personal grooming: A global Nielsen consumer report,* http://www.acnielsen.co.in/news/20070402.shtml (accessed May 3,2007).

Ntambwe, Malangu. 2004. Mirror on the wall, who is the fairest of them all? *Science in Africa, Africa's First On-Line Science Magazine,* March. http://www.scienceinafrica.co.za/2004/march/skinUghtening.htm (accessed May 1, 2007).

Ntshingila, Futhi. 2005. Female buppies using harmful skin lighteners. *Sunday Times, South Africa,* November 27. http://www.sundaytimes.co.za (accessed January 25, 2006).

NYC Health Dept 2005. NYC Health Dept warns against use of "skin lightening" creams containing mercury or similar products which do not list ingredients. http://www.nyc.gov/htmydoh/html/pr/pr008-Q5.shtini (accessed May 7, 2007).

O'Farrell, Michael. 2002. Pressure mounts to have soap plant shut down. *Irish Examiner,* August 26. http://archives.tcm.ie/irishexaminer/2002/08/26/story510455503.asp (accessed May 1, 2007).

Parrenas, Rhacel. 2001. *Servants of globalization: Women, migration, and domestic work.* Palo Alto, CA: Stanford University Press.

Peiss, Kathy. 1998. *Hope in a jar: The making of America's beauty culture.* New York: Metropolitan Books.

Ribane, Nakedi. 2006. *Beauty: A Black perspective.* Durban, South Africa: University of Kwa-Zulu-Natal Press.

Runkle, Susan. 2004. Making "Miss India": Constructing gender, power and nation. *South Asian Popular Culture* 2 (2): 145–59.

———. 2005. The beauty obsession. *Manushi* 145 (February). http://www.indiatogether.org/manushi/issuel45/lovelyJitm (accessed May 5, 2007).

Russell, Kathy, Midge Wilson, and Ronald Hall. 1992. *The color complex: The politics of skin color among African Americans.* New York: Harcourt Brace Jankovich.

Saskatchewan Business Unlimited. 2005. Prairie plants take root in cosmetics industry. *Saskatchewan Business Unlimited* 10 (1): 1–2.

Sheriff, Robin E. 2001. *Dreaming equality: Color, race and racism in urban Brazil.* New Brunswick, NJ: Rutgers University Press.

Stepan, Nancy Ley. 1991. *The hour of eugenics: Race, gender, and nation in Latin America.* Ithaca, NY: Cornell University Press.

Synovate. 2004. In:fact. http://www.synovate.com/knowledge/infact/issues/200406 (accessed March 21, 2007).

Tabbada, Reyna Mae L. 2006. Trouble in paradise. Press release, September 20. http://www.bulatlat.com/news/6-33/6-33-trouble.htm (accessed May 5, 2007).

Telles, Edward E. 2004. *Race in another America: The significance of skin color in Brazil.* Princeton, NJ: Princeton University Press.

Thomas, Iyamide. 2004. "Yellow fever": The disease that is skin bleaching. *Mano Vision* 33 (October): 32–33. http://www.manovision.com/ISSUES/ISSUE33/33skin.pdf (accessed May 7, 2007).

Thomas, Lynn M. (in press.) Skin lighteners in South Africa: Transnational entangle and technologies of the self. In *Shades of difference: Why skin color matters,* edited by Evelyn Nakano Glenn. Stanford, CA: Stanford University Press.

Unilever. 2006. Annual report. http://www.unilever.com/ourconnpany/investorcentre/annual_reports/archives.asp (accessed May 6, 2007).

U.S. Food and Drug Administration. 1996. *FDA warns consumers not to use Crema De Belleza.* FDA statement, July 23. Rockville, MD: U.S. Food and Drug Administration.

Views on article—Complextion. n.d. http://www.indiaparenting.com/beauty/beauty041bookshtml (accessed November 2005).

Winders, Jamie, John Paul Jones III, and Michael James Higgins. 2005. Making gueras: Selling white identities on late-night Mexican television. *Gender, Place and Culture* 12 (1): 71–93.

Wong, Stephanie. 2004. Whitening cream sales soar as Asia's skin-deep beauties shun Western suntans. *Manila Bulletin,* http://www.mb.com.ph/issues/2004/08/24/SCTY2004082416969 .html# (accessed March 24, 2007).

Part III

Music

What Key?

Chapter Ten

Bad Sistas

Black Women Rappers and Sexual Politics in Rap Music

Tricia Rose

Black women rappers interpret and articulate the fears, pleasures, and promises of young black women whose voices have been relegated to the margins of public discourse. They are integral and resistant voices in rap music and in popular music in general who sustain an ongoing dialogue with their audiences and with male rappers about sexual promiscuity, emotional commitment, infidelity, the drug trade, racial politics, and black cultural history. By paying close attention to female rappers, we can gain some insight into how young African-American women provide for themselves a relatively safe free-play zone where they creatively address questions of sexual power, the reality of truncated economic opportunity, and the pain of racism and sexism. Like their male counterparts, they are predominantly resistant voices that at times voice ideas that are in sync with elements of dominant discourses. Where they differ from male rappers, however, is in their thematic focus. Although male rappers' social criticism often contests police harassment and other means by which black men are "policed," black women rappers' central contestation is in the arena of sexual politics.

Female rappers have been uniformly touted as sexually progressive, anti-sexist voices in rap music. Given the prominence and strength of these black women's voices in the popular terrain, it is not surprising that they have been heralded as rap's politically correct underdogs.[1] Their media status as anti-sexist rappers is necessarily accompanied by an understanding of male rappers as uniformly sexist. This opposition between male and female rappers serves to produce imaginary clarity in the realm of rap's sexual politics, rather than confront its contradictory nature.

The complexity of male and female sexual narratives rarely, if ever, finds its way into discussions of sexism or feminism in rap. In the case of critical writing on male rappers, nonsexist and pro-women commentary about women and gender are virtually nonexistent. Instead, discussions of sexual references in male rappers' work are limited to considerations of the nature of rap's sexism. Similarly, critical commentary on female rappers rarely confronts the ways in which some of their work affirms patriarchal family norms and courtship rituals.

Repositioning women rappers as part of a dialogic process with male rappers (and others), rather than in complete opposition to them, I want to consider the ways black women rappers work within and against dominant sexual and racial narratives in American culture. For example, some female rappers affirm aspects of sexual power relationships as they raise incisive questions that seriously challenge the current distribution of power between men and women. Works by black women rappers that place black women's bodies in the spotlight have a similarly contradictory effect; they affirm black female beauty and yet often preserve the logic of female sexual objectification.

Three central themes predominate in the works of black female rappers: heterosexual courtship, the importance of the female voice, and mastery in women's rap and black female public displays of physical and sexual freedom. Here, these themes are contextualized in two ways; first, in dialogue with male rappers' sexual discourses, and then in dialogue with larger social discourses, including feminism. Clearly, female rappers are at least indirectly responding to male rappers' sexist constructions of black women. However, female rappers' sexual discourse is not simply part of a dialogue with male rappers but also responds to a variety of related issues, including dominant notions of femininity, feminism, and black female sexuality. At the very least, black women rappers are in dialogue with one another, black men, black women, and dominant American culture as they struggle to define themselves against a confining and treacherous social environment.

The concept of dialogue, exchange, and multidirectional communication is a useful way to understand the contradictory aspects and partiality of means of communication in popular music and cultural expression. In his application of Russian philosopher and literary critic Mikhail Bakhtin's concept of dialogism to popular music, George Lipsitz argues that: "Popular music is nothing if not dialogic, the product of an ongoing historical conversation in which no one has the first or last word. The traces of the past that pervade the popular music of the present amount to more than mere chance: they are not simply juxtapositions of incompatible realities. They reflect a dialogic process, one embedded in collective history and nurtured by the ingenuity of artists interested in fashioning icons of opposition."[2] Lipsitz's interpretation of popular music as a social and historical dialogue is an extremely important break from traditional, formalist interpretations of music. By grounding cultural production historically and avoiding the application of a fixed inventory of core structures, Lipsitz in his use of dialogic criticism is concerned with how popular music "arbitrates tensions between opposition and co-optation at any given historical moment." Linking popular musical discourses to the social world, Lipsitz's use of dialogic criticism in popular music shares a number of similarities with James Scott's interpretation of the hidden and public transcripts in rituals, gossips, folktales, and other popular practices. Both approaches examine power relationships as they are acted out, resisted, and affirmed in popular practices, and each understands that popular practices enter into and revise dialogues already in progress.[3]

Lipsitz's use of dialogic criticism is especially productive in the context of black women rappers. Negotiating multiple social boundaries and identities, black women rappers are in dialogue with one another, with male rappers, with other popular musicians (through sampling and other revisionary practices), with black women fans, and with hip hop fans in general. Dialogism resists the one-dimensional opposition between male and female rappers as respectively sexist and feminist. It also accommodates the tension between sympathetic racial bonds among black men and women as well as black women's frustration regarding sexual oppression at the hands of black men. As Cornel West aptly describes it, "the pressure on Afro-Americans as a people has forced the black man closer to the black woman: they are in the same boat. But they are also at each other's throat. The relation is internally hierarchical and often mediated by violence: black men over black women."[4] In addition, dialogism allows us to ground apparent inconsistencies and contradictions in rap's sexual politics within the complexity and contradictions of everyday life and protest, and it also allows us to make sense of the contradictory modes of resistance in women rappers' work.

Unfortunately, most discussions of rap's sexual politics and black women rappers do not account for these real-life complexities. Instead, discussions of women rappers can be divided into two related positions: (1) women rappers are feminist voices who combat sexism in rap; and/or (2) the sexist exclusion or mischaracterization of women's participation in rap music devalues women's significance and must be countered by evidence of women's contributions. In the former position, female rap are lyrics are frequently offered as indirect critiques of infamous such works as those of the 2 Live Crew, Geto Boys, NWA, and others. In this battle between the sexes, male rappers are constructed as sexist and female rappers are constructed as feminist or womanist.[5] For example, Michelle Wallace's *New York Times* article, "When Black Feminism Faces the Music and the Music is Rap," concludes with a call for dialogue between male and female rappers regarding sex and sexism; yet the bulk of the piece, in fact, describes male rapper's references to sex as displaying "little regard for the humanity of the black woman" and positions female rappers in opposition to these male rappers.[6]

There are at least two problems with the monolith of male sexism and women rapper's opposition to it. First, and most obviously, it places female rappers in a totalizing oppositional relationship to male rappers. This is not to say that women rappers do not directly criticize sexist male rap lyrics, but their relationship to male rappers cannot be characterized as one of complete opposition. For example, during the height of the 2 Live Crew controversy over obscenity in popular music, a number of prominent female rappers were asked to comment on 2 Live Crew and the sexist content of their lyrics. I only observed Salt from Salt 'N' Pepa speaking out against 2 Live Crew, and she did so in terms that resembled familiar black nationalist calls for "respecting" black women, rather than calling for an end to sexism. MC Lyte, Queen Latifah, Sister Souljah, and Yo-Yo refused to criticize their male colleagues—not necessarily because they did not find the lyrics offensive, but because they were acutely aware of the dominant discursive context within which their responses would be reproduced. Cognizant that they were being constructed in the mainstream press as a progressive response to regressive male rappers, these female rappers felt that they were being used as a political baton to beat male rappers over the head, rather than being affirmed as women who could open up public dialogue to interrogate sexism and its effects on young black women. Furthermore, they remain acutely aware of the uneven and sometimes racist way in which sexist offenses are prosecuted, stigmatized, and reported. And so, in several public contexts, women rappers defended male rappers' freedom of speech and focused their answers on the question of censorship rather than on sexism in rap lyrics.[7] This is not to say that their evasive tactics are not problematic in so far as they may implicitly sanction verbal attacks on women in rap. My point here is that women rappers cannot be situated in total opposition to male rappers; they support and critique male rappers' sexual discourse in a number of contradictory ways.[8]

Second, this way of thinking cannot account for the complexity and contradictory nature of the sexual dialogues in rap, not only those taking place between male and female rappers but also within male sexual themes and within female sexual themes in rap: male rappers' sexual discourse is not consistently sexist, and female sexual discourse is not consistently feminist. Not only do women rappers defend male rappers' sexist speech in a larger society that seems to attack black men disproportionately, but their lyrics sometimes affirm patriarchal notions about family life and the traditional roles of husbands, fathers, and lovers. Similarly, there are many lyrics in male rappers' work that not only chastise men for abusing women but also call for male responsibility in childrearing and support the centrality of black women in black cultural life. For example, several male rappers' works take an explicit stand against sexual violence toward women. De La Soul's "Millie Pulled a Pistol on Santa" is a brilliant and poignant story about a young girl whose father's sexual abuse of her and her inability to convince adults of his crime drives her to kill him. A Tribe Called Quest's "Description of a Fool" defines a fool as, among other things, a man who hits a woman; and Tribe's "Date Rape" takes a decidedly pro-woman position about the coercive power men have in date rape situations. Some examples are not so easily positioned as progressive or regressive. In a single lyrical stanza in Tim Dog's "Fuck Compton," Tim Dog criticizes and chastises NWA producer Dr. Dre for his cowardly real-life physical abuse of female rapper and video host Dee Barnes; yet, a few phrases later he solidifies his power over Dr. Dre by bragging about how he "fucked" Dr. Dre's girlfriend behind his back. Gangster rapper Ice Cube calls for killing police officers and then turns his rage on black women, calling for slaying "bitches" in the same phrase. Cube's lyrics suggest that state authority figures and black women are similarly responsible for black male disempowerment and oppression. Similar contradictions appear in women rappers' work. Yo-Yo's "Don't Play with My Yo-Yo" features Ice Cube repeating the song's title as part of the chorus, a move that allows Yo-Yo to be possessed by Ice Cube, albeit as a way to protect her from enemies and unwanted male advances. Salt 'N' Pepa's "Independent" attacks a man whose weakness is a product of his incapacity to provide material possessions and his limited economic means, a move that sustains the link between masculinity and economic privilege. In a number of raps by women, men who are being insulted are referred to as "fruity" or "punks," hinting at their possible homosexuality as a way to emasculate them. This sort of homophobia affirms oppressive standards of heterosexual masculinity and problematizes a simplistic reading of female rappers' sexual narratives.[9]

The second approach to black women rappers and rap's sexual politics, the sexist exclusion or mischaracterization of black women's participation in rap music, has two faces. Either analyses of rap are aggressively masculine and render women rappers invisible, or black female contributions are rightfully and extensively presented to counter previous deletions. A subtle but important example of the former is Houston Baker's "Hybridity, the Rap Race and Pedagogy for the 1990s," in which Baker explains rap's emergence as, in part, a "resentment of disco culture and a reassertion of black manhood." To define rap's emergence as a reassertion of black manhood not only affirms the equation of male heterosexuality with manhood, but also renders sustained and substantial female pleasure and participation in hip hop invisible or impossible. The centrality of heterosexual male pleasure and identity in his construction is not the problem; it is, instead, his formulation of male pleasure in rap coupled with the total absence of women at the conceptual level that render his analysis incorrect and problematic. [10]

Nelson George's 1989 ten-year anniversary tribute to rap is a much more explicit case of what I call the "what women?" syndrome. In honor of rap's birthday in the recording industry, George, a black music historian and pro–hip hop music critic, published a sentimental rap retrospective in which he mourned rap's movement from a street subculture into the cold, sterile world of commercial record production. [11] George pointed out that, until recently, music industry powers have maintained a studied indifference to rap music. And now that rap's "commercial viability has been proven," many major recording companies are signing any halfway decent act they can find.

What worries George is that corporate influence on black music has led, in the past, to the dissolution of vibrant black cultural forms and that rap may become the latest victim. The problem is complex, real, and requires analysis. However, Nelson George and media critics generally embed their descriptions of "authentic rap" and fears of recent corporate influence on it in gender-coded discourse that mischaracterizes rap and silences women rappers and consumers. In his tenth-anniversary piece, George traces major shifts in rap, naming titles, artists, and producers. He weaves over twenty rap groups into his piece and names not a single female rapper. His retrospective is chockfull of prideful urban black youths (read men) whose contributions to rap reflect "the thoughts of city kids more deeply than the likes of Michael Jackson, Oprah Winfrey et al." His concluding remarks make apparent his underlying perception of rap: "To proclaim the death of rap is to be sure, premature." But the farther the control of rap gets from its street corner constituency and the more corporations grasp it—record conglomerates, Burger King, Minute Maid, Yo MTV Raps, etc.—the more vulnerable it becomes to cultural emasculation." For George, corporate meddling not only dilutes cultural forms, but also it reduces strapping, testosterone-packed men into women! Could we imagine anything worse? Nelson George's concluding remarks are extreme but not unusual; his is but one example of media critics' consistent coding of rap music as male in the face of a significant and sustained female presence. Furthermore, George's mindboggling, yet emblematic, definition of rap as a "ultra-urban, unromantic, hyperrealistic, neonationalist, antiassimilationist, aggressive Afrocentric impulse," not only simplifies the complexity of masculinity, but his definition is also designed to conjure only a heterosexual masculine subject without drawing critical attention toward *how* black male heterosexuality is socially constructed. For George, and for media critics in general, it is far easier to regender women rappers than it is to revise their own masculinist analysis of rap music. My immediate reaction to this article took the form of a letter to the editor of the

Village Voice, which was published with the name tag "Lady Complainer," a petty and sexist attempt to devalue my criticism while retaining the appearance of being committed to open critique and dialogue. . . .

Many of the articles that have attempted to address the deletion of women in rap have been written by women and offer feminist analyses of the contributions of women to hip hop. [12] As several of these writers point out, the marginalization, deletion, and mischaracterization of women's role in black cultural production is routine practice. Nancy Guevara charges that the "exclusion and/or trivialization of women's role in hip hop" is no mere oversight. In response to these exclusions, Guevara's "Women Writin', Rappin' and Breakin'" documents black and Latino female participation in hip hop from the earliest stages in the mid-1970s and it articulates the ways in which young women were discouraged from participating in hip hop youth culture. [13]

Two essays began to draw on the dialogic aspects of popular music via an exploration of the nature and character of black women's popular musical production in relationship to black culture and to larger cultural discourses. In her article, "Black Women and Music: A Historical Legacy of Struggle," Angela Davis puts forth three related arguments of particular importance. First, she challenges the marginal representation of black women in the documentation of African-American cultural developments and suggests that these representations do not adequately reflect women's participation. Second, she notes that music, song, and dance are especially rich places to look for the collective consciousness of black Americans. And third, she calls for a close reexamination of black woman's musical legacy as a way to understand black women's consciousness. She writes: "Music has long permeated the daily life of most African-Americans; it has played a central role in the normal socialization process; and during moments characterized by intense movements for social change, it has helped to shape the necessary political consciousness. Any attempt, therefore, to understand in depth the evolution of women's consciousness within the Black community requires a serious examination of the music which has influenced them—particularly that which they themselves have created. [14] Davis's argument is important, because it links black music to black politics; more important, it links black music to black women's racial, sexual, and political identities. Davis's approach identifies black music as a critical factor in the fashioning of a black collective consciousness—to which Lipsitz might add, a critical factor that "contributes to an on-going historical conversation in which no one has the first or last word."

Addressing similar issues regarding the absence or misrepresentation of black women's musical production, Hazel Carby charges that white-dominated feminist discourse has marginalized nonwhite women and questions of black sexuality. In responding to the reliance on black women's fiction as

primary texts for analyzing black female discourse, Carby argues forcefully
that representations of black women's sexuality in African-American literature differs significantly from representations of sexuality in black women's
blues. Stating that "different cultural forms negotiate and resolve different
sets of social contradictions," Carby suggests that many literary and cultural
studies scholars have perhaps allowed black women writers to speak on
behalf of a large segment of black women whose daily lives and material
conditions may not be adequately reflected in black women's fiction. For
example, the consumption patterns and social contexts for reception of popular music differ significantly from those of fiction.[15] The dialogic capacity of
popular music, particularly that of rap music, seems especially suited for
engaging many of the social contradictions and ambiguities that pertain specifically to contemporary urban working-class black life.

Carby and Davis are calling for a multifaceted analysis of black women's
identity and sexuality with special attention paid to their musical production.
Placing black popular music and black women's musical production at center
stage, Carby and Davis lay a foundation for analyses of black women rappers
that can confront the complex and contradictory nature of popular expression
and black female social identities.

Although there are significantly fewer female than male rappers, they
have a prominent role in rap and a substantial following. It is difficult to
ignore the massive increase in record deals for women rappers following Salt
'N' Pepa's double platinum (2 million) 1986 debut album *Hot, Cool and
Vicious*. Such volume album sales, even for a rap album by a male artist,
were virtually unprecedented in 1986. Since then, several female rappers,
many of whom have been rapping for years (some since the mid-1970s) have
finally been recorded and promoted.[16] Says female rapper Ms. Melodie: "It
wasn't that the male started rap, the male was just the first to be put on wax.
Females were always into rap, and females always had their little crews and
were always known for rockin' house parties and streets or whatever, school
yards, the comer, the park, whatever it was.[17] In the early stages, women's
participation in rap was hindered by gender-related considerations. M.C.
Lady "D" notes that because she didn't put a female crew together for regular
performances, she "didn't have to worry about getting (her) equipment
ripped off, coming up with the cash to get it in the first place, or hauling it
around on the subways to gigs, problems that kept a lot of other women out
of rap in the early days.[18] For a number of reasons, including increased
record industry support and more demand for rappers generally and female
rappers specifically, women have greater access to production and transportation resources.

MC Lyte's 1988 release "Paper Thin" sold over 125,000 copies in the
first six months with virtually no radio play. Lady B, who became the first
recorded woman rapper in 1978, has since become Philadelphia's top rated-

DJ on WUSL and is founder and editor-in-chief of *Word Up!*, a tabloid devoted to hip hop.[19] Salt 'N' Pepa's first single "Expressions," from *Black's Magic,* went gold in the first week and stayed in the number one position on Billboard's Rap Chart for over two months. Most of these songs address black women's rejection of black male domination, an assertion of new terms for heterosexual courtship, and the centrality of black women's voices.

NOTES

1. Jon Parales, "Female Rappers Strut Their Stuff in a Male Domain," *New York Times*, 5 November 1989, p. C19; Jon Parales, "The Women Who Talk Back in Rap," *New York Times*, 21 October 1900, p. C33; Marcus B. Marbry, "Rap Gets a Woman's Touch," *Emerge*, February 1990, pp. 62–65; David E. Thigpen, "Not for Men Only," *Time*, 27 May 1999, pp. 71–72. See footnote 12 for further citations.

2. George Lipsitz, *Time Passages* (Philadelphia: Temple University Press, 1988), p. 99. See also Mikhail Bakhtin, *Speech Genres and Other Late Essays* (Austin: University of Texas Press, 1986).

3. This refers to my use of Jim Scott's work. James C. Scott, *Domination and the Arts of Resistance: Hidden Transcripts* (New Haven: Yale University Press, 1990).

4. Anders Stephanson, "Interview with Cornel West," in Andrew Ross, ed., *Universal Abandon: The Politics of Postmodernism* (Minneapolis: University of Minnesota Press, 1988), pp. 269–86.

5. Paula Ebron, "Rapping between Men: Performing Gender," *Radical America*, vol. 23, no. 4, 1991, 23–27. Although she is primarily concerned with gendered discourse in Public Enemy—even when such discourse does not refer to black women—she does cite women rappers as respondents to sexism who "contest the most regressive ideas about the role of Black women in the process of cultural production" (p. 26). What is more interesting about the piece, however, is her exploration of the way black men are in dialogue with white men, particularly in regard to women as sexual property.

6. Michelle Wallace, "When Black Feminism Faces the Music and the Music Is Rap," *New York Times*, 29 July 1990, p.12. This kind of generalized characterization of sexism in rap is also made glaringly apparent in the misquotation of my reference to sexism in the work of 2 Live Crew. In the interview she conducted with me for the article, I told Wallace that the 2 Live Crew's lyrics are basically male locker-room discourse with a beat. In the article, I was quoted as saying that *rap music* is basically locker-room discourse with a beat.

7. Notes from the *New Music Seminar* conferences July 1990 and 1991; *Hip Hop at the Crossroads*, Howard University conference February 1991; Rose interviews with MC Lyte and Salt, 7 September 1990.

8. In her piece, "Beyond Racism and Misogyny: Black Feminism and the 2 Live Crew," Kimberle Crenshaw stakes out a position that addresses similar concerns regarding black feminists who are asked to respond to cases of sexism that have been selected for larger social scrutiny. She interrogates the single-axis opposition between race and gender as "the" most important aspect of the 2 Live Crew issue. She explores from a legal perspective the politics of selective prosecution and definitions of pornography. I raise her work here to point out the wide range of black women who find themselves in this difficult bind and to suggest that black women rappers' refusal to roundly condemn 2 Live Crew may be based in a larger, more complex dynamics regarding black female subjectivity. *Boston Review* 16, no. 6, 6–33, 1991.

9. There are also similar examples of homophobic lyrics by male rappers, but I have not enumerated them because they do not pertain to the point I am making here.

10. Houston A. Baker, "Hybridity, the Rap Race, and Pedagogy for the 1990's," in Andrew Ross and Constance Penley, eds., *Technoculture* (Minneapolis: University of Minnesota Press, 1991), pp. 197–209. In addition, disco's relationship to rap was not one of resentment—rap

music was based on disco music and culture. Although some of the more upscale downtown New York clubs excluded black and Latino teenage b-boys, this was not a break from traditional class and racial hierarchies in New York nightlife, and plenty of uptown disco clubs were in operation. Instrumental disco singles served as the musical accompaniment for several early raps, and disco's transformation of the role of the DJ into a "master of musical ceremonies" set the stage for rap's DJs' providing much of the inspiration for rap's collage-oriented mixes. For a discussion of the substantial link between disco and rap, see Nelson George, *The Death of Rhythm and Blues* (New York: Pantheon, 1990), pp. 188–91. For a discussion of disco as a black and a black gay musical culture, see Reebee Garofalo, "Crossing Over: 1939–1989," in Jannette L. Dates and William Barlow, eds., *Split Image: African Americans in the Mass Media* (Washington, DC: Howard University Press, 1990)

11. Nelson George, "Rap's Tenth Birthday," *Village Voice*, 24 October 1989, p. 40.

12. Dominique Di Prima and Lisa Kennedy, "Beat the Rap," *Mother Jones*, September–October 1990, pp. 32–35; Jill Pearlman, "Rap's Gender Gap," *Option*, Fall 1988, pp. 32–36; Marisa Fox, "From the Belly of the Blues to the Cradle of Rap," *Details*, July 1989, pp. 118–24; Judith Halberstam, "Starting from Scratch: Female Rappers and Feminist Discourse," *Revisions*, 2 no. 2 (Winter 1989): 1–4.

13. Nancy Guevara, "Women Writin', Rappin', Breakin'," in Mike Davis, et al., *The Year Left 2: An American Socialist Yearbook* (London: Verso, 1987), pp. 160–75.

14. Angela Davis, "Black Women and Music: A Historical Legacy of Struggle," in Joanne M. Braxton and Andree Nicola McLaughlin, eds., *Wild Women in the Whirlwind: Afro-American Culture and the Contemporary Literary Renaissance* (New Brunswick, NJ: Rutgers University Press, 1990, pp. 3–21.

15. Hazel V. Carby, "it jus Be's Dat Way Sometime: The Sexual Politics of Women's Blues," *Radical America* 20, no.4 (1986): 9–22.

16. Roxanne Shame was the first commercial breakthrough female artist. Her basement-produced single was "Roxanne's Revenge" (1985). See also more recent works by Yo-Yo, Monie Love, Ms. Melodic, Harmony, Antoinette, Oak-town 3-5-7, and Shazzy.

17. Cited in Jill Pearlman, "Rap's Gender Gap," *Option* (Fall 1988): 23–36, 34.

18. Cited in Di Prima and Kennedy, "Beat the Rap," p. 34.

19. Pearlman, "Rap's Gender Gap," p. 34.

Chapter Eleven

Jennifer as Selena

Rethinking Latinidad in Media and Popular Culture

Frances R. Aparicio

In cultural studies and the expressive arts, Latinidad has been partly defined as the ways in which the entertainment industry, mainstream journalism, and Hollywood have homogenized all Latinos into one undifferentiated group, thus erasing our historical, national, racial, class, and gender subjectivities.[1] While the resistance to, and the political/theoretical ambivalence toward, Latinidad as a conceptual framework on the part of many Chicano/a and Latino/a scholars has had to do with the anxiety toward erasing the national identities (and academic fields) that have taken so long to claim as part of the American body politic (and the university), the fear of the erasure of our cultural specificities and complexities through the discursive construct of Latinidad finds its justification in the reiteration of egregious stereotypes and images that continuously populate advertising, television, and films, despite our historical and systematic attempts at critical deconstruction.

In *Latin Looks*, Clara Rodríguez (1998) identifies some of the most egregious realities of Latino representation in U.S. media. Our underrepresentation, coupled with the criminalized stereotypes of Latinos, reveals a politics of representation that seems to worsen as the demographic changes increase our presence. The title of the book, *Latin Looks*, was "purposely chosen to underscore the tendency to view Latinos as if they all looked the same." (6) Indeed, Spanish Cable TV as much as Hollywood have not taken into account, nor recognized, the particularities of each national group. Therefore, a Latina actress is discursively defined in the public sphere because of her generalizability as a Latina rather than because of her uniqueness as a Boricua or Mexican American or Cuban American. For instance, the Latin music boom, while specifically constituted by Caribbean and Puerto Rican, East

201

Coast figures—Jennifer López, Ricky Martin, Marc Anthony—was never articulated as a Boricua boom, but rather as a Latin music boom. The term itself, Latin music, in contrast to Latino music—or, for that matter, Puerto Rican music, Afro-Caribbean music—is a central signifier of the dominant constructions of Latinidad. Yet, if the so-called Latin music boom is a direct result of the demographic growth of U.S. Latinos as a consumer power, and Mexican Americans constitute about 60 percent of that sector, why do the music figures that metonymically represent this sector happen to be mostly Puerto Rican and Caribbean? This phenomenon is the result of the direct, historical colonial relations between the United States and the Hispanic Caribbean. It is informed by the diachronic continuity of dominant representations that have cannibalized the local cultural productions, and particularly the music and rhythms that have emerged, ironically, as forms of resistance to those dominant institutions and hegemonic powers that be. The term Latin music boom *deflects* the social, demographic, and cultural realities of everyday life among U.S. Latinos and *replaces* what is socially real Latino with historically familiar, acceptable, and contained images of Latinos that the United States can integrate into its own logic. Yet we also know that the systematic exclusion of Mexican-American musical productions from most of the Latin music boom, which is historically informed by their exclusion from national citizenship as "illegals," has been also duplicated by the hegemonic, Miami-based, Latino musical industry in the first presentation of the Latin Grammy Awards.

Another dominant construct about Latinidad is the more recent image of the Latino "cultural wars," as articulated in a 2002 *New York Times* article (Kugel) that attempted to examine the social transformations and cultural tensions between Puerto Ricans in New York and the newer immigrant groups there. Titled "Latino Cultural Wars," this piece addresses the impact that the influx of so-called "other" Latino groups have had on the cultural public presence of Puerto Ricans in New York. I mention this article because it frames the social interactions among various Latino groups exclusively as conflictive competitions for cultural hegemony. It describes contemporary and new forms of cultural negotiations taking place among various Latin American national groups in specific urban spaces, such as New York, Chicago, Los Angeles, and Miami, as "cultural wars," a term that echoes the right-wing attacks against multicultural education throughout the 1980s. While the "cultural wars" in the 1980s were, in effect, struggles of power enacted by Anglo-dominant sectors in positions of public power and within institutions, the "cultural wars" suggested in this article are not equivalent, or even comparable, to its original referent. Indeed, power dynamics among Latinos in the United States still need to be teased out and understood, given the complexity of social positionings, class differences, race, gender identities, colonial histories, immigration status, and a myriad of other factors that can produce or reduce power. These inter-Latino negotiations do not mirror the "cultural wars" of the 1980s because the majority of Latinos are not positioned in major sites of institutional power, although of course certain groups such as the Cuban exile and many Latin-American immigrant professionals and elites do hold power in their respective fields. Because of the diverse ways in which U.S. Latino/as exercise and articulate power, and because of the multiple subjectivities and identities that we embody, the processes of interlatino transculturations are much more complex than what this article on "cultural wars" suggests. While I have previously explored what I called the "competing authenticities" that constitute the larger space of Latinidad (Aparicio, 1999), it is equally true that there are still numerous forms of negotiations, mutual transculturations, cultural divergences, and power hierarchies that need to be identified as these are themselves socially emerging in the new Latino urban spaces and in other smaller cities and rural areas. The *New York Times* article, for instance, refers to the fact that a recent Guatemalan immigrant girl named Gabriela Minueza, age 9, sang "Preciosa," one of the most significant, patriotic hymns that praise Puerto Rico, to her Latino school community. It uses this event to argue that the Puerto Rican cultural hegemony in New York is obscuring or oppressing other Latino cultural identities. However within a decolonial imaginary and logic, to use Emma Pérez's (1999) theoretical proposal for understanding women's agency in Chicano history, I want to propose that this event could also be iconic of the analogous forms of colonialism and ensuing hybridity that Latino groups may share, despite the specific historical differences between their national countries, their immigration histories, and the political relations to the United States. The fact that a Guatemalan immigrant sings "Preciosa" is a testament to the ways in which cultural texts, such as this patriotic Puerto Rican song, are multiply layered semantically within the context of their local performances. Gabriela does not stop being a Guatemalan at that moment, nor does she become a Boricua. This very moving example of Latinidad, in effect, reveals to me that such a song, as a cultural text, evokes in its audience, and perhaps in its interpreter, an analogous structure of feeling having to do with the pain of exile and of geocultural displacements. What the author of the *New York Times* article missed in his unilateral reading of such a moment of Latinidad is the palimpsest of displacements and migrations that have been effected by the history of colonialisms in the Americas, a multiple layering that indeed brings Guatemalans and Puerto Ricans closer together. That Rafael Hernández composed most of his songs in Mexico and in New York, that Marc Anthony has performed "Preciosa" in a salsa version to reaffirm his Boricua identity as a Nuyorican, and that now a Guatemalan immigrant would sing it to her schoolmates constitute three historical layers of an articulation of the pain of colonialism.

Rather than deploying Latinidad in its two extremes—as a site of homogenization or as a site of cultural wars—in this essay I propose to approach Latinidad as a concept that allows us to explore moments of convergences and divergences in the formation of Latino/a (post)colonial subjectivities and in hybrid cultural expressions among various Latino national groups. This approach allows us to rethink the ways in which national categories of identity have limited and elided the new forms of identity formation emerging in Latino/a communities as a result of inter-Latino affinities, desires, and conflicts. By exploring such inter-Latino sites, that is, those sites where two or more Latinos from various national origins encounter, construct, and transculturate each others critics can reinfuse the term "Latinidad" with alternative ways of knowing the content of our lives and why we do what we do. It is an approach that moves us beyond the cautious demonizing of the term itself because it tends to homogenize all sectors, or because it is a term that has partly been deployed by the media and the entertainment industry. By rethinking Latinidad through media and popular culture as a site through which we produce knowledge about a Latino other and we explore our (post)colonial analogies, we are, in fact, proposing a "decolonial imaginary," to use Emma Pérez's term, in two ways: we are constructing inter-Latino knowledge that allows Latino/as from various national groups to understand their Latino counterparts, a knowledge that itself represents an alternative discourse given the silenced knowledge about each other that has been our educational legacy; secondly, an approach to "Latinidad" that searches for the analogous (post)colonial conditions and experiences among the various national groups allows us to appropriate the exhausted term and to reinvigorate it with an oppositional, decolonizing ideology that will be much more liberatory than what previous approaches to the term have yielded. If Emma Pérez proposed the term "decolonial imaginary" in the context of reclaiming that "third feminist space" (33) in which the historical agency of Mexican-American women would not be silenced or elided, I would like to use it here to frame an analysis of inter-Latina identifications in the context of popular music and film. The case of Jennifer López performing—and being transformed into—Selena for the film by Gregory Nava brings forth certain dynamics of identification and disidentification among two women, one Tejana singer, Selena, and Jennifer López, a Nuyorican from the Bronx. This, in turn, suggests how both Jennifer López and Selena, as U.S. Latinas (an identity constructed through their audiences, the industry, and the content of their work, but also through the history of ethno-racialization), have shared similar historical experiences as colonized subjects. In addition, their respective bodies also became the object of various cultural gazes and dominant, patriarchal forces, in the public space. They are both, then, embodiments of the colonial conditions of U.S. Latino/as and of "the publicly performing Latina body" (Paredez, 2002: 84).

IDENTITY POLITICS IN CASTING, OR THE RE-CASTING OF JENNIFER INTO SELENA

The death of Selena in 1995 triggered numerous forms of memorialization: the funeral itself, attended by thousands of fans from all over the country; a statue in Corpus Christi; the re-recording and anthologizing of her songs; the line of clothing that she had designed; the photo of her face imprinted on t-shirts sold on the streets of Texas, in her boutiques, and through mail orders; issues of *People, Texas Magazine,* and other print media dedicated to her life and musical career; films, such as Gregory Nava's *Selena,* Lourdes Portillo's feminist documentary, *Corpus: A Home Movie for Selena,* and *Selena Remembered* (made for TV), among others; and books that were written and published like fast food immediately after her death: *Selena: La última canción* (in bilingual format), written by Geraldo Ruiz and recipient of the Premio International de Crónica y Reportajes, appeared in 1995 and was partially endorsed by the Quintanilla family (Ruiz, 1995); and Joe Nick Patoski's (1996) *Selena: Como la Flor,* which contextualizes the role that she played in the larger history of Tex-Mex music and the significance of her persona as a cultural hero and role model for the Mexican-American community in Texas and the Southwest. Among these publications, we also have Maria Celeste Arrarás' (1997) *El Secreto de Selena,* which should also be examined as another instance of a Latina reconstructing another Latina in the public sphere.

Selena's role as a cultural hero for the Mexicano community in Texas, and as role model for thousands of young Mexican-American girls, can be understood in various ways. First, she was the first woman in the male-dominated industry of Tex-Mex music who broke the record in terms of sales (Vargas, 2002: 117; Patoski, 1996: 101–44) In this light, the potential for identification between her young female, Mexican-American fans and the singer was tapped, thus creating a larger audience than what was traditionally expected for this musical genre and style. Second, Selena's mythification after her death as a saint, martyr, and healer (compared to Pedrito Jaramillo and others) was a direct result of the way in which she died, her young age, and the charisma that she had exerted throughout her life, a social power and attractive personality that allowed a largely disempowered community to feel a sense of hope in their own futures. Thus, the power that she held with her largely Mexican-American audiences has been examined in the context of the postmodern condition in Latin America and the United States. Chicano anthropologist José Limón (1998: 188–91), for instance, has examined the displacement and failure of the traditional intellectual and the ensuing ascendance of media figures, singers, and the visual image as central figures and sites in the development and definition of cultural politics and identity formation. Limón has argued, in the context of Tejano culture, that Selena's popularity was established as a result of the disillusionment of the Texas Mexican community with its own politicians and leaders. The sense of hope that Paul Gilroy (1993: 132–34) describes among fans and listening audiences, the politics of fulfillment as he calls it, derives by default, then, in a sort of metonymic relationship to the failures of the state as these are embodied in the figures of elected officials.

It has been commonly argued that Selena's popularity outside of the Mexican-American community was a direct result of her untimely death. In addition, it has also been suggested that Selena became a "Latina" public figure as the result of the production of a larger national audience that came to know her and her music posthumously. Deborah Paredez, moreover, has argued that Selena's tragic death, memorialization at the national level, and in particular the musical based on her life, were sites through which "Selena provided many Latina/os with a compelling discursive space in which to decry both past and concurrent tragic consequences they faced as a result of new nativist hysteria that marked the decade as well as to imagine a future wherein Latina/os would gain significant political, economic and representational ground in the light of the 2000 Census projections and findings" (Paredez, 2002: 67). In this political context, then, Selena's figure, music, life, and death were deployed by Tejanos, Mexican Americans, and other Latino/as as symbolic sites for the claiming of Latino/as as full American citizens.

This process by which Latino and Latina listeners "discovered" Selena's musical work, and thus reconstructed her within the larger space of a United States "Latinidad," was also the direct result of the film, *Selena*, starring Jennifer López. I clearly remember the first time I watched the film at the movies, hearing others in the theater comment that they didn't know that this was based on a real life story. While many non-Latinos came to see the movie without any knowledge of Selena's historical existence, many non-Mexican-American Latinos were in the same situation. Frances Negrón-Muntaner (1997) observes, in the opening lines of "Jennifer's Butt," that the Puerto Rican families in suburban Philadelphia who came to the movie were perhaps moved by "an intense necrophilia, momentarily followed by spasms of melancholia and sadness for the loss of a young life, a frequent occurrence in inner-city Latino-America" (181) and perhaps also by the ways in which Selena exemplified the American Dream and its tragic demise simultaneously (182). Thus, a space for the potential identification and disidentification among and between Latino/as of various national origins was carved by her untimely and tragic death, not only because of the national coverage that it received, but because this coverage and memorialization allowed non-Tejano Latinos to both grieve for themselves (as Paredez and Negrón-Muntaner suggest) and to imagine a more powerful future as Latino/as. It is also significant that the immediate news programming and coverage that ensued immediately after her shooting on March 31, 1995 and the national coverage of the trial against Yolanda Saldivar was predominantly produced by Univisión's Miami crew of newscasters and journalists. Maria Celeste Arrarás's book-length *testimonio* of her role in this coverage, of her experiences in South Texas as a Puerto Rican journalist and public figure within the predominantly Cuban enterprise of Univisión, is another instance of an inter-Latino historical moment mediated through the central figure of Selena. The fact that the Bronx-born Boricua actress Jennifer López was chosen to visually re-embody Selena in the Gregory Nava film, the film that made itself into the authoritative visual narrative of her life, into its master narrative, is also significant for understanding inter-Latino identifications as sites of postcolonial affinities and recognitions, as "decolonial imaginaries."

As Deborah Vargas argues, while Selena reaffirmed a Tejana identity through her repertoire, her fashion and style, and her persona, it is also true that her musical selections, arrangements, and hybrid fusion of Tejano music with other musical forms, allowed Selena to create a larger, Latin American and Latino/a audience that identified with her. In fact, according to Vargas, "Selena's music was popular in various parts of Latin/o America, particularly Mexico, El Salvador, and Puerto Rico. As such, the history and culture that mark the music of Tejas discursively engaged the histories and cultures of new populations" (121). Her musical collaborations with the Barrio Boyz, with Honduran pop singer Alvaro Torres, her musical arrangements and incursions into "disco, funk, glam, and new wave" (120), are indexes of these inter-Latino articulations and of the transnational circulation of sounds that made them possible. Thus, that Selena could reaffirm and maintain her Tejana identity, while simultaneously constructing a larger Latino/a identity through her music and audience, is evidence of the multiple subjectivities that traverse and inhabit the space of Latinidad. It is also a clear instance of how identities are the result of the construction by others of a public self. These multiple identities defy the linear conceptualizations of identity shifts that Negrón-Muntaner, for instance, proposes when she writes (184): "Selena went from being a Tejana (a territorialized "regional" identity) to being a Latina (an "ethnic minority")."

If it is true, as Clara Rodríguez argues, that there is a homogenized "Latin look" produced by the entertainment industry, isn't it also true that Jennifer López and Selena's physical similarities are not necessarily only a result of this dominant homogenization, but perhaps, as I argue here, visual embodiments of the colonial conditions and historical experiences of second-generation U.S. Latinas who have been public objects of racial sexualization? While the film *Selena* is clearly the product of Hollywood, it was also largely influenced by two powerful Latino men, Gregory Nava and Abraham Quintanilla. Thus, gender ideologies within Latino cultures, beauty standards and patriarchal notions (both Mexican and Anglo) of the Latina body, all played a role in the ways in which Jennifer López "became" Selena for the film. These gender ideologies are overtly discussed in Lourdes Portillo's documentary, while in the Nava film they are silently, but visually articulated.

Latina scholars have been so preoccupied with differentiating ourselves to the larger Anglo world that we have overlooked the fact that there are physical similarities among some of us. The similarities of the real bodies of both Selena and Jennifer López speak to the reality of a "Latina look" that is, in this case, not a homogenized result of Hollywood, but in fact two concrete, real Latina bodies. The uncanny coincidences between the body measurements of Jennifer López and Selena at the time of the filming were foregrounded by Selena's seamstress, who remarked: "All the costumes in the movie were made from the original patterns. So when they told me what to make, I just went into my boxes." "Jennifer had only an inch difference in her waist, but she brought a trainer in and she lost it." Manuel Peña (1999: 203–7) has argued that Selena played a double function in terms of her physicality and body. He frames this doubleness in terms of "use value" and "exchange value" to explain how Selena served both as a cultural hero with which her community could identify, at the same time that she was capitalizing on her sexuality to serve as an object of desire for mainstream audiences. The double-edged sexuality, constituted both through the virginal, good daughter image and the emerging sexual symbol that Selena constructed for herself through her "bustiers" and revealing costumes, is not necessarily informed by a segmented audience, as Peña suggests, but rather by patriarchal discourses that, through processes of racialization and erotization, objectify Latinas' bodies. It is interesting that according to some of the theories above, Selena could only be "sexual" for Anglo or non-Latino audiences, a cultural projection that masks the potential desire of the Mexican male for the young Tejana singer.

In the cultural realm, the body curvature, the long, dark hair, the full lips, and the rear end of both Latina entertainers, Jennifer López and Selena, have become symbols of their pride in their racial and ethnic identities, a pride that both singers articulated as part of their public personae. If critics recall López's moment of reaffirmation of her sexualized and racialized "butt" in Cristina's talk show when she responded that "todo es mio, it's all mine" (Negrón-Muntaner, 1997; Paredez, 2002), Selena was consistently remembered for having reaffirmed her Tejana identity, for having resisted the colonial beauty standards of both Mexico and the Anglo industry (in Mexico she was called a *naca*, derogatory term used by dominant Mexicans to refer to those who are "Indian" looking). Yet the social, cultural, racial, and gendered meanings of these two public Latina bodies are not exclusively sites for resistance to colonization and to patriarchy. Their social meanings are much more complex. For instance, Negrón-Muntaner asserts in her "epistemology of the butt" that "a big *culo* does not only upset hegemonic (white) notions of beauty and good taste" (189) but also that Jennifer López's rear end allows the "Puerto Rican diaspora" to have "a big *culo* to call our own, ending a long stretch of second-class citizenship in both the United States and Puerto Rico" (191). This claim can only be valid at the level of symbolic speculation, for Puerto Rican subordination continues to be strong despite López's fame and fortune. Because the bodies of Latinas, Afro-Caribbeans, and women of color have been historically constructed so as to satisfy the erotic desires of men in dominant society as well as the labor needs of colonial and imperial economies, one can not dismiss the sedimented patriarchal and racialized values that Selena and Jennifer López's butts still trigger for many non-Latino viewers as icons of cultural subalternity, not to mention their status as "patriarchal synechdoques" (Aparicio, 1998: 142–53) in the larger grammar of masculinist discourses.

In the film *Selena* the young Tejana's body had to be reproduced through the analogous figure of a Boricua whose live butt resurrected notions of racialized and gender differences and "excesses" in Selena's own musical career. Yet these "excesses" were muted and undermined by the film's patriarchal directives, which represented Selena as a mostly virginal, good daughter rather than as a young woman with sexual desires and needs of her own. The movie scene when Selena is eating pizza with Chris Pérez and she comments that she never diets is an attempt to "naturalize" her body weight and to undermine Selena's own constructedness of her sexuality on stage, attempts that were also foregrounded by her radical introduction of the "bustier" onto the stage but that were consistently disparaged by the patriarchal authority of her father. The historical fact is that both Selena and Jennifer López ultimately experimented with transforming their curvaceous bodies into more acceptable white notions of beauty (Selena had liposuction and Jennifer López has significantly transformed her body and her hair since the movie). This reveals the difficulties of said resistance in the entertainment industry. (Shakira's case and controversial blonde hair is another case in point). My point here is that the bodies of both Selena and Jennifer López were literally sites through which hegemonic notions of physical beauty and value were being contested and struggled. Both bodies were public enactments and physical embodiments of simultaneous colonial desire and subaltern resistance. While internet and journalistic accounts of the process of casting, make up, costume making, and other aspects of the production of the movie foregrounded the physical similarities between Selena and Jennifer López, none of these narratives accounted for the ways in which the struggles over these bodies and body parts articulated the historical experiences of second-generation Latinas in the United States as racialized subjects.

Yet these similarities were offset by the debates and controversies around national identity: why was a boricua from the Bronx chosen to play the lead role of a Tex-Mex singer? If casting has been a process inflected with identity politics and with the expectations that actors and actresses from one national group can only perform another subject from that same group, as reflected in the discussion about Benjamin Bratt's role as Miguel Piñero (Kim, 2002), then the case of the selection of Jennifer López to play Selena was inevitably wrought with debates around the Puerto Rican/Mexican divide. On the one hand, the casting call to select the actress who would interpret Selena in the movie triggered the participation of 20,000 young Latinas in five major cities in the United States. This is the second largest casting call in the history of Hollywood (texmexqueen.com/selenamovie.htm). When Gregory Nava called Jennifer López to see if she would be interested, "she did, and the rest was history" (texmexqueen). I quote this phrase because it suggests that López's personality, style, and charisma was comparable to that of the Tex-Mex singer. Yet, in contrast to other Mexican actresses who were also considered for the role, there are, in fact, similarities between the Bronx Boricua and the Tex-Mex singer, that were articulated in and through the casting process and that reveal the effects of colonialism on Puerto Ricans and Mexicans as historical minorities.

The differences between a Mexican-American Latina such as Selena, and other Mexican actresses such as Bibi Gaytan and Selma Hayek, were evident at the level of language, culture, and national location. Bibi Gaytan was automatically eliminated once it was known that the film would be produced in English. Selma Hayek "had too deep of an accent" (texmexqueen). This is significant evidence of the heterogeneous social, linguistic, and cultural locations between Selena and these Mexican superstars. Despite the geographical proximity to the U.S./Mexico border, Texas-born Selena's identity as a Mexican-American young girl, and as a Tejana, shares more with Bronx-born Jennifer López than with Hayek or Gaytan. The linguistic gaps foregrounded in the coverage about casting decisions indicate that Mexicans and Mexican-Americans are not the same thing. (Is it a coincidence that El Show de Johnny Canales is very popular among New York Puerto Ricans?) The visibility of Hayek and Gaytan in Hollywood also reveals the transnational importation of Mexican superstars into Hollywood, a phenomenon that in many ways displaces and replaces the need for the development of local, national, Mexican-American talent in the acting profession. In fact, this planned migration of stars from Mexico to the United States mirrors the importation of programming from Latin America into the United States that is the base for Spanish Cable television (Davila, 2001a: 178). There is, then, a Latina experience constituted by a history of cultural, linguistic, and economic colonization that both Selena and Jennifer López have embodied, particularly in terms of their dominant language as English-speaking Latinas who did not necessarily identify with the major issues of their respective homelands. Likewise, the inverse colonization, one may say, of Spanish-cable television programming, suggests that U.S. Latino/as as audiences still do not have media productions that are controlled nationally or mostly produced by our own communities. While it is true that the debates around casting foregrounded Jennifer López as a Puerto Rican rather than as a Latina (Negrón-Muntaner, 1997: 184), they also allowed López to articulate her affinities with Selena as U.S. Latinas: "Selena and I are both Latinas and both had the common experience of growing up Latina in this country. This was good enough" (Negrón-Muntaner 1997: 184).

FROM HIP HOP TO *CUMBIA* AND BACK

However, it is not only the body that makes the actress or the singer. The narratives that summarize the process through which Jennifer López was transformed into Selena foregrounded regional differences that surfaced most evidently in the dancing. While both bodies were very similar in physical terms, curvature, and in the dominant gaze that they both have triggered, it is clear that each of these bodies was socialized into a particular set of movements, rhythms, and footwork that originated in the heritage and traditions of their local and regional cultures. Narratives about the casting process summarize the following:

"The part also gave López a chance to showcase her natural talents as a live stage/musical performer." She broke into entertainment as one of the kinetic Fly Girls on Fox's comedy series "In Living Color," and playing Selena allowed her to revisit her dance training. López rehearsed extensively with choreographer Miranda Garrison to faithfully recreate Selena's fluid, natural style. López remembers, "One of the biggest challenges was the dance part. It's very hard to unlearn everything your body is accustomed to doing and that it does naturally. I had to learn what Selena did, which is very different from my own dance instincts." These comments reveal the ambiguous ways in which dance is defined: it is both "natural" and "instinctive" yet it is also locally, regionally, and culturally inflected and "learned." Dance as a performance of cultural identity has played a central role in the career development of both Jennifer López and of Selena. If the movie itself dedicated a scene to the moment when Selena's mother teaches her to dance the *cumbia* (an interesting musical tradition transmitted here from woman to woman), Jennifer López's own musical career has also been based on her dance performances in videos. Yet López's beginnings with "In Living Color" and the musical arrangements of her cuts locate her more centrally in the pop, R&B, and hip hop categories. Although Selena and Los Dinos capitalized on merging Tex Mex with pop styles and arrangements, her *cumbia* dancing and choreographic movements still retained the basic, traditional footsteps of this dance form so popular among *nortenos*. Yet the regional identities between these dance traditions and styles may mask some of the commonalities between them. If *cumbias* originated as one of the many rhythms developed by African slaves in the eighteenth century in the Atlantic coast of Colombia, then its hip-swaying moves are historically analogous to those of salsa dancing. In fact, while the trotting foot movements of *cumbias* may differ from the more syncopated footwork of salsa dancing, *cumbias* also feature "repeating keyboard patterns" which are in fact borrowed from salsa. While Tex-Mex *cumbias* are supposedly "simpler than the Columbian counterpart, the "shuffling steps . . . come, as folklore tells us, from slaves who were dancing while wearing leg irons and chains" (Burr, 1999: 78). Thus, the common African elements of cumbias, Afro-Caribbean dance styles, and hip hop could be foregrounded as a common racial genealogy that has been partially silenced by the national values associated with these dance forms. In the case of Tex-Mex music, this Africanness is transculturated into Mexicanness through the shift to the accordion, while in the urban East Coast the Africanness of hip hop and salsa dancing is mediated by the Hollywood, mainstream images that are incorporated into the musical videos. (In Jennifer López's case, her somatic transformation into lighter hair, less butt, and weight loss serves as a reminder of these whitening impulses constantly at work, while the framing of musical videos such as "Waiting for Tonight" as a tropical jungle speaks to the historically cemented, lingering, hegemonic constructions of Latin American identity.) It is not unsurprising that Willie Colón, whose musical projects have explored the historical processes of ra-cialization and whitening ("Color americano"), performs a song entitled "Cumbia bomba," which merges both Afro-Puerto Rican bomba rhythms with the Colombian *cumbia*. Yet this production has emerged out of his relocation to Mexico City, and to me it serves as another example of the Puerto Rican/Mexican analogies that can be found through an oppositional genealogical project that uncovers the African, subaltern elements in both cultural canons.

The fact that Jennifer López paid homage to Selena in her first touring concert, which began in San Juan, Puerto Rico, speaks of the ways in which Latinidad and inter-Latina affiliations are realized not only at the level of symbolic discourse but in more concrete, real ways. López sang "I Could Fall in Love," and "apparently when she sang the song she began to cry as they flashed images of Selena on a big screen." It has been reported that "it was the best Jennifer sounded all night in her concert" (pub50.exboard.com/ftejanorosefrm1.show . . .). This homage to Selena and the "emotional" performance triggered by it has, on the one hand, rescued Jennifer López from some of the vestiges of the debates on the politics of identity behind the casting process. One fan writes:

I gotta say that a lot of Selena fans have held bad feelings against Jennifer because it seems like she forgot that it was Selena that gave her her big break, but apparently Jenni has surprised us all and showed that she remembers very well who Selena is and even did a tribute in her first concert ever. My hat is off to Jennifer. (pub50.exboard.com)

But what does this performative decision suggest? In the contest of this previous discussion on Latinidad, it seems that Jennifer López's embodiment of and transformation into Selena is a revealing instance of, first, a Latinidad feminista that is enacted through their resistance to dominant social constructions of both Latina bodies and vis-à-vis the dominant, objectifying gaze. The Jennifer López/Selena dyad also reveals that U.S. Latinas will continue to explore their commonalities as colonized subjects, as historical minorities that continue to engage in struggles of discourse and power with dominant institutions. Thus, the fact that Jennifer sang Selena's songs in San Juan, Puerto Rico, is quite meaningful. It parallels the uncovering of analogous forms of colonialism that continue to affect the everyday lives of many U.S. Latinos across national groups. The presense of Selena in San Juan represents, also, a continuation of, and a foregrounding of, the silenced history of Mexicans in Puerto Rico, a historical presence that dates back to 1810 and earlier (Picó, 1994: 19).

The case study of Jennifer López and Selena proposes itself as a model for using Latinidad as an approach that unveils the affinities between and among historical minorities such as Mexican-Americans and Puerto Ricans. The identification of Jennifer López with Selena, an individual one, as well as the potential identificatory process of Latino/a audiences with Selena and with Jennifer López, open up as possible spaces through which Latino/a cultural critics can advance the knowledge about U.S. Lations as we begin to face the challenge of our demographic diversification and our inter-Latino dynamics and interactions. To dismiss Latinidad as an exclusively hegemonic site is to dismiss the potential for continuing to explore our (post)colonial historical experiences and for finding affinities and similarities that may empower us rather than fragment us. Jennifer's performance as Selena, her visual resurrection of the slain Tex-Mex singer was perhaps one way of achieving such an awareness. This form of oppositionality may have been masked by the identity politics of casting decisions and by the privileged economic position that López holds as the best paid Latina in the history of Hollywood, a status that the film *Selena* ironically made possible. These power differentials are still to be identified and more fully understood.

NOTE

1. While it is impossible to trace here a genealogy of the term "Latinidad" as it has been deployed by major Latino/a scholars, I want to emphasize that the multiple meanings of the term have to do with the fact that it has been defined in various contexts and from various disciplinary vantage points: from Felix Padilla's social and political approach to "Latinismo" (1985) that stressed the strategic, collective mobilizations between Puerto Ricans and Mexicans in Chicago, to Arlene Dávila's (2001a, b) analysis of Latinidad as a transnational, hemispheric imposition of Latin American programming on U.S. Latino viewers, to diachronic analyses of the shifts from the cultural nationalism paradigms of the 1970s to pan-Latino imaginaries during the 1990s (Gaspar de Alba, 1998; Dávila, 2001b), to Mérida Rúa's (2001) proposal of a "Puerto Rican Latinidad" based on the everyday lives, encounters, and affiliations between Puerto Ricans and other Latino groups in Chicago. "Latinidad" refers then to a diversity of processes and cultural interactions based on the disciplinary approach from which it is defined. See also Sandoval-Sánchez (1999), Aparicio and Chávez-Silverman (1997), Laó-Montes (2001), the Latina Feminist Group (2001), and Obolei (1995).

REFERENCES

Aparirio, Frances R. (1999). "Reading the "Latino," in Latino Studies: Toward Re-imagining Our Academic Location," *Discourse: Journal for Theoretical Studies in Media and Culture* 21, no. 2: pp. 3–18.

Aparicio, Frances R. (1998). *Listening to Salsa: Gender, Latin Popular Music, and Puerto Rican Cultures.* Hanover and London: Wesleyan University Press/University Press of New England.

Aparicio, Frances R. and Chavez-Silverman, Susan (1997). "Introduction," in Frances R. Aparicio and Susan Chavez-Silverman, editors, *Tropicalizations: Transcultural Representations of Latinidad.* Hanover and London: University Press of New England, pp. 1–17.

Arraras, Maria Celeste (1997). *El secreto de Selena.* New York: Simon and Schuster.

Bun; Ramiro (1999). *Tejano and Regional Mexican Music.* New York: Billboard Books.

Davila, Arlene (2001a). *Latinos Inc.: The Marketing and Making of a People.* Berkeley, Los Angeles and London: University of California Press.

Davila, Arlene (2001b). "Culture in the Battlefront: from Nationalist to Pan-Latino Projects," in A. Laó-Montes and A. Davila, editors, *Mambo Montage: The Latinization of New York.* New York: Columbia University Press, pp. 159–182.

Gaspar de Alba, Alicia (1998). *Chicano Art Inside/Outside the Master's House: Cultural Politics and the CARA Exhibition.* Austin: The University of Texas Press.

Gilroy, Paul (1993). *Small Acts: Thoughts on the Politics of Black Cultures.* London and New York: Serpent"s Tail.

Kim, Jae-Ha (2002). "Bratt finds rhyme, reason in poet role," *Chicago Tribune.* January 20, 1D, 10D.

Kugel, Seth (2002). "The Latino Culture Wars," *New York Times.* February 24: pp. 7–8F.

Laó-Montes, Agustín (2001). "Mambo Montage: The Latinization of New York City," in A. Laó-Montes and A. Davila, editors, *Mambo Montage: The Latinization of New York.* New York: Columbia University Press, pp. 1–52.

Latina Feminist Group (2001). *Telling to Live: Latina Feminist Testimonios.* Durham: Duke University Press.

Limón José, E. (1998). *American Encounters: Greater Mexico, the United States, and the Erotics of Culture.* Boston: Beacon Press.

Negrón-Muntaner, Frances (1997). "Jennifer"s Butt," *Aztlán* 22, no. 2 (Fall): pp. 181–94.

Obolei, Suzanne (1995). *Ethnic Labels, Latino Lives: Identity and the Politics of (Re)Presentation in the United States.* Minneapolis: University of Minnesota Press.

Paredez, Deborah (2002). "Remembering Selena, Re-membering Latinidad," *Theater Journal* 54, pp. 63–84.

Patoski, Joe Nick (1996). *Selena: Como la Flor.* Boston: Little, Brown and Company.

Peña, Manuel (1999). *Música Tejana: The Cultural Economy of Artistic Transformation.* College Station: Texas A & M University Press.

Pérez, Emma (1999). *The Decolonial Imaginary: Writing Chicanas into History.* Bloomington: Indiana University Press.

Picó, Fernando (1994). "Los mexicanos en Puerto Rico," *Claridad,* 18–24 November, p. 19.

Rodríguez, Clara E., editor (1998). *Latin Looks: Images of Latinas and Latinos in the U.S. Media.* Boulder, CO: Westview Press.

Rúa, Merida (2001). "Colao subjectivities: PortoMex and MexiRican perspectives on language and identity," *Centro: Journal of the Center for Puerto Rican Studies* 2, pp. 116–33.

Ruiz, Geraldo (1995). *Selena: La última canción.* New York: El Diario Books.

Sandoval-Sanchez, Alberto (1999). *Jose, Can You See?: Latinos On and Off Broadway.* Madison: University of Wisconsin Press.

Tracy, Kathleen (2000). *Jennifer López.* Toronto, Ontario: ECW Press.

Vargas, Deborah R. (2002). "Bidi Bidi Bom Bom: Selena and Tejano Music in The Making of Tejas," in M. Habell-Pallan and M. Romero, editors, *Latino/a Popular Culture,* New York: New York University Press, pp. 117–26.

Chapter Twelve

Passed into the Present

Women in Hawaiian Entertainment

Amy Ku'uleialoha Stillman

Since the late nineteenth century, Hawaiian music and dance have been enjoyed by residents and visitors to Hawai'i and have served as a promotional tool for performers who toured and played nightspots outside Hawai'i. Women were an integral part of Hawaiian entertainment. Yet, on close examination, women's contributions cluster into two principal areas: featured soloists and caretakers of knowledge. In this chapter, my purpose is to provide a historical overview of women in Hawaiian entertainment, particularly in the twentieth century, in order to show how women's contributions have been absolutely essential to the perpetuation of Hawaiian music and dance.

Hawaiian entertainment is inscribed in the historical record of Hawai'i's peoples. Indigenous legends attribute the hula tradition to Hi'iaka, favored younger sister of the volcano goddess Pele. The opening scene in the epic tale of Pele and Hi'iaka takes place on the beach at Puna, where Hi'iaka's friend Hōpoe and her companion Hā'ena are engaged in a dance. Upon Pele's request for a dance from her sisters, Hi'iaka responds, dancing to a song that, according to the legend, marks the invention of the hula.[1]

> Ke ha'a la Puna i ka makani
> Ha'a ka ulu hala i Kea'au
> Ha'a H ā' ena me Hōpoe
> Ha'a ka wahine
> 'Ami i kai o Nānāhuki la
> Hula le'a wale i kai o Nānāhuki e!

> Puna dances in the breeze
> The pandanus groves at Kea'au dance Hā'ena and Hōpoe dance

The woman dances
Hip-swaying in the waters of Nānāhuki
Dancing with enjoyment in the waters of Nānāhuki![2]

The saga of Pele and Hiāʻiaka details how the sisters confront love, betrayal, loyalty, and vengeance, as Hiāʻiaka is sent on a journey to fetch Pele's lover from Kauaāʻi island. Throughout her journey, Hiāʻiaka's adventures are memorialized in both narrative prose and poetry. The epic is a foundational text for hula students, both in its relating of the genesis of hula and in its encasing of numerous pieces of hula repertoire, many of which have passed into the present.

Out of this episode emerged the hula tradition, the performance of which combines dance movement, poetic composition, vocal recitation, and percussive instrumental accompaniment. Other legends relate the arrival of the shark skin-covered temple drum with the chief Laʻa-mai-Kahiki at around the twelfth century. The religious system associated with these settlers and the sacred drum required the observation of elaborate ritual practices, among them the safeguarding of sacred and esoteric knowledge. The hula's mythic origins were encompassed by restrictions surrounding the training of performers and the transmission of sacred repertoire.

While specific details of how the elaborate state religious system intersected with gender in Hawaiian society are beyond the scope of this essay, what is important here is that women were involved in hula performance from its beginnings. After the arrival of Europeans in 1778 and the subsequent success of American Calvinist missionaries in converting Hawaiians to Christianity by the mid-1820s, Hawaiian society underwent radical social transformation throughout the nineteenth century. Hawaiian performance was transformed as Hawaiians embraced Anglo-American Christian hymns, and missionaries promoted musical literacy in the use of musical staff notation; yet, despite missionary-inspired prohibitions of the hula, adherents quietly took it underground until later in the nineteenth century, when its performance was once again encouraged. The visual record throughout is rich with images of women performers, in drawings, photographs, and postcards. By the late nineteenth century, women composers were enriching the historical record with songs, and the advent of sound recording added the dimension of women's voices by the start of the twentieth century.

The contrast of foreground and underground provides a convenient conceptual frame for considering two areas of women's contributions to Hawaiian entertainment that I wish to focus on here. As featured soloists, whether as singers or dancers, women are foregrounded by virtue of being onstage. Likewise, in photographic sources, women are foregrounded in a purely statistical manner, outnumbering men performers on postcards by a landslide, for reasons that are elaborated below.

Although the notion of foreground is usually contrasted with background, I suggest that "underground" offers greater nuance. Over the course of the twentieth century, the primary lens through which Hawaiian music and hula have been openly accessible, especially outside Hawaiā'i, has been that of tourist entertainment. There is no one moment that can be designated as the advent of tourism to the islands, for the archipelago became an intended destination from the moment the British sea captain James Cook charted the islands' location in 1778 (and he himself was the first return visitor later that year).

Throughout the nineteenth century, published travel accounts enjoyed a broad public readership in the United States and Europe. Many readers aspired to visit the islands eventually. Scheduled visits became possible with the establishment of regular transportation routes, in place by the 1880s; this was followed immediately by government-sponsored promotional efforts that continue in the present, as tourism has become Hawai'i's top economic sector. In this context, activities not directly related to onstage performance become part and parcel of workings intended to be transparent to the gaze of tourists, not essential to their appreciation of performance activity. The notion of underground is taken here in reference to tourism. What are underground, then, are activities that are community-based, church-based, and research-based—activities critical to the perpetuation of the performance tradition but virtually invisible outside their own arenas.

Women's contributions to Hawaiian entertainment have been absolutely crucial to its perpetuation. Women have been involved in a broad spectrum of roles, not only as singers and dancers but as composers, instrumentalists, teachers, educators, scholars, and policymakers. Importantly, in numerous cases, women's impact begins within their own families, and the descendants of prominent matriarchs embody the fruits of their teaching and practice. While the lens of foreground offers an opportunity to view the valorizing of women singers and dancers as a focal point, the lens of underground reveals the more crucial contribution of women in keeping the Hawaiian performance tradition truly alive. Moreover, this case underscores the importance of looking past that which is foregrounded, in plain view, to identify women's contributions in domains not in plain view yet crucial to that which is foregrounded.

FEATURED SOLOISTS

In Hawaiian entertainment, featured performers take front and center stage. Arguably, women featured as soloists are appreciated not only for vocal skill but for visual appearance as well. Photographs of women soloists with male instrumental ensembles emphasize the contrast in dress and adornment: women singers attired in floor-length dresses, often either white or bright colored floral fabrics, stand out against men in suits, and the women's abundance of floral adornment in lei and hairpieces is countered by minimal floral adornment on men—with the exception of men who are featured soloists and thus stand out from men whose roles are accompaniment. One variant that has highlighted women performers is their attire in hula costumes—raffia skirts—in contrast to male musicians wearing western-style suits or dress shirts, trousers, and shoes.

Pitch is another dimension in which women soloists stand out. Women's voice ranges rise above men's and even above many instruments, giving women a sonic foregrounding in the musical texture. In the Hawaiian music tradition, there are two distinct subtraditions of women soloists who sing in the high ranges.

The first subtradition can be termed "art songs," the performance of which originally aspired to concert-style presentation by singers whose voices demonstrated training and cultivation. This trained-voice style of performance was particularly associated with the genre of songs called *mele Hawai'i*, which prevailed in the late nineteenth century; many songs of that period remain widely known. *Mele Hawai'i* were songs that were modeled on the alternating verse-chorus song form of the gospel hymns initially introduced by Protestant missionaries, starting in the 1820s.

By the 1860s, Hawaiian composers were composing songs with secular (i.e., non-Christian) lyrics. Moreover, many of the composers were musically literate in western musical notation, which they used to notate their songs. In the late nineteenth century, new songs were premiered in concert recitals that were announced in the newspapers. These events usually included selections of western classical music, and the *mele Hawai'i* songs were performed with piano accompaniment—in the manner of German *lieder* and French *chanson*.

Mele Hawai'i songs have been a prominent part of the repertoire of the Royal Hawaiian Band, an institution in the history of Hawaiian music, formed under royal patronage in the late nineteenth century and continued in the present under municipal auspices. Initially an all-male ensemble, women were accepted as instrumentalists only after the mid-twentieth century. However, the band apparently has always featured a woman vocalist. Included in this cadre are such singers as Nani Alapai, Julia Chilton, Annie Lei Hall, Jennie K. Akeo, Lena Machado, Lizzie Alohikea, Yvonne Perry, and Nalani Olds Napoleon. To this day, women vocalists featured in the band's weekly concerts stand in front of a group of instrumentalists who remain overwhelmingly male, and no woman has yet been appointed as bandmaster. Yet the sonic presence of women is unmistakable, with soprano voices soaring above the majority of the instruments.

The second subtradition is associated with the repertoire and performance of *hula ku'i* songs. In contrast to the literate composition of *mele Hawai'i* songs that circulated as published sheet music, *hula ku'i* songs circulated mostly orally, and their performance incorporates vocal techniques that emanate from the older, indigenous system of chant. *Hula ku'i* songs were staples in party and nightclub entertainment, removed from the rarified realm of concert and recital halls, where *mele Hawai'i* songs reigned. The headlining women singers who emerged after World War II projected a self-confident panache manifested as earthy vocal flamboyance. The flair corresponded to the penchant in *hula ku'i* songs for double meanings in the lyrics, which singers would emphasize vocally through the use of chant-derived articulatory techniques.

The recordings of Genoa Keawe exemplify the vocal earthiness applied to *hula ku'i* songs. Her nearly six-decade recording career began in the late 1940s with the Honolulu-based 49th State Record Company, and her clear, bell-like voice, crisp enunciation, and widely admired use of yodeling, referred to as *ha'i*, have constituted a standard against which other singers are often compared.[3] Other singers who have enjoyed headliner status in the *hula ku'i* subtradition of Hawaiian music include Nora Keahi Santos, Pauline Kekahuna, Linda Dela Cruz, Myra English, Myrtle K. Hilo, Leinaala Haili, Kealoha Kalama, Leilani Sharpe Mendez, Karen Keawehawai'i, Darlene Ahuna, and Amy Hanaiali'i Gilliom.

There are some notable qualifications to the dichotomy drawn above. First, despite the contrasting performance practices commonly associated with *mele Hawai'i* and *hula ku'i* songs, the repertoire is not mutually exclusive with respect to singers' abilities. Singers select their repertoire on the basis of the subject matter of the lyrics and the musical materials (melody, harmonizations, tempo, etc.). Yet certain singers tend to gravitate toward a certain repertoire, depending on what their vocal techniques allow them to exploit—be it the rarified elegance of mele Hawai'i songs or the rambunctious *joie de vivre* of *hula ku'i* songs.

In this respect, the singer Lena Machado stands out as exceptional, in excelling in both repertoires. A featured soloist with the Royal Hawaiian Band in the 1930s, she was also an admired singer of *hula ku'i* songs to whom many would correctly point as the model for subsequent vocalists. Even more extraordinary, Lena Macado was also an accomplished song composer, and her *hula ku'i* songs—which constitute the bulk of her recordings currently circulating as reissues—were particularly suited to showcasing her skill in the *ha'i* yodeling technique.[4]

Moreover, while a majority of featured women singers are noted for singing in the high soprano range, the contralto Haunani Kahalewai enjoyed three decades of prominence as one of the featured singers on live weekly broadcasts of the *Hawaii Calls* radio show, which ran from 1935 into the early 1970s. Her low, sultry voice was featured on dozens of commercial recordings; successors could conceivably include Marlene Sai, Melveen Leed, and Ku'uipo Kumukahi.

In hula, women dancers have been foregrounded since the late 1800s. It is not difficult to understand why. As objects of desire, native Hawaiian women engaged the fascination of visiting European and American men. These men were among the earliest visitors to the islands in the late 1700s and the early 1800s; even as women travelers and settlers to the islands increased, especially after the arrival of the first party of American missionaries in 1820, men exerted a definite edge in publishing accounts of their travels and in taking photographs, contributing to a greater overall interest in images of women subjects than in men. And because entertainment provided a break from the activities of everyday subsistence, hula enjoyed the preference of artists and photographers over more pedestrian activities such as cooking or fishing.[5]

Hence in historical photographs and postcards since the 1860s is traceable a gradual disappearance of men as dancers. Photographs from the 1880s include men dancing alongside women or men dancers posing in studio portraits alongside women dancers. By the turn of the century, poses of hula troupes were dominated by women; when men were included in photographs, it was most often as accompanists.

The most widely circulated images of women dancers are those associated with the Kodak Hula Show. This show, which ran from 1932 to 2002, was intended to provide an opportunity for tourists to take their own souvenir photographs of hula performances, during daylight hours and in an outdoor setting; this was to compensate for the fact that the lighting in nightclub shows was too low for amateur photographers. Over the decades, numerous commercial hula-related products have been issued, ranging from photographs and postcards to slides, viewcards, 8 mm film, and VHS videotape. The commercial photos capture the three kinds of hula costumes used in the show: (1) the knee-length hula skirt made of ti leaves, worn with a shoulder-less fabric blouson; (2) the floor-length figure-hugging holoku gown with train; and (3) the loose long gown with a kerchief tied around the hips, used by comediennes.

Also emerging in the 1930s was the figure of the featured solo hula dancer, who stood out from the typical chorus line of the troupe. Performers who achieved soloist stature were not only graceful dancers; they embodied a particular exotic beauty that tourism marketing was quick to harness graphically on travel posters and advertisements. The ideal was a slender long-limbed mixed-race woman of medium color, not too fair yet not dark.[6] In shows, soloists often perform dances set in a slow tempo that emphasize grace and control; they are attired in glamorous gowns and an abundance of floral ornamentation in neck lei and hairpieces. It is interesting to note that the connections between hula and celebrated ideals of feminine beauty are most clearly seen in beauty pageants, where so many contestants elect to perform hula as their talent—not only at the Miss Hawai'i state pageant level but also in the Miss America pageant.[7]

The role of the featured hula soloist had its counterpart in Hollywood movies, where non-Hawaiian starlets were showcased in hula production numbers. Despite coaching in many instances by authoritative consultants, many starlets ended up shimmying fairly meaninglessly in numbers that showcased them visually but still cause trained hula dancers to cringe at their lack of technique. In one notable exception, tap dancer Eleanor Powell, in the 1940 film *Honolulu*, starts out the finale production number in a pseudo-hula that very quickly dissolves into a tap-dancing display only costumed to look like hula.

In the wake of the cultural revival of the 1970s and the establishment of hula competitions as premier venues for hula troupes, contestants for the title of Miss Aloha Hula in the oldest and most prestigious event, the Merrie Monarch Hula Competition, have altered the rules of the game. Contestants are judged not only on technique but also on Hawaiian language competence, demonstrated in chanting, and the extent to which their dancing conveys an understanding of what they are dancing about.

In the cultural world of hula competitions, in different spotlights from those of tourist entertainment venues, soloist contestants are not eye candy but rather knowledgeable exponents of hula technique. Headshot portraits of soloist contestants are included in the program book; those portraits often show poses associated with glamour photography, and subjects are dressed in elaborate attire and coiffure. Since talent and technique are valued above appearance, however, there is a wider range of body size and appearance among the contestants—all of whom represent competing troupes—and the winners. In a venue decidedly antithetical to tourist commodification, hula competitions have helped restore a broader visual spectrum more representative of contemporary Hawaiian women. But the ideal of featuring a woman dancer as soloist is still upheld: contests for male soloists are fewer, far less prominent (the Merrie Monarch competition, for example, does not include a solo men's category), and virtually ignored in the media.

MATRIARCHS OF TRADITION

Watching a formal performance of Hawaiian music or hula involves viewing a finished product. The performers must possess a minimum level of skill in singing, playing instruments, and dance; those skills are focused on specific songs that are taught and rehearsed. The formal performance adds two additional elements: costuming and staging. Performers must be attired in costumes that complement the program of songs that will be presented, particularly in the choice of floral materials for the neck, wrist, and ankle wreaths that adorn dancers. Staging involves how performers are spatially arranged on stage and how they enter and exit.

What is presented onstage constitutes the foreground of Hawaiian music and hula performance. For the vast majority of tourists, this is all that is visible. Among audiences of Hawai'i residents, some will see only the finished performance, while others may have opportunities to observe parts of the teaching and preparation (especially parents of children enrolled in hula classes). In this sense, what happens backstage is analogous to what happens underground, out of sight. And this is precisely where women have reigned supreme. Throughout the twentieth century, it is possible to trace not only the staging of Hawaiian entertainment but also the continuity of the performance tradition in the hands of women.

To focus on women is not to deny or denigrate the contributions of men in the teaching and perpetuation of Hawaiian music and hula. A handful of men commanded respect as teachers of hula, such as Pua Ha'aheo, Antone Ka'o'o, Bill Lincoln, Tom Hiona, Henry Pa, Samuel Naeole, George Na'ope, and Darrell Lupenui. Men also clearly dominated as instructors as well as performers on instruments such as guitar and 'ukulele. Men dominated music publishing as well: Henry Berger, Charles Hopkins, A. R. "Sonny" Cunha, Charles E. King, Ernest Kaai, and Johnny Noble all published major collections of song compositions and individual sheet music.[8] From the perspective of historical distance, however, one thing becomes apparent: despite the prominence of men as performers and publishers, it has been largely the work of women that has borne fruit into succeeding generations.

Consider some statistics. In 1970, the University of Hawai'i Committee for the Preservation of Hawaiian Language, Art and Culture identified five masters as *Loea Hula* (literally, skilled hula expert) for their deep knowledge of rarely taught aspects of the hula tradition. All five were women: Lokalia Montgomery, Mary Kawena Pukui, Iolani Luahine, Eleanor Hiram, and Kau'i Zuttermeister. In 1984, the Kalihi-Palama Culture and Arts Society published a volume, *Nānā i Nā Loea Hula*, that documented profiles of prominent hula teachers; women were the focus of sixty of the book's seventy-eight profiles. The follow-up volume with the same title, published in 1997, reflects a nurturing of men hula teachers: twenty-one of the book's fifty-seven profiles are of men.

The dominance of charismatic women teachers brings into view the concept of hula lineages, of tracing one's knowledge through prior generations of teachers. In the twentieth century, another aspect of lineage comes to the foreground, and that is the matriarchal nurturing of one's blood descendants among the students to whom the traditions and knowledge are passed.

Lineages of prominence in the history of Hawaiian music and dance are too numerous to enumerate fully here. Through four case studies, we can see many of the ways in which the teachings of matriarchal figures continue in the present. The two figures whose impact on Hawaiian music is detailed below are Vicki I'i Rodrigues and Imrgard Farden Aluli. Both women were heirs to family legacies in Hawaiian music and hula. Both women have achieved renown as composers whose work has been widely recorded and performed. Both women gave birth to children who grew up to carry on their traditions. And both women have nurtured generations of students who also carry on their traditions.

Vicki I'i Rodrigues was a highly regarded musician and a respected authority on Hawaiian music. Like many musicians and enthusiasts, "Auntie Vicki" (as she was affectionately known) maintained a personal book of songs. Some were compositions by her grandmother, Katie Stevens I'i; others were compositions by her grandfather, Thomas Sylvester Kalama. To this legacy she has added her own compositions, which have, in turn, passed on to her children and students. Her five children have all worked as entertainers; three in particular—Nina Keali'iwahamana, Boyce Ka'ihi'ihikapu, and Lani Custino—were long-standing performers with the *Hawaii Calls* radio show and have appeared on the numerous commercial recordings issued under the show's auspices.

In the late 1950s, Auntie Vicki and her five children collaborated on an LP titled *Na Mele Ohana*,[9] which called attention to the multigenerational contributions of her family in Hawaiian music. Auntie Vicki's legacy as a teacher extends to many students, among whom two in particular stand out. Contemporary *kumu hula* (hula master) Leimomi Ho credits Auntie Vicki as her only hula teacher and evolved her own styling of hula movement and choreography that for many years stood out as distinct from the stylings of kumu hula from other lineages. The accomplished falsetto singer Tony Conjugacion has served as a musical repository of Auntie Vicki's vast repertoire, which he has been recording in his own prodigious output; his 1996 recording *O Ka Wd I Hala* (Of the Time Past)[10] consisted mostly of Auntie Vicki's own compositions.

Irmgard Farden Aluli was one of thirteen siblings who were born into a musical household, grew up to be accomplished musicians, and are the subjects of a book-length biography.[11] Throughout her life, Auntie Irmgard composed hundreds of songs. One in particular has become standard for all musicians and dancers: the song "Puamana" praises her family's home of that name in Lahaina, Maui.

Puamana, ku'u home i Lahaina	Puamana is my home at Lahaina
Me n ā pua 'ala onaona,	With fragrant flowers,
kuu home i aloha 'ia	My home is beloved.

Ku'u home i ka ulu o ka niu,	My home in the coconut tree groves
'O ka niu kū kilakila,	The coconut trees stand upright
e napenape m ā lie.	And wave gently

Home nani, home i ka 'ae kai la	Beautiful home on the beach
Ke kōnane a ka mahina	The reflection of the moon
Ke kai hawanawana	Shines on the whispering sea.

Ha'ina 'ia mai ka puana	The story is told
Ku'u home i Lahaina	My home in Lahaina
I piha me ka hau'oli	Is filled with happiness. [12]

The song is well suited for beginning hula dancers, as it is filled with basic images to depict using hand and arm gestures: a home is depicted by showing the angled roof pitch with both hands; the coconut trees standing tall are depicted by holding one forearm across the chest, supporting the other arm held straight upright; the beach and ocean are depicted by hand gestures placed below the waist that sketch gentle waves washing onto the shore; and happiness is a playful shrug of the shoulders. [13]

Professionally active in entertainment throughout her life, Auntie Irmgard founded a quartet in the 1960s, which she named Puamana after her family home and the song about it. After years of inactivity, Puamana was resurrected in the 1980s with an all-family membership: daughters Mihana Aluli Souza and 'A'ima McManus and niece Luana McKenney. The group maintained an active performance schedule in the community and issued one CD, *From Irmgard with Love*, [14] consisting of Auntie Irmgard's songs. After Auntie Irmgard's passing in 2001, Mihana Souza issued a solo CD, [15] and her daughter Mahina Souza formed a duo, Kahala Moon, with cousin Kahala Mossman; they issued their debut CD, *Collage*, [16] in 2002. Mahina Souza represents yet another musical generation to come out of a family lineage of musical households.

In hula circles, women have had an even greater impact on the survival of traditional styles of performance that contrasted with the westernized styles in which Auntie Vicki I'i Rodrigues and Auntie Irmgard Aluli excelled. Hula in the performance tradition that supposedly predates westernization has always been more closely guarded by knowledgeable exponents. Attributes of sacredness permeate much of the material necessary for continuing ritual aspects of hula, particularly in the process of transmission and in the preparation for performances. By the mid- to late 1800s, many Christianized Hawaiians felt that Hawaiian ritual beliefs and practices were best left to pass. Some exponents took it on themselves to continue to teach these things clandestinely, especially to students who demonstrated a commitment to respect these traditions and to exercise appropriate caution in passing them further.

When, in the late 1960s and 1970s, Hawaiians began to reclaim those aspects of culture that had almost been suppressed out of existence, it was through the efforts of a handful of women teachers that this knowledge could be accessed and the practices brought back out into view. Two teachers in particular, Lokalia Montgomery and Edith Kanaká ole, exemplify the perpetuation of traditional hula practices not generally staged for tourist consumption and entertainment. These teachers are important not only because they transmitted their knowledge but because their students have also been extremely active in bringing about widespread participation in these traditions, in a pyramid kind of effect.

Lokalia Montgomery conducted classes in the living room of her Kapahulu home for years. In her classes, Lokalia focused on pre-twentieth-century repertoire not generally presented in tourist entertainment venues. At a time in the twentieth century when Hawaiians were raised as native speakers of English, Lokalia emphasized understanding of the poetic texts, many of which contained esoteric cultural knowledge. And at a time when westernized Hawaiian music provided the public soundscape, Lokalia's teachings kept alive the older, pre-hula *ku'i* chanted styles.

Among the legions of students who passed through her door, one in particular, Maiki Aiu Lake, was notable for training students who would continue to expand on Lokalia's teachings. Auntie Maiki clearly stands out as having exerted a major significance on hula generally: around 1970, she took the unprecedented step of opening a class specifically to train students who would go on to become teachers themselves. The first class graduated in 1972; over the next eleven years, she graduated forty-two students as teachers.[17]

The new cadre of teachers emerged precisely at the time when interest in studying hula had suddenly multiplied exponentially, and the respect for hula traditions that she instilled in her students became a cornerstone in their teaching of hula: in the orbits of Auntie Maiki's students, hula was not merely casual recreation but a serious endeavor to gain understanding of culturally rich traditions. Furthermore, her students included men who went on to establish schools that brought a vigorously masculine look to dancing and that were significant in drawing increasing numbers of men back to hula.

Most important, Auntie Maiki understood that living traditions are changing traditions. To this end, she instilled in her students a deep respect for what was handed down from the past; she drilled mastery of basic technique, and then she stood back and encouraged her graduates to innovate, confident that they would do so on a firm foundation. It was a potent combination of training, talent, and daring that Auntie Maiki had unleashed on the hula world, but one that has ultimately contributed to the flourishing of a truly vibrant range of idiosyncratic hula stylings.

A number of Auntie Maiki's students have, over the course of the years, directed award-winning hula troupes and made successful recordings that include notable amounts of traditional, as opposed to westernized, material. Although Auntie Maiki had also recorded her chanting, the recordings were only released posthumously in 1992 and clearly encapsulate a conservative approach to performing hula repertoire when placed next to the innovations of her students. [18]

Another example of a prominent hula lineage—and one that clearly dismandes any suggestion of an Oʻahu-island dominance in Hawaiian entertainment—is the Kanakaʻole family in Hilo, Hawaiʻi. Auntie Edith Kanakaʻole brought her family's tradition into the late twentieth century, having inherited it from her mother and grandmother and having trained her own daughters, especially Nalani Kanakaʻole and Pualani Kanakaʻole Kanahele, who assumed directorship of the school after Auntie Edith's passing in 1979. Auntie Edith's chanting and traditional repertoire were released on a 1977 recording, *Haʻakuʻi Pele i Hawaiʻi*;[19] this was followed by a recording of Auntie Edith's singing of her own compositions, HiʻipoiikaʻAina Aloha. [20]

The Kanakaʻole family's tradition is of particular significance for hula, because it is through the hula practice in this family that the repertorie associated with Pele, goddess of the volcano, has been transmitted continuously into the present (including the text cited at the beginning of this chapter, "Ke haʻa la Puna"). The family's proximity to Kilauea volcano accounts for a continuity of ritual practices surrounding the hula. The volcano, whose destructive eruptions gives birth to new land, is also clearly understood as the energizing source for the school's deep-bent-knee, bombastic hula style, low to the ground. In the wake of the vigorous cultural revival of the 1970s, the Kanakaʻoles' style has been widely emulated in hula schools throughout the islands and even in hula troupes in the continental United States.

In 1993, the National Endowment for the Arts honored the two sisters as National Heritage Fellows. Throughout the 1990s, they have turned their creative energies toward theatrical innovations in the presentation of the hula legacy that they guard. To date, two full-length shows have been staged, *Holo Mai Pele* and *Paiʻea*. The latter production toured California in 1998. The earlier production debuted in 1995, and in the fall of 2001 a one-hour film version was broadcast on PBS's Great Performances series, underscoring hula as a serious cultural tradition in a national venue. [21]

As the two direct heirs of Auntie Edith Kanakaʻole's traditions advance in age, the next two generations of the family have blossomed onto the hula scene. Kekuhi Kanahele, daughter of Auntie Pua, trained in the family hula traditions since childhood and designated as a co-successor (along with cousin Huihui Mossman) to her mother in directing the school, has come into her own as a singer, recording artist, and composer, having released three compact discs since 1996.[22] Kekuhi's son Lopaka Santiago, of college age at this writing, was also trained in the family hula traditions since childhood and has emerged as an award-winning vocalist in the falsetto tradition. He is preparing his first recording.

There are numerous other families who have been prominent in perpetuating Hawaiian music and dance, and whose eminence can be traced to the efforts of women who safeguarded the knowledge they received. Names such as Beamer, Puku'i, and Zuttermeister come to mind immediately. While space limitations do not allow a full consideration of those families' contributions, suffice it to note that in all cases, knowledge was passed into the present through the hands and voices of women.

In the context of hula competitions—venues of prestige that have emerged since the early 1970s[23] —there has emerged yet another way in which family dynasties are visibly manifested. At the start of the 1970s, an overwhelming majority of hula teachers actively teaching were women. Among women teachers, many of their daughters have since grown up around hula and have started to succeed their mothers in teaching hula and running the hula schools. For mother-daughter teams, competitions for solo titles have become a goal toward which to aspire. In the Merrie Monarch Hula Competition, the contest for the title Miss Aloha Hula has become a venue in which the daughters of prominent hula teachers do very well.

The most well known example is Aloha Dalire, *kumu hula* of Keolalaulani Halau 'Olapa o Laka. She was the very first winner of the soloist contest in 1971, when her mother was teaching hula; in the 1990s, all three of Aloha's daughters who have entered the contest have also won the title—Kapualokeokalaniakea in 1991, Kau'imaiokalaniakea in 1992, and Keolalaulani in 1999.[24] Other daughters of *kumu hula* who have won the title include Twyla Ululani Mendez (1984), daughter of Leilani Sharpe Mendez; Natalie Noelani Ai Kamau'u (1990), daughter of Olana Ai; Pi'ilani Smith (1989), daughter of Alicia Smith; Maelia Loebenstein (1993), granddaughter and successor of Mae Loebenstein; and Ku'ukamalani Ho (1996), daughter of Leimomi Ho. The prevalence of daughters of *kumu hula* being strong contenders drew much media commentary in 2002, when three contestants vying for the tide were daughters of well-regarded *kumu hula*.

The prominence of women guardians of the hula tradition is not limited to Hawai'i. Indeed, the relocation of Hawaiians to the continent has spurred the growth of hula schools, especially in California and Washington State. Again, women have dominated in the organization of schools and community events since the 1960s, and daughters are moving into positions of responsibility. In Hayward, California, *kumu hula* 'Ehulani Lum founded a hula school in the 1970s and launched the annual Iā 'Oe Ka Lā Hula Competition in 1981; her work is continued by her daughter Gordean Lum Villiados. Across the San Francisco Bay in San Mateo, longtime teacher Esther Correa has handed the reins of her school, Hula Halau 'o Ku'uleinani, to her daughter, Renee Kuʻuleinani Price. In Los Angeles, *kumu hula* Sissy Kaʻio was featured with her sons and daughters in the 1992 production titled *California Generations*, which toured the state; this program highlighted how cultural traditions are being perpetuated through multiple family generations. In San Diego, longtime teacher Auntie Barbara Finneran has been co teaching for years with her daughter, Karen Kealoha Finneran, as has the mother-daughter team of Kauʻi Brown and Donna Merghart.

TRACKING WOMEN'S HISTORY IN HAWAIIAN MUSIC AND HULA

Space limitations required focusing on a handful of case studies rather than systematically surveying the richness of women's contributions in Hawaiian music and dance. In general, however, it is possible to sketch two broad contours. Onstage, women are featured soloists, as much for their visual appearance as for their technical skill in singing or dancing. Behind the scenes, out of casual sight lines, and despite challenges that have threatened the continuity of hula (for example, conversion to Christianity in the early 1800s, when hula was deemed pagan and targeted for suppression), deep knowledge of esoteric traditions has been passed into the present by women. Not only did women safeguard knowledge of older ways when those ways were out of fashion; women exerted matriarchal authority in ensuring that students they trained would be respectful and responsible caretakers of knowledge they received. In the case of Auntie Maiki Aiu Lake, students were grounded in traditions so that they would be appropriately cautious as well as informed about how they chose to innovate.

The history of Hawaiian music and dance is replete with strong women who exerted significant influence on the careers of many entertainers. Moreover, it is clear that a history of native Hawaiian women must be viewed in terms of both what is publicly visible "onstage" and what is carefully guarded underground. Many aspects of Hawaiian culture have survived because one or more women held them close until they decided to pass on whatever they were protecting. The case of Hawaiian music and dance is particularly suggestive, because so much performance has been publicly visible. It is always difficult to know whether what is plainly visible is all that there is, or whether there is a bigger backdrop framing it. How much one can see then becomes a matter of where one is standing—inside, among the accepted acolytes, or outside, among the neophytes.

Hawaiian music and hula offer yet another dimension for further consideration. Hawaiʻi's multiethnic population, along with liberal incidents of interethnic marriages, suggests that Hawaiian performance traditions may be of interest to historians of Asian American women. Not only is it the case that Hawai'i residents include people of various ethnic heritage; the historical trend of interethnic marriages and the customary Hawaiian practice of adoption have blurred many lines between ethnicities and cultural practices. The very names of various hula teachers, such as Beverly Muraoka, Victoria Holt Takamine, and Denise Ramento, inscribe a multitude of complex histories of interaction. What is visible is perhaps not all that there is to know about how women in Hawaiian music and hula have passed tradition into the present.

NOTES

1. Nathaniel B. Emerson, *Pele and Hiiaka: A Myth from Hawaii* (Honolulu: Advertiser, 1915), xv–xvii, 1–2. Emerson's published version has been the basis for contemporary knowledge of this saga and of the poetic repertoire associated with hula. Recent research by S. Ku'ualoha Ho'omanawanui has identified multiple versions of the Pele and Hi'iaka legends, which are already revising our reception of Emerson's published version.

2. The Hawaiian text is based on Emerson with some revision of punctuation; the translation is mine.

3. Genoa Keawe's discography includes hundreds of songs on 78 rpm, 45 rpm, LP, cassette, and CD. Two highly recommended recordings are *Party Hulas* (Hula Records H-507, 1965) and *Luau Hulas* (Hula Records H-514, 1967); both have been reissued on compact disc (http://www.hawaiian-music.com/). Individual songs recorded on the 49th State label have been reissued on various compact discs in the series "Vintage Hawaiian Treasures," produced by Cord International (http://www.cordinternational.com/).

4. Lena Machado's recordings of her song compositions, dating from 1935 to 1962, have been reissued on *Hawaiian Song Bird* (Hana Ola HOCD29000, 1997; http://www. cordinternational.com/wahine.htm).

5. Several rich collections of photographs of hula since the mid-1800s have been published in recent years: see especially Mark Blackburn, *Hula Girls and Surfer Boys* 1870–1940 (Atglen, PA: Schiffer Publishing, 2000) and *Hula Heaven: The Queen"s Album* (Atglen, PA: Schiffer Publishing, 2001). Popular culture iconography of hula girl figurines and representations appears in Chris Pfouts, *Hula Dancers and Tiki Gods* (Atglen, PA: Schiffer Publishing, 2001). To place postcards depicting hula dancers in the context of postcards of Hawai'i generally, see Keith Steiner, *Hawai'i's Early Territorial Days 1900–1915 Viewed from Vintage Postcards by Island Curio* (Honolulu: Mutual Publishing, 2001).

6. Jane Desmond has painstakingly traced these visual formations in relation to racialization and the marketing of Hawaiian entertainment. See her *Staging Tourism: Bodies on Display from Waikiki to Sea World* (Chicago: University of Chicago Press, 1999), 34–121.

7. Interestingly, the first Miss Hawai'i to win the Miss America title, in 1991, was not a hula dancer. When pageant producers decided to institute a salute to the home state of the outgoing Miss America in 1992, Carolyn Sapp was cast as a central focus in an elaborate hula production number with the Brothers Cazimero and dancers associated with their show, then at the Royal Hawaiian Hotel.

8. For a bibliographic survey of Hawaiian songbooks and a historical contextualization of these particular compilations, see Amy K. Stillman, "Published Hawaiian Songbooks," *Notes* 44:1 (December 1987), 221–39.

9. Hula Records H-501.

10. Mountain Apple Company MACD 2031.

11. Mary C. Richards, *Sweet Voices of Lahaina: The Life Story of Maui's Fabulous Fardens* (Aiea: Island Heritage, 1990).

12. Chikao Toriyama, *Musical Images of Hawai'i* (Honolulu: Chikao Toriyama, 1996), 77. Translation is mine.

13. The song "Puamana" was also the structuring device used in the documentary film of the same name about Auntie Irmgard, produced by Les Blank, Meleanna Aluli Meyer, and Chris Simon. See *Puamana* (El Cerrito, CA: Flower Films, 1991).

14. Mountain Apple Company MACD 2049, 1998.

15. I. Mihana, *Rust on the Moon* (IM Records 777, 2001.

16. Kahala Moon, *Collage* (Keala Records 1218, 2002).

17. Rita Ariyoshi, *Hula Is Life: The Story of Halau Hula o Maiki* (Honolulu: Maiki Aiu Building Corporation, 1998), 66–67.

18. Maiki Aiu Lake and the Kahauanu Lake Trio and Singers, *Maiki: Chants and Mele of Hawaii* (Hula CDHS-588, 1992). Chant recordings by her students include three by Keli'i Tau'a—*The Pele Legends* (Pumehana PS-4903, 1977), *Kamehameha Chants* (Pumehana PS-4918, 1979), and *Pule Mua* (Mountain Apple Company MACD 2032, 1996)—and two by John R. Kaha'i Topolinski—*Na Mele Kupuna* (Pumehana PS-4906,1978) and *Nou E Kawena* (Pumehana PS-4926,1986). Robert Cazimero can be heard on over twenty recordings issued by the popular Brothers Cazimero duo, but his creative work with traditional hula is not yet represented on commercial sound recordings. The work of Auntie Maiki's students can be seen in commercial videotapes of televised broadcasts of hula competitions, in particular the prestigious Merrie Monarch Hula Competition.

19. Hula Records HS-560, 1977.

20. Hula Records HS-568, 1979.

21. The companion book by Pualani Kanaka'ole Kanahele, *Holo Mai Pele* (Honolulu: Pacific Islanders in Communication and Hilo: Edith Kanaka'ole Foundation, 2001), contains song texts, translations, and explanations of the Hawaiian-language repertoire seen on film. The school also issued a compact disc, *Uwōlani* (Liko Records LRCD-2003, 1998), which includes more traditional material in the troupe's repertoire.

22. *Hahani Mai* (Punahele PPCD004, 1996), *Kekuhi* (Mountain Apple Company MACD 2054, 1998), and *Honey Boy* (Mountain Apple Company MACD 2089.

23. For an overview of hula competition events, see Amy Stillman, "Hawaiian Hula Competitions: Event, Repertoire, Performance, Tradition," *Journal of American Folklore* 100 (1996): 357–80.

24. For newspaper coverage, see Cynthia Oi, "Dancing across the Generations," *Honolulu Star Bulletin*, April 9, 1999; online at http://starbulletin.com/1999/04/09/news/story2.html.

Chapter Thirteen

Cibo Matto's *Stereotype A*

Articulating Asian American Hip Pop

Jane C. H. Park

In 1996 Yuka Honda and Miho Hatori, of the now defunct independent hip hop/alternative pop band Cibo Matto, appeared on a special food segment of MTV's *House of Style*. The Japanese-born female musicians served as guides on a culinary tour of fashionable ethnic cuisines in New York City. The stint followed the release of their debut album, *Viva! La Woman* by Warner Bros. Records, which contained songs heavily laced with food themes and imagery. A few years later, Hatori and Honda performed on PBS's *Sessions on West 54th* to promote their second album, *Stereotype A*. In response to host John Hyatt's question, "Do you consider New York your spiritual home?" Hatori replied in the affirmative, saying the group's cultural and musical roots lay in the multicultural milieu of downtown New York. Apparent in these two media representations is a distinct shift in the popular perception of Cibo Matto—from the latest Japanese novelty band in 1996 to a serious Japanese American alternative pop group three years later. How and why did this shift take place? And what strategies does the band's short history provide for dealing differently with gender and racial stereotypes in popular culture?

INTRODUCTION

This essay looks at how Cibo Matto (hereafter CM) was marketed to appeal to an American alternative pop and hip hop audience. What racial, sexual, and cultural terms did the music press use to frame and sell CM? How do these terms relate to historical representations of Asian and Asian American women in the United States? Finally, how did the band acknowledge and engage with these representations in its songs? I try to answer these questions by positioning the group within the larger stories of hip hop and women in popular music and by showing how its unique identity as an Asian American female band contributes to these histories. More specifically, I consider the ways in which CM's music and their image as technologically savvy female artists suggest a new way to critique existing racial and gender stereotypes of Asian and Asian American women in the United States.

No extended academic analysis has been done on this particular group, and little scholarship exists on Asian Americans in popular music. My work on CM does not claim to represent the experiences of minority groups in U.S. media or those of contemporary Japanese female pop bands. Rather, it provides a case study of one such band and its members' attempts to negotiate the double legacy of racism and sexism in the American popular music industry. However, before attempting to answer larger questions about the band's social and political significance, it is necessary to provide some background on its conception, development, and reception.

NOT ANOTHER SHONEN KNIFE

Journalist Yuka Honda and student Miho Hatori met in New York during the early 1990s while playing in an avant-garde punk band called Leitoh Lychee. When the group broke up, the two decided to start their own band and christened it Cibo Matto ("food crazy" in Italian). Their first self-titled CD was released in 1995 through the Japanese independent label, People's Records, and sold twenty thousand copies.[1] Given the publicity of their recording ventures, their connections with Yoko Ono, the Beastie Boys and the Lounge Lizards, and their growing New York fan base, CM was recruited by Warner Bros. Records in 1996.

Viva! La Woman (hereafter *Viva*) was released and appeared on the lists of top ten hip hop albums for 1996 in *Spin* and *Rolling Stone*. In the album Hatori raps fiercely in broken, heavily accented English against Honda's cool sonic patchwork—eclectic, upbeat samples of popular musical kitsch. Critics seized upon the food imagery in the album and the group's ethnic and gender identities to link them with Shonen Knife (hereafter SK), another alternative Japanese female band, which also sang about food. The comparison works to a point. Both bands use highly metaphoric, often surrealistic language to evoke a mixture of English and Japanese cultural sensibilities and to conflate lyrically tropes of food, sex, and nation. As well the bands demonstrate a similar kind of musical hybridity in their layering of pop, rock, and punk elements into a kind of uncannily familiar sonic pastiche. This pastiche seems to resonate for an American audience due in part to the bands' ambivalent performance styles—not quite "straight" but not outright parody either.

Outside these similarities, however, the bands had little in common. SK's punk-pop sound and DIY approach affiliated them with the West Coast punk and grunge music scene, while CM's music and image linked them to the alternative hip hop and electronica scene in New York.[2] SK songs revolve around supergirly, childlike topics like cats, Barbie dolls, and junk food. Their sound is consistent and easily recognizable: the songs are short with minimalist punk chords, tinny guitar, and heavily accented lyrics that carry a chirpy carpe diem message. CM's songs, on the other hand, show a broader stylistic range, mixing different cultural genres—from bossa nova, disco-fimk, and jazz to rap, R&B, down tempo, and heavy metal.

Also, unlike SK members, who remain based in Osaka and identify as native Japanese, Honda and Hatori refer to themselves as an "American band run by Asian people."[3] Hatori makes a connection between their ambiguous national and cultural affiliations and the formal syncretism of their music—a connection I elaborate on later. She jokes, "People always expect you to choose sides between digital or analog, old school or new school, even between Chinese or Italian food. Well, we eat everything."[4]

Finally, while SK is friends with feminist-identified bands L7 and Bikini Kill, its members take a nonfeminist stance, preferring to see themselves as musicians before women: "We never thought of ourselves as a female band."[5] CM members, on the other hand, are quick to identify as feminists and to recognize the sexist and racist stereotypes the press sometimes has conferred on them. Take for instance Yuka Honda's musings in a 1999 interview with Heidi Sherman:

> It's hard for people to take us seriously. We are girls, so they ask us who writes our music. We have all these food titles, so people kind of put us in this novelty band category. With the last album [*Viva*] people would ask us, "Do you think you're stereotyped?" But afterward they would ask, "What's your favorite food?" You know, things they would never ask me if I were the drummer of The Roots.[6]

CUTESY J-POP, WITH AN EDGE

As Honda points out, critics often lumped CK with bands like SK and Pizzicato 5 based on the bands' shared national origin, ambiguous "cute" image, and penchant for food and pop culture themes. One example appears in a 1998 article by music critic Neil Strauss in the *New York Times*. "New Sounds from Japan: A Starter's Kit" presents a kind of Western ethnomusicologist's guide to the obscurely hip music scene of a culture that has become synonymous with high-tech gadgetry, video games, and Japanese animation. It lists several new and upcoming Japanese artists, the majority of them male, in various musical categories.[7] Strauss legitimates these artists by likening their inevitable "invasion" of the U.S. popular music scene to the British rock invasion led by the Beatles in the 1960s. The taxonomy of Japanese musicians ends with a category Strauss labels *kawaii*, which contains the only two female bands in his guide: Shonen Knife and Cibo Matto.

The Japanese term *kawaii* translates as "cute" and is used to describe a gendered aesthetic style that melds the image of the underaged, sometimes coyly innocent nymphet with the pleasures of consumer capitalism. Japanese imports in the United States bearing the mark of the *kawaii* style include the Sanrio family of toys, and anime [Japanese cartoon] television programs such as *Sailor Moon* and *Pokemon*. The schoolgirl look so popular in Japan has found its U.S. equivalent in the explicitly sexual versions of the "bubblegum pop" star personae epitomized by young female musicians like Britney Spears and Christina Aguilera.

Rather than unwittingly or willingly falling under this category, Honda and Hatori playfully critique it. They do so by exploring—in their lyrics, music, and performance styles—the complex set of questions about female objectification, subjectivity, and agency raised by this image of infantilized female sexuality. From the start, CM members quite consciously engaged with the widespread stereotype of Asian women generally and Japanese women specifically as cute, naive, and girlish—a stereotype that links the desirable "innocence" of Japanese women to that of the early 1960s all-American girl. Some critics seemed to comprehend their strategy:

> The bare description of Cibo Matto sounds like a gimmick or a put-on: two Japanese women from the Lower East Side of Manhattan, a vocalist (Miho Hatori) and a sound manipulator (Yuka Honda), with an entire album of songs about food, from "White Pepper Ice Cream" to "Beef Jerky." But in Cibo Matto's songs, food encompasses love and sensuality, memory and anticipation.[8]

Others missed it altogether:

> It's just what you'd expect from a novelty act whose name means "food crazy" in Italian and whose every song is about love, cuisine and love of cuisine.[9]

> The group is two Japanese women, Miho Hatori and Yuka Honda, who live in New York and are infatuated with contemporary pop music that uses "sampling"—a technique that treats a song like a tossed salad, lacing the melody with exotic and arresting sound effects. But that's just the start. Cibo Matto also has a major food fixation. The group's name is Italian for "food crazy."[10]

Others seemed to like what CM was doing, but weren't quite sure what to make of it:

> Imagine that Beck and Bjork had a love child in Tokyo, and you might get some idea of this delightful blend of hip-hop, scat-rap, scraps of reggae and experimental ambient noise. . . . These songs are either very deep or very silly, but either way they often come across like a string of Japanese haiku poems tacked together.[11]

> Listening to Cibo Matto's global-economic synthesis feels like crashing into some cartoon netherworld where Abba waltzes with Kraftwerk at Studio 54. In other words, it sounds fake—but not in a bad way. . . . Like a spoonful of sorbet, Cibo Matto dazzles the tongue for an instant, then melts.[12]

LOST AND FOUND IN TRANSLATION

Most likely, the ambivalent framing of CM results from the relative invisibility of Japanese popular music in mainstream America. Japanese female musicians whose work has migrated to the United States include the pop duo, Pink Lady; the "Japanese Madonna," Matsuda Seiko; the lead singer of postmodern pop group Pizzicato 5, Maki Nomiya; and the indie rock trio, Buffalo Daughter. Of this short list, those who have managed to succeed in the United States, Shonen Knife, Pizzicato 5, Buffalo Daughter, and Cibo Matto, tend to attract an alternative audience that emphasizes the groups' distinctly "Japanese" look and sound.[13] The audience base for these bands seems to differ little from the critics in their attraction to the "exotic" element of the bands' representation.

What is significant here is not so much that these bands self-consciously perform Oriental tropes but that critics and fans have been so quick to conflate these performances with the musicians' racial and gender identities. To a large extent, this kind of reception can be seen as the outcome of the "Japanese chic" trend that began in the early 1980s—a new kind of consumer Orientalism which exploded in the late nineties due to the rising popularity of East Asian aesthetic forms in Hong Kong action cinema, Japanese animation, video games, and fashion. While this kind of crossover brings visibility to Japanese and East Asian peoples and cultures in the West, it often tends to mark them as permanently foreign, since their salability depends on their difference from the perceived norm. Alvin Liu, assistant arts editor for the *San Francisco Bay Guardian*, notes this double bind: "Japanese artists who succeed in the United States . . . offer a new spin on old forms, combining once-familiar pop formulas in ways that may not have occurred to an artist in the United States or Europe." He goes on to mention that the potential danger for groups that do find an audience in the West lies in their almost inevitable exoticization as "novelty acts" by fans and critics. [14]

CM differs from the other Japanese-born groups mentioned in that, with the release of *Stereotype A* (*SA*), they self-identified as Asian American. By doing so, they challenged the traditional idea of Asian Americans as individuals born in the United States who have assimilated culturally and can speak English fluently. They point instead to a new kind of "Asian American" represented by the growing number of transnational immigrants from East Asia who seem able to negotiate and bridge more easily the "Asian" and "American" elements of their identities. They also point to a growing acceptance in the United States, especially among American youth who have been raised on Japanese and Hong Kong popular culture, of East Asian peoples and styles as not so solidly foreign, but rather uncannily familiar. This acceptance—which often rides a dimly discernible line be appropriation and appreciation—appears heavily in hip hop culture: in the lyrics and styles of groups as diverse as the Wu Tang Clan, Common, Dead Prez, the Beastie Boys, and DMX. The established presence of Asian references in hip hop and CM's association with the alternative hip hop scene in downtown New York laid the groundwork for Hatori and Honda to make their musical debut by deconstructing hip hop, the now global language of youth and popular culture, using another, older global language, that of food and consumption.

In *Representing*, Craig Watkins discusses the cross-marketability of hip hop in social and political terms. He defines hip hop as a social movement in that it "enables its participants to imagine themselves as part of a larger community"—both through the creative use of technology in songs, performances, and recordings and the synergistic production and consumption of hip hop "lifestyles."[15] A group like CM provides a way to look at how this political element of hip hop double translates, to Japan in the 1990s and then back to the United States via Japanese American immigrant artists. In "Hip Hop and Racial Desire in Contemporary Japan," Nina Cornyetz asserts that hip hop provides a political use-value for young Japanese fans—but one different from the use-value for hip hop audiences in other places and times. To explain, she turns to sampling, the process of entering analog sound sources (usually loops from older songs, though for more abstract artists, snippets can come from primary sounds such as recorded traffic noise or the din of restaurant conversations) into the sampler, an instrument that records these sources in digital form, allowing them to be edited, manipulated, and sutured into new compositions.[16]

According to Cornyetz, sampling can be linked to the production of Japanese national subjectivity in two ways. First, it echoes cultural and economic strategies that Japan has used to reposition itself in the global order since World War II. In the same way that disenfranchised black and Latino Bronx youth in the 1970s created a new expressive form by rearranging the musical materials around them, Japan used Western economic and cultural models to assert its identity in the postindustrial transnational world order. Second, contemporary Japanese hip hop fans, like most youth, are positioned outside the dominant culture. In Japan, this culture tries to interpolate them as corporate drones ("sararimen") and well-behaved housewives. Through its musical and visual style, hip hop gives these Japanese youth a tool with which to critique the dominant culture and to construct a future wherein they might reclaim subjectivity on their own terms. [17]

As native-born Japanese women who call New York City home, CM members Hatori and Honda occupy a transnational space that cuts across subculture and dominant culture, Japan and America, commercial and old school hip hop. . . . It is a position fraught with misunderstanding and prone to misinterpretation as evidenced by the band's reception. Clearly, the lumping together of CM with other Japanese and female bands on the basis of a combined racial, national, and sexual identity fits squarely into Edward Said's definition of orientalism. [18] At the same time, it also recalls similar ghettoizations in contemporary U.S. popular music—in particular, the commercialized reduction of female groups and musicians such as L7, Hole, P. J. Harvey, and Liz Phair under the banner of "Women in Rock," [19] and the invisibility of female musicians as producers and DJs relative to their vocalist and MC counterparts.

As the Grammy Awards ceremony demonstrates every year, ghettoizations in the music industry continue to exist along the lines of both gender and race. At the same time, the use of new technologies to create and express different musical styles has begun to challenge the racist and sexist assumptions that undergird the marginalization of women, people of color, and musicians who fit both categories. It is to these technologies and their potential for social and political change that I now turn.

TECHNOLOGY, RACE, GENDER, . . . AND MUSIC

In her article, "Just a Girl?" Gayle Wald describes how the music press used the construction of "innocent" femininity to pit SK and CM against their less "girly" Riot Grrl counterparts. Wald's primary argument is that Riot Grrls strategically reappropriate the site of girlhood to "construct alternative modes of visibility for women in independent rock." In a brief, provocative section at the end, she contrasts the gendered roles assumed in the music scene by Riot Grrl and these Japanese bands:

In short, such a deliberate performance [by the Riot Grrls] assumes a subject for whom girlishness precludes, or is in conflict with, cultural agency. But what of women whose modes of access to, and mobility within, the public sphere depend on their supposed embodiment of a girlish ideal?[20]

In other words, what of nonwhite, non-American women whose only form of visible subjectivity within the Western context is one that simultaneously infantilizes them and marks them as "other"? The opposition that Wald describes displaces the prefeminist notion of "girl" from the bodies of white women onto those of Japanese women specifically and Asian women generally. The trivialization of Japanese female bands like CM recalls and troubles the discursive segregation of "pop" and "rock" music that began with the arrival of the Beatles and subsequent ousting of the girl groups in the United States. In her essay "(R)evolution Now," Norma Coates gives a concise summary of the relationship between pop and rock that followed this shift:

In this schema, rock is metonymic with "authenticity" while "pop" is metonymic with "artifice." Sliding even further down the metonymic slope, "authentic" becomes "masculine" while "artificial" becomes "feminine." Rock, therefore, is "masculine," pop is "feminine," and the two are set in a binary relation to each other, with the masculine . . . on top.[21]

Coates's point on gender applies as well to race and nationality in the context of CM's initial reception as exotic Japanese "others" putting a quaint spin on hip hop. In this perception of the group, the stereotype of Japan specifically and East Asians generally as clever imitators of Western styles connects neatly to the sexist association of female musicians with pop and artifice. CM easily could have succumbed to the rock-pop, authentic-inauthentic binary by producing a second album that clearly went one way: either explicitly commercial bubblegum pop or "serious" alternative rock. Instead, Hatori and Honda followed in the footsteps of friends like Prince Paul, Dan the Automator, and Yoko Ono by producing, in *SA*, a generically hybrid work that refuses categorization. As in *Viva*, they do so through an expert manipulation of musical technologies during recordings and performances.

Later in her essay, Coates could be referring to CM when she posits a potential rethinking of the male, authentic rock-female, inauthentic pop binary based on the use of new musical technologies by marginal groups:

The onset of new musical trends such as techno, digital sampling, and the increased reliance upon studio technologies to enhance and stimulate musi production has provoked a rethinking of the concept of authenticity.[22]

Coates is referring here to attitudes toward and uses of technology that define hip hop and electronica, an umbrella category for genres such as techno, drum-and-bass, house, and down tempo (formerly trip-hop), which rely heavily on technological instruments: samplers, sequencers, and synthesizers. Consider as well the following description of rap as "a complex fusion of orality and postmodern technology" in Tricia Rose's *Black Noise*:[23]

> The arrangement and selection of sounds rap musicians have invented via samples, turntables, tape machines, and sound systems are at once deconstructive (in that they actually take apart recorded musical compositions) and recuperative (because they recontextualize these elements creating new meanings for cultural sounds that have been relegated to commercial waste bins).[24]

To put it another way, hip hop and electronica use various technologies to deconstruct and reconstruct sound fragments in much the same way that marginal subjects create identities for themselves in a society that refuses to acknowledge them as wholly human. These subjects recontextualize the cultural labels that have been thrust upon them—poor, female, immigrant, black, Latina, queer, Asian—to create powerful new identities whose truth and strength reside in the continued acknowledgment of their painful histories. In this way, the process of reclaiming marginal identity or experience can be likened to the construction, performance, and reception of hip hop and electronic music. Furthermore, the techniques of sampling, rapping, recording, and sequencing can help create a type of layered, polyglot voice that offers an alternative interpretation of authenticity, the big idea underlying and perpetuating the rock-pop binary. Hip hop and electronica—when it is good and it works—consists of questioning this binary and the notion of the "authentic" self and text as fixed, coherent, and comprehensible.

RACIALIZED CYBORG-GIRLS

This section begins a discussion that attempts to tie many of the ideas presented so far, particularly issues of nation, gender, and technology. As such, it functions as a kind of preliminary theoretical road map for exploring how female artists of color might produce trenchant social critique through stylistic and cultural juxtapositions that stem from a genuine appreciation for difference. The link between music as art-in-process and self as subject-in-process is a major theme in most of CM's songs, which incorporate a conscious, innovative use of digital technologies. The two project an image of cosmopolitan sophistication, reinforced by the Dada quality of their lyrics and the hip, futuristic image they project on their album covers, music videos, and live performances. For instance, the inside cover of *Viva* foregrounds Hatori and Honda in a studio cluttered with recording equipment, skateboards, and computers. This image runs counter to traditional ideas of the female musician as technologically incompetent, fit only to head a band with her voice and sex appeal or to occupy the background as a backup singer or dancer.

In a *New York Times* article on the 1998 Winter Musical Conference in Miami, Evelyn McDonnell notes the absence of female musicians in electronica. After listing artists such as Bjork and Beth Orton, McDonnell points out that they are mostly vocalists who do not fit the image of the male electronica musician—the "science nerd, madly fiddling with a wall of machines"—now a fixture in the popular music scene thanks to folks such as David Byrne, the Chemical Brothers, Moby, and Fatboy Slim. According to McDonnell, female artists such as Pauline Oliveros, Laurie Anderson, and Cibo Matto who do fiddle with walls of machines disprove the stereotype of women as technophobic. However, when the press does acknowledge such artists, it frames them as exceptions to the general rule: "When women run the gizmos, they are considered . . . iconoclastic loners—performance artists. When men do it, they create a genre in their own image."[25]

While the sexy female geek remains marginal in popular music, alternative-minded artists like CM, Le Tigre, DJ Shortee, and others, along with a burgeoning group of younger female electronica musicians, [26] *have* started to create a genre in their own image, albeit one yet to be widely acknowledged. Consider, for example, the following scene: an October 30, 1999, performance on *Sessions at West 54th*. Yuka Honda, wearing wired bunny ears, nonchalantly inserts floppy disks into a computer synthesizer while a pigtailed Hatori sings soulfully into the microphone. The boys—Timo Ellis, Duma Love, and Sean Lennon—provide backup. The camera focuses on the two Japanese women performing their artistic and commercial negotiations with "*kawaii*," jumping up and down, punk-pogo style, shooting quick smiles at each other across the stage.[27] This scene heralds the arrival of what I call the active racialized cyborg-girl, a subject that speaks through, with, and as a new kind of human-machine.

Donna Haraway defined the cyborg in 1991 as an entity simultaneously organic and inorganic, human and machine. In the "Cyborg Manifesto," she uses the trope of the cyborg primarily to critique and trouble hetero-normative notions of gender and sexuality, and in *Modest_Witness* (1997) she attempts to do the same with race and ethnicity. CM members perform Haraway's concept of the gender-transgressive cyborg but put a different spin on it as diasporic Japanese female artists. They do so first by defying musical categorization, revealing the inherent instability of genre categories in popular music, and second by using technology as image and instrument to critique historical stereotypes of Asian women in the United States.

YOKO, THE PIONEER

The lineage of the racialized cyborg-girl can be traced back to Yoko Ono, the Japanese American musician, poet, and performance artist whom Beatles fans still vilify as the "dragon lady" who stole John Lennon away from his British musical brethren. As an incomprehensible Dragon Lady who refused to play the Lotus Blossom, Ono received brutal treatment from the media in the 1960s and 1970s. As she put it in an interview with Amei Wallach, "I think the image of the Asian woman up until me was Madam Butterfly. . . . I was touching a sacred cow, but I also didn't seem to be that vulnerable woman who is going to commit suicide. I was coming right at your face." This rebellious attitude earned Ono labels like "John Rennon's Excrusive Gloupie" from Esquire magazine in 1961. After years of condemnation from Beatles fans, Ono is finally being acknowledged as an artist in her own right with her role in the band IMA, which she founded with her son Sean Ono Lennon, and art exhibitions such as "Yes Yoko Ono" at the Whitney Museum in fall 2000.[28]

Lennon and Ono first met at her one-woman show in London's Indica Gallery in 1966 when she was an up-and-coming New York avant-garde artist associated with the Fluxus art movement. Fluxus members John Cage, Nam June Paik, Walter De Maria, Richard Maxfield, Terry Riley, and others were interested in dissolving the barriers between media forms. Their work led eventually to the creation of what is now known as performance art. After marrying Lennon, Ono continued her experiments in sound, video, and image by collaborating with him on B-sides and albums such as *Double Fantasy* and *Yoko Ono/Plastic Ono Band*. She was also a vocal activist in the women's movement and the antiwar movement, and she and Lennon performed their political views with controversial events such as bed-ins, bagism, "happenings," and the scandalous *Two Virgins* album cover, which featured the newlyweds nude.[29] As a cofounder of Fluxus, a collaborator with Lennon, and an undervalued artist who, like Andy Warhol, turned her celebrity into art, Ono paved the way for many contemporary Asian American female artists, including Cibo Matto.

Like Ono, Honda and Hatori posit a new kind of gendered racial den for Asian Americans. At the same time, like Ono, they remain stuck in a web of old stereotypes that continue to be reproduced in slightly different forms. They engaged with these stereotypes by openly acknowledging and playing with them in their second album.

PLAYING (WITH) STEREOTYPES

Critical reception for *SA* mostly reflected the shift in the band's narrative and formal focus. In this album, the group tried to shake off its image as a food-obsessed novelty band. Honda and Hatori ousted former producers, Mitchell Froom and Tchad Blake, to produce the songs themselves, with the help of several musical friends, including Timo Ellis, Sean Lennon (whom Honda was dating at the time), Marc Ribot, Medeski, Martin & Wood, Soul Coughing, and Buffalo Daughter, another Japanese American female band.[30] Unlike *Viva* the songs in *SA* seldom refer to food and tend to veer toward self-consciously crafted art pop rather than staying within a more recognizably hip hop aesthetic. In the first week of its release, the album shot up to the top of the *College Music Journal* (*CMJ*) Chart, the official monitor of alternative radio. A few reviewers continued to take CM less seriously than their male counterparts. The comment below, for example, attributes CM's elevation to "proper band" status to the addition of two new male members, Sean Lennon and Timo Ellis:

> The 2-year-old Cibo Matto scrambles cocktail music, jazz, funk, hip-hop, punk. . . . They were cute and precious early; midway they were joined by "guests, friends and semi-permanent members, like family," bassist Sean Lennon (famous lineage, plays in IMA) and drummer Russell Simons [sic] (John Spencer Blues Explosion/IMA). The sound became more ferocious, and they emerged from the "novelty" shroud.[31]

> The most obvious change, though (between VLW and CM) is that they actually sound like a proper band now, thanks to the presence of Sean Lennon and Timo Ellis.[32]

However, most critics at this point seemed to "get" the band's use of complex cultural juxtapositions and their "knowing wink" at an audience that also presumably "got" the message. Note the use of the adjective "faux" in the comment below, which indicates that the reviewer knows the group is performing a staged form of innocence for a smart, appreciative audience.

> They (Hatori and Honda) were giggly faux naifs, especially onstage. Fans with New York predilections enjoyed picking up all the allusions, letting the concept carry the group when the music grew thin.[33]

SONIC FUSION CUISINE: TYING IT TOGETHER

According to Honda, the primary concept behind *Stereotype A* was the work of locating and constructing the self (or selves) in sound rather than in image. Like taste, sound has been relegated to a subordinate position vis-a-vis sight in Western epistemology. The privileging of sight is most evident in the rationalist equation of visibility sometimes with power (the assumption that making visible the histories of marginalized groups automatically grants those groups an equal "voice" in dominant discourse) and at other times with powerlessness (Mulvey's still relevant concept of the male gaze objectifying the "to-be-looked-at" female body in Hollywood cinema).

CM explores the radical possibilities of sound both as art and communication by drawing from and articulating various types of music in new ways. Hip hop, electronica, pop, punk, metal, disco, and noise are ju a few of the musical styles showcased in their songs. CM produces a kind of sonic fusion cuisine in both albums. While the fusion element is most apparent in the culinary references in *Viva! La Woman*, the same fascination with throwing together different, sometimes wildly disparate sound fragments—like ingredients in an impromptu recipe—is also evident in *Stereotype A*. Honda talks about the food imagery in *Viva* as universal metaphors: "Food is a great metaphor, because everybody eats. Everybody knows the feeling when you're hungry for five hours and you have some kind of junk food and it tastes so amazing. It's a common experience." And Hatori adds that food and the experience of eating can provide a universal narrative language: "When I wrote the songs on the album, my vocabulary was limited, and using food is the easiest way to tell a story."[34] In both albums, Hatori and Honda try to create an affective language based on eclectic sonic ambience—a language that elicits a particular visceral and emotional response that cannot be contained or adequately described through words and images alone. *Viva* uses food allusions to create this language (stressing the sense of taste and smell), while *SA* uses allusions to popular musical styles (stressing sound).

CM members contend that like taste, sound is one way of breaking down racial and sexual stereotypes, which historically denigrate others' phenotypical traits such as skin color, facial features, and secondary sex characteristics rather than listening to what the others have to say. Honda suggests that people focus less on sight and more on "communication" to locate themselves in relation to others within their social and cultural environments.

> Stereo is . . . what tells you where you are located. Dolphins can see what is happening with their sense of hearing. . . . We have to learn to listen for ourselves. . . . and not just believe everything we're told.[35]

And in "Birthday Cake" Hatori deconstructs feminine cuteness by using it to close a flippantly violent history of the 1960.

Like Ono, CM publicly identify as political activists in interviews. Their friends include members of feminist bands such as Le Tigre and Buffalo Daughter as well as musicians like Mike D of the Beastie Boys who are well known for their activism in the environmental and Free Tibet movements. In the summer of 1999 CM demonstrated its support for political causes by performing at Lilith Fair and the Tibetan Freedom Concert. And in the fall of 2001 the band participated in benefit concerts in New York for the New York Women's Foundation, the New York Association of New Americans, and the American Red Cross Disaster Relief Fund.[36] Regardless of the publicity motive behind such appearances, the band's overt association with such causes bespeaks a political consciousness.

However, Honda and Hatori's political views are most effective when they are performed, subtly and metaphorically, in their songs. Like Honda's creative sampling, which makes up so much of CM's unique sound, Hatori's lyrics create a new kind of identity and home for the transnational subject. Home is a virtual, aurally created space that exists between the first and third worlds as a pastiche of different sounds and languages. In some sense, it exists as memory, which music is able to evoke more immediately than any other medium. And it is this version of home as memory and process that one encounters in the song, "Sci Fi Wasabi." Of all the songs on the new album, "Sci Fi Wasabi" best falls under the genre of hip hop for which CM is known. As such, it acts as a kind of bridge between the quirky hip hop "food band" of 1996 and the more seriously kitschy, musically diverse image of CM in 1999.

In "Sci Fi Wasabi," CM appropriates various trappings of rap and mixes them with Japanese cultural signifiers and slang. For example, the song opens with a homonym and double entendre: "What's up B," followed by what sounds like a repetition but isn't—"wasabi." The expression "what's up B" is a fairly standard one in hip hop culture with "B" standing for break-boy. "Wasabi" is the hot green mustard mixed with soy sauce used for dipping sushi and sashimi, two distinctly Japanese foods that acquired popularity and cultural cachet in the United States in the 1980s. It alludes here to CM's past association with the food motif even as it collapses cultural differences through a simple speech act. The song then races the listener through the streets of downtown New York, which are defamiliarized and rendered virtual through technical, pop-futuristic references: "start buttons," Obi Wan Kenobi, earning "points" as in a video game. The beat mimics sonic speed as Miho rushes on her bike to a destination and a goal. However the goal becomes more and more insignificant as she absorbs the pulsing rhythm of her surroundings.

The final image, of the singer metaphorically flying up to the sky, precludes narrative closure. Miho does not find the key because that was never really the point anyway. If the "key" that Miho has been looking for is "identity," by the end of the song it has become clear that identity cannot be reified, "found," or even "made." Instead, like so many of the other songs in the album, "Sci Fi Wasabi" suggests that identity is a never-ending process undergone over and over again in different emotional, physical, and spiritual states.

Since *Stereotype A*, Honda and Hatori have worked together and separately on various projects including *Butter 08* (Grand Royal, 1996) with Russell Simins and Jamey Staub, and *Handsome Boy Modeling School* (Tommy Boy, 1999) with Prince Paul and Dan the Automaton. At present the band is on "indefinite hiatus." In 2002 Hatori assumed the role of "Noodle," the nineteen-year-old Japanese female member of the animated band, Gorillaz, whose industry in-joke debut album went multiplatinum and snagged an Emmy nomination. Currently Hatori is performing bossa nova with Beck's former guitarist Smokey Hormel as part of the duo, Smokey & Miho.[37] Honda broke up with Lennon and released her first solo record, *Memories Are My Only Witness*, in spring 2002 on John Zorn's label Tzadik. Described as "moody" and "cinematic," Honda's recent work focuses more on sonic texture and experimentation and less on the dance beats and melodic choruses that characterized CM's style.[38]

CONCLUSION

By contextualizing Cibo Matto in the arenas of hip hop, women in electronic music, and Asian American representational history, I have tried to show how stereotypes of Asian women in the United States are being performed and negotiated in one small corner of popular music. In response to racial, sexual, and generic stereotyping, Cibo Matto has turned to politically nuanced lyrics, eclectic melodies, and sampling techniques, and a technologically astute girly image that defies any monolithic gender or racial identity. Honda and Hatori together and now separately critique the racist and sexist labels conferred upon Asian American women with humor and style—aesthetic strategies that have yet to be adequately theorized as the strong political weapons they can be.

NOTES

1. Carrie Bell, "Warner Bros. Positions Cibo Matto to Break Its 'Stereotype.'" *Billboard*, 1 May 1999, Expanded Academic Database, 28 January 2003.

2. Nirvana and Red Kross were prominent players in the scene. Both groups were also avid fans and friends of SK.

3. J. D. Considine, "Band Builds Lyrical Bridge between Japan and the U.S.," *Los Angeles Times*, 11 August 1999, Calendar, Part F, 4.

4. The official Cibo Matto website: www.wbr.cibomatto.com.

5. Ibid.

6. *Nylon*, fall 1999, 214–15.

7. Neil Strauss, "New Sounds from Japan: A Starter's Kit," *New York Times*, 12 July 1998, home ed.: C9.

8. Jon Pareles, "Cibo Matto: *Viva! La Woman*," *New York Times*, 28 January 1996, 24.

9. Glenn Kardy, "Cibo Matto's Musical Feeding Frenzy," *Daily Yomiyuri*, 1 August 1996, 10.

10. Steven Rosen, "If It Sounds Like Tossed Salad, It Might Be Cibo Matto," *Denver Post*, 17 May 1996, GT-16.

11. Steve Davy, "A Crazy Feast of Food-Centricity," *South China Morning Post*, 17 May 1996, 5.

12. Jeff Gordimer, "Japanese Kitsch—Fake but Groovy," *Fortune*, 21 June 1999, 139(12): 56.

13. See Jeff Yang, Dina Gan, and Terry Hong, *Eastern Standard Time: A Guide to Asian Influence on American Culture*, New York: Houghton Mifflin, 1997, and Mark Schilling, *The Encyclopedia of Japanese Pop Culture*, New York: Weatherhill, 1997.

14. Alvin Liu, "Tired U.S. Pop Looks East," *Asahi Evening News*, 25 March 1999, home ed.: C9+.

15. Ibid.

16. Shout out to my girl Tara Rodgers, editor of electronica webzine *Pinknoises*, for providing me with this concise definition. E-mail correspondence, 13 July 2000.

17. The historical situation in Japan is more ambiguous and complex than that of other Asian countries, since it has also played both colonized (by the West) and colonizer (of the East).

18. See Edward Said, *Orientalism*, New York: Vintage Books, 1979, 12.

19. See *Rolling Stone*, 13 November 1997, cover story.

20. Gayle Wald, "Just a Girl? Rock Music, Feminism, and the Cultural Con of Female Youth," *Signs*, spring 1998, 23:599.

21. Norma Coates, "(R)evolution Now," in Sheila Whiteley, ed., *Sexing the Groove: Popular Music and Gender*, New York: Routledge, 1997, 52.

22. Ibid., 53.

23. Tricia Rose, *Black Noise: Rap Music and Black Culture in Contemporary America*, Hanover, NH: Wesleyan University Press, 1994, 85.

24. Ibid., 65, emphasis added.

25. Evelyn McDonnell, "Why Aren't More Geeks with the Gizmo Girls?" *New York Times*, 12 April 1998, 2.

26. See www.pinknoises.com.

27. Wald, 604–5.

28. Amei Wallach, "The Widow Peaks: Yoko Ono Gets Her Own Moment in a New Avant-Garde," *New York Times Magazine*, 24 September 2000, 58–61.

29. Arion Berger, "Yoko Ono," in *Trouble Girls: Women in Rock*, ed. Barbara O'Dair, New York: Random House, 1997, 246.

30. Bell.

31. Jim Sullivan, "Gourmet Music," *Boston Globe*, 2 May 1996, city ed.: Calendar.

32. Andy Gill, "Pop: Food for Thought; Cibo Matto's First Album Was an Enigmatic Hors d'Oeuvre. Now the Japanese Duo Has Served Up a Sumptuous Main Course," *Independent*, 9 July 1999, features: 15.
33. Jon Pareles, "Novelty Act? Not If Things Go Their Way," *New York Times*, 15 June 1999, late ed.: E9.
34. Elysa Gardner, "Cibo Matto's Food for Thought," *Los Angeles Times*, 5 May 1996, Sunday home ed.: Calendar, 61.
35. The official Cibo Matto website: www.cibomatto.com.
36. Ibid.
37. Joan Anderman, "Brazilian Sound Gives New Life to Smokey, Miho," *Boston Globe*, 15 November 2002, 3d ed.: C12+.
38. Cory Vielma, "Yuka Honda: Memories Are My Only Witness (Tzadik)," *SF Weekly*, 17 April 2002; *Lexis Nexis*, 28 January 2003.

WORKS CITED

Anderman, Joan. "Brazilian Sound Gives New Life to Smokey, Miho." *Boston Globe*, 15 November 2002, 3d ed.: C12+.
Bell, Carrie. "Warner Bros. Positions Cibo Matto to Break Its 'Stereotype.'" *Billboard*, 1 May 1999. Expanded Academic Database. 28 January 2003.
Berger, Arion. "Yoko Ono." In *Trouble Girls: Women in Rock*, ed. Barbara O'Dair (New York: Random House, 1997).
Cibo Matto. *Stereotype A* (Warner Bros. Records, 1999).
———. *Viva! La Woman* (Warner Bros. Records, 1996).
Coates, Norma. "(R)evolution Now? Rock and the Political Potential of Gender." In *Sexing the Groove: Popular Music and Gender*, ed. Sheila Whiteley (London: Routledge, 1997), 50–64.
Considine, J. D. "Band Builds Lyrical Bridge between Japan and the U.S." *Los Angeles Times*, 11 August 1999, home ed.: F4.
Cornyetz, Nina. "Fetishized Blackness: Hip Hop and Racial Desire in Contemporary Japan." *Social Text* 41 (winter 1994).
Davy, Steve. "A Crazy Feast of Food-Centricity." *South China Morning Post*, 17 May 1996: 5.
Dower, John. *War without Mercy: Race and Power in the Pacific War* (New York: Pantheon Books, 1986).
Felder, Rachel. *Manic Pop Thrill* (Hopewell, NJ: Ecco Press, 1993).
Gaar, Gillian. *She's a Rebel: The History of Women in Rock & Roll* (Seattle: Seal Press, 1992).
Garner, Elysa. "Cibo Matto's Food for Thought." *Los Angeles Times*, 5 May 1999, home ed.: 61.
Gill, Andy. "Pop: Food for Thought; Cibo Matto's First Album Was an Enigmatic Hors d'Oeuvre. Now the Japanese Duo Has Served Up a Sumptuous Main Course." *Independent*, 9 July 1999, home ed.: F15.
Gordimer, Jeff. "Japanese Kitsch—Fake but Groovy." *Fortune*, 25 June 1999, 139(12): 56.
Haraway, Donna. "A Cyborg Manifesto." In *Simians, Cyborgs, and Women: The Reinvention of Nature* (New York: Routledge, 1991).
———. *Modest_Witness@Second_Millennium.FemaleMan©_Meets_OncoMouse™: Feminism and Technoscience* (New York: Routledge, 1997).
Kang, Connie K. "Sunday Report: At a Crossroads; Rising Numbers Bring Greater Influence—and Sometimes Greater Problems—for the State's Asian Americans." *Los Angeles Times*, 12 July 1998, home ed.: A1+.
Kardy, Glenn. "Cibo Matto's Musical Feeding Frenzy." *Daily Yomiyuri*, 1 August 1996, 10.
Kondo, Dorinne. *About Face: Performing Race in Fashion and Theater* (New York: Routledge, 1997).
Lee, Robert. *Orientals: Asian Americans in Popular Culture* (Philadelphia: Temple University Press, 1999).

Lipsitz, George. *The Possessive Investment in Whiteness* (Philadelphia: Temple University Press, 1998).

Liu, Alvin. "Tired U.S. Pop Looks East." *Asahi Evening News*, 25 March 1999, home ed.: C9-K

McDonnell, Evelyn. "Why Aren't More Geeks with the Gizmo Girls?" *New York Times*, 12 April 1998, 2.

Pareles, John. "Cibo Matto: *Viva! La Woman*." *New York Times*, 28 January 1996, 24.

———. "Novelty Act? Not If Things Go Their Way." *New York Times*, 15 June 1999, E9.

Rose, Tricia. *Black Noise: Rap Music and Black Culture in Contemporary America* (Hanover, NH: Wesleyan University Press, 1994).

Rosen, Steven. "If It Sounds Like Tossed Salad, It Might Be Cibo Matto." *Denver Post,* 17 May 1996, G7–16.

Said, Edward. *Orientalism* (New York: Vintage Books, 1979).

Schilling, Mark. *The Encyclopedia of Japanese Pop Culture* (New York: Weatherhill, 1997).

Strauss, Neil. "New Sounds from Japan: A Starter's Kit." *New York Times*, 12 July 1998, home ed.: C9.

Sullivan, Jim. "Gourmet Music." *Boston Globe*, 2 May 1996, city ed.: C29.

Tajima, Renee. "Lotus Blossoms Don't Bleed." In *Making Waves*, ed. Asian Women United of California (Boston: Beacon Press, 1989).

Vielma, Cory. "Yuka Honda: Memories Are My Only Witness (Tzadik)," *SF Weekly*, 17 April 2002; *Lexis Nexis*, 28 January 2003.

Wald, Gayle. "Just a Girl? Rock Music, Feminism, and the Cultural Construction of Female Youth." *Signs* 23 (Spring 1998): 599.

Wallach, Amei. "The Widow Peaks: Yoko Ono Gets Her Own Moment in a New Avant-Garde." *New York Times Magazine*, 24 September 2999, 58–61.

Whiteley, Sheila, ed. *Sexing the Groove: Popular Music and Gender* (New York: Routledge, 1997).

Yang, Jeff, Dina Gan, and Terry Hong. *Eastern Standard Time: A Guide to Asian Influence on American Culture* (New York: Houghton Mifflin, 1997), 263.

Part IV

Television

Changing Channels

Chapter Fourteen

"Made to Be the Maid"?

An Examination of the Latina as Maid in Mainstream Film and Television

Rosa E. Soto

I was watching films one day when I noticed something similar throughout them that I never noticed before. I wondered how this similarity spoke to the way in which narratives are complicit in perpetuating a negative image of the Latina experience. Each of the films I was watching had a Latina maid. A few of these films, in just the last twenty years, include *Down and Out in Beverly Hills* (1986), *First Wives Club* (1996), and *Maid in Manhattan* (2002).[1] Just a few television shows include *Designing Women* (1986–1993), *Veronica's Closet* (1997–2000) and *Will & Grace* (1998–2006). Latina maids also appear in secondary roles in shows like *Who's the Boss, Sex and the City, CSI: Miami, Seinfeld, Bones, Nip/Tuck,* and a plethora of other TV shows and films.

Understanding just how the Latina maid functions in this popular discourse leads to an understanding of the politics of racial relationships and the politics of a Hollywood discourse. Thus, it is essential to explore the ways that the Latina maid or servant functions for mainstream Anglo—and sometimes Latino—audiences. My goal in taking a closer look at the significance of Latina representation is suggested in Krin Gabbard's (2004) *Black Magic: Anglo Hollywood and African-American Culture*, which examines the complicated politics of African Americans in films. Gabbard's book sheds light on the ways in which Angloness or Anglo people remain in "unquestioned centrality" in American films (p. 7). As Richard Dyer (1997) noted in his text Anglo, "Research—into books, museums, the press, advertising, films, tele-

253

vision . . . shows that in Western representation Anglos are overwhelmingly and disproportionately predominant, have the central and elaborated roles and above all else are placed as the norm, the ordinary, the standard" (p. 3).

UNDERSTAND HOW RACIAL "OTHERS" ARE CONSTRUCTED

It is in recognizing how Angloness is presented as a standard, and in analyzing it, that we can come to understand how racial "others" are constructed. Gabbard (2004) further argued that, "there is no better way of looking at how Angloness is constructed in movies than by examining how blackness makes these constructions work" (p. 8). Looking at the image of the Latina maid in film, television, and in culture in general allows us to understand the role of the marginalized Latina in Hollywood and the racial mythology about the nature of the Latina in general. And although the number of Latina maids in film and television may seem a coincidence, the overwhelming representation of them in that role suggests an ideological need for them by mainstream, Anglo audiences.

The image of the Latina servant or maid in film and television, from the beginning of the 1980s to today, performs a number of different narrative purposes, some of which have been fulfilled by different ethnic or racial groups in the past. Each, however, speaks to the ways in which the Latina maid is a necessary character for her Anglo counterparts. First, the Latina maid or servant clarifies the generally Anglo main protagonist, who most often is her employer, as a "classed" individual in that she signifies the class status that the Anglo protagonist has achieved. For example, in the 2002 film *The Banger Sisters*, the Latina maid serves to illustrate just how much Susan Sarandon's character, Lavinia Kingsley, has come up in the world. In the TV show *Veronica's Closet*, the Latina maid serves as an indicator of the wealth Veronica Chase has achieved through modeling.

Second, the Latina maid serves the function of allowing Anglo protagonists and characters to see themselves and to be represented as good and altruistic individuals worthy of care and devotion from their servants even in light of obvious character flaws. For example, in *First Wives Club*, Cynthia (an upper-class woman played by Stockard Channing) gives Teresa, her Latina maid, an expensive pearl necklace as thanks for years of loyal service right before Cynthia jumps out of a window. The present indicates that Cynthia cares about her servant, even as she is preserved as a martyr for first wives everywhere. In *Maid in Manhattan*, the Latina maid, played by Jennifer Lopez, foregrounds the male Anglo character's dedication to the working class, helping to establish his worthiness as he struggles against an abusive political system. Lopez's character provides Chris Marshall (played by Ralph

Fiennes) with an understanding of a class oppression that allows him to gain the trust of and help minority residents of a working-class neighborhood and thus become the film's hero.

Additionally, the function of the Latina maid serves to allow Anglo protagonists a sense of altruism as they help Latinas/os gain employment and provide for their own families. In *Down and Out in Beverly Hills*, the Anglo protagonists, David and Barbara Whiteman (played by Richard Dreyfuss and Bette Midler) proclaim themselves "good people" who have helped the underclass minority by employing them as maids and gardeners in their homes, as well as factory workers in David's hanger factory. On *Will & Grace*, Karen often forces Rosario, the Latina maid, to acknowledge all that she has done for her, from giving Rosario a job to getting her a green card. [2]

Third, the Latina maid serves as ethnic flavor for the Anglo protagonists. Ethnic "flavor" is how we understand that the Anglo characters are hip to the world, understanding culture and ethnicity in an ever-changing society. As such, having a Latina maid helps them achieve a perceived global perspective. In *Down and Out in Beverly Hills*, Barbara provides Carmen (played by Elizabeth Pena) with a job, and Carmen provides language and food lessons to Barbara, thus establishing Barbara's hipness in terms of a global sense of "culture." Thus, the Whitemans can present themselves as caring about the social welfare of Latinos/as while at the same time demonstrating that a personal relationship can exist that is mutually beneficial for both employee and employer.

Finally, Latina maids are often sexy servants (a throwback to the 1930s' Latina "spitfires") who threaten the status quo of the Anglo upper middle class and middle class. Their exuberant sexuality is both an ethnic threat to the assumed purity of sexuality within the Anglo household (specifically that of the Anglo woman), and also a threat if she uses that sexuality to break up the marriage and, hence, the value system of the Anglo household and Anglo society. In both the film *Big Trouble* and *Down and Out in Beverly Hills*, the Latina maid threatens the seemingly secure and untouchable status of the Anglo marriage. These Latina maids are used by Anglo male protagonists as sexual relief from the hum-drum reality of their suburban lifestyles. Additionally, they are used by the Anglo female protagonists as the reason their marriages fail. These maids serve as scapegoats for the Anglo middle class, who would displace blame onto the Latina maid for their descent from privilege rather than fault political, economic, and social realities.

It is important, however, to explain that these roles are often conflated within one another. Therefore, a Latina maid like Carmen in *Down and Out in Beverly Hills* provides ethnic flavor in lieu of cultural lessons while simultaneously serving as a visual marker of the upper middle-class status of the Anglo family. At the same time, she is the sexy Latina temptress who threatens the Whitemans' marriage. When not threatening to break up a marriage, the Latina maid may function in film to affirm the power of love to resolve all manner of inequality. For example, as the ethnic "other" in *Maid in Manhattan*, Marisa confirms for an Anglo audience that ethnic and class differences will melt away in the light of love.

These characterizations of the Latina maid are used to complicate, problematize or situate Anglo middle-class or upper middle-class value systems as privileged and desirable, as well as to naturalize the social location of Latinos/as. I begin with an analysis of the film *The Banger Sisters*, which addresses the ideological process of denial that undergirds a classed sense of "Angloness," and then return to *Down and Out in Beverly Hills* to show how one character in one film can embody all of the functions and characterizations of the Latina maid that are described here.

MAID TO BE INVISIBLE

In the 2002 film *The Banger Sisters*, actress Goldie Hawn plays Suzette (no last name given), a bartender whose life has never measured up to her expectations in the 1960s, when she "banged" (slang for "having sex with") well-known rockers for a living. She seeks out her left-it-all-behind friend, Lavinia Kingsley (played by Susan Sarandon), an upper middle-class conservative who neither acknowledges her old life nor the reality that her current situation is stultifying. Suzette becomes frustrated by what she imagines is Lavinia's pretend existence, and she questions Lavinia's recollection of history, her position as a woman and her views about class oppression. One crucial scene establishes both Suzette's superiority as a working-class woman who understands "true oppression" and explains the taken-for-granted system of exploitation in which the upper middle class depends on the work of invisible servants. Suzette lectures Lavinia's spoiled children, Hannah and Ginger, because they refuse to wash their own dishes. As they argue about the dishes, one of the young girls points out to Suzette that it is Rosa who normally does them. Suzette then asks the girls if they know Rosa's last name,[3] to which they reply, "No." Suzette then states, "You have people wiping your ass, and you don't even know their names." After this confrontation, she calls them spoiled brats, and they begin to clean the dishes.

Implicit in this scene is the moral of the film—that privileges must be earned, and without hard work, one is destined to become irrelevant, as Lavinia has become to her daughters and husband. This scene also elucidates how complicit Lavinia and her daughters are in a world that oppresses "workers," and begins the true focus of the narrative, Lavinia's awakening and self-discovery. Rosa, the maid, is spoken of but never seen, which says much about the invisibility of Latinos/as both within the film industry and society. The film's narrative had made Rosa, her history and her subjectivity invisible. However, *The Banger Sisters* uses the maid's invisibility to emphasize an Anglo, upper middle-class reality that refuses to see or acknowledge the ethnic "others" who make their privileged lives possible. Her subjectivity is displaced onto Suzette, whose work as a bartender through the years has been taken for granted by people like Sarandon's character. The invisible Latina maid was never significant to the narrative; she exists only to initially establish the Anglo family in the film as classed and clarifies how oblivious they are to the needs of ethnic "others."

Another film that includes remarkably similar dialogue and narrative purpose is *Clueless*, with Alicia Silverstone in the role of a clueless young girl named Cher Horowitz. In this film, Cher asks Latina maid Lucy (played by Aida Linares) to tell Jose the gardener to trim the bushes. Lucy replies that Cher should tell him herself, and Cher then says that she does not speak Mexican, to which Lucy replies, "I no a Mexican," and Cher is then admonished by her step-brother, who clarifies for her that Lucy is from El Salvador. Similar to *The Banger Sisters* is the fact that Cher is initially oblivious to the lives and realities of the ethnic "others" that make her privileged life possible. And, as with The Banger Sisters, it is Cher's growth in the film that is significant and not the Latina maid's ethnicity, politics, or heritage. The Latina maid merely serves as a marker for Cher's "cluelessness." The narrative, which includes a scene with a background Latina maid, foregrounds the subtle politics of the film in establishing that the Anglo protagonist is both naive and capable of change. The presence of the Latina maid, even an invisible one, provides evidence for the growth of an Anglo consciousness. As Richard Dyer argued in *Anglo*, "Anglo discourse implacably reduces the non-Anglo subject to being a function for the Anglo subject, not allowing her/him space or autonomy, permitting neither the recognition of similarities nor the acceptance of differences except as a means for knowing the Anglo self" (p. 13). It is also interesting to note that movie critics who reviewed *The Banger Sisters* and *Clueless* did not discuss the scenes with the Latina maids either, even though both scenes are positioned as critical junctures which foreground the politics of the film.

Therefore, the choice to position these maids as Latina reinforces the notion of Latinas/os as "background." Mary Romero (1990) stated that they are "shadow figures, walk-on props in films and TV programs celebrating family life among Texas oil barons or Wall Street executives" (p. 2). Additionally, the Latina/o worker is similarly effaced in Hollywood, where the assumption, with few exceptions, is that Latinas can only be seen in the role of the maid, not the role of the lead.[4] The film *Maid in Manhattan*, indicates a relatively new trend for the Latina maid in contemporary film in that she is clearly framed within the concept of upward mobility. The possibility of escaping the drudgery and subservience of manual labor, however, appears limited to the infrequent instances in which the maid is played by a star (Jennifer Lopez).

FICTIONAL SERVANTS: HOW NECESSARY ARE LATINA MAIDS?

Mary Romero (1990) argued that Latinos/as are necessary because they ful-fill a specific economic need in upper middle-class families: "Not only are they less expensive than employees hired by agencies who pay benefits, but they are easily exploited for additional work" (p. 6). Furthermore, Romero stated that the importance of the Latino/a worker to the upper-income family extends beyond that of the household maid. "Citizenship, race, ethnicity, class and gender continue to mark the boundaries of domestic service—an occupation that extends from the rare household staff that includes butler, driver, cook, maid, and nanny to the day worker who cleans 4 to 9 hours for a different employer each day" (p. 3). Romero's argument acknowledges a changing culture that threatens Anglo middle-class and upper middle-class security, for without servants, they face the threat of being positioned as part of the underclass themselves. Without servants, they would have to fulfill the obligations of child care and household now done by those they hire. Indeed, the hiring of a Latina maid is often represented as an altruistic act by the upper middle class, for they appear to be helping the underclass minority as well as their own financial bottom line and sense of security. In hiring ethnic help, upper middle-class individuals are able to assuage liberal guilt over their exclusion of Latinas/os as they perpetuate the myth that hiring ethnic labor is an altruistic act. As an example of this myth-making, Romero (1990) wrote about Linda Chavez, the former nominee for secretary of labor under President George W. Bush. As Romero explained, Chavez claimed that "the 2 years she provided shelter and cash to Marta Mercado, an undocumented Guatemalan, was not an employment arrangement, but rather an act of char-ity and compassion" (p. 14). Thus, Chavez, a politically conservative Latina, characterizes the relationship as a personal one unregulated by the law and not a public one that should be regulated.

The background Latina maid in real life and film is no new pattern. For years, servants, field hands, caretakers, and others have fulfilled the purpose of clarifying quickly the classed position of Anglos in mediated narrative and in real life. Furthermore, they serve to clarify and reaffirm hierarchal societal realities that are necessary for the upper middle class to feel good about their wealth and success. They also allow individuals to feel good about "helping" the ethnic "other." This is true for mainstream film and television produc-tions and social reality. The wealthy individual today needs the ethnic servant. And the ethnic servant may feel he or she needs the Anglo patron for real-life economic realities and upward mobility. The film connection between Anglo employers and ethnic servants (played historically by Black characters) speaks to the real-life relationship between Anglos and people of color, which may appear today, in film and reality, to be built on altruism and mutual codependence, but elides a legacy of racism and gender inequalities.

THE HISTORICAL LEGACY OF THE ETHNIC MAID IN FILM

The representation of the Latina maid exists within the context of other ethnic maids in films of the twentieth century, often serving as a trope for the structuring of an Anglo, classed identity. In the early decades of film (1910–1930), the visible servant was often an Irish immigrant. According to Faye E. Dudden (1983), "When the famine immigration poured into the United States from Ireland in the late 1840s and early 1850s, it began to look as though every servant was Irish, at least in the major seaboard cities" (p. 60). This trend of hiring Irish women continued throughout the nineteenth century and found its way into the twentieth century. Hiring Irish women was often convenient for Anglo women because the Irish spoke the same language, unlike Russian, German, or Scandinavian workers. As Dudden (1983) stated, "Facing no language barrier, they could find ready acceptance as servants, and entering service solved the problem of finding housing" (p. 60). The trend of hiring Irish servants made its way into early cinema, along with the stereotype of the female, Irish servant as the "Irish biddy" who was helpless and problematic:

> The Irish domestic, stereotypically referred to as "biddy," which dominated the labor market at mid-century and therefore drew the blame for servant problems, tended to make an unsatisfactory servant. She carried to extremes what were, in the eyes of the employers, the characteristic faults of domestics. Among "faithless strangers" the immigrant woman was most faithless, not just personally but culturally. (p. 65)

This reinforced for upper middle-class women, both in reality and in film, the belief that they were helping or rescuing immigrant women from their inability to take care of themselves. At the same time, by hiring these women, they were taking care of their families. The domestic servant allowed the Anglo, upper middle-class woman to "welcome the prospect of more elevated activities than constant domestic drudgery" (Dudden, 1983, p. 47).

However, Irish immigrant women became increasingly unwilling to work for low wages and often viewed domestic service as a temporary working condition before marriage, which David M. Katzman (1978) attributed to an assimilation of Anglo, cultural values in the next generation of Irish Americans, the first to be born in the United States. "Clearly," he stated, "for Irish immigrants, service had provided the vehicle for entry into American society and for upward mobility" (p. 70).

As Irish women began moving into the middle- and upper middle-class, Black servants, who had been commonplace in the South due to slavery, moved to large, Northern cities in search of work, and Black women soon "comprised nearly a majority of servants and laundresses nationally" (Katzman, 1978, p. 72). Therefore, reflecting what was happening in real-life upper middle-class homes in the 1930s and throughout the 1950s, the servant in film was more often than not African American. This 1930s servant is most typified by actress Hattie McDaniel, the first Black woman to win an Oscar—for best supporting actress—for her role as Mammy in the 1939 film *Gone With the Wind.* [5]

The change in the ethnic makeup of maids in film and television, from African Americans to Latinas came from the changing economic structure in African American families. As Patricia A. Turner (1994) said:

> Starting in the late 1950s and through the 1960s and 1970s, a window was broken in the kitchen to which African-American women had been confined. Suddenly they had increased opportunities to seek work outside their own and other people's homes. Educational opportunity grants afforded access to higher education, and employers were eager to display their liberal credentials by hiring African-American employees. (p. 56)

As African American families began their upward mobility into the middle class, the opening for domestic servants in the home was again filled by new immigrants who, because of a lack of education, language barriers, and ethnic discrimination, often found themselves working as servants in Anglo households. It is important to note that this system of hiring is grounded in geographic realities reflected in film and television shows. For example, films like *Forrest Gump*, *Clara's Heart*, and *Corrina, Corrina* more often feature African American servants because they are set in the South. Films or TV shows set in New York City, like *Will & Grace*, or *Miami*, like *Big Trouble*, often feature Latina or Central/South American workers. Films set in California, like *Hollywood Homicide* or *Big Fat Liar*, often feature Mexican maids. Additionally, films situated in a particular historical period, such as during the U.S. Civil War, tend to feature African-American servants, as in *Gone With the Wind*. Implicit, no matter what the decade or geographic setting, is that the hired hand will almost always be ethnic—the rare exception being au pairs and cooks, who tend to be Anglo, more educated, and of unidentifiable European lineage, all of which suggest a division of labor according to ethnicity and skin color.

THE SEXY LATINA MAID AS THE NEW LATINA SPITFIRE

The sexy Latina maid is a segue from the Latina spitfire roles of the 1930s through the 1950s. These roles, best exemplified in the work of actresses Lupe Velez, Dolores Del Rio, and Rita Hayworth, emphasized sensuality and frivolous behavior. The spitfire in early Western films functioned as a temptress who threatened the basic moral values of the Anglo, male protagonist. She is set in direct contrast to the morally upstanding, Anglo female heroine who ultimately saves the male protagonist from the Latina temptress. These spitfires are often superficial characters, generally not developed beyond their basic sexual desires and needs, whereas Anglo actresses in the film are generally fully developed characters with clear moral values and honest and correct ethics. Historically, the role of the early spitfire or Latina temptress has been in direct contrast to that of the morally upstanding, Anglo, female character, and in many films the male protagonist had to choose between them. The function of the spitfire was obvious; for the Anglo male protagonist, redemption was found in resisting those treacherous "spitfire" women.

Today, the Latina spitfire has been updated and transformed but is nonetheless still evident within the role of the Latina maid in many films and television shows—for example, in the 1986 film *Down and Out in Beverly Hills*, starring Richard Dreyfuss, Bette Midler and Nick Nolte, and 2002's *Big Trouble*, starring Tim Allen and Rene Russo, with Sofia Vergara as the Latina maid Nina. Evidence of how this ideology permeates television also includes an episode of the television show *Bones*, which reconfigures the historical spitfire as a Latina maid. In the episode entitled "The Woman in the Garden," the Latina maid is killed by the Latino manager of the household who feels that she had tempted the young, wealthy, Anglo man of the house with her sexuality. Upset that she has overstepped her bounds, he argues that he killed her to maintain the status quo in the relationship between employees—the Latino men and Latina women evident everywhere in the garden and inside the house—and their Anglo employers. Implicit is that the Latina maid has somehow corrupted the young Anglo male and by extension his upper middle-class values.

In *Down and Out in Beverly Hills*, Elizabeth Peña plays the Latina maid Carmen, who provides the most memorable role of the spitfire in contemporary films. As a temptress who threatens the stability and upper middle-class values of the Anglo family for whom she works, Carmen is a reconfigured Latina spitfire. Even film critics positioned her as such: Most discussed Carmen in terms of her representation as a sexy spitfire. For example, Pauline Kael (1986) from the *New Yorker* called her "the Whitemans's hot live-in maid" (p. 105) and discussed her physical attributes rather than any social significance she may have to the politics of the film. She stated, "Elizabeth

Peña plays Carmen as tantalizing and sulky; she has a bedroom mouth, and when it says no to Dave, the rejection is brutal, because that mouth looks as if it were made to say nothing but yes" (p. 106).

Down and Out in Beverly Hills, directed by Paul Mazursky, is a remake of a 1932 French film by famed director Jean Renoir. In *Boudu sauve des eaux*, translated in English as *Boudu Saved from Drowning*, Renoir follows the story of Boudu (played by Michel Simon), a tramp who jumps into the Seine River after he loses his dog and is rescued by Edouard Lestingois (played by Charles Granval), a bookseller who gives him shelter and hopes to redeem him through induction into a bourgeoisie life of work and family. The young maid, Anne-Marie (played by Séverine Lerczinska), has sex with Edouard Lestingois in exchange for the possibility of upward mobility. Later, she sleeps with Boudu and appears allied with the Lestingois family's goal of making Boudu a respectable member of the community. The fact that Boudu ultimately decides to forego an upper middle-class existence, as he throws his bourgeois hat in the Seine River and swims, both literally and metaphorically, away from the Lestingois and all they represent, situates this film as class criticism. In the end, the tramp wants nothing to do with the compromises associated with living for and up to society's expectation for the bourgeoisie.

The 1986 remake by Mazursky of Renoir's film fails to maintain the class critique of its predecessor. Whereas the maid in the original attempts to change her class status by seducing Lestingois, the remake positions the Latina as less powerful, for she is seduced rather than being the seducer, and she is framed as being dependent on her employers for her green card. Being a mainstream Hollywood film, *Down and Out in Beverly Hills* backs down from any attempt to explore or negotiate complicated class politics, even though it sets itself up to do so. In this version, Jerry the bum ends up a class convert, adopting the Whiteman family's bourgeois value system and lifestyle. Thus, any satire of the prevailing upper middle-class values that might have been suggested is eliminated. As Janice Morgan (1990) argued in "From Clochards to Cappuccinos: Renoir's Boudu is 'Down and Out' in Beverly Hills," "Though at first the rebel had promised liberation from the relentless cycle 'work produce consume work produce consume' we are led to the cynical conclusion that he has, in fact, only eliminated the first two terms of the above three" (pp. 8–9). Morgan continued her critique of the Mazursky film: "Properly defused, stripped of any revitalizing potential to change or to challenge the social order . . . the Outsider is more than welcome to be co-opted into the system. Whatever promise, threat, or possibility Jerry's presumed otherness might have represented has, for the price of a cappuccino, been overruled" (p. 11). The film, in true mainstream Hollywood style, never follows through on its potential to satirically explain Jerry's opposition to the Whitemans' way of life as an opposition to greed.

When he joins the fold, he joins their ideology. As Andrew Kopkind (1986) stated, "Mazursky exploits the myth but never exposes it" (p. 252). The film fails in its promise to expose problems inherent in class systems. However, an analysis of the role of the Latina maid Carmen moves us towards an understanding of class and racialized politics in this film.

Initially, I must explain how it is that we know Carmen is Latina. First, she speaks Spanish and has a clear accent throughout the film.[6] Second, she is often in her room watching Hispanic television shows and news. Third, she is often positioned as ethnic by the Whitemans throughout the film, as Barbara Whiteman frequently asks Carmen to correct her Spanish and David Whiteman talks often about his helping the ethnic poor, exemplified by Carmen.[7] Carmen is first seen in the background of the film, cleaning and cooking. As she cooks, she helps Barbara with her Spanish and they talk about the upcoming Thanksgiving dinner, which Carmen is invited to and which quickly situates the family as caring and generous enough to invite the help.

However, the narrative becomes more complicated as she dines with the Whiteman family on Thanksgiving.[8] Her function there, as the audience is reminded, is as the maid which is foregrounded as she serves the meal. In one scene, one of the guests—all of whom are affluent friends of the Whitemans—asks Carmen in a familiar tone how her family is doing. Although it may seem that the interest is genuine—which supports the idea that the Anglo, upper middle class is concerned about the real problems of poor Latinos/as—when she responds that her family is not doing well and that her brother, a sugar cane worker, is out of work, the guests laugh at his misfortune. The response from one of the diners—that "there's not much of a call for that in Los Angeles"—re-affirms the stereotype that Latinos do not want to work, for if the brother did, he would learn some other trade besides the useless one (at least, in Los Angeles) of cutting sugar cane. This moment in the film establishes the superiority of the Anglo, upper middle-class work ethic and related values. However, it quickly glosses over the struggle of ethnic help and we quickly forget that Carmen and her family are in difficult financial straits. As Bonnie Thornton Dill (1986) explained, "Racial ethnics were brought to this country to meet the need for a cheap and exploitable labor force. Little attention was given to their family and community life except as it related to their economic productivity" (p. 15).

What is important in the narrative of *Down and Out in Beverly Hills* is the problems of the Whiteman family, and it is clear that Carmen (like the spitfire of the 1930s) is one of those problems. The family's breakdown is hinted at in the initial scene, in which the married couple is positioned far from each other in their bed. Following are allusions to a sexually ambiguous son, an anorexic daughter, Barbara's obsession with shopping, and David's guilt about his success. As clear as the allusions are to the instability of the family, the reasons for this are more subtle. What is clear is that the situation isn't helped by the Latina maid, who is sleeping with David.

The plot of the film revolves around David Whiteman attempting to help Jerry, a homeless, hungry bum (played by Nick Nolte) who has just lost his dog and attempts to drown himself in the Whitemans' pool. As in the Renoir film, the narrative positions the Whitemans' upward mobility, prosperity and value system in direct contrast to that of the bum they are trying to "help." Although the problems of the Latina maid and her family are dismissed, the situation of this Anglo man is taken far more seriously, for it represents the upper middle-class fear of downward mobility. It is clear in the film that what scares the family most is the possibility that they could become this bum, that they can and still have the possibility of one day being in the same position. As David Whiteman states, "There by the grace of God go you and I." Carmen and her brother's obviously similar situation are negated by the more serious situation of the Anglo man out of work, for this threatens the status quo. In this way, the film reaffirms the idea that Latinos are where they should be and are there because of their own lack of motivation. David Whiteman becomes obsessed with finding out how Jerry became homeless and destitute. As Richard Dyer (1997) pointed out, ethnic concerns or issues are often displaced by Anglo concerns in films.

Furthermore, as the sexy maid, the Latina here reinforces the idea of the immorality of Latinos/as today. Their sexuality is problematic, and they therefore must be punished for it. Thus, Carmen is in the film to be used sexually by her employer and the bum. The fact that Carmen is an immigrant, dependent on David for a green card, positions her as a prostitute, for she is selling her body for the possibility of staying in the United States. The film positions the morality of the Anglo woman as superior to the degraded morality of the Latina woman, which is again a characteristic of past spitfire roles. Furthermore, Carmen's lack of morals and seeming promiscuity are reaffirmed when she sleeps with Jerry.

Nonetheless, the Latina maid in films seems to have no individual identity; her narrative function is to expose the problems of the Anglo, middle or upper middle-class family, thereby revealing that the seeming domestic bliss of the family is not blissful after all. For example, in *Down and Out in Beverly Hills*, the Whitemans' relationship has become dysfunctional as a result of Barbara's preoccupation with maintaining the image of wealth and David's sense of entitlement, which extends to the body of the maid. What is made evident in the film is that the Latina maid is incapable of bettering herself on her own, that she needs the guidance and direction of the Anglo world to escape poverty and develop a sense of self. This need for Anglo definition and guidance is evident when Carmen takes a Marxist stance in response to David's questioning her about having had sex with Jerry. Carmen tells him that she can see "the big picture" now, and that he is an "imperialist" who sees Carmen as "the Third World," ripe for exploitation. Furthermore, Carmen states: "Struggle is a great teacher. You see I am nothing. I am the worker and you are the capitalist. The only way we change this is revolution." When David Whiteman denies having oppressed her and tells her that he thought they were having fun, Carmen replies that fun is decadent. And when David points out that his father was a communist, Carmen calls him a traitor to his class. In this scene, Carmen is given agency and subjectivity. However, her newfound class consciousness is thanks to Jerry, who has introduced Carmen to Marxist class analysis and given her books about Marxist theory. Thus, it is an Anglo male who is responsible for Carmen's agency.

In past films, Anglo employers were often able to see themselves as altruistic and generous when they gave their maids time off, clothes, money or other support to facilitate their growth or individuality. Although it appears that Carmen has gained subjectivity and agency, it continues to be negated; she exists in the film primarily to underscore the goodness and honesty of the Anglo characters. At the end of the film, when we find out that Jerry is a scam artist who he has lied about his past, we understand Carmen's Marxist stance to be as contrived and insignificant as Jerry's bum impersonation. Ultimately, his lies and her misguided Marxist arguments are not as important as the allegiances Carmen, Jerry, and the Whitemans have created together. Carmen and the Whitemans continue to have a common purpose—to save Jerry from his misguided path and position him to reap the benefits of a bourgeois existence.

David Whiteman's claims to generosity toward poor Mexican immigrants are undercut by his overarching concern for the welfare of the Anglo, male character, Jerry. This is clear from another scene in the film, when a black homeless man who is Jerry's friend approaches them while they are dining. David is clearly upset by the man's intrusion into his private discussion with Jerry. Again, his concern is not with the struggles of the black man, whom he dismisses as seeming crazy. It is Jerry who is most in need of salvation because of the threat of Anglo, downward mobility. Interestingly, it is Jerry, who has sex with Barbara, who is regarded as worth saving—unlike Carmen, who has sex with David but is seen as potentially causing the moral breakdown of the family. She is vilified, while Jerry is idolized in the film. Her seeming lack of morality, which reaffirms the moral ambiguity of ethnic workers, is evident when she has sex with Jerry, further making her problematic because she has now become responsible for the moral degradation of two Anglo males.

What is important in this film is how the Latina maid functions for Angloness and not how she may function for herself. Her problems are never resolved. Carmen is offered no chance for upward mobility. If, in fact, she is allowed to escape her role (suggested but never fully realized), it is because the Anglo protagonist helped her to do so. In fact, Carmen becomes aligned with the Anglo, upper middle class when, in the film's final scenes, Carmen joins the Whiteman family (visually side by side in the scene) in asking Jerry to stay and help them out of the fallible, upper middle-class world in which they live. The Anglo homeless man is saved, and because of this, so is the Anglo family.

What we ultimately have to acknowledge about the Latina maid is that she is a necessary character in film and television today not simply because she positions the family that she works for as classed. Her figure also is necessary because she is intrinsic to structuring the economic and class privilege of "Angloness" in multiple ways. She exists in the narrative to allow Anglo people to see themselves as altruistic, as good moral individuals who care for their communities and are worthy of all the privileges that come with their race and class. In looking more closely at what media representations say about people of color, the underlying ideology is laid bare. In the United States, Mary Romero (1990) reminds us, maid's work "remains women of color's work, and it is never done" (p. 22).

NOTES

1. A more inclusive list is as follows: *The Incredible Shrinking Woman* (1981), *El Norte* (1983), *Goonies* (1986), *Troop Beverly Hills* (1989), *Regarding Henry* (1991), *Cape Fear* (1991), *Leap of Faith* (1992), *Universal Soldier* (1992), *Clueless* (1995), *Ransom* (1996), *As Good As it Gets* (1997), *Liar, Liar* (1997), *Enemy of the State* (1997) , *Dr. T and the Women* (2000), *Don't Say a Word* (2001), *Storytelling* (2001), *Two Weeks Notice* (2002), *Big Trouble* (2002), *Mr. Deeds* (2002), *Big Fat Liar* (2002), *Mr. St. Nick* (2002), *Hollywood Homicide* (2003), *Man on Fire* (2004), *Dirty Sexy Money* (2007–), *Noah's Arc* (2004–), *Gossip Girl* (2007–), *The Last Shot* (2004), *Win a Date with Tad Hamilton* (2004), *The Sisterhood of the Traveling Pants* (2005), *Spanglish* (2005), *Crash* (2005), and *Materials Girls* (2006). Just a few television shows include *Charlie's Angels* (1976–1981), *I Married Dora* (1987–1988), *21 Jump Street* (1987–1991), *Designing Women* (1986–1993), *Dudley* (1993), *Veronica's Closet* (1997–2000), *Dharma & Greg* (1997–2002), *Pasadena* (2001), *Will & Grace* (1998–2006), *Curb Your Enthusiasm* (2000–), *Ed* (2000–2004), *Reba* (2001–2006), *24* (2001–), *O.C.* (2003–2007), *Whoopi* (2003–2004) and *Arrested Development* (2003–2006), as well as television shows on HBO and Showtime: *Entourage* (2004–), *Weeds* (2005–) and *Dexter* (2006–).

2. Admittedly, Will & Grace is a situation comedy that sets itself up as a satire of society. Rosario is often cheeky, and Karen often looks the fool for her outlandish behavior.

3. Suzette is given no last name, which positions her with the Latina maid, Rosa, who also is without a last name. Suzette, also like Rosa, is aligned with the working class because she is a bartender.

4. A small number of Latina stars, such as Jennifer Lopez and Salma Hayek, are among the few exceptions. However, it is worth noting that Lupe Ontiveros, a Mexican actress, has played more than 150 maids in film. She narrated a 2005 documentary, *Maid in America*, which examines the experiences of maids in society.

5. In fact, McDaniel portrayed the mammy figure in more than eighty-two films. According to Carlton Jackson (1990), McDaniel refused to play mammy roles during the 1950s and as a result was boycotted by producers. Ironically, she subsequently became a real maid to make a living.

6. See Keller (1985) for further examination of early spitfire roles and their historical function within films.

7. It is probable that Carmen is Mexican as the film is set in Beverly Hills.

8. The name of the family appears to be a pun about how truly Anglo its value system is.

REFERENCES

Dill, B. T., (1986). *Our mothers grief: Racial ethnic women and the maintenance of families.* Memphis, TN: Memphis State University Press.

Dudden, F. E. (1983). *Serving women: Household service in nineteenth-century America.* Middletown, CT: Wesleyan University Press.

Dyer, R. (1997). *Anglo.* London: Routledge.

Gabbard, K. (2004). *Black magic: Anglo Hollywood and African-American culture.* New Brunswick, NJ: Rutgers University Press.

Jackson, C. (1990). *Hattie: The life of Hattie McDaniel.* Lanham, MD: Madison Books.

Kael, P. (1986). The current cinema: Anglo and gray. *The New Yorker,* 61, 105-110.

Katzman, D. (1978). *Seven days a week: Women and domestic service in industrializing America.* New York: Oxford University Press.

Kopkind, A. (1986). Films: Down and out in Beverly Hills. *The Nation,* 251–252.

Keller, G. D. (1985). *Chicano Cinema: Research, reviews, and resources.* New York: Bilingual Review/Press.

Morgan, J. (1990). From clochards to cappuccinos: Renoir's Boudu is "Down and out" in Beverly Hills. *Cinema Journal* 29, 23–35.

Romero, M. (1990). *Maid in the U.S.A.* New York: Routledge.

Strum, P., and Tarantolo, D. (2003 September). Women immigrants in the United States. Proceedings of the Woodrow Wilson Center for Scholars and the Migration Policy Institute. Washington DC: Woodrow Wilson International Center.

Turner, P. A. (1994). *Ceramic uncles and celluloid mammies: Black images and their influence on culture.* New York: Anchor Books.

Chapter Fifteen

The Burden of History

Representations of American Indian Women in Popular Media

S. Elizabeth Bird

In summer 1995, U.S. toy stores were flooded with dolls, books, play-sets, costumes, and games carrying the name of Pocahontas, the Indian princess. The Walt Disney marketing juggernaut was selling images of American Indians as never before, and the face and body of an Indian woman in particular.[1]

The animated feature, *Pocahontas*, was the first mainstream movie in history to have an Indian woman as its leading character. It seemed ironically appropriate that this role was a cartoon—the ultimate in unreality. For although women from other ethnic groups have had varied but definite success in transforming stereotypical media representations, American Indian women have continued to appear in a limited range of roles and imagery. More than a decade after Disney's *Pocahontas*, there has been little significant change in that situation. Indeed, it is striking that the most pervasive representations of Indian women in contemporary U.S. culture are stereotypical images in such places as comic books, advertising, toys, "collectables," and greeting cards.

The mainstream media visibility of American Indians in general has declined since the 1990s, a decade that saw a rise in "Indian" movies and a few TV shows, following the unexpected success of *Dances With Wolves* in 1990. Even in that decade, Indian women were conspicuous by their absence, appearing (with some exceptions) in small, supporting roles, as loyal wives or pretty "maidens," while the plot lines belonged to the men. To understand why this happened, and to interpret the current state of representation, we must understand one basic point: Mass images of American Indians are images created by White culture, for White culture, and the representation of Indian women carries the double burden of stereotyping by both ethnicity and gender. American Indians have only recently (although quite successfully) begun to influence the production of images of themselves, and the range of available imagery of Indians is remarkably small.

This was demonstrated eloquently in the classic work by Berkhofer (1979):

> the essence of the White image of the Indian has been the definition of Native Americans in fact and fancy as a separate and single Other. Whether evaluated as noble or ignoble, whether seen as exotic or downgraded, the Indian as an image was always alien to the White. (p. xv)

As Berkhofer noted, interest in American Indians has ebbed and flowed over time. Depending on the era, the Indian male has usually been either the "noble savage" or his alter ego, the "ignoble savage." As White cultural images of themselves change, so does the image of the Indian change—now becoming everything Whites fear, in the person of the marauding, hellish savage, then becoming everything they envy, in the person of the peaceful, mystical, spiritual guardian of the land who was in vogue in the 1990s. However they are pictured, Indians are the quintessential Other, whose role in mass culture is to be the object of the White, colonialist gaze. And a central element in that gaze has been a construction of the Indian as locked in the past.

WOMAN AS PRINCESS OR SQUAW

Although this limited view of Indians has affected the representation of both men and women, it has curtailed the presentation of women more. Again, to understand that, we need to go back in time to see how the current imagery developed. Just as male imagery alternates between nobility and savagery, so female Indian imagery is bifurcated. From early times, a dominant image was the Indian Princess, represented most thoroughly by Pocahontas, the seventeenth-century sachem's daughter who, according to legend, threw herself in front of her tribe's executioners to save the life of colonist Capt. John Smith. Even before this, the Indian Queen image had been used widely to represent the exoticism of America, evolving into the dusky princess who "continued to stand for the New World and for rude native nobility" (R. Green, 1975, p. 703).

As Tilton (1994) described it, the Pocahontas/princess myth became a crucial part in the creation of a national identity: "On a national level . . . it had become clear by the second decade of the nineteenth century that Pocahontas had rescued Smith, and by implication all Anglo-Americans, so that they might carry on the destined work of becoming a great nation" (p. 55). The Indian princess became an important, nonthreatening symbol of White Americans' right to be here because she was always willing to sacrifice her happiness, cultural identity and even her life for the good of the new nation. Endless plays, novels, and poems were written about Pocahontas, extolling her beauty and nobility, and illustrating the prevailing view of the princess— gentle, noble, nonthreateningly erotic, virtually a White Christian, and yet different because tied to the native soils of America. As Tilton explained, the Princess Pocahontas story enabled the White United States, but especially the South, to justify its dominance, providing a kind of origin myth that explained how and why Indians had welcomed the destiny brought to them by Whites.

The "Indian princess" as a stereotype thrived in the nineteenth century and into the twentieth. For example, Francis (1992), in his study of the "Imaginary Indian" in Canadian culture, described the late nineteenth-century success of author and poet Pauline Johnson, the daughter of a Mohawk chief. Dressed in a "polyglot" costume of ermine tails, knives and beads, the "Mohawk princess" declaimed melodramatic tales of doomed love between Indian women and White men. Audiences "saw in her the personification of Pocahontas. . . . The original Miss America, Pocahontas came to represent the beautiful, exotic New World itself. Her story provided a model for the ideal merger of Native and newcomer" (pp. 120–21). Similarly, Deloria (2004) described the fascinating career of early twentieth-century Creek singer Tsianina Redfeather, who, as a classic buckskin-clad princess, entranced audiences with her mixture of musical refinement and Native identity.

But just as popular imagery defined White women as either good or bad, virgin or whore, so it forced images of Indian women into a similar bipolar split. According to R. Green (1975), the Indian "princess" is defined as one who helps or saves a White man. But if she actually has a sexual relationship with a White or Indian man, she becomes a "squaw," who is lower even than a "bad" White woman. The squaw is the other side of the Indian woman—a drudge who is at the beck and call of her savage Indian husband, who produces baby after baby, who has sex endlessly and indiscriminately with Whites and Indians alike. R. Green documented the sad history of this image in popular songs and tales of the nineteenth century, and King (2003) offered a thorough analysis of the multiple derogatory connotations of the word, arguing that "it is best understood as a key-word of conquest" (p. 3). The perception of Indian women as sexual conveniences is demonstrated with graphic horror in the eyewitness accounts of the 1865 Sand Creek massacre of Cheyenne, after which soldiers were seen to move the bodies of Indian women into obscene poses, and to cut off their genitals for display on their saddle horns (Jones, 1994).

The inescapable fact about this dual imagery of Indian woman is that the imagery is entirely defined by Whites. From early contact, White observers brought their own categories and preconceptions to indigenous American cultures, and "authoritative" sources defined the role of the Indian woman in ways that bore little relationship to reality. Thus, James Hall and Thomas McKenney (who was the chief U.S. administrator of Indian affairs from 1816 to 1830) wrote in 1844: "The life of the Indian woman, under the most favourable circumstances, is one of continual labour and unmitigated hardship. Trained to servitude from infancy, and condemned to the performance of the most menial offices, they are the servants rather than the companions of man" (McKenney & Hall, 1844/1933, p. 199). No actual Indian culture saw women in these limited terms; in fact the range of Indian cultures offered a variety of roles for women, many of them holding a great deal of honor and prestige.[2] As Denetdale (2001) pointed out, for example, "In contrast to popular stereotypes about Native American women that have cast them into the dichotomies of princess and squaw drudge, the few Navajo women in the historical record are noted as autonomous and self-assured" (p. 1). The complexity of these roles has been elided from both mainstream history and popular culture because they were not comprehensible to White culture. Thus, as R. Green (1975) argued, stereotypes of male and female American Indians "are both tied to definition by relationships with white men, but she (woman) is especially burdened by the narrowness of that definition" (p. 713).

THE WESTERN AS DEFINING GENRE

As popular media evolved, the definitions of Indian women remained oppressively narrow. As I have noted, representations of Indians have stayed locked in the past, and the popular genre that has ensured that is the Western (Leuthold, 1995). Western film and television simply took over where dime novels and Wild West shows left off, endlessly reliving the myth of the late nineteenth-century frontier. The Western genre was hard on American Indians, imprisoning them in their roles as marauding savages, and later as noble, doomed braves. Although we think of Westerns as "cowboys and Indians," during the great era of Western film from the 1930s to the 1950s, actual Indian characters were surprisingly rare. Rather, they appear as yelling hordes, scenery, or in occasional bit parts. And, as Tompkins (1992) pointed out, the Western is overwhelmingly male, dealing with male quests and challenges. Women may be there as an incentive or a reward, but they are not subjective participants in the story. Indian women, above all, disappear. If they surface occasionally, they are minor plot devices, like the character from the famous 1956 western *The Searchers*: "Her name was 'Look.' This woman is treated so abominably by the characters—ridiculed, humiliated, and then killed off casually by the plot—that I couldn't believe my eyes. The movie treated her as a joke, not as a person" (p. 8).

Thus, in the "golden age" of the cinema Western, the "squaw" was the most common image of Indian women. At the same time, the sacrificing princess stereotype was still salient, as it had been at the birth of cinema. Marsden and Nachbar (1988) described the princess image in such early films as the 1903 *Kit Carson*, in which an Indian woman helps Kit escape and is killed by her own chief. "For the next 10 years this romantic figure, young, beautiful and self-sacrificing, would come to the aid of Whites almost as often as the savage Reactionary would murder or capture them" (pp. 609–10). Although Pocahontas herself is portrayed in many movies, the theme is replayed in other guises—*The Squaw's Sacrifice* (1909), *The Heart of the Sioux* (1910), *The Indian Maid's Sacrifice* (1911), *The Heart of an Indian* (1913). As Deloria (2004) put it, in these films, Indian women offered White men "access through marriage to their primitive authenticity and their land. Having transformed their White partners, the Native spouses then voluntarily eliminate themselves so that reproductive futures might follow White-in-White marriages" (p. 84).

From the 1920s to 1940s, the portrayal of the princess declined. She returned with the "sensitive" Westerns of the 1950s and beyond, led especially by director Delmer Daves' *Broken Arrow*, released in 1950. This told the story of a White man (played by James Stewart), who in the course of setting up a peace accord with Apache chief Cochise, falls in love with and marries Sonseeahray, or "Morning Star" (played by Debra Paget), an Apache woman who is, naturally, a princess. Sonseeahray dies, after being shot by a White man who is breaking the peace, but, as always, her death is not in vain. As the Stewart character speaks over the final scenes in the film, "The death of Sonseeahray put a seal on the peace." The Princess figure again went into decline in the 1960s, seeming outdated and of less importance to White culture. Although the graphically obscene dimension of the "squaw" did not translate into the movie era, the remnants of it remained in the few, tiny roles for Indian women in Westerns from the 1950s onwards. Without the princess stereotype, White culture had only the squaw, and she was by definition unimportant and uninteresting.[3] Like her princess predecessor, the newer squaw was devoted to a White man, but she had even less importance to the plot, and was easily sacrificed if necessary. As Marsden and Nachbar (1988) pointed out, none of the famous "Indian" movies of the early 1970s had substantial roles for women: "*A Man Called Horse* (1970); *Little Big Man*

(1971); *Jeremiah Johnson* (1972); and *The Man who Loved Cat Dancing* (1973)—all have Indian women married to Whites who die either during the film or in the background of the film's story" (p. 614).

Thus, the most obvious and overwhelming aspect of portrayals of American Indians (male and female) is that these portrayals reflect a White gaze. Ironically, this has become even more pronounced in recent years, even as portrayals of Indians have become more "authentic," in terms of accurate detail, language, and above all, the use of Indian actors. When non-Indian Hollywood stars played Indians, there were occasional films that purportedly saw events from the point of view of an Indian character. Thus, in Robert Aldrich's 1954 *Apache*, Burt Lancaster is cast as Massai, an Apache warrior who first defies White authority, but eventually learns to farm, and sets the stage for peace. His wife, a classic Indian princess, also played by a White actress, Jean Peters, is a woman who sacrifices everything, and almost dies for love of Massai. ("If I lost you, I would be nothing," she mourns at one point in the film.) Like the casting of Debra Paget and Jeff Chandler in *Broken Arrow*, these many ludicrous casting choices are insulting, consigning actual Indian actors to minor roles.

However, contemporary filmmakers, aware that it is no longer acceptable to cast Whites as Indians, seem to have simply abandoned central roles for Indian characters. Clearly, this is an economic as well as a cultural decision—no Indian actor apparently has the drawing power that Burt Lancaster or Jeff Chandler had in their era. Inevitably, the lead roles go to White characters playing White roles. Even the television movie, *The Legend of Walks Far Woman* (1982), would probably not have been made without a star like Raquel Welch in the (Indian) title role. Thus, ironically, although Hollywood now realizes that Indian roles must be played by Indian actors, those actors often find themselves playing only side-kick roles. The films look more "authentic" now, but as Leuthold (1995) wrote, issues of representation go far beyond accurate detail into "questions of whether (Indian) women are depicted with a full sense of humanity" (p. 178). One device producers have used is to create a central role for a White actor to play a mixed-blood Indian—Tom Berenger in *At Play in the Fields of the Lord* or Val Kilmer (who does have Indian heritage) in *Thunderheart* (1992). But, once again, there have been none of these roles for women; the female role in *Thunderheart*, played with conviction by Sheila Tousey, is small and, predictably, ends in death.

CONTEMPORARY MEDIA REPRESENTATIONS OF INDIAN
GENDER

Meanwhile, Indian men have fared somewhat better in media depictions. It is not insignificant that the most recent collection of essays on the Hollywood Indian (Rollins & O'Connor, 2003) rarely mentions women. Indian men also have been consigned to the past, defined by the Western genre. But Westerns are about men, and Indian men since the 1950s have had roles as side-kicks to the hero. Most significant, however, Indian men were the focus of the wave of fascination with things Indian that first crested in the 1960s and 1970s when the counter-culture embraced Indians (Brand, 1988). Although mainstream media interest subsided somewhat in the 1980s, the Indian "wannabee" phenomenon was gaining momentum in New-Age-tinged popular culture (R. Green, 1988b), and rose again in the 1990s, this time in a more mainstream, ecologically minded form. The Indian elder who is wise beyond White understanding first began to appear in films like *Little Big Man* and *One Flew Over the Cuckoo's Nest* (1975), and returned in force after *Dances With Wolves*. In the 1990s, as never before, Indians were chic—mystical, wise, earth-loving, and tragic. New Age culture appropriated Indian religious practices, clothing, music, and myths, whereas Indian-inspired art and design became all the rage.[4] In this trend, Indian culture is yet again commodified and made the object of White consumption, as it has been for centuries (Castile, 1996).

This fascination is consistently associated in popular imagery with Indian men—artists, warriors, shamans. Indeed, in a study of male Indian imagery in film, romance novels, and other popular media, Van Lent (1996) convincingly shows that the image of the Indian male became an important cultural icon in the 1990s. Perhaps in response to cultural uncertainties about "correct" male roles, the Indian man, usually placed in a "dead" historical context, bifurcated in a slightly new way. Young men are handsome and virile, with the potential for decisive action when pressed, yet tender, loving, and vulnerable. Thus, Indian or mixed-blood men prove incredible lovers for White women in romance novels, whereas Indian women are invisible. Handsome young Indian men fight alongside White heroes in 1990s movies like *Dances With Wolves*, *Last of the Mohicans*, and *Squanto*. Meanwhile, older men act as wise sages in the same period pieces, and they provide a similar spiritual dimension in more contemporary films like *Free Willy*, *Legends of the Fall*, and even *Natural Born Killers*. They were stereotypical roles, they were usually subordinate to White storylines, and they served White cultural needs—but at least they were there (Bird, 2001).

In contrast, roles for Indian women in mainstream film and television have been meager at best. It is instructive to look, for example, at the Indian woman who became most familiar on both the large and small screen in the 1990s. Tantoo Cardinal, a Metis (mixed-blood) woman from Canada, had roles in several movies, including *Black Robe*, *Dances With Wolves*, and *Legends of the Fall*. She also played a recurring role in the television series *Dr. Quinn, Medicine Woman*, to which I return later; first, I consider Cardinal's movie roles.

In *Dances With Wolves*, Cardinal plays Black Shawl, the wife of Kicking Bird, the medicine man who befriends Lt. John Dunbar, the lead character played by director Kevin Costner. Black Shawl is a definite advance on the sacrificial princesses of the past—she admonishes her husband when he is too curt with his ward, Stands with a Fist, and nudges him into authorizing the marriage of Dunbar and Stands with a Fist. Kicking Bird and Black Shawl are permitted an enjoyable sex life, and their marriage is seen as warm and loving. Nevertheless, it is clearly a minor, supporting role. The lead female role is Stands with a Fist, a White woman who has been adopted into the tribe. This fact does make it plausible that she can speak English, and thus can interpret for Dunbar and Kicking Bird. However, one wonders why some other device did not occur to Michael Blake, the author of the book and screenplay, that would have made a Lakota woman a central character.

In *Black Robe* (1992), Cardinal again plays the wife of a more prominent character, although with less humor and light relief. Her character is killed midway through the film. The one other role for an Indian woman in the film is that of the chief's daughter Annuka, with whom a young subsidiary character falls in love—an unrewarding role played by Sandrine Holt, who is Eurasian, not Native American. The film, although praised by critics for its accuracy, misrepresented the important role of Iroquoi women in political decision making (Churchill, 1994). Worse, perhaps, it resurrected the squaw in Annuka. Churchill commented on "Annuka's proclivity, fair and unmarried maiden though she is, to copulate voraciously with whatever male she happens to find convenient when the urge strikes. More shocking, she obviously prefers to do it in the dirt, on all fours" (p. 128). Only when she falls in love with Daniel, a young Frenchman, does she learn how to enjoy love and the civilized "missionary position." Once again, the message is that sexuality among Indians is casual and animal-like, although an Indian can be uplifted by a real love relationship with a White.

Legends of the Fall (1994) is a classic example of Indian identity being appropriated to add mystery and resonance to White characters' life problems. The film is narrated by Gordon Tootoosis as a Cree elder who frames the life of hero Tristan Ludlow (played by Brad Pitt). Cardinal plays Pet, an Indian woman married to a hired hand on the Ludlow ranch. She is clearly loved and respected, but speaks hardly at all. Eventually, her daughter (played by Katrina Lombard) marries Tristan, but is killed in a random act of violence, setting in motion a new twist in the main, White characters' lives.

Cardinal has spoken about her supporting roles and the frustrations that go with them: "If you've got those small roles, you're there on the (production) set but you're barely ever used" (cited in Greer, 1994b, p. 152). She describes building the characters in her mind, giving them histories and trying to make the experience more fulfilling this way: "You have to give yourself a reason for being there, a whole history where you live, what the whole place looks like, what your everyday life is like" (p. 152). One can only think how frustrating it must be for other Indian women, having to do their best with tiny, underwritten, and stereotypical roles. For example, Kimberley Norris, an Indian woman who had a small role in the 1980s TV miniseries *Son of the Morning Star*, reports how she was told to redo a scene in which she wept for the slain leader Crazy Horse. Instead of her tears, she was told, "Let's do it again and just take it with that dignified stoicism of the Indians" (cited in Greer, 1994a, p. 144). As Norris commented, "That was a real quick lesson in their perception of how we don't have those natural human emotions" (p. 144).

THE DUAL BURDEN OF GENDER AND RACE: *DR. QUINN, MEDICINE WOMAN*

Even in the 1990s and into the twenty-first century, American Indians are still rare on popular television, largely because of the demise of the Western as a major TV genre. They did appear occasionally, frequently as stereotypical "mystical wise men," in action adventures such as CBS's *Walker, Texas Ranger*, where the supposedly part-Native hero (Chuck Norris) was advised and inspired by his Indian uncle and mentor on a semi-regular basis. *Northern Exposure*, which ran on CBS from 1990 to 1995, did succeed in challenging some stereotypes, and I shall return to that show later.

Aside from *Northern Exposure*, the only other show that included Indians as regular characters over a sustained time period was CBS's *Dr. Quinn, Medicine Woman*, a frontier drama set in the late 1860s. Generally despised by critics for its formulaic and sentimental predictability, and dismissed by Jojola (2003) as "an awful, awful, apologist's series" (p. 19), *Dr. Quinn* nevertheless proved very successful, lasting several seasons in the 1990s. The show featured a crusading woman doctor, Michaela Quinn (played by Jane Seymour), who fought the bigotry and sexism of the people of Colorado Springs on a weekly basis. The show was especially popular with women, and one reason for this was its essentially feminist point of view (Bird, 2003;

Dow, 1996). Created and produced by Beth Sullivan, the show was populated by a cast of strong women, surrounded by a group of rather weak and bigoted men. As Dow suggested, the show took many of the standard Western formulas, such as the hero battling for justice, and transformed the hero into a woman. And unlike traditional TV Westerns, American Indians were included in the form of a Cheyenne village. However, these Cheyenne were largely anonymous, functioning as plot devices to showcase the central White characters. Indeed, *Dr. Quinn* illustrated perfectly the point that the Indian of popular culture is a White creation (Bird, 1996).

Perhaps most striking of all, the show had not one strong female Cheyenne character. In fact, *Dr. Quinn* threw into sharp focus the double burden of race and gender stereotyping that erased Indian women from popular imagery. It demonstrated that in popular media, the traditional, restricted images of White women have often been challenged and transformed; virtually all the strong characters were women, with men generally presented as ignorant buffoons (with the exception of the glamorous Indian "Wannabe," Sully, Michaela's love interest). Yet even within this context, there was no space for a significant Indian woman. The Cheyenne, although presented "authentically," and generally favorably, were not well-drawn characters with their own stories. Rather they were beautiful, serene, and spiritual, reflecting the 1990s fascination with New Age-tinged mysticism.

The one Cheyenne who had a significant presence was medicine man Cloud Dancing, the epitome of the stoic, strong, noble male Indian, who suffered horrendous personal losses with dignity and forgiveness, fitting right into a permitted role for Indian men—the noble wise man. There was no such role allowed for his wife, Snowbird, played until the character's death by the long-suffering Tantoo Cardinal. Her main role was to look wise and wifely, offering smiling advice to Cloud Dancing, just as she did as Kicking Bird's wife in *Dances With Wolves*. Mostly, however, she appeared briefly to allow Dr. Quinn to make a point—she suffered a miscarriage so that Michaela could become indignant about the Indians' lack of food; she looked on as Michaela vaccinated Indian children, uttering lines like, "You bring us strong medicine."

Cardinal must have had shows like *Dr. Quinn* in mind when she commented, "Native people are not brought into the foreground, or even accepted as an everyday part of life, not anywhere in the American media. It is rare, rare, rare that you see anything about Native people as human beings" (Greer, 1994b, p. 153). Other Cheyenne women drifted around the village, smiling and carrying babies. In one memorable episode, the show displaced Indian women completely, while trying to use their cultural experience to make a 1990s moral point. It focused on a woman who is the sole survivor of an Army raid on her Cheyenne village. She is brought to town, where she faces the ignorance and racism of the local people, and meanwhile proves to be a temporary rival for Sully's affections. This story offered a chance to develop a Cheyenne female character more fully, and yet this was avoided— the woman is White, and was merely raised Cheyenne. She fits perfectly into the pattern of White female Indian adoptees or abductees that we have seen in movies from *Soldier Blue* to *Dances With Wolves*, drawing on the long popular tradition of the captivity narrative (Bird, 2001). In this context, the White woman essentially stands in for the Indian woman, apparently making the character more interesting for White viewers, who can vicariously enjoy "going Indian," without having to engage with a real Indian woman. Toward the end of the 1994–1995 season, the producers of *Dr. Quinn* apparently found the strain of incorporating Indian characters too much, bringing to the screen the real historical massacre of Cheyenne at the 1868 "battle" of Washita. Snowbird and most of the villagers died, and Snowbird's dying words to Michaela were typically designed to assuage White guilt: "One day, perhaps many seasons from now, my people and your people will come to understand each other and no longer be afraid." After that episode, audiences saw Indian land being sold off, and the Cheyenne largely disappeared from the program. The notion that viewers might have been interested in following the fate of the survivors apparently did not occur to the producers.

RETURN TO POCAHONTAS

So it seems that by the mid-1990s, living, breathing Indian women had become so invisible and irrelevant that the only way mainstream White culture could insert an Indian woman back into the cultural picture was to return to Pocahontas—and make her a cartoon. And despite being touted as a feminist rendering of the tale, with Pocahontas as a free-spirited, courageous, and strong-willed young woman, the story clearly echoed the old imagery. Pocahontas persuades her father to make peace, although it is not clear why this is in her best interests. Even though she loses her lover, she learns to recognize the inevitability of "progress," a crucial and guilt-reducing element in the White image of Indians. In the cartoon, Disney tells us also that Pocahontas taught John Smith respect for nature, implying that she had a profound impact on how the nation developed—representing a kind of collective fantasy that is strikingly close to the sentimental image of Pocahontas embraced in the nineteenth century. Disney's version harks back to Victorian imagery in other ways—the cartoon character is notably voluptuous and scantily clad, as were the earlier images. As R. Green (1988a) pointed out, "the society permitted portrayals to include sexual references (bare and prominent bosoms) for females even when tribal dress and ethnography denied the reality of the reference" (p. 593). Combining "superwoman" imagery of women as both strong-willed and eminently desirable to men, alongside the current image of Indians as guardians of the Earth, "Disney has created a marketable New Age Pocahontas to embody our millennial dreams for wholeness and harmony" (Strong, 1996, p. 416).

"Our dreams," of course, refers to White dreams, for Pocahontas was still a White fantasy. Indeed, as Tilton (1994) wrote, "We might argue that if one were to formulate the narrative from an Indian perspective, Pocahontas would have to be presented as an extremely problematic character" (p. 90). Yet Disney's *Pocahontas* breathed new life into an Indian Princess stereotype that never really disappeared. We still see it, on Pocahontas-inspired merchandise in gifts shops and flea markets—"collector plates," dolls and figurines, greeting cards, and gaudy artwork. The image lives on in local legends about Indian maidens/princesses who leaped to their deaths for love of a handsome brave or a White man (DeCaro, 1986). But it has nothing whatever to do with the lived experience of American Indian women in the late twentieth/early twenty-first centuries. As R. Green (1975) argued, "Delightful and interesting as Pocahontas' story may be, she offers an intolerable metaphor for the Indian-White experience. She and the Squaw offer unendurable metaphors for the lives of Indian women" (p. 714).

Not surprisingly, then, *Pocahontas* did not break ground for innovative representations of American Indian women. Indeed, in many ways, the film marked the high point of mainstream media's interest in exotic female Indian identity. Into the 1990s, interest waned; *Dr. Quinn* and *Northern Exposure* ended, and the miniboom in Westerns spawned by *Dances With Wolves* fizzled out. Richard Attenborough's *Grey Owl* (1999) told the story of Englishman Archie Belaney, who masqueraded as an Indian in Canada in the 1930s and became an international sensation as an environmentalist speaker and writer. Starring Pierce Brosnan, it was conceived as a major movie, but was not well received. The film is worth noting because it did have a significant role for an Indian woman. Annie Galipeau portrayed Anahareo, Grey Owl's common-law wife, who in reality encouraged him to write and market the books that made him famous, and clearly was a major force in his life. Unfortunately, in the movie she is presented as a young woman who, although strong-willed, will go to almost any lengths to win over and keep her Indian wannabe partner.

By 2006, the mainstream media interest in American Indian themes had all but disappeared, as evidenced in the lukewarm reaction to critically acclaimed director Terrence Malick's 2005 film *The New World*. The movie, which experienced serious production delays, was billed as "an epic adventure set amid the encounter of European and Native American cultures during the founding of the Jamestown Settlement in 1607," in which we witness "the dawn of a new America" (www.thenewworldmovie.com). The movie starred Colin Farrell as John Smith, Christian Bale as John Rolfe, and 14-

year-old newcomer Q'Orianka Kilcher as Pocahontas, in yet another retelling of the classic legend. Despite its highly bankable cast and esteemed director, *The New World* made little impact. Many critics praised its stunning and evocative cinematography, but it lacked dramatic punch. The film perpetuated the fiction of a physical love affair between Smith and the "princess," and in an odd way it seemed to echo the style of the Disney cartoon, as much of the film involves Pocahontas educating Smith on the beauty of nature and her perfect, harmonious culture. The filmmakers were constrained by the discomfort of showing the 14-year-old Kilcher and 27-year-old Farrell as lovers, so the love story depends on endless scenes in which the two exchange lingering looks, platonic embraces, and rather chaste-looking kisses, while frolicking in the pristine Virginia scenery. Kilcher, whose heritage is part indigenous Peruvian, presents Pocahontas as strong, striking, and independent-minded, although totally consumed by love. The film cannot escape the problematic nature of the story, in that she asserts her independence by effectively renouncing her family and tribe, and throwing in her lot with the English, resulting in her banishment. And despite numerous decorative roles for Indian extras, there are few Indian roles of any consequence, and none for other women, most of whom float mutely around the camp. Only one matters—the woman who helps create the "new America" that will largely exclude her own people. Malick's relatively unsuccessful Pocahontas version seems to mark the end (for the time being) of the small wave of "Indian" movies and television.

BREAKING THE STEREOTYPE

Although mainstream popular culture still offers little subjectivity to the Indian, male or female, the impetus for change grew steadily in the 1990s and into the twenty-first century. The day of the blockbuster Indian movie seems over, but that was never the venue for innovation anyway; in mainstream movies Indians continue to be trapped in the past, or in a conception of Indians as "traditional." Instead, we may look for change in smaller, independent films, and nonmainstream television. More honest portrayals of Indian life have developed in such "small" movies as *Powwow Highway* (1989), which became a very popular video rental among American Indians, and "came closest to revealing the 'modern' Indian-self" (Jojola, 2003, p. 15). Writing in 1998, Jojola (2003), predicted that the cycle of blockbuster "Indian sympathy" films would have to wane before space could open up for innovation in Indian representation. "Such invention will only come when a bona fide Native director or producer breaks into the ranks of Hollywood" (p. 21). That moment came with the 1998 release of the critically acclaimed

Smoke Signals, directed by Chris Eyre from stories by noted Spokane/Coeur d'Alene writer Sherman Alexie. As Cobb (2003) wrote, *Smoke Signals* breaks new ground in that it is ultimately about Indian people telling their own stories without any reference to White/Indian relationships: "*Smoke Signals* was not merely a part of the continuum of Native Americans and film; it was a pivot point" (Cobb, 2003, p. 226). Eyre went on to direct the more somber *Skins* (2001), while Alexie himself made *The Business of Fancy Dancing* (2002), which addressed the issues faced by a gay central character.

These productions, rooted in the reality of contemporary reservation life, have shattered the stereotypes of American Indian screen roles. At the same time, women have not had major roles in these films. Both *Powwow Highway* and *Smoke Signals* focus on road trips that tell the story of two male buddies. Female roles are by no means stereotypical, but are limited. *Skins* also concentrates on the relationship between two brothers, Mogy and Rudy, played by Graham Greene and Eric Schweig. There are three tiny female roles, two played by well-known actors, Lois Red Elk and *Northern Exposure*'s Elaine Miles. Michelle Thrush plays Stella, ostensibly Rudy's love interest, but the relationship (and Stella's character generally) is barely explored, with Thrush getting only a few minutes of screen time.

Women fared a little better in *Dance Me Outside* (1995), set on a contemporary Canadian reserve. Although the film's central characters are young men (Indian actors Ryan Black, Adam Beach, and Michael Greyeyes), there are several interesting and nonstereotypical female roles, notably girlfriend-turned-activist Sadie (played by Jennifer Podemski) and the hero's sister, Ilianna (played by Lisa LaCroix), who is torn between her old flame and a new, White husband. Finally, one other 1990s independent film deserves a mention—*Where the Rivers Flow North*. Jay Craven, the non-Indian director, coproducer, and cowriter, adapted it from a novella by Vermont author Howard Frank Mosher. Although not "about Indians" at all, it finally provided a major, costarring role for an Indian woman—Tantoo Cardinal. This film tells the story of a couple, an aging White logger (Rip Torn) and his Indian housekeeper/common-law wife Bangor (Cardinal), as they fight against the acquisition of their land in the 1920s. Bangor is written as an Indian woman, and there are moments in the film where that is clear, such as when the developers' strong-man refers to her as a squaw. But her ethnicity is not the issue—her complicated, bickering relationship with Tom's character is. In a reversal of the usual pattern, the male character dies in his quest for independence, leaving Bangor alone, not victorious but at least surviving. The film, by its nature and subject matter, could never be a "big" movie, but at least it may point to the possibility of roles for Indian women that acknowledge their ethnicity while being "about" larger human issues.

Conventional wisdom also is challenged in other nonmainstream media. Independent documentary Indian filmmakers are telling their stories (Prins 1989; Weatherford, 1992), and Indian women such as Loretta Todd, Sandra Osawa, and Jolene Rickard have emerged as among the strongest of them (Ginsburg, 2003). Noncommercial television has also led the way to change; for instance the National Film Board of Canada produced many films, beginning with a series of four 1-hour television movies in 1986, called "Daughters of the Country," which told four different stories of Indian or Metis women from the eighteenth century to the present. Although still set in the past, these were extraordinary in that they told their stories from the point of view of the women. Suddenly, instead of a movie that gazes at Indians through the eyes of White settlers, soldiers, or trappers, we saw those Whites as interlopers, whose ways are strange and alien. So accustomed are we to the standard way of seeing things, that it takes time to adjust. I found myself expecting to have the story of Ikwe told through the eyes of the White man she is forced to marry. Instead, he remains peripheral and, ultimately, dispensable. Life in the Ojibwa village is simple and mundane, concentrating more on survival and everyday tasks than on mystical ceremonies. The women who play the lead roles, such as Hazel King as Ikwe, or Mireille Deyglun as Mistress Madeleine, are neither voluptuous princesses nor dumpy squaws, but ordinary women who face human dilemmas not defined by their ethnicity.

Canada has also led the way in producing TV series and movies that represent contemporary Native experience, something that has not happened at all in the United States. Canadian Broadcasting Corporation series such as *The Rez* and *North of 60* have had a national impact that has transcended their identity as First Nation or "Indian" productions and made their stars nationally known. Native musicians have also had an impact, with singers such as Inuit Susan Aglukark and the Innu band Kashtin, who have also gone beyond an indigenous market.

U.S. network television went some way in expanding the imagery of Indian women in the CBS series *Northern Exposure*, which ran from 1990 to 1995. As Taylor (1996) wrote, *Northern Exposure*, which was set in contemporary Alaska, "casts its native population as alive, well, and flourishing, part of the dominant White society and modernity, yet still practicing traditional ways" (p. 229). As part of an ensemble cast, the show included two native Alaskan characters, Ed Chigliak (played by Darren E. Burrows) and Marilyn Whirlwind (played by Elaine Miles). Like all the characters on the show, neither was simple and one-dimensional, but rather displayed idiosyncratic, quirky characteristics. Marilyn was large, and yet was allowed to be sexual without being portrayed as "loose" or "squaw-like." At the same time, Taylor pointed out that the program was vague and inconsistent about Marilyn's cultural heritage; she seemed to move between the distinctly different

Haida, Tlingit, and Athabascan cultures, whereas White characters are consistently rooted in specific ethnicities. "Television would never consider giving cajuns Russian accents, (or) putting Islamic women in bikinis," (p. 241), yet *Northern Exposure*'s producers moved Marilyn and Ed's tribal affiliation with abandon.

In the long term, it's doubtful if *Northern Exposure* had any major impact on mainstream portrayals of Indians. The show was so distinctive, dreamlike and "unrealistic" that it may be remembered as a unique and nonrepresentative moment in television. Yet when I asked Indian viewers to compare *Northern Exposure* and *Dr. Quinn*, which is ostensibly presented as more "realistic," they all agreed that *Northern Exposure* was more "real," reflecting a sense of identification with the Native Alaskans as human beings, rather than cardboard characters (Bird, 1996). In that respect, *Northern Exposure* was in a different class from any U.S. television show, before or since.

We also saw a hopeful sign in the 1994 Turner Broadcasting series on "The Native Americans," which attempted to dramatize historic moments in Indian history in a series of feature-length TV movies. Although Geronimo and *The Broken Chain* were dismissed by at least one Indian critic as "feeble" (Merritt, 1994), the same writer had more encouraging words for *Lakota Woman: Siege at Wounded Knee*, a dramatization of the autobiography of Mary Crow Dog, who took part in the 1973 American Indian Movement (AIM) siege at Wounded Knee. The movie was made with a 90 percent Indian cast, and 40 percent of the crew were Indians, offering unprecedented opportunities for Indian people to gain experience in film-making techniques. Executive producer Lois Bonfiglio described the filming as "an extraordinary spiritual and emotional experience" for everyone involved. Indeed, the movie proved exceptional in that, like the smaller budget Canadian films, it told the story from the point of view of Mary Crow Dog, played by Irene Bedard (the voice of Disney's Pocahontas). The film does not glamorize Indian women—Mary is seen to sink into a life of alcoholism and promiscuity before being transformed by the message of AIM. Neither does it stereotype her as a degraded squaw; she is simply a human being, dealing with a set of problems and issues, many of which confront her because of her ethnic heritage. Although some may be cynical that Ted Turner and Jane Fonda were merely jumping on the Indian bandwagon (Merritt, 1994), *Lakota Woman* did offer an encouraging step in the right direction.

In 1996, HBO offered a groundbreaking mini-series *Grand Avenue*, based on the novel by Greg Sarris, which follows five generations of Pomo Indians as they leave the reservation to deal with life in Santa Rosa, California. Again, this production offers much more well-drawn roles for women than most feature films, giving rich opportunities to Irene Bedard, Sheila Tousey, and the inevitable Tantoo Cardinal. And perhaps the most high-profile effort of all has been the PBS *Mystery* productions of the very popular Tony Hillerman Navajo novels, starring Adam Beach and Wes Studi as Navajo police officers Jim Chee and Joe Leaphorn. An earlier film attempt to make one of the novels, *Dark Wind* (1993), which cast non-Native actors in the central roles, was widely derided. However, PBS signed Chris Eyre to direct *Skinwalkers* (2002) and *Thief of Time* (2004), which were much more successful. Although the main roles again were male, Alex Rice as lawyer/love interest Janet Peete and Sheila Tousey as Emma Leaphorn gave fine performances in rich, nuanced and nonstereotypical roles.

Meanwhile, American Indian women novelists and poets have worked hard to cast off the old imagery. Leslie Silko, Paula Gunn Allen, Joy Harjo, and others "have established a 'voice' and an 'identity' for the Indian woman which are grounded in the realities of the present, rather than the stereotypes of the past" (Tsosie, 1988). An interesting intervention in the world of comic book production, a notoriously stereotypical industry, is Bluecom Comics, which produces *Peace Party*, a "multicultural comic book featuring Native Americans" and also maintains a comprehensive Web site with pages on stereotypes and how to combat them (www.bluecomcomics.com). Even so, the *Peace Party* series centers around two leading male characters, with women generally taking subordinate roles. Nevertheless, it can be hoped that eventually, just as White and African-American women now have at least some voice in creating mass imagery, American Indian women will break into the consciousness of the mass culture industry. As Tantoo Cardinal said, "We have to get to a place where our Native women have a sexuality, a sensuality, an intelligence" (cited in Greer, 1994b, p. 153). But the stereotypes of Indians, male and female, will be hard to shatter—their role as the exotic, fascinating "other" is so entrenched and so naturalized.

DOES IT MATTER?

Over the last twenty years or so, feminist media criticism has moved past earlier, simplistic studies of media imagery—the kind of study that described media portrayals and discussed whether they reflected reality or perpetuated stereotypes. Classic studies offered a rich discussion of female "resistant" and "subversive" readings, suggesting that women can find pleasure in a range of unexpected texts (see, e.g., Ang, 1985; Bird, 1992; Brown, 1990; Press, 1991; Radway, 1984). Additionally, as more women take part in the production of media—as scriptwriters, directors, producers, and actors—we see the opportunity to celebrate some of the huge advances that have been gained in the representation of women. As Cook (1993) wrote, these female media makers "speak for themselves and not necessarily for all women: but they insist on their right to speak differently, and for that difference to be recognised" (p. xxiii).

Yet overwhelmingly, these gains have been made by White and African-American women, with American Indian women still almost invisible in mass culture in other than stereotypical representations. Ironically, "Indianness" is pervasive in U.S. culture, as a style that has embraced particular icons, such as the ubiquitous dream-catcher, or Kokopelli, the South West's hump-back flute player, both of which now appear on everything from T-shirts to earrings. A contemporary restless quest for spirituality continues to fuel demand for sweat lodges, sand-paintings, and carved fetishes—all disconnected from specific tribal identity and context. Indians seem to be the last ethnic group that still can be freely stereotyped in the most grotesque ways. As recently as 2004, American Indians were outraged by a CBS Grammy Award broadcast featuring the hip-hop duo OutKast, who performed their hit "Hey Ya" against a backdrop of smoke, teepees, and other Indian pop culture symbols. Singer Andre "3000" Benjamin, in a lime-green "Indian" costume and wig, was backed by scantily clad, gyrating dancers in feathers and green "princess" outfits. An introductory voice-over intoned that "the Natives are getting restless." A staff writer for the newspaper *Indian Country Today* commented, "These may have been costumes to OutKast and the producers . . . but to American Indians they were the latest in a long line of insults, caricatures drawn from history" (http://www.indiancountry.com). The performance drew protests from many Indian nations, individuals, and well-known Indian voices, such as writer and columnist Suzan Shown Harjo. AIM member Vernon Bellecourt commented that the performance was analogous to portraying African Americans "with a grass skirt, a bone through their nose, a war lance in hand and balancing a watermelon and pork chop in the other" (www.bluecomcomics.com).

But does the limited picture of Indian women (and men) actually matter? After all, most people are surrounded by real men and women; they know that media imagery is not everything, and their understandings of gender are formed not only by media but also by day-to-day interactions. In many parts of the country, however, non-Indians never see or encounter a real, living Indian person (McGuire, 1992). Media representations take on an added power in this situation, filling a knowledge vacuum with outmoded and limited stereotypes, as several studies suggest (see Riverwind, n.d.). In my study of *Dr. Quinn*, for example, White viewers found the portrayal of the Cheyenne "authentic" and believable, especially when the Cheyenne behaved in ways that are, indeed, stereotypical—stoic, silent, and spiritual. It was these very aspects of behavior that Indian viewers found most problematic. Furthermore, one of the most striking findings in my later study (Bird, 2003), which offered participants the chance to create a hypothetical television show with an Indian character, was that White participants had a particularly hard time developing a nonstereotypical female role—even in a region of the country that has one of the largest populations of Native people. Perhaps the reality is trumped by the endless parade of buckskin-clad "princesses" on comic books, greeting cards, "collectables," and gift shop paraphernalia.

In 1993, Williams introduced an anthology that in many ways was a celebration of the transformations women have brought about in popular filmmaking. She presented the collection as the beginning of an answer to her own question: "So what happens when marginalised or repressed stories come to the fore? What happens when fantasies of power or tales of difference . . . become the conscious, overt, marketable stuff of mainstream cinema?" (p. xxv). When it comes to representations of American Indian women, the answer to this question is sadly clear. We don't know what happens, although the examples of independent film and television offer an encouraging way forward. More than a decade after Williams' question, American Indian men and women in the United States have little public identity as everyday Americans. Only when we find room for their tales will our mediated realities be finally able to break the lock of a mythic past.

NOTES

1. Although some prefer to use the term *Native Americans*, I have generally chosen to use *American Indians*, since this is the more commonly used self-description in Minnesota where I resided when first writing this.

2. Tsosie (1988) discusses the range of traditional roles for women in several indigenous cultures. For a discussion of accepted alternative female roles in specific cultures, see Lewis (1941) and Medicine (1983). Many Native American cultures also offered alternative social roles for men (see Callender and Kodrens, 1983). Foster (1995) describes how strong female roles have been erased from the historical literature on the Iroquois.

3. Indian actress Lois Red Elk commented in 1980 that of the many small roles she has played in her career, almost none of her characters was given a name (Leuthold, 1995).

4. For a discussion of appropriations of Native culture, see Whitt (1995) and Meyer and Royer (2001). A. Green (1991) took issue especially with white feminists who appropriate Indian spirituality.

REFERENCES

Ang, I. (1985). *Watching Dallas*. London: Methuen.

Berkhofer, R. F. (1979). *The white man's Indian*. New York: Vintage Books.

Bird, S. E. (1992). *For enquiring minds: A cultural study of supermarket tabloids*. Knoxville: University of Tennessee Press.

Bird, S. E. (1996). Not my fantasy: The persistence of Indian imagery in *Dr. Quinn, Medicine Woman*. In S. E. Bird (Ed.), *Dressing in feathers: The construction of the Indian in American popular culture* (pp. 245–62). Boulder, CO: Westview Press.

Bird, S. E. (2001). Savage desires: The gendered representation of American Indians in popular media. In C. J. Meyer & D. Royer (Ed.), *Selling the Indian: Commercializing and appropriating American Indian cultures* (pp. 62–98). Tucson: University of Arizona Press.

Bird, S. E. (2003). *The audience in everyday life: Living in a media world.* New York: Routledge.

Brand, S. (1988). Indians and the counterculture, 1960s–1970s. In W. E. Washburn (Ed.), *The handbook of North American Indians* (Vol. 4, pp. 570–72) Washington, DC: Smithsonian Institution Press.

Brown, M. E. (Ed.). (1990). *Television and women's culture: The politics of the popular.* Newbury Park, CA: Sage.

Callender, C., & L. M. Kodrens (1983). The North American berdache. *Current Anthropology,* 24, 443–90.

Castile, G. P (1996). The commodification of Indian identity. *American Anthropologist* 98(4), 743–49.

Churchill, W. (1994). *Indians are us: Culture and genocide in Native North America.* Monroe, ME: Common Courage Press.

Cobb, A. J. (2003). This is what it means to say Smoke Signals. In P. C. Rollins & J. E. O'Connor (Eds.), *Hollywood's Indian: The portrayal of the Native American in film* (pp. 207–28). Lexington: University Press of Kentucky.

Cook, P. (1993). Border crossings: Women and film in context. In P. Cook & P. Dodd (Eds.), *Women and film: A sight and sound reader* (pp. ix–xxiii.). Philadelphia: Temple University Press.

DeCaro, F. (1986). Vanishing the red man: Cultural guilt and legend formation. *International Folklore Review* 4, 74–80.

Deloria, P. J. (2004). *Indians in unexpected places.* Lawrence: University Press of Kansas.

Denetdale, J. N. (2001). Representing Changing Woman: A review essay on Navajo women. *American Indian Culture and Research Journal* 25(3), 1–26.

Dow, B. (1996). *Prime time feminism: Television, media culture, and the women's movement since 1970.* Philadelphia: University of Pennsylvania Press.

Foster, M. H. (1995). Lost women of the matriarchy: Iroquois women in the historical literature. *American Indian Culture and Research Journal* 19(3), 121–40.

Francis, D. (1992). *The imaginary Indian: The image of the Indian in Canadian culture.* Vancouver: Arsenal Pulp Press.

Ginsburg, F. (2003). Indigenous media: Negotiating control over images. In L. Gross, J. S. Katz, & J. Ruby (Eds.), *Image ethics in the digital age* (pp. 295–311). Minneapolis: University of Minnesota Press.

Green, A. (1991). For all those who were Indian in a former life. *Ms.* 2(3), 44–45.

Green, R. (1975). The Pocahontas perplex: The image of the Indian woman in American culture. *Massachusetts Review,* 16(4), 698–714.

Green, R. (1988a). The Indian in popular American culture. In W. E. Washburn (Ed.), *The handbook of North American Indians* (Vol. 4, pp. 587–606). Washington, DC: Smithsonian Institution Press.

Green, R. (1988b). The tribe called wannabee: Playing Indian in America and Europe. *Folklore* 99(1), 30–55.

Greer, S. (1994a). Imagining Indians: Native people voice their concerns, beliefs, and action plans at Arizona film festival. *Winds of Change* 9(4), 142–44.

Greer, S. (1994b). Tantoo Cardinal: A part of all nations. *Winds of Change* 9(4), 150–153.

Jojola, T. (2003). Absurd reality II: Hollywood goes to the Indians. In P. C. Rollins & J. E. O'Connor (Eds.), *Hollywood's Indian: The portrayal of the Native American in film* (pp. 12–26). Lexington: University Press of Kentucky.

Jones, M. E. (Ed.). (1994). The military savagely destroys Indians: Testimony from U.S. Congressional investigations. In *The American frontier: Opposing viewpoints.* San Diego: Greenhaven Press.

King, C. R (2003). De/scribing squaw: Indigenous women and imperial idioms in the United States. *American Indian Culture and Research Journal* 27(2), 1–16.

Leuthold, S.M. (1995). Native American responses to the Western. *American Indian Culture and Research Journal* 19(1), 153–89.

Lewis, O. (1941). Manly-hearted women among the South Peigan. *American Anthropologist* 43, 173–87.

Marsden, M. T., & Nachbar, J. (1988). The Indian in the movies. In W. E. Washburn (Ed.), *The handbook of North American Indians* (Vol. 4, pp. 607–616). Washington, DC Smithsonian Institution Press.

McGuire, R. H. (1992). Archeology and the first Americans. *American Anthropologist* 94(4), 816–36.

McKenney, T. L, & Hall, J. (1933). *The Indian tribes of North America.* Edinburgh: John Grant. (Original work published 1844).

Medicine, B. (1983). "Warrior women": Sex role alternatives for Plains Indian women. In P. Albers & B. Medicine (Eds.), *Hidden half: Studies of Plains Indian women* (pp. 267–80). Lanham, MD: University Press of America.

Merritt, J. (1994). Lakota Woman: Authentic culture on film or exploitation. *Winds of Change* 8(2), 90–93.

Meyer, C. J., & Royer, D. (2001). *Selling the Indian: Commercializing and appropriating American Indian cultures.* Tucson: University of Arizona Press.

Oneida Nation Response to OutKast Performance. (2004). *Indian Country Today.* Retrieved September 1, 2006, from http://www. indiancountry.com/content.cfm?id=1076426250.

Press, A. (1991). *Women watching television.* Philadelphia: University of Pennsylvania Press.

Prins, H. (1989). American Indians and the ethnocinematic complex: From Native participation to production control. *Visual Sociology* 4(2), 85–89.

Radway, J. (1984). *Reading the romance: Women, patriarchy, and popular literature.* Chapel Hill: University of North Carolina Press.

Riverwind, J. (n.d). The basic Indian stereotypes. Retrieved September 1, 2006, from http://www.bluecorncomics.com/stbasics.htm.

Rollins, P. C., & O'Connor, J. E. (Eds.). (2003). *Hollywood's Indian: The portrayal of the Native American in film.* Lexington: University Press of Kentucky.

Strong, P.T (1996). Animated Indians: Critique and contradiction in commodified children's culture. *Cultural Anthropology* 11(3), 405–24.

Taylor, A. (1996). Cultural heritage in Northern Exposure. In S. E. Bird (Ed.), *Dressing in feathers: The construction of the Indian in American popular culture* (pp. 229–244). Boulder, CO: Westview Press.

Thenewworldmovie.com. Synopsis of film *The New World.* Retrieved September 1, 2006, from http://www.thenewworldmovie.com

Tilton, R. (1994). *Pocahontas: The evolution of an American narrative.* Cambridge: Cambridge University Press.

Tompkins, J. (1992). *West of everything.* New York: Oxford University Press.

Tsosie, R. (1988). Changing women: The cross currents of American Indian feminine identity. *American Indian Culture and Research Journal* 12(1), 1–38.

Van Lent, P. (1996). Her beautiful savage: The current sexual image of the Native American male. In S. E. Bird (Ed.), *Dressing in feathers: The construction of the Indian in American popular culture* (pp. 211–28) Boulder, CO: Westview Press.

Weatherford, E. (1992). Starting fire with gunpowder. *Film Comment* 28, 64–67.

Whitt, L. A. (1995). Cultural imperialism and the marketing of Native America. *American Indian Culture and Research Journal* 19(3), 1–32.

Williams, L. R. (1993). Everything in question: Women and film in prospect. In P. Cook & P. Dodd (Eds.), *Women and film: A sight and sound reader* (pp. xxiv–xxix). Philadelphia: Temple University Press.

Chapter Sixteen

The Eurasian Female Hero(ine)

Sydney Fox as Relic Hunter

Yasmin Jiwani

In contrast to previous historical periods, contemporary Western television programs and films have increasingly incorporated the racialized Other as heroes rather than simply as villains. The successes of Jennifer Lopez, Lucy Liu, and Jessica Alba as recent female heroines attest to the allure of the exotic other and its ability as a viable social and cultural currency to attract particular audience segments. The changing representations of women of color in popular Western television reflect responses to the larger forces of globalization as well as the growing economic power exercised by Asian and other minorities in the United States. Furthermore, in this article, I argue that, although these representations have changed considerably, they still draw on a collective stock of sedimented knowledge that results in the construction of an Other reminiscent of standard colonialist and orientalist representations. In discussing the notion of the racialized heroine as typified in shows such as *Relic Hunter*, the trajectory of the female heroine continually involves hybridity, that is, the mixing of various forms of power to enhance the physical, psychological, and social prowess of these women. As a result, these hybrid heroines end up being symbolically recuperated as signs of an emancipated femininity and an assimilated ethnicity.

The notion of "Asian" women or "women of color" as a representational category is highly problematic, beginning with the tropes inherent in colonial literature that tend to collapse differences between women to produce a homogeneous categorization of women of color. Such a categorization not only reflects a particular set of political influences but is dependent on the nature of the relationship between the dominant colonizing nation and its subject nation. In addition, the links between these earlier representations and their contemporary avatars shed light on how heroic women of color are represented in current Western television programming, particularly American and Canadian-American coproductions. *Relic Hunter* and its principal character, Sydney Fox, reveal the underlying ideological premises informing the changing representations of women of color. It also suggests possible reasons for these changes in representations while underscoring their continuities with previous historically inscribed representations.

Representations not only tell us about the world in which we live, they also categorize that world, giving it an order that is intelligible and makes common sense. Himani Bannerji defines media representations of Others as images that describe and prescribe social reality. Similarly, Stuart Hall underscores how media representations not only provide us with the language by which to name the world but also inform our understandings of categories such as "race" ("Narrative" 20). These representations are also used to legitimize particular policies and practices (Hall, "Narrative," *Representation*, "Whites of Their Eyes: Racist") to nurture a sense of national identity and, as Benjamin Anderson argues, to foster an "imagined community."

PROBLEMATIZING "ASIAN" WOMEN

Methodologically, it is problematic to speak of "Asian" women as a monolithic or homogeneous category, particularly given the wide differences within in Asia as a continent and within the communities that are typified and categorized as "Asian." Even within these communities, the term "Asian" has different meanings in different postcolonial settings.[1] In examining visual media such as films and television programs, the category "Asian" appears to be rather nebulous and all encapsulating. Women of color appear as "Asians" when their skin tone is brown, unless their appearance is accompanied by other culturally specific signifiers that suggest a specific Native, Hispanic, or Pacific Islander identity. However, even here, their representations tend to be visually collapsed into the category of "women of color" and, within that category, Hispanic/Asian/Indian women are often represented as being interchangeable, much like "natives" were considered interchangeable in colonial discourse (JanMohamed 64). Bearing this in mind, I attempt to capture representations that spill into the category of an "Asian"/Eursian identity.

However, critical approaches to media representations of Hispanic and mixed-race women are also relevant in analyzing these images, given that many of the traits they are seen to possess are also attributed to Asian and Eurasian women. The rationale for so doing lies in the very fact that these images are still considered interchangeable and, thus, communicate a dominant ideological perspective that resonates with the embedded and historically sedimented colonial stock of knowledge. As Edward Said argues, constructions of Others, which are framed and organized around particular worldviews and dominant discourses such as orientalism, derive their power from the citational nature of this discourse—that is, via the mechanism by which representations are constructed, articulated, and defined in reference to previous representations, sometimes in conformity with them and, at other times, in opposition. Thus, they cumulatively constitute a systematic body of knowledge about these Others (see, for instance, Yegenoglu).

HISTORICAL REPRESENTATIONS—THE LEGACY

Representations of people of color (or the colonized) varied depending on the empire that was in power and the particular historical point of colonization. Undoubtedly, there were differences in French, Spanish, and British representations. Images that circulated during the heyday of the British Empire, many of which were then absorbed into the stock of knowledge that informed and underpinned American imperialism, constitute an important point of departure.

Early representations of women of color tended to portray them as exotic, erotic, and dangerous (Jiwani). Especially dangerous when they appeared solo, they were represented as treacherous distractions seducing the white hero into abandoning his civilizing "mission" and reducing him to nativity. En masse, they were often represented as passive and colorful backdrops to the daredevil exploits of the quintessential white male adventurer central to the imperialist narrative (Shohat and Stam). One has only to think of the old James Bond films or the exploits of Indiana Jones as examples of this tradition. These representations were grounded in old British colonial images in which the fecundity of native women was seen as a danger to the empire, and taboos against miscegenation were seen as necessary so that the strength of the empire (i.e., its soldiers) would not be drained through conversion to native ways or through the reproduction of a mixed race (Burney; Greenberger; McBratney). Thus, if the women were signified as dangerous, forbidden, evil, and lustful, their unsuitability as wives or mothers would be communicated. These sentiments were current both in the popular media and policy documents. For instance, Chandra Mohanty cites a memo, the "concubinage circular," disseminated by Lord Crewe in 1909 to colonial officers in Africa, which urged them not to consort with native women, as this diminished their authority and reduced their effectiveness as administrators (17).

Representations of women of color as highly sexualized, extremely fe-
cund, and as objects of the white, male gaze were, thus, a significant trope in
the dominant British colonial narrative. These representations contrasted
sharply with those of the virginal or sexually repressed white female sexuality. This juxtaposition of innocent white women with the excessive and aber-
rant women of color helped to reinscribe the hegemonic worldview of the
"civilized" superiority of the white race (see also hooks). William Schneider
describes how native women were exhibited in circuses and sideshows in
Europe. As well, Shohat and Stam underscore the sexualization of native
women in their discussion of the anatomical obsession with Saartjie Baart-
man, popularly known as the "Hottentot Venus," whose body was exhibited
widely and whose body parts were subsequently dissected by George Cuvier
and held as examples of the animality of the "savages" (see also Abraham;
Beltrane; Gilman).

Negative representations of Asians—notably the Chinese and Japanese—
were also abundant in the Western popular press. For example, the *New York
Daily Tribune* of September 29, 1854, had a column that described the Chinese as "uncivilized, unclean, filthy beyond all conception, without any of
the higher domestic or social relations; lustful and sensual in their disposi-
tions; every female is a prostitute, and of the basest order; the first words they
learn are terms of obscenity or profanity, and beyond this they care to learn
no more. Clannish in nature, they will not associate except with their own
people." (qtd. in Rath, par. 11; see also Lim). These observations were made
without any reference to the exclusionary laws prevailing in America at the
time, which constrained Asian immigration such that women were not allowed to enter except as dependents or chattel labor (see, for instance, Abu-
Laban; Backhouse; Chen). [2] Of all the various traits attributed to Asian wom-
en in columns like the one in the *New York Daily Tribune*, their heightened
sexuality and profanity were emphasized most. This emphasis often resulted
in a more intense scrutiny of the sexual behavior of Asian women, as well as
a focus on them as spreading venereal diseases.

In speaking to representations of Asian women, Ronald Takaki notes that

> Chinese women were condemned as a "depraved class" and their depravity
> was associated with their almost African-like physical appearance. While their
> complexions approached "fair," one writer observed, their whole physiogno-
> my indicated "but a slight removal from the African race." (qtd. in Pieterse
> 25–26)

Noting, too, how Chinese men, for their part, "were denounced as threats to
white women" (Takaki, qtd. in Pieterse 25–26), it is interesting to see how
South Asian men were similarly constructed as threats to white women along
the West Coast of the United States. In Canada, these kinds of representa-

tions subsequently were used to rationalize laws that prohibited men of color from using white women as laborers in their business enterprises (K. Anderson; Backhouse). However, aside from their strategic uses, these representations also reflect the racial hierarchies that were (and are) present both within U.S. and Canadian societies.

The taboo against miscegenation underpinned many of these negative colonial representations. Early and even recent Hollywood films have emphasized the negative outcomes of miscegenation (Ito). The woman of color usually dies a tragic death or is transformed into a horrible hag (see, for instance, She, Ayesha). As for the white male hero, he inevitably stages a miraculous escape from the claws of the evil dragon lady. All of these dastardly "fates," as I have outlined elsewhere, reinforce the notion of Asian women, like other women of color, as exotic, erotic, and dangerous (Jiwani).

Harold Isaacs has traced some of these early representations to the phenomenon of the "yellow peril," arguing that American (and Canadian) fears were rooted in what was seen as a growing Asian population that would soon engulf the country. Similarly, the fear of "difference" also underpins many economic and political policies of exclusion that were articulated in the colonies against Asians and other non-European immigrants (Huttenback). The way that this "difference" was framed varied according to the prevailing political sentiments of the day. As a result, representations of Asians oscillated between the image of "hordes" invading the American and Canadian landscape and images that emphasized their spirituality, mysticism, and lives of abject poverty (Buchignani and Indra).

It appears that the more sympathetic, though highly patronizing, representations were often—but not always—articulated by Western feminists whose preoccupation with their long-suffering sisters in the colonies resulted in lurid tales of the cultural backwardness of the colonized. For example, in writing about Indian women, prominent British feminist Josephine Butler defined them as caught

> between the upper and nether millstone, helpless, voiceless, hopeless. Their helplessness appeals to the heart, in somewhat the same way that the helplessness and suffering of a dumb animal does, under the knife of a vivisector. Somewhere, halfway between the Martyr Saints and the tortured "friend of man," the noble dog, stand, it seems to me, these pitiful Indian women, girls, children, as many of them are. They have not even the small power of resistance which the western woman may have . . . who may have some clearer knowledge of a just and pitiful God to whom she may make her mute appeal. (qtd. in Burton 144)

Although other more egalitarian sentiments were articulated by some of the lesser-known feminists, the dominant discourse of the day emphasized the barbarism of Asian cultures and the oppressed conditions of Asian women.

Western feminism was often communicated as the dominant "rescue" meta-narrative (Cooke; Razack). This theme continues to inform contemporary representations of Asian women in popular Western television programming.[3]

Stuart Hall ("Whites of Their Eyes") argues that these colonial representations were characterized by a structure of ambivalence. Thus, representations of black women often cohered around the image of the kindly and maternal Aunt Jemima in contradistinction to their representations as Jezebels. Similarly, representations of the loyal house slave contrasted with representations of the field slaves as cunning and rebellious. Representations of faithful, submissive, and self-sacrificing Asian women contrasted with other representations, which highlighted them as cunning figures of the underworld. This ambivalence has enabled the continuities and ruptures to exist simultaneously in contemporary representations of Asian women in popular Western media. It has also served to strategically "deactivate" the transgressive element of their difference, thereby containing its immanent threat and facilitating its commodification as an exotic difference that can be easily consumed (Beltrane; Lalvani).

CONTEMPORARY REPRESENTATIONS

Over the past few years, popular representations of Asian women have changed remarkably. In part, this change may be due to the economic and demographic power of the Asian population in the United States. As Tom Kagy points out, in 1993 there were more than eight million Asians living in the United States, and the average income of the Asian household was higher than the national average. Moreover, Asian representation in managerial positions, colleges, and universities has increased tremendously. The consuming power of Asians is similarly high. Kagy notes that "a survey of counter people of premium cosmetic brands like Estee Lauder, Chanel, Lancome and Christian Dior in top-flight California department stores shows that 20–65% of all sales are to Asian women" (3). As well, there is the lure of the Asian markets, especially for syndicated shows. Kagy estimated that by 2001 the Asian market would "account for 50% of all world box office revenues" (4). Added to this is the popular representation of Asian communities as "model minorities"—assimilating rapidly and acquiring economic power without insisting on cultural retention in the public sphere of politics and business.

In other words, economics may be an important driving force contributing to the change in representations. However, the positioning, ideologically and materially, of some Asian communities as model minorities in the United States may be a more critical factor. Certainly, in light of the contemporary racialized stratification order that positions Native, black, and Hispanic minorities (or majorities) on the lower rungs, the use of a model minority to maintain the stratification order becomes paramount and is predicated on a "divide and rule" strategy. As suggested earlier, another possible explanation for these changes is the influence of Asian markets outside the United States that, as Zhao and Schiller point out, cannot be ignored in light of the access afforded to them by various international trade agreements under the aegis of the World Trade Organization.

Finally, it could be argued that such changes may be the result of increasing momentum on the part of media advocacy organizations in the last decade. In the last few years alone, the intensity of media education and literacy combined with the work of organizations such as the Media Action Network for Asian Americans (MANAA) have advanced the issue of media representations to a broader arena. These advocacy initiatives have relied on annual research reports published by the Screen Actors Guild, as well as on the extensive cultural indicators project of the Annenberg School of Communications. The latter reports have consistently demonstrated the under-representation and "misrepresentation" of Asian Americans in American film and television.[4] Likewise, the 1998 Screen Actors Guild report, *Casting the American Scene: Fairness and Diversity in Television*, emphasizes the under-representation of Asian Americans in television programming—both daytime and prime time. Based on "weeklong samples of prime-time network drama recorded from 1994 to 1997 and daytime serial drama from 1995–1997" (Gerbner), the report indicates that Asian representation (in terms of the number of television characters) increased from 0.8 percent in the 1982–1992 period of analysis to 1.3 percent in the 1994–1997 period. However, the Asian population also increased during this period, thus detracting from any real significant increase in television representation.[5]

For the communities concerned, as well as for media activists, this under-representation is compounded by the concentrated representation of minorities in stereotypical roles. In an open letter to Hollywood, MANAA identified a list of media stereotypes and urged Hollywood to dismantle these by offering suggested alternatives. Those findings have been echoed by other scholars and critics (e.g., Chen; Chung; Feng; Hagedorn; Lim; Marchetti; McAllister; Shu; Tajima). Common stereotypes that MANAA identified included the portrayal of Asian Americans as unassimilable immigrants and as exploitive of others. The Media Action Network also found that Asians were repeatedly cast in supporting roles in which their features, style, and comportment were communicated as being inferior, comical, or ominous. Furthermore, MANAA argued that Asian males were consistently emasculated in the media, as epitomized by their frequent portrayal as either asexual or feminine. For their part, Asian women were represented as the "China dolls/geisha girls or lotus blossoms"—as "exotic, subservient, compliant, industrious, eager to please." Recounting her experiences growing up in the Philippines and being exposed to American representations of Asian women, Jessica Hagedorn speaks to these often contradictory stereotypes when she suggests that she

> was mystified and enthralled by Hollywood's skewed representations of Asian women: sleek, evil goddesses with slanted eyes and cunning ways, or smiling, sarong-clad South Seas "maidens" with undulating hips, kinky black hair, and white skin darkened by makeup. (33)[6]

These prevailing representations, in other words, are constructed as binary oppositions. Thus, the implacable China doll is contrasted with the "inherently scheming, untrustworthy, and back-stabbing" dragon lady (Media Action Network); the self-sacrificing Asians, like the faithful Gunga Dins of the Kipling era, or the man of color sidekick to the Robinson Crusoe type of white hero (Zackel), or the obedient and submissive "Asian" heroine in *The Good Earth*, are contrasted with the rebellious Others who undermine the moral order and suffer the fateful consequences of their actions.[7]

FROM DRAGON LADY TO WARRIOR WOMAN

From the hard-edged and sarcastic Lucy Liu in *Ally McBeal* to the martial arts expert Kelly Hu in *Martial Law* and *Shanghai Noon*, Asian women are increasingly visible on television screens and in Hollywood films.[8] That said, many of these Asian women are in fact Eurasian and, in some cases, are used to fill in for Native women. For instance, Kelly Hu represents an Aboriginal woman in *Shanghai Noon*. In *The Joy Luck Club*—a film ostensibly about Chinese women—Tamlyn Tomita, who is part Japanese and part Filipino, plays one of the characters.

The homogeneity that marks these representations is itself telling of how the interchangeability of Others remains a dominant feature of contemporary media discourses dealing with representations. This casual blurring of boundaries lends itself to the various combinations and permutations that are possible to tell a story—whether this is told from the perspective of the Other or from the perspective of the dominant self. What is critical, however, is how these representations are drawn from myriad cultural traditions as fodder to be recirculated and recombined in the interests of satiating the thirst for novelty and, at the same time, the need for familiarity. Thus, the figure of Mulan can be derived from a particular tradition, divested of certain particularities of that tradition, and then reinscribed with familiar characteristics to create a hybrid that is at once different and the same (for an insightful take on this phenomenon, see Lang).

Contemporary representations of Asian women reflect this interplay between sameness and difference. Often embodying a Xena warrior princess kind of style—beautiful, talented, and skilled in martial arts—their pedigree not only reaches far back but is emblematic of the syncretistic tendencies of postmodern popular culture. Amidst this pastiche of styles glued together from a variety of sources, the syncretism is further reflected in their own mixed-race heritage. Tia Carrere, for instance—the actor who plays the main character in *Relic Hunter*—is Filipina born in Hawaii. The positioning of Carrere (whose actual name is Althea Janairo) as Sydney Fox, "relic hunter," is quite a departure from the traditional portrayal of Asian women as powerless, submissive, and docile victims, or alternatively as exotic, evil, and scheming dragon ladies.

RELIC HUNTER

Relic Hunter lasted for three seasons and generated a total of sixty-six episodes. It began in September 1999 and ended in May 2002; the reruns are still being shown. Originally produced by Fireworks Entertainment Inc., a subsidiary of Can-West Inc. and Gaumont Television (France), the program was filmed in Toronto, Paris, Spain, and England. Subsequent seasons were produced by Fireworks Entertainment Inc. and Farrier Ltd. and distributed by Paramount Domestic. The series is reflective of a growing tendency of different countries to collaborate on coproductions—a strategic move on the part of Western telecommunication companies hoping to capture the ever-expanding non-European market (see Zhao and Schiller). In terms of genre, *Relic Hunter* can best be described as a comic adventure action program.

Relic Hunter deserves analysis because of both its popularity and its strategic use of an Asian woman as the main heroine/actor. Furthermore, the very notion of the Asian woman as a relic hunter merits attention because such a role has, historically, been confined to white males playing such heroes as Allen Quartermain and Indiana Jones. In a sense, placing a woman—and an "Asian" woman at that—in such a dominant position signals a reversal of roles. But it also speaks to the widespread belief (heavily promoted by the Western media) that women have achieved equality and often have even surpassed males in achieving power and dominance—especially if they are allowed to flourish in the democratically fertile soil of the liberal West.

In *Relic Hunter*, Sydney Fox is a swashbuckling explorer searching for the lost and time-forgotten relics of the past. Although the term "relic" has religious origins, Sydney is not a Madonna-like figure in any way. She is an extremely intelligent history professor teaching at Trinity University—an institution that resembles one of the Ivy League schools in the United States. Sydney's background information (posted on the popular *Relic Hunter* Web site) indicates that she is a child of an Asian mother and a white father. Her mother died when she was very young (likely as a result of miscegenation, if we are to believe old Hollywood's edicts!), and she grew up with her civil engineer father, traveling with him as he worked his way around the globe. Her origins, in other words, conform with Franklin Wong's argument that "most Hollywood Eurasians have Caucasian fathers and Asian mothers, symbolically naturalizing the western male's sexual access to the Asian female" (qtd. in Marchetti 68).

Sydney's access to the privileges of her white father is most apparent in her educational background, her familiarity with other cultural and linguistic traditions, and her hybrid beauty—symbolizing in its totality a seductive femininity traditionally associated with the East and the honor, integrity, and intelligence commonly associated with the West (see, for instance, Said). As a history professor teaching ancient civilizations, she has no problem appropriating different traditions and dances and exhibiting these to her students. As a relic hunter, she is often hired by private investigators, rich families, governments, and a host of other parties to find elusive objects. However, not all the relics she recuperates are ancient. For instance, in one episode, Sydney is hired by a collector to retrieve Elvis Presley's original guitar. Hence, she crosses the boundaries between a retriever of ancient treasures and a finder of local Americana.

In the series, Sydney is flanked by a white British male research assistant, Nigel, who is as weak as she is strong and as passive as she is assertive. Interestingly, most of the chat room discussions focus on his cuteness, and most of the Web sites focus on her sexuality. Nigel is timid about venturing into strange lands. He is the antithesis of the white male explorer, whereas Sydney is the female counterpart of this explorer. Yet, Nigel maintains his masculinity, as signified by his constantly roving eyes and his appreciation for the female secretary, as well as for any other attractive female who crosses his path. Sydney, on the other hand, maintains her focus and is relentless in her pursuit of the particular artifact she has been hired to retrieve. Many of these artifacts subsequently become the property of the university—especially if they are in the realm of public works of art—and, in turn, the university not only benefits financially from Sydney's exploits but uses this as a rationale to retain her as faculty while overlooking her numerous absences from the classroom.

Completing this unusual character triad is a blonde secretary/clerical assistant named Claudia, who is described by the show's Web site as the "ditzy" undergraduate. Her interests extend to her personal appearance and an obsession with an appropriately hunky male. The official Web site indicates her expertise as being "popular culture." She represents the present, whereas Sydney travels between the past and present.[9]

A number of interesting points about the current state of race, nationhood, and gender roles can be made with regard to *Relic Hunter*'s cast. Sydney clearly signifies the modern, middle-class, university-educated American woman of color; Nigel represents a feminized British white male. As for Claudia, she—like Sydney—is American. However, she is white, younger than Sydney, and not all that accomplished. Thus, if the two share the privileged status of being American, Claudia signifies the youthful, self-interested, and not-so-worldly aspect of this status, whereas Sydney typifies the American Dream: the self-made woman whose professional and material success can be attributed to a combination of the innate race and class privilege imparted by her father and that certain *je ne sais quoi* afforded by her mother's cultural legacy. Sydney, in other words, epitomizes the liberal ideology of equality that is enshrined in the whole notion of the American Dream.

In terms of gender roles, Nigel's positioning as the lone male in this triad allows the two women to enact the dual legitimized aspects of femininity. Sydney is always protecting Nigel, chiding him for his negligence, and supporting him through his many weaknesses. She becomes, in relation to Nigel, a mother-like figure. Claudia, on the other hand, titillates Nigel, luring him into making advances that are laughable as they belie his ability to mimic the more acceptable "macho" notions of masculinity. Yet, in an important sense, Claudia represents Nigel's female counterpart—a companion from his peer group who has the potential to be "girlfriend material." She is, thus, more like a potential girlfriend or companion. These symbolic inversions are thrown into relief when viewed against the backdrop of colonial tropes. . . .

The relationship among these three characters can also be read as one in which Western superiority in terms of intelligence and physical prowess meets with Eastern exotica as exemplified in such qualities as beauty, agility, grace, and cunning. As suggested earlier, Sydney—the woman-of-color heroine—is positioned in the "in-between" zone of hybridity. This is a hybridity, as Young argues, that "makes difference into sameness, and sameness into difference, but in a way that makes the same no longer the same, the different no longer simply the different" (26). Hybridization, in other words, symbolizes an intervention—one designed to contain the excesses of the original sign but also to assimilate its difference in a way that is non-threatening (Minh-ha).[10] Central to this understanding of hybridity is its assumption of a first-order—a "pure race"—that is then altered or transformed (Mahtani).

Religion and science traditionally have been the patriarchal pillars that have served to influence and define women's bodies and status (Balsamo: Haraway). In both traditions, women have been defined in terms of a quintessential "lack," and the challenge has been one of rectifying this "lack" through mechanical and biological interventions. In the case of *Relic Hunter*, the assumed lack within women of color is rectified through hybridity— through a literal mixing of traditions and genes that, when molded through the Western educational system, end up fashioning an Other that is more like "us." Science and orientalism come together to forge the contemporary Asian woman. Unlike her black sisters, the hybridized Asian woman is able to transcend the structural barriers of racism and sexism. This resonates with the neocolonial strategy identified by Ono when he argues that the "media rely on racial hierarchicalization of people of color" (179).

For the disempowered, Sydney Fox represents the hope that there is a way out: If one tries hard enough and is disciplined enough, one can succeed. In the context of a climate of backlash against feminism and the fight for women's rights, this message reinforces the illusion of equality and suggests that any setbacks women experience can be overcome through sheer will and determination and, if all else fails, training in martial arts. In other words, there is no talk here of dismantling systemic structures. Patriarchy in the world of *Relic Hunter* exists only in an institutionalized form and that form, as represented here by the mythical Trinity University, is portrayed as being harmless—a benign force that can be overridden by intellectual brilliance, meritocracy, and the "foxiness" of the Fox. This latter characteristic is also reflected in the ease with which Sydney Fox traverses numerous and varied cultural terrains, simply donning the appropriate garb to "pass" and, in so doing, find her relics. In these exotic cultural landscapes, the natives are merely the colorful backdrops against which she enacts her heroism; the natives' backwardness and barbarism merely a foil to her own enlightened humanity (or, as Jhally and Lewis might put it, her own "enlightened racism").

As a "bronzed Barbie doll" or the "multinational other" (Bogle 210–11), Sydney Fox represents the quintessential assimilated Asian American woman. Many of the relics she rescues from corrupt officials and obscure places span the continuum from the exotic (a genuine article purportedly belonging to the Buddha in "Buddha's Bowl") to the patriotic (an old, authentic American map salvaged in small-town America in "Flag Day") to the trivial (Elvis's original guitar). In the latter two cases, the settings are highly localized and parochial. However, in these settings, Sydney's race is of no consequence. She can brazenly walk through a deserted Western town in her cowboy boots, easily taking on the crude beer-drinking white males with her martial arts that, though incongruous in such a setting, still get her out of a bind. Alternatively, she can single-handedly take on the natives in the jungles of a generic Asia.

Able to travel the myriad cultural landscapes, Sydney represents the American arrogance of "knowing it all," and yet, at the same time, her race and ethnicity give her the passport to be able to enter otherwise forbidden spaces with impunity and immunity. Her appropriation of artifacts from these sites is permitted under the guise of benevolent Western intrusion motivated by the higher moral goal of protecting that which the natives do not value—their own history. In such a way, she reaffirms the colonial narrative of Western superiority, but this time as its heroine.

CONCLUSION

The popular success of television programs such as *Relic Hunter* lies in their ability to resonate with a wide and global audience. In part, these resonances draw on the larger meta-narratives of the female hero as warrior or as goddess. At the same time, these contemporary representations—although framed as being "positive" as they depart from traditional iconic representations of Asian women—perpetuate many of the old imperial tropes discussed at the beginning of this article.

The market rationale for including "positive" representations is clearly a major motivating factor behind programs such as *Relic Hunter*, as is the growing population of Asians in America. Yet, by containing "difference" through the kinds of strategies identified throughout this article, popular media render such differences palatable for the consuming audience. The underlying message of assimilation, the lack of cultural ties and identity, and the emphasis on individual skills all play into the ideological narrative that underlies the American Dream of upward mobility. The dragon lady has been tamed. And she has been tamed by an inclusion that is itself predicated on Asians constituting a formidable economic and demographic force within America as a result of migration, intermarriage, and socialization. As heroine, she represents the resolution of Western anxieties and dreams.

An implicit message in these programs is that Asian women can have strength only if they are shaped by the prevailing dominant Western influences—whether these be of a technological nature (i.e., superiority in bioengineering)[11] or of a value-based social nature. Difference is then contained and shaped according to the West's own needs. Thus, the Asian woman has entered the nexus of signs to become an iconic representation of the West's success story—she is the hybrid hero. As such, she lends herself easily to a kind of ideological recuperation in the dominant Western paradigm of the successful, self-made woman—a status helped along by the structural positioning of Asian communities as model minorities in the American landscape (see Palumbo-Liu). The economic success of these communities and their self-reliance (often because of exclusion and ghettoization) are features that have not only legitimized these communities but have also allowed them to be used as token examples of the veracity of the American Dream.

Generic Western values (and, by extension, generic Asians) form the backdrop of these programs, which, although produced by different countries such as Canada and France, do not reflect the specificities of these national entities. Rather, there is a homogenizing tendency at work in these representations—a tendency that is only offset by the simultaneous but limited production of cultural products specific to national cinemas and indigenous cultural industries. However, even these latter tend to internalize and reproduce dominant Western modes of thought and self-representation, thereby contributing to a global consumer culture or what Shu has termed a kind of "managed multiculturalism." In the Canadian context, for instance, the resonance of the program may lie in its packaging of cultural difference within the rubric of the state policy of multiculturalism and its interpellation of hybridity through the hyphenated identity of racialized and immigrant Canadians. As Mahtani has observed, in such a context "a vacant celebration of cultural hybridity veils gendered and racialised power dynamics" (74). In this way, the sign of the Asian—now Eurasian—woman is emptied of its historical materiality and filled with a dose of liberal sameness so as to signify not only Western liberal traditions but also to render American penetration of other markets economically viable and justifiable. And all this in the name of "the hero."

NOTES

1. For instance, "Asian" in Britain often refers to South Asians (from India, Pakistan, and the Indian diasporic peoples). On the other hand, in Western Canada, notably in British Columbia, the term "Asian" refers specifically to the Chinese, with other South East Asian peoples being popularly referred to as "East Indians."

2. In the United States and Canada, specific laws were enacted to curtail Asian immigration, for example, the Pacific Barred Zones Act (1917) in California and the Continuous Voyage Act (1908) in Canada.

3. For example, in a recent episode of the popular series *Stargate SC-1*, which is produced in Vancouver, British Columbia, the white woman officer on the Star Gate team goes out to "rescue" her alien sisters who are being oppressed by the males of their culture. This interplanetary rescue mission succeeds in communicating the superiority and "progressiveness" of Western feminism as compared to the oppressiveness of "other" cultures. These Others are visibly different in their appearance and clothing.

4. While the issue of "misrepresentation" relies on the argument that an accurate ontological representation exists, its import in the debate about self and Other representation lies in public policy consequences of negative representations. Furthermore, a key concern of the debate rests on the power of the dominant Others to define a community rather than empowering that community to define itself (see also Parmar for a discussion of this point).

5. The Screen Actors Guild's report concludes that "People of color, the vast majority of humankind, estimated to reach a majority in America by the year 2000, are 18.3% of the major network prime time cast. African Americans are 12.3% of prime time, but Latino/Hispanics, over 10% of the U.S. population, are about 2.6% of prime time and 3.7% of daytime serials. Americans of Asian/Pacific origin, 3.4% of the U.S. population, also suffer conspicuously by their virtual absence as 1.4% of prime time and 0.4% of daytime roles" (Gerbner 7).

6. Many of these roles were played by white women fitted with prosthetics and made up to look like Asians (Ito).

7. These portrayals have been artfully captured by Valerie Soe in *All Orientals Look the Same* and *Picturing Oriental Girls, A (Re) Educational Videotape*, and Deborah Gee's *Slaying the Dragon*.

8. Although television and film differ in terms of media formats, there is a certain amount of slippage of representations between the two. The latter is particularly evident in the reformatting of films for screening on television and in the use of VCRs, which make the viewing of films more accessible within the domestic sphere.

9. In later episodes, Claudia is replaced by another female character who is somewhat more intelligent and who never fails to use her sexual charms to achieve her goals. This latter tactic proves especially effective in protecting Professor Sydney Fox from the newly arrived, ruthless, budget-cutting university administrator.

10. For a further discussion of the containment of ethnicity, see Diane Negra's discussion of Marisa Tomei.

11. As exemplified in the representation of Jessica Alba in *Dark Angel* (see McConnell).

WORKS CITED

Abraham, Christiana. "Deconstructing the Legacy of the 'Savage' Woman: The Politics of Displacing Boundaries in Panache Magazine." Thesis, Concordia University, 2001.

Abu-Laban, Yasmeen. "Keeping 'em Out: Gender, Race, and Class Biases in Canadian Immigration Policy." *Painting the Maple: Essays on Race, Gender, and the Construction of Canada*. Ed. V. Strong-Boag, S. Grace, A. Eisenberg, and J. Anderson. Vancouver: University of British Columbia Press, 1998. 69–82.

Anderson, Benjamin. *Imagined Communities*. London and New York: Verso, 1983.

Anderson, Kay. *Vancouver's Chinatown: Racial Discourse in Canada, 1875–1980*. Montreal: McGill-Queen's University Press, 1991.

Backhouse, Constance. *Color-Coded: A Legal History of Racism in Canada, 1900–1950*. Toronto: University of Toronto Press, 1999.

Balsamo, Anne. *Technologies of the Gendered Body*. Durham, NC: Duke University Press, 1999.

Bannerji, Himani. "Now You See Us/Now You Don't." *Video Guide* 8 (1986): 40–45.

Beltrane, Mary C. "The Hollywood Latina Body as Site of Social Struggle: Media Constructions of Stardom and Jennifer Lopez's 'Cross-over Butt.'" *Quarterly Review of Film and Video* 19 (2002): 71–86 .

Bogle, Donald. *Toms, Coons, Mulattoes, Mammies and Bucks: An Interpretive History of Blacks in American Films* . New York: Continuum, 1989.

Buchignani, Norman, and Doreen Indra, with Ram Srivastava. *Continuous Journey*. Toronto: McLelland and Stewart, 1985.

Burney, Sheila. "The Exotic and the Restless: Representation of the 'Other' in Colonialist Discourse." International Institute of Semiotic and Structural Studies, University of British Columbia, Vancouver. 1988.

Burton, Antoinette M. "The White Woman's Burden: British Feminist and the 'Indian Woman,' 1865–1915." *Western Women and Imperialism, Complicity and Resistance*. Ed. Nupur Chaudhuri and Margaret Strobel. Bloomington: Indiana University Press, 1992. 137–57.

Chen, Victoria. "The Construction of Chinese American Women's Identity." *Women Making Meaning: New Feminist Directions in Communication*. Ed. Lana F. Rakow. New York: Routledge, 1992. 225–43.

Chung, Sue Fawn. "From Fu Manchu, Evil Genius to James Lee Wong, Popular Hero: A Study of the Chinese American in Popular Periodical Fiction from 1920-1940." *Journal of Popular Culture* 10.3 (1976): 534–47.

Cooke, Miriam. "Saving Brown Women." *Signs* 28.1 (2002): 468–70.

Feng, Peter. "Redefining Asian American Masculinity: Steven Okazaki's 'American Sons.'" *Cineaste* 22.3 (1996): 27–29.

Gee, Deborah. *Slaying the Dragon*. NAATA/Cross Current Media, 1988.

Gerbner, George. "Casting the American Scene: A Look at the Characters on Prime Time and Daytime Television from 1994–1997." Media Awareness Network 1998. August 5, 2000 http://www.media-awareness.ca/ena/issues/minreD/resource/reports/aerbner.htm.

Gilman, Sander. "The Hottentot and the Prostitute. Toward an Iconography of Female Sexuality." *Race-ing Art History*. Ed. K. N. Pinder. New York: Routledge, 2002. 119–38.

The Good Earth. Dir. Sidney Franklin. Perf. Paul Muni, Luise Rainer, Walter Connolly, Keye Luke, and Tillie Losch. Prod. Irving Thalberg. 1937. Videocassette. Warner Home Video.

Greenberger, Allen J. *The British Image of India. A Study in the Literature of Imperialism 1880–1960*. London: Oxford University Press, 1969.

Hagedorn, Jessica. "Asian Women in Film: No Joy, No Luck." *Facing Difference: Race, Gender and Mass Media*. Ed. S. Biagi and M. Kem-Foxworth. Thousand Oaks, CA: Pine Forge, 1997. 32–37.

Hall, Stuart. "The Narrative Construction of Reality." *Southern Review* 17 (1984): 3–17.

Hall, Stuart, ed. Representation, *Cultural Representations and Signifying Practices* . London: Sage, 1997.

Hall, Stuart. "The Whites of Their Eyes." *The Media Reader*. Ed. Manuel Alvarado and John O. Thompson. London: British Film Institute, 1990. 10–21.

Hall, Stuart. "The Whites of Their Eyes: Racist Ideologies and the Media." *Gender, Race and Class in Media, a Text Reader*. Ed. Gail Dines and Jean M. Humez. Thousand Oaks, CA: Sage, 1995. 18–22.

Haraway, Donna. "A Manifesto for Cyborgs: Science, Technology and Socialist Feminism in the 1980s." *Socialist Review* 80.2 (1985): 65–108.

hooks, bell. *Outlaw Culture: Resisting Representations*. New York: Routledge, 1994.

Huttenback. Robert A. *Racism and Empire: White Settler and Colored Immigrants in the British Self-Governing Colonies, 1830–1910*. Ithaca, NY: Cornell University Press, 1976.

Isaacs, Harold. *Scratches on Our Minds*. Westport, CT: Greenwood, 1958.

Ito, Robert B. "A Certain Slant: A Brief History of Hollywood Yellowface." *Bright Lights Film Journal* 18 (1997). August 5, 2000 http://www.brightlightsfilm.com/18/18 yellow.html.

JanMohamed, Abdul R. "The Economy of Manichean Allegory: The Function of Racial Difference in Colonialist Literature." *Critical Inquiry* 12.1 (1985): 59–87.

Jhally, Sut, and Justin Lewis. *Enlightened Racism: The Cosby Show, Audiences and the Myth of the American Dream*. Boulder, CO: Westview, 1992.

Jiwani, Yasmin. "The Exotic, the Erotic and the Dangerous: South Asian Women in Popular Film." *Canadian Woman Studies* 13.1 (1992): 42–46.

Kagy, Tom. "Money, Media and the Asian American Image." *Goldsea Features* 1997. August 5, 2000 http://Qoldsea.com/Mediawatch/Monevmedia/moneymedia.html.

Lalvani, Suren. "Consuming the Exotic Other." *Critical Studies in Mass Communication* 12 (1995): 263–86.

Lang, Feng. "The Female Individual and the Empire: A Historicist Approach to *Mulan* and Kingston's *Woman Warrior*." *Comparative Literature* 55.3 (2003): 229–45.

Lim, Shirley Geok-lin. "Gender Transformations in Asian/American Representations." *Gender and Culture in Literature and Film East and West: Issues of Perception and Interpretation.* Ed. Nitaya Masavisut, George Simson, and Larry E. Smith. Honolulu, HI: College of Languages, Linguistics and Literature, University of Hawaii and the East-West Centre, 1994. 95–112.

Mahtani, Minelle. "Interrogating the Hyphen-Nation: Canadian Multicultural Policy and 'Mixed Race' Identities." *Social Identities* 8.1 (2002): 67–90.

Marchetti, Gina. *Romance and the "Yellow Peril": Race, Sex, and Discursive Strategies in Hollywood Fiction.* Berkeley and Los Angeles: California University Press, 1993.

McAllister, Kirsten Emiko. "Asians in Hollywood." *CineAction* 30 (1992): 8–13.

McBratney, John. "Images of Indian Women in Rudyard Kipling: A Case of Doubling Discourse." *Inscriptions* 3.4 (1988): 47–57.

McConnell, Kathleen. "Dark Angel: A Recombinant Pygmalion for the Twenty-First Century." *Gothic Studies* 4.2 (2002): 178–90.

Media Action Network for Asian Americans. *A Memo from MANAA to Hollywood: Asian Stereotypes, Restrictive Portrayals of Asians in the Media and How to Balance Them.* August 5, 2000 http: //www.manaa.ora/a stereotypes.html.

Minh-ha, Trinh T. *Woman, Native, Other: Writing Postcoloniality and Feminism* . Bloomington: Indiana University Press, 1989.

Mohanty, Chandra Talpade. "Cartographies of Struggle: Third World Women and the Politics of Feminism." *Third World Women and the Politics of Feminism.* Ed. Chandra Talpade Mohanty, Ann Russo, and Lourdes Torres. Bloomington: Indiana University Press, 1991. 1–47.

Negra, Diane. *Off-White Hollywood: American Culture and Ethnic Female Stardom.* London, Routledge, 2001.

Ono, Kent A. "To Be a Vampire on *Buffy the Vampire Slayer*: Race and ('Other') Socially Marginalizing Positions on Horror TV." *Fantasy Girls: Gender in the New Universe of Science Fiction and Fantasy Television* . Ed. Elyce Rae Helford. Lanham, MD: Rowman & Littlefield, 2000. 163–86.

Palumbo-Liu, David. *Asian/American Historical Crossings of a Racial Frontier.* Stanford, CA: Stanford University Press, 1999.

Parmar, Pratibha. "Hateful Contraries, Media Images of Asian Women." *Ten* 8, 16 (1984).

Pieterse, Jan Nederveen. "White Negroes." *Gender; Race and Class in Media, a Text Reader.* Ed. Gail Dines and Jean M. Humez. Thousand Oaks, CA: Sage, 1995. 23–27.

Rath. Sura P. "Home(s) Abroad: Diasporic Identities in Third Spaces." *Jouvert, a Journal of Postcolonial Studies* 4.3 (2000). August 5, 2000 http://social.chass.ncsu.edu/iouvert/v4i3/rath1.htm.

Razack, Sherene H. *Looking White People in the Eye: Gender, Race, and Culture in Courtrooms and Classrooms* . Toronto: University of Toronto Press, 1998.

Said, Edward. *Orientalism.* New York: Random House, 1978.

Schneider, William. "Race and Empire: The Rise of Popular Ethnography in the Late Nineteenth Century." *Journal of Popular Culture* 11.1 (1977): 98–109.

Shohat, Ella, and Robert Stam. *Unthinking Eurocentrism: Multiculturalism and the Media.* London: Routledge, 1994.

Shu, Yuan. "Reading the Kung Fu Film in an American Context: From Bruce Lee to Jackie Chan." *Journal of Popular Film and Television* 31.2 (2003): 50–59.

Soe, Valerie. *All Orientals Look the Same.* NAATA/Cross Current Media, 1992.

Soe, Valerie. *Picturing Oriental Girls: A (Re) Educational Videotape.* NAATA/Cross Current Media, 1992.

Tajima, Renee. "Lotus Blossoms Don't Bleed: Images of Asian Women." *Making Waves: An Anthology of Writing by and about Asian American Women.* Ed. Asian Women United of California. Boston: Beacon, 1989. 308–17.

Yegenoglu, Meyda. *Colonial Fantasies: Towards a Feminist Reading of Orientalism.* Cambridge: Cambridge University Press, 1998.

Young, Robert J. C. *Colonial Desire: Hybridity in Theory, Culture and Race.* London: Routledge, 1995.

Zackel, Frederick. "Robinson Crusoe and the Ethnic Sidekick." *Bright Lights Film Journal* 30 (2000). August 5, 2000 http://www.briahtliahtsfilm.com/30/crusoe1.html.

Zhao, Yuezhi, and Dan Schiller. "Dances with Wolves? China's Integration into Digital Capitalism." *Info: The Journal of Policy, Regulation and Strategy for Telecommunications Information and Media* 3.2 (2001): 138–51.

Chapter Seventeen

The Maddening Business of Show

Beretta E. Smith-Shomade

[Beulah] . . . spends most of her time in the kitchen but never seems to know what's cookin'.
—Louise Beavers, "Beulah Helps the Hendersons," *The Beulah Show*

I used to do a character, a little black girl who wanted blonde hair. Everyone on television was blonde.
—Whoopi Goldberg, *Book*

Whether it's Beulah, Julia, Gel Christy Love, Thea, or Moesha, one of the most pervasive problems with black representation on American television has been the lack of scope and depth offered in its purview. African-Americans' furious responses to images of themselves have been directed less toward specific programs than toward perpetually limited roles, histories, and reflections of black life portrayed on American and world television monitors. Historically, one show on television every few years has borne the burden of reflecting all of black American culture. Thus, both quality and quantity of representation have been, and remain, an issue.

In fact, black image dearth continued so egregiously at the end of the twentieth century that the National Association for the Advancement of Colored People (NAACP) felt compelled once again to take the television networks to task for their 1999 fall season's literal black-out of African-American characters. The NAACP's attack on the quantity of colored representation—both in front of and behind the camera—is an ongoing struggle in the visual media.[1] Yet quality issues continue too. Representations that approximate the diversity and complexity of those called black Americans and of America itself are scant.

According to Jannette Dates, black programs have followed "the pattern set in minstrelsy, which . . . [seems] destined to continue ad infinitum."[2] The minstrelsy ethos resounded on American television before 1980 and, some argue, since. Yet, as much as visual history discounts their presence, African-Americans frame every picture of the United States—despite disfiguration and disguise. Thus, this chapter traces the representations of African-Americans as part of American entertainment, their place in its historical memory, and their function in a racist and sexist society.

HISTORICAL ANTECEDENTS

Early black performers played roles that primarily satiated white audiences. Slave performance, minstrelsy, and later vaudeville introduced Negro performance as a commodity for white consumption. Cinema perpetuated that same type of blackfaced utility. For example, in an early silent Edison film, *What Happened in the Tunnel* (1903), a Negra (actually a white woman in blackface) literally buttresses a play on black women's (a)sexuality. The short film features a white woman and her Negra maid on a train. A white male passenger makes advances toward the white woman. As the train enters the tunnel, he leans forward to kiss her. Once outside the tunnel, however, he discovers that the women switched seats. The maid received his affection. The man expresses revulsion as the women laugh.

Beyond its obvious racist implications, the "racist and sexist joke" is complicated, according to Miriam Hansen, by the women's laughter and the white man's objectification through ridicule. Hansen contends that "[w]hile the figure of the prankster falling prey to his own prank is quite common in the genre of mischief comedy, the maid's direct glance at the camera suggests not only that she was not merely a prop but that she, rather than her mistress, might have authorized the substitution."[3] Yet as we know, a black maid "authorizing" anything in 1903 is ridiculous. The joke remains squarely on the maid. The pun, based on the man's confusion, can ultimately only contribute to the maid's disillusionment. With the maid's large and dark presence, the possibility of the kiss's voluntary sanction by either the man or the maid seems ludicrous, at least in public. The maid, in her Colored, non-sexualized construction, possesses neither the authority nor evident desire implicit in Hansen's suggestion, unless one subscribes to the idea that black women harbor unrequited desires for their oppressors.[4] These types of images, nevertheless, emblematized the nation's early cinematic efforts.

Such images did not appear only in Caucasian cinema. Although films such as *The Birth of a Nation* (Griffith, 1915) and its antecedents further demonized the figure of the black woman and man in feature-length films, early filmmakers like Oscar Micheaux, Spencer Williams, and the Lincoln Brothers made films that followed Hollywood's problematic constructions. Although their films attempted to answer Hollywood's racism, they perpetuated sexist, classist, and color-struck ideas.[5]

In these decades before television's arrival, Negras appeared in film as servants, harlots, mammies, tragic mulattoes, and religious zealots. The nation's carefree attitude during the 1920s forwarded the Harlem Renaissance and launched the Colored woman as feature performer on screen. Nina Mae McKinney distinguished herself as the silver screen's first Colored harlot. She played in King Vidor's 1929 sound film *Hallelujah* as a jezebel, of course, bamboozling a good man. In *Toms, Coons, Mulattoes, Mammies, and Bucks: An Interpretive History of Blacks in American Films*, Donald Bogle describes McKinney's character, Chick, as a black, exotic sex object, half woman, half child: "She was the black woman out of control of her emotions, split in two by her loyalties and her own vulnerabilities. Implied throughout the battle with self was the tragic mulatto theme. The white half of her represented the spiritual; the black half, the animalistic."[6] This and the other aforementioned screen stereotypes presented themselves in both mainstream and early black cinema. They stood as Negras' predominant roles.

During the Depression years Negro actors appeared more regularly, perhaps as a comfort to the economically strapped majority. "[W]hether that face was seen for two minutes or three and a half hours, it was invariably there to tidy up the house, cook a meal, or watch over the livery stables."[7] Even within the highly publicized *Imitation of Life* (1934), in which Louise Beavers earns the title of Partner, her lot remains cast to service. Actresses such as Beavers and McKinney, Fredi Washington, Josephine Baker (mostly abroad), and Thelma "Butterfly" McQueen all helped shape certain descriptors of black women during cinema's first fifty years. Limited opportunities for other film roles surfaced and none focused on black women specifically.[8] After all, Peola's (Fredi Washington) passions (and thus the story in *Imitation of Life*) revolve around a white woman's life—a lie for a woman scientifically rendered Colored.

To bolster black participation in the World War II effort, the U.S. Department of War (with the prodding of the NAACP) worked with Hollywood to create more favorable images of America's "problem people." Films like *The Negro Soldier* (1944), *Home of the Brave* (1949), and the *Why We Fight* series all attempted to lure blacks into the war effort by ignoring America's atrocities and elevating Hitler's.[9] This linking of patriotism to representation obviously negated Colored women—a fact not missed by filmmaker Julie Dash several decades later.

A retrospective look at wartime Hollywood, Dash's film *Illusions* (1983) tells the story of a rising entertainment executive, Mignon Dupree (Lonette McKee), who "passes" in order to make critical decisions within a major film studio. But in one touted and poignant scene Dash illustrates the impotence of blacks' and women's imagery and highlights the illusionary lives real folks led during the 1940s. In the scene Dash layers images of Mignon at a recording session with a white actress lip-synching in a Hollywood film. Between the two screens (one fabric, the other glass) stands a young black singer, Ester Jeeter (Rosanne Katon), doing the actual singing. The scene depicts the confinement of most black women's representation—between screens, without credited voice, and virtually invisible. Ella Shohat and Robert Stam characterize the scene as "Black talent and energy . . . sublimated into a haloed White image."[10] These processes occur while a white male technician orchestrates and controls the entire production. The scene aptly illustrates black women's cinematic history and legacy of powerlessness.

Whereas 1940s films cursorily examined societal concerns, early television generally ignored serious social issues altogether, choosing to show happy people with happy problems. Although perhaps, as some surmise, programs featuring black characters or themes were considered inappropriate,[11] the *Amos 'n' Andy* series offered white ideals of appropriate blacks and their concerns. The program featured caricatured African-Americans who emerged from the minds and mouths of two white southern men. In the radio program (which preceded the television series) black women existed as phantoms—invisible (because it was radio) but also voiceless. Melvin Ely explains: "For years the program presented [women characters] through the male characters, who discussed the women, 'conversed' with them on the telephone, and occasionally read aloud from their letters. Amazingly, Godsen & Correll managed to give each of these silent female figures a vivid personality of her own and, at times, a crucial part in the drama."[12] Personalities and actualities, it seems, characterized sufficiently and in exchange for tangible colored actresses.

When the program appeared on television in 1951, producers cast Ernestine Wade as Sapphire Stevens and Amanda Randolph as Mama. According to Ely, Mama "epitomized both the race-transcending battle-ax and the hard-edged version of the familiar black 'mammy.' [Her] considerable heft, baleful stare, and enormous hats rendered that image even more vivid on television than it had been on radio."[13] Wade's Sapphire spawned a character type of its own. In essence, this Sapphire-type translated to an updated, shrewish mammy. J. Fred MacDonald calls the pair "less than picturesque images of black femininity."[14]

Arriving in 1950 just before the televised *Amos 'n' Andy*, *The Beulah Show* appeared, starring Ethel Waters (and later Louise Beavers). Beulah's centrality came through her guidance of the white family through crisis. This black maid "restored balance and normalcy to the household."[15] To give shows like *Beulah* and *Amos 'n' Andy* credibility for white television audiences, "rural black dialect, malapropisms, mispronunciations, and misinterpretations" transferred from their earlier predecessors of radio, cinema, vaudeville, and minstrelsy to television.[16] The NAACP condemned both programs in its 1951 national convention, claiming, among other things, "Negro women are shown as cackling, screaming shrews, in big-mouth close-ups using street slang, just short of vulgarity."[17] Because of the NAACP and other external pressures, both shows were canceled by the fall of 1953. This, however, failed to alter substantially the portrayals of blacks, especially black women. Nor did it eliminate blacks' appearance on television.

Black musical artists began emerging on television as singers, dancers, and comedians on variety shows such as Ed Sullivan's *Toast of the Town* (1948–1971), the *Colgate Comedy Hour* (1950–1955), and the *Jackie Gleason Show* (1952–1970). For one year (1956–1957) Nat King Cole hosted his own network variety program, the first black performer to do so.[18] MacDonald suggests that the arrival of black musical artists signaled a new era of racial fairness absent prior to the war.

In 1951 members of the National Association of Radio and Television Broadcasters pledged: "Racial or nationality types shall not be shown on television in such manner as to ridicule the race or nationality."[19] Bolstered by the 1954 *Brown v. Board of Education of Topeka* decision, by black achievements in sports and sciences, and by Negro entertainers on television, Colored communities felt poised to assert their civil and social rights. With continued urban migration, undereducated blacks occupied abundant manufacturing jobs, creating social divisions that would lead to increased economic disparity between black haves and have-nots.[20] Institutionalized racism, however, proved a formidable force in maintaining cultural norms, particularly in television. People who produced television remained unconvinced of the profitability of black television faces.

Yet by the 1960s worldwide attention centered on blacks in America. With extensive civil unrest, protests, and frequent televised injustices, the living conditions of the nation's black community burst across screens and into homes. During this tumultuous period black representation erupted mostly within the genre of television news. Having done without previously, networks scrambled to recruit black news reporters like Charlayne Hunter-Gault and Carole Simpson to cover those areas unknown to the television world.[21] Stories featuring beautiful, militant black women with Afros vaulted into American homes. The images were often situated in a context of confrontation, characterizing perhaps some aspect of the Black Panther Party or children being attacked by dogs, city fire hoses, or bombs. Never before had America and the world been privy to such atrocities against U.S. citizenry. In 1964, pressured from within and without, President Lyndon B. Johnson signed legislation giving federal protection to Negroes in employment, voting, and civil rights. The legislation ended legalized segregation and illuminated a formerly hidden segment of society, all witnessed via television.

Capitalizing on both the uprisings of the period and Melvin Van Peebles's flawed protest film, *Sweet Sweetback's Baadasssss Song* (1971), Hollywood rediscovered black America.[22] Studios found that black power could translate into green power with negligible regard to context or content. Further, the 1960s brought the dismantling of the Production Code and implementation of the Ratings System. These developments virtually guaranteed cinema full freedom of expression.

Consequently, films aimed at black audiences circulated from 1971 to the mid-1970s. This "blaxploitation" era characterized peoples of African descent as monolithic balls of anger, trapped in urban jungles, forever relegated to the margins. The films substantiated much of Daniel Patrick Moynihan's report on the Negro family.[23] Moreover, some argue that the Ratings System itself contributed to the rise of exploitative sex and violence in the new "R" and "NC-17" categories. Most black exploitation films fell under this rubric and were directed and produced by white men. While demonizing blackness, the scripts often overlooked or subverted African-Americans', and particularly black women's, legitimate anger.

For example, *Cleopatra Jones* (Julien, 1973) and her many adventures, *Coffy* (Hill, 1973), and its sequel, *Foxy Brown* (Hill, 1974), featured two angry black women. These films' releases coincided not only with the black nationalist and women's movements but also with the box office successes of their male counterparts such as *Shaft* (Parks, 1971), *Superfly* (Parks, 1972), and *The Mack* (Campus, 1973). Bogle suggests, "These macho goddesses answered a multitude of needs and were a hybrid of stereotypes. . . . They lived in fantasy worlds—of violence, blood, guns, and gore—which pleased, rather than threatened, male audiences."[24]

Antithetical to Hollywood film product depicting segregated and violent black worlds, 1970s television delivered blacks assimilated and functioning well in American society, as in the programs *Julia* (1968–1971), *The Flip Wilson Show* (1970–1974), and *The Jeffersons* (1975–1985). This alternative image was mandated in part by broadcast standards and practices departments, who policed all material for broadcast. *Julia*, in particular, operated fully within the American, safe, white, and middle-class mainstream.

Beginning in September of 1968, Diahann Carroll portrayed Julia Baker, the first black nondomestic female character on television.[25] Julia lived in an integrated California environment as a widowed, professional nurse raising her son. This fictional integration aired across a real-life backdrop of white homeowners fleeing neighborhoods where blacks moved. With government funds made available for the construction of federal freeways leading out of the city and government assistance for those who wanted to buy homes in the suburbs, whites left the city in droves—taking their dollars with them. The Bradys, the Partridges, the Tates, the Douglases, the Mediterraneans of Brewster Place, and even Lucille Carmichael headed for the hills—where "farm livin'" or at least colorless existence prevailed.[26] *Julia* never alluded explicitly to this phenomenon nor to the civil and social unrest raging on American streets. This became one of the most potent criticisms leveled at the show from both the media and outside advocates. The show implied that the fires were mythical—harmony could be achieved if we could all just get along. Look, watch Julia do it. Julia ran for three years, with Julia never having a steady companion, promotion, or confrontation.[27] This blind-eye approach paved the way for 1990s "no color lines" programming.[28]

The Flip Wilson Show began airing on September 17, 1970, and became the first successful black variety series.[29] Wilson's brand of humor was perceived as particularly ethnic, which appealed to a wide (read white) audience. More important to this work, Wilson's character, Geraldine, became an American icon. S/he, with her "rotary drive hips," made the phrases "the devil made me do it" and "what you see is what you get" household expressions. This character served as a model and ideal for the characters Sheneneh and Mama in Martin Lawrence's *Martin* . . . .

In a limited fashion "television attempted to draw on film's blaxploitation notion of strong black women. In the police drama *Get Christie Love!* (1974–1975) Teresa Graves plays an undercover cop for the Los Angeles Police Department. J. Fred MacDonald suggests that for its one season "the series was marred by an unbelievable character acting out poorly written scripts in a tired genre."[30] Although Graves's character was tough, smart, and sexy, she provided nothing new. Her character did, however, provide a modicum of empowerment to those who rarely saw physically strong and attractive black women in visual culture. Young women, including myself, saw the possibility for a convergence of strength, respect, and femininity. The program also coincided with television's expanding view of black life.

To their credit television executives attempted to explore different aspects of Afro-American life. They focused on working-class families. Yet that exploration confined itself primarily to female-dominated spaces and to humor. Programs like *Good Times* (1974–1979), *That's My Mama* (1974–1975), *The Jeffersons* (1975–1985), and *What's Happening!!* (1976–1979) limited black women to the primary role of mammy or sapphire.[31] Qualities of strength, direction, and chutzpah, if you will, turned into Mother Jefferson's constant nagging; Dee and Florence's wisecracking, lazy remarks; and Florida's exasperated complaints.[32] The African-American women on these sitcoms emerged as domineering and consistently oppressive.

In its updated 1979 report on the status of minorities and women on television, the United States Commission on Civil Rights surmised that "[t]he black situation comedies and 'jiggly' shows, while certainly not the only ones in which minorities and women are portrayed, nevertheless represent recent and important trends in the portrayal of members of these groups on network television drama during prime time."[33] That trend was a marked lack of improvement. Yet with cable's rise in the 1980s, a shift in the labor market, and the browning of the country, networks began to alter their demographic focus and to recognize a new segmenting of the audience. This shift led to a transition from Reagan-Bush Willie Horton imagery to the hip-hop, colored Clinton reign.

EN ROUTE TO THE EIGHTIES

Historian W. E. B. Du Bois maintained that the "problem of the Twentieth Century [was and] is the problem of the color-line."[34] At the dawn of the millennium, no matter how this country skirts, circumvents, or denies it, race stands as the most critical malady of American society, particularly for those besieged by its ideological and social implications. According to Gerald David Jaynes and Robin M. Williams Jr. of the National Research Council, five major events transformed American race relations over the past forty years. Three decades of South-North and rural-urban migration by Negroes produced conditions leading to profound changes in their social status. The civil rights revolution moved Coloreds toward full citizenship rights, producing critical changes in the nation's political and educational institutions. During World War II and for twenty-five years afterward, the United States' economy grew at unprecedented high and sustained rates, facilitating efforts to improve blacks' status throughout society. Yet during the early 1970s the rate of economic growth slowed, with thirty years of black migration coming to a halt. Subsequently, the improved status of blacks slowed significantly. Finally, rapid changes in the family living arrangements of children, beginning in the 1960s, split most of the black population into two groups: those living in families with one adult head—overwhelmingly poor—and those living in families with two adult heads—largely middle income.[35] These five distinct but related events dramatically altered American life.

In 1980 the African-American population represented approximately 11.7 percent of the United States total population, or twenty-six million people. In 1998 that figure reached 13 percent, or thirty-four million.[36] Politically and culturally the 1980s marked the rise of buppiedom (black urban professionals), the benefits of affirmative action, and a renaissance in black intellectualism. Jesse Jackson bid persuasively for the presidency in 1984 and 1988, and multiculturalism (mostly commodified) reigned. Yet this period also ushered in the presidency and policies of Ronald Reagan.

Reagan's inauguration emerged from and fostered a new wave of conservatism with his encouragement of racial division and his celebration of the dominance of United States capitalism in the world. By the end of his term, in 1989, critics had lambasted him for the savings and loan scandal, environmental abuses, civil rights reversals, and consumer victimization. Ironically, however, according to a *New York Times* poll he left office with 68 percent of the American people (40 percent of blacks, 72 percent of whites) approving of the way he handled his job since 1981.[37] The Reagan worldview reproduced itself largely by way of television.

Coco Fusco suggests that during the Reagan-Bush era a form of social engineering transpired. She calls it the "commodification of ethnicity"—a commodification fostered through media production that claims a stake in maintaining multicultural diversity: "In this depoliticised version of the '60s, ethnic identity becomes the focus of ongoing spectacle and aestheticisation, and subaltern popular memory is its terrain. This simulation of ethnic diversity keeps each group in a fixed place, since we each have the spotlight only for as long as we express our difference."[38] Or, it remains profitable. The spotlight on African-American ethnicity advanced largely by way of two groups: one that Americans termed the "black middle class" and the other contemptuously called the "black urban underclass."

E. Franklin Frazier wrote derisively about a Negro elite in his 1969 revised text *Black Bourgeoisie*, suggesting that their behavior and mentality reflected white American values. Calling this group "exaggerated Americans," he proposed, "What may appear as distortions of American patterns of behavior and thought are due to the fact that the Negro lives on the margin of American society. . . . [The bourgeoisie] lacks a basis in the American economic system . . . [and has] shown no interest in the 'liberation' of Negroes except as it affected their own status or acceptance by the white community. . . . [T]hey have attempted to conform to the behavior and values of the white community in the most minute details."[39] Franklin's disdain notwithstanding, contemporary versions of his black bourgeoisie, Buppies, include black business owners, educated white-collar workers, professional athletes, entertainers (including media workers and politicians), and academics. Inclusion is based largely on income, attitude, and visual presentation. Members of the other group, the urban underclass (particularly men), garner a surfeit of scholarly articles, studies, and even political agendas. Rappers rap about them, news characterizes them, and politicians capitalize on their presence during depressed economic times. Despite this deluge of information on the urban underclass, coverage of the causes for, the tangible impact of media on, and solutions for this segment of American society is limited.

Black American income levels resembled a pyramid—a small portion at the top widening out to a large poverty base. Conversely, white American incomes replicated a diamond—a small top and base with a wide middle. In 1985, for example, 31 percent of black families (10 million) and 11 percent of white families (29 million) lived below the federal poverty line.[40] Although the numbers were quite small, membership (or perceived membership) in the black middle class encouraged a mind-set of much greater numbers and influence. This Negro nouveau riche produced a unique form of individualism, different even from that described in Franklin's analysis.[41]

Beginning in the early 1980s, many members of the black middle class began to assume behaviors that were culturally anomalous to previous ones held by black Americans and their ancestors. Their behavior exacerbated the chasm between blacks with privilege and blacks in poverty. In West African philosophy, the foreknowledge of African-Americans, a part of the notion of self was tied to the notion of community. As described by psychologist Wade Nobles, "the traditional African's view of himself; his self-concept is that he believes: 'I am because we are; and because we are, therefore, I am.'"[42] Thus in the U.S. past, because of smaller numbers of people actually in the middle and upper classes and because of restrictions on where people could work, survival for African-Americans meant cooperation. But with desegregation the requirement of contact with other Negroes no longer existed. A degree of disdain has grown between the two groups that actually furthers regressive conditions for both. Cornel West offers an explanation for a certain nihilistic behavior consistent with this widening gap of the two groups. In *Race Matters* his comments refer to the black lower class, but I submit, they apply also to the bourgeoisie: "our black foremothers and forefathers . . . [created] buffers to ward off the nihilistic threat, to equip black folk with cultural armor to beat back the demons of hopelessness, meaninglessness, and lovelessness. These buffers consisted of cultural structures of meaning and feeling that created and sustained communities; this armor constituted ways of life and struggle that embodied values of service and sacrifice, love and care, discipline and excellence."[43] These buffers seem to be wearing away rapidly and readily with the assimilation of buppies and the misrepresentation of the poor.

Affirmative action gains helped create and sustain the bourgeois mentality by many who began to occupy upper- and middle-management positions in the late 1970s, particularly in the government sector.[44] Ironically, although affirmative action policies actually advanced mostly white women, the program became the whipping post for unemployed and reactionary white men, the Christian right, and new-niche-needing scholars.[45] Much of the monetary benefit of these advances fell to the young people sarcastically labeled Generation X, many of whom have seen only what the new status brings materially. In cities like Los Angeles, New York, Atlanta, and Washington, D.C., prominent black families struggled to keep up with the Joneses—two pay-checks from poverty. They pursued the American dream relentlessly—a dream constructed during the time of their ancestral enslavement. Some of these same people formed the black intelligentsia.

Affirmative action opened university doors to blacks that previously had been closed. Yet some of those who got in identified themselves as racially black but were philosophically anti-black. Those who earned Ph.D.s received university positions, book contracts, and network consultations. Despite this trend, the late 1980s saw a third wave in progressive black intellectualism blossom alongside the conservatism. [46] Promoted by university presses and sometimes, necessarily, the scholars themselves, African-American academicians came to public consciousness as Sam Fulwood describes: "the acclaimed and celebrated to the obscure and ridiculed; the ultra-left to neo-conservative to the reactionary right; the Afro-centrists to the Classicists; the B-boy and go-girl posse to the buppie and Jack-N-Jill clique; the radical feminists and lesbians to the engendered men and gay paraders."[47] This new era of black thought produced the likes of Houston Baker, Kimberlé Crenshaw, Patricia Hill Collins, Henry Louis Gates, bell hooks, Todd Boyd, Tricia Rose, Robin D. G. Kelley, Valerie Smith, and Cornel West. Unlike others of their economic and professional status, many of these new scholars at least reintroduced problems and concerns of African-Americans along the multiple axes of race, gender, class, ethnicity, sexual orientation, and generation.

In this cultural landscape, black women (such as Maya Angelou) became celebrities within academia. Within much popular discourse, however, they also became the corrupters of the black family, the straw on the backs of black men, and the primary pilferers of America's welfare coffers. All of the critiques laid a foundation for a real-life phenomenon in which by the end of the century 63 percent of all blacks attending college were female, fourteen black women served in the 107th United States Congress,[48] and Sheryl Swoopes became the first woman to have shoes (Nike) named in her honor. The 1980s provided a noticeable increase in black women's television representations with the introduction of Black Entertainment Television (BET) in 1980, *The Cosby Show* in 1984, *The Oprah Winfrey Show* in 1986, and *The Arsenio Hall Show* in 1989. Black images doubled in number during the 1990s via all genres, profiling African-Americans in large numbers. Programs created venues formerly (and formally) closed to African-Americans and began a new trajectory for black representation in the television spectrum.

CONTEMPORARY TELEVISION

In the 1980s the incestuous relationships among networks, advertisers, and production companies became further entangled with deregulation and the infiltration of cable, forcing television networks to reexamine their ability to be profitable. In the 1990s corporate mergers reduced media offerings to essentially five companies.[49] Television executives began to see "narrow-casting" as one way to retain some of their dispersing audiences.

As defined by cable and accelerated in the 1980s, narrowcasting suggests entire programming devoted to a defined audience by elements such as gender, race, and ability to consume. The idea actually emerged in earlier years, with network programs like *Mary Tyler Moore* (1970–1977) and its spin-offs *Rhoda* (1974–1978), *Phyllis* (1975–1977), and *The Betty White Show* (1977–1978), the first example of gender counterprogramming. For example, by 1986, to counter ABC's *Monday Night Football*, CBS scheduled a distinctive women's night with the programs *Kate and Allie* (1984–1989), *My Sister Sam* (1986–1988), *Designing Women* (1986–1993), *Cagney and Lacey* (1982–1988), and, later, *Murphy Brown* (1988–1998).[50] This successful gendered counterprogramming strategy translated racially also, particularly on NBC. As early as 1981 Thursday night found *Diff'rent Strokes* (1978–1986), *Gimme a Break* (1981–1987), and *Hill Street Blues* (1981–1987) in the prime-time lineup.[51] In the two subsequent years, NBC continued to lead with black majority casts or focus for one evening. With the introduction of *The Cosby Show* in 1984 and its spin-off, *A Different World* three years later and directly preceding it in the lineup, NBC's Thursdays became television's black night. When Fox introduced *In Living Color* (1990–1994), *Roc* (1991–1994), *Martin* (1992–1997), and *Living Single* (1993–1998), it followed that same pattern.[52]

Postmodernist rhetoric played a significant part in the text and context of the programming subsequently offered. Talk of waning historical relevance, parody's lapse into pastiche, and level playing fields danced with American capitalistic euphoria. Network television felt empowered by this new diversity dollar. Yet not all applied evenly. From the promotion to the opening credits of these new black programs, an explicitness marked their positioning. In all four television comedies that I focus on—*Fresh Prince of Bel-Air*, *Martin*, *Living Single*, and *Moesha*—urban (read black) rhythms, dancing, or rap announce their arrival. Commercials for corporations sponsoring these programs, such as McDonald's, Nike, and Revlon, limit black faces to eating, running, or simply needing makeup—at least before ten o'clock EST. After that time those faces disappear.

Television promotions for this night of black programs introduced the hilarity of the black faces awaiting both the colorized and Anglo consumer. For example, print advertisements for *Martin* and *Living Single* showed cast members grinning and wide-eyed, yet with chic and hip clothing—for whites (who were not a large part of the viewing audience) that meant performing darkies; for blacks (the majority of the audience) it was a chance to see what younger generations do with their contemporary privilege. Even the printing font used for these shows' promotion marks a difference—intimating a lower (read ethnic) type of humor. John Berger suggests, "Publicity helps to mask and compensate for all that is undemocratic with society. . . . Publicity explains everything in its own terms."[53] For the Negroes in this new era the terms of televisual blackness emerged quite defined and limiting. In some ways they reintroduced the minstrel mantra from film.

Moreover, during the 1990s a spate of black gangster films emerged following the success of *Boyz n the Hood* (Singleton) and *New Jack City* (Van Peebles) in 1991, which served to situate and confine blacks to violent, urban ghettos. More successful films like *Juice* (Dickerson, 1992) and *Menace II Society* (Hughes, 1993) gave Hollywood fodder and incentive to reproduce 1970s cinema. These films were different because they employed black directors and writers, but they were also much like the black films of the past. These films largely position African-American women in the space of bitch, gangster, hoe, hoochie, or welfare-receiving single-parent mother (or, in many cases, a combination). These films, along with the rise of rap music, particularly define black women's representations. Prime-time television followed this same pattern of profit at the expense of black women's imagery.

BLACK WOMEN FOR BEGINNERS

As I suggested earlier, black women's visual presence intensified during the 1980s and 1990s. In literature African-American women were accused of usurping the black males' voice and position. Yet this literary takeover contrasted starkly with television programs that heralded predominantly black male protagonists and executive producers, as well as many predominantly male film directors. Black urban America's musical sound, largely expressed by the male voice, provided a lyrical check on black women's supposed power. All these male-dominated media factored heavily in the visual representations of African-Americans and women. Yet the media and Negro men pointed to literature, film, and television programs as evidence of women's ascension to power at the black man's expense. *The Color Purple, The Oprah Winfrey Show, The Women of Brewster Place*, and *Waiting to Exhale* all bore crosses for alleged black male-bashing.

Beyond the media realm significant political and economic power within Negro communities remained with black men (for example, Congressional Black Caucus, Urban League, Southern Christian Leadership Council, NAACP, and the black church). African-American men routinely led economic enterprises and held corporate seats. According to the popular press, 1992 ushered in the "Year of the Woman," in which black women gained or retained ten congressional seats. This proliferation occurred while black men retained or gained thirty House seats. This imbalance resounded even more poignantly in work and domestic spaces.

Economist Julianne Malveaux suggests that black women work in a multitiered system. This system positions women in either nontraditional jobs, professional jobs (as teachers, nurses, and social workers), clerical jobs, marginally employed service and private household jobs, or in positions that cycle women between work and welfare.[54] Black women find themselves congregated within the lower three strata. This contrasts with the fact that during the past twenty years more black women have completed high school with declining dropout rates. Yet black women lag behind their white counterparts.[55]

Furthermore, research suggests that although black families headed by women are more likely to be on welfare, less than 10 percent of the composite income of these families comes from public assistance.[56] The average number of children in black female-headed families is 1.89, about the same as other families. Little evidence suggests that these women have children to get on welfare or that the size of welfare benefits increases the likelihood of their being on welfare.[57] However, news coverage of women and welfare paints a vastly different, colorful picture.

Determining which group, black men or black women, suffer oppression more in the United States is neither necessary nor a goal here. Both endure it. Yet the aforementioned forms of institutional exclusion persist alongside the myth of female takeover. Black women's survival in such dichotomous realms defies understanding, unless one knows the history of black women in the United States of America.

Afro-American women emerged in 1980s television comedy as upper and middle class (as represented by the Huxtables and the young coeds of *A Different World*). They embodied the black bourgeoisie. Women play material-driven individualists who possess the education, ability, and means to achieve goals, all through their own efforts. Even Claire (of *The Cosby Show*) was shown as someone who could have and do it all, effortlessly. She could care for the family and laugh about her children buying $90.00 shirts because she had already made it to the top. Hooray for the black superwoman!

Yet, as I mentioned earlier, individualistic tendencies that exclude overt homages to trailblazers, community, and familial responsibilities have traditionally been absent in Colored communities—placing these images in opposition to African-centered ways of being. Black women's television behavior fueled renewed debates/doubts about the need for affirmative action and collaborated with the popular perception/deception of black women single-handedly destroying the black community. Significantly, most roles for African-American women (and men) on television remained outside of drama and within situation comedy—making people laugh and perpetuating the image of black women as sidekicks to leading men.[58]

Knowing black women's difficulties, one should acknowledge their resiliency and constant resistance to oppressive forces. For example, bell hooks suggests that black women's communities function as sites of critique and resistance that stand against forces that tend to objectify their members. She maintains that in these places the idea of specialness (exoticizing) is kept in check. Accordingly, your sister-friends may tell you that your "shit is just common." Much of this analysis seeks not to hold women back or devalue their contributions but to pay tribute to those preceding and to check manipulative moves to power and assumption of individualism. Although community appraisals reduce objectification and exoticism's existence, hooks maintains that in racially integrated spaces, where white, male gazes are favored, it becomes easy for "individual black females deemed 'special' to become exoticized, objectified in ways that support types of behavior that on the home turf would just be considered out of control."[59] Those behaviors lend ammunition to those same white men who label assertive black women crazy (needing containment) or supermammas who care for all those around them (and bear the burden of the work).

. . . I argue that objectification of black women exists yet can be undercut by showing moments of subjectivity achieved within television texts and within the audience's own subjectivity and identification with the character. In other words, I advocate moments of agency conferred upon and taken up by black women within their circumscribed roles and within the audiences' readings of the text—defining agency as the mode of visual and content awareness of women's authority, voice, and vision. Subjectivity enables black women to "define their own reality, establish their own identities, [and] name their history."[60] It implies action and effectiveness either orally, visually, narratively, or consciously. Investigating representations of black women situated in the political, economic, and cultural contexts of post-1980 helps to both rewrite television history and forward a womanist agenda.

Despite the obvious economic, political, critical, and theoretical disparities that exist between Colored men and women, perhaps a word more is needed about why black men have been decentered in this study. Racialized discourses have received validation in postmodern academia—discourses that now circulate within both popular and scholarly media outlets. African-Americans and other marginalized people have been allowed dialogic space in almost all arenas: sports (oh, but not management), domestic affairs (well, not policy and only limitedly in foreign affairs),[61] crime (but not punishment), and white-collar positions (but not merit-based compensation). These openings include visual representations.

These gaps have placed a poignant focus on African-Americans, but, significantly, this focus has centered primarily on black men. Scholarly film texts, the popular press, New Jack cinema, and television all validate, condemn, or otherwise spotlight black men. It is a rare entity that does otherwise. With this deluge of materials on the representations of African-American men and the lacuna of similar material concerning black women, I believe a focused study on African-American women is desperately called for, solo.

NOTES

1. See "NAACP Blasts TV Networks' Fall Season Whitewash," in *NAACP Convention News*, July12, 1999, http://151.200.0.60/president/releases/naacp_blasts_tv_networks.htm (accessed September 28, 2001).

2. Jannette L. Dates and William Barlow, eds., *Split Image: African Americans in the Mass Media* (Washington, DC: Howard University Press, 1990), 265.

3. Miriam Hansen, *Babel and Babylon: Spectatorship in American Silent Film* (Cambridge: Harvard University Press, 1991), 39.

4. Ella Shohat and Robert Stam, Donald Bogle, and James C. Scott all argue for "liberatory possibilities" or "hidden transcripts" in marginalized people's performance. Although I agree with these nuanced ideas and their potential, they fail to apply in this instance.

5. For more on early black cinema and its participants see Charlene Regester, "Lynched, Assaulted, and Intimidated: Oscar Micheaux's Most Controversial Films," *Popular Culture Review* 5, no. 2 (February 1994); Thomas Cripps, *Slow Fade to Black: The Negro in American Film, 1900–1942* (New York: Oxford University Press, 1993); and Daniel Bernardi, ed., *The Birth of Whiteness: Race and the Emergence of U.S. Cinema* (New Brunswick, NJ: Rutgers University Press, 1996). For a good filmography see Larry Richards, *African American Films through 1959: A Comprehensive, Illustrated Filmography* (Jefferson, NC: McFarland, 1998).

6. Donald Bogle, *Toms, Coons, Mulattoes, Mammies, and Bucks: An Interpretive History of Blacks in American Films* (New York: Continuum, 1991), 31–33.

7. Ibid., 36.

8. I have found no Hollywood film that centers black women or their lives before *Imitation of Life*. During this period, however, Josephine Baker stars in *La Sirene des Tropiques* (1927), *Zou Zou* (1934), and *Princess Tam Tam* (1935). Yet these films were made in France and were shown most successfully there. Although films by Oscar Micheaux—e.g., *Within Our Gates* (1919), *Body and Soul* (1925), and *The Scar of Shame* (1927)—all centered around colored women, these films were created and shown exclusively for African-American audiences outside of Hollywood.

9. For an in-depth analysis of the war and Hollywood see Thomas Cripps's *Making Movies Black: The Hollywood Message Movie from World War II to the Civil Rights Era* (New York: Oxford University Press, 1993). Cripps constructs a historical and cultural look at how Hollywood aided the war effort.

10. Ella Shohat and Robert Stam, *Unthinking Eurocentrism: Multiculturalism and the Media* (New York: Routledge, 1994), 225.

11. See Dates and Barlow, *Split Image*, 254.

12. Melvin Patrick Ely, *The Adventures of "Amos 'n' Andy": A Social History of an American Phenomenon* (New York: Free Press, 1991), 98.

13. Ibid., 208.

14. J. Fred MacDonald, *Blacks and White TV: African Americans in Television since 1948* (Chicago: Nelson-Hall, 1992), 32.

15. Dates and Barlow, *Split Image*, 262.

16. Ibid., 264.

17. MacDonald, *Blacks and White TV*, 29.

18. I examine *The Nat King Cole Show* in "I Got Your Bitch!: Colored Women, Music Videos, and Punnany Commodity, pp. 69–109 in Beretta E. Smith-Shomade, *Shaded Lives: African American Women and Television* (New Brunswick, N.J: Rutgers University Press, 2002).

19. MacDonald, *Blacks and White TV* 4.

20. Daniel R. Fusfeld and Timothy Bates, "Black Economic Well-Being since the 1950s," in *A Turbulent Voyage: Readings in African American Studies*, ed. Floyd W. Hayes III (San Diego, CA: Collegiate Press, 1997), 491–516.

21. For one particular reporter's story see Charlayne Hunter-Gault's *In My Place* (New York: Farrar, Straus, Giroux, 1992).

22. Television diminished an already declining film audience, and Hollywood searched for solutions to improve movie attendance.

23. The Department of Labor and Daniel Patrick Moynihan released a report in 1965 called *The Negro Family: The Case for National Action* (Washington, DC: GPO, 1965). The report suggested that matriarch-led families lay at the foundation of black communities' weakness and that "at the heart of the deterioration of the fabric of Negro society is the deterioration of the Negro family" (5). This factor, according to the department's criteria, fostered the racial unrest in urban America.

24. Bogle, *Toms*, 251. For how this phenomenon of black women's anger was translated in 1990s cinema see Tricia Rose, "Rock-a-Block, Baby!:" Black Women Disrupting Gangs and Constructing Hip-Hop Gangsta Films," *Cinema Journal* 42, no. 2 (Winter 2003): 25–40.

25. Donald Bogle, *Blacks in American Films and Television: An Illustrated Encyclopedia* (New York: Simon and Schuster, 1988), 284–85.

26. For a look at 1970s white flight see Nathan Glazer, "The Hard Questions: Life in the City," *New Republic,* August 19, 1996, 37; George C. Gaister, "White Flight from Racially Integrated Neighbourhoods in the 1970s: The Cleveland Experience," *Urban Studies* 27, no. 3 (June 1990): 385–99; and Heather Ann Thompson, "Rethinking the Politics of White Flight in the Postwar City: Detroit, 1945–1980," *Journal of Urban History* 25, no. 2 (January 1999): 163–98.

27. In the short-lived *Harris and Company* (March–April 1979), the show's creators strove to project "new images of African Americans in order to introduce a different perspective, a framework for thinking about black people based on their own African-American inspired vision of black reality" (Dates and Barlow, *Split Image*, 258). Although it received good reviews, NBC dropped it from the schedule after only four episodes. Dates forecasted that the "death of relevancy helped to ensure the stifling of television programs or stories treating serious issues affecting African-Americans" (ibid., 266). A pattern of devaluing black stories in visually unfamiliar contexts continues, as seen by the short runs of the series *Under One Roof, Frank's Place,* and *City of Angels.* These series ran in the latter part of the century. Dates believes that their early demise not only reflects a changing network commitment to programming in general but, more insidiously, to its method of justifying not carrying this type of programming because "people just don't want to see that." *Under One Roof* ran from March to April 1995, *Frank's Place* from September 1987 to October 1988. *City of Angels* ran from January 2000 to December 2000. For an analysis of *Frank's Place's* unique ability to show black life see Herman Gray's *Watching Race: Television and the Struggle for "Blackness"* (Minneapolis: University of Minnesota Press, 1995), chap. 7.

28. Interestingly, too, *Julia* left the air just as *The Mary Tyler Moore Show* arrived. Moore's show came without the baggage and racial yoke of *Julia*. It aired for seven years and spawned three series. I thank Deborah Jaramillo for bringing this irony to my attention.

29. Bogle, *Illustrated Encyclopedia*, 272.

30. MacDonald, *Blacks and White TV*, 206.

31. *Good Times* creator Norman Lear initially envisioned the program with a single-mother household, but veteran actress Esther Rolle refused the role unless a husband/father, John Amos, was added. Lear accepted these terms. The young, wisecracking son, J. J. (Jimmie Walker), however, began to dominate the program. Based on this reconfigured family balance, Amos left the show. Shortly thereafter Rolle left too. A similar reconstitution of the black family existed in the long-running *Family Matters* (1989–1998).

32. Mother Jefferson (Zara Cully) and Florence (Marla Gibbs) appeared on *The Jeffersons,* Dee (Danielle Spencer) on *What Is Happening!!* and *What's Happening Now!!*, and Florida (Esther Rolle) on *Good Times*.

33. United States Commission on Civil Rights, *Window Dressing on the Set: An Update* (Washington: GPO, 1979), 6.

34. W. E. B. Du Bois, *The Souls of Black Folk* (1903; reprint, New York: Norton, 1999), 5.

35. Gerald David Jaynes and Robin M. Williams Jr., eds., *A Common Destiny: Blacks and American Society* (Washington, DC: National Academy, 1989), 35–36.

36. In 1980 the United States population stood at approximately 228 million, with 180 million whites, 26 million blacks, and more than 14 million Latinos. Census 2000 results showed a nation of over 281 million inhabitants, with 198 million whites, almost 35 million blacks, and more than 33 million Latinos. Of that total, black women constitute more than 18 million. Figures are taken from James B. Person Jr., ed., *Statistical Forecasts of the United States* (Detroit: Gale Research, 1993); the *Statistical Abstract of the United States, 1994*, by the U.S. Department of Commerce (Washington, DC: GPO, 1994); and *Census 2000*, available from http://factflnder.census.gov/serylet/BasicFactsSerylet.

37. See Steven V. Roberts, "Washington in Transition: Reagan's Final Rating Is Best of Any President since '40s," *New York Times*, January 18, 1989, A1.

38. Coco Fusco, "About Locating Ourselves and Our Representations," *Framework* 36 (1989): 9.

39. E. Franklin Frazier, *Black Bourgeoisie* (London: Collier, 1969), 192–93.

40. Jaynes and Williams, *Common Destiny*, 274–75.

41. In *Common Destiny* Jaynes and Williams insist that the new black bourgeoisie possess a predilection toward alignment with a black lower class. They suggest that this may be the result of "structural liberalism," which stems from a shared interest, thus reinforcing considerations of ideology or race solidarity in seeing the public sector expand (169). Yet statistics in black flight from Negro communities, the widening chasm of income, and the "look" of television force me to disagree with their assessment.

42. Wade W. Nobles, "African Philosophy: Foundations for Black Psychology," in *A Turbulent Voyage: Readings in African American Studies*, ed. Floyd W. Hayes III (San Diego, CA: Collegiate Press, 1997), 303.

43. Cornel West, *Race Matters* (Boston: Beacon Press, 1993), 15.

44. Conceived and carried out by President Johnson's civil rights legislation of 1968, affirmative action was to correct centuries of discriminatory employment, housing, and education practices. In 1980s cultural currency affirmative action was used as a code for whites to scapegoat African-Americans, particularly for the nation's economic downfall, unemployment, and the increase in perceived unqualified Colored faces in corporate spaces.

45. On affirmative action see Darien A. McWhirter, *The End of Affirmative Action: Where Do We Go from Here?* (New York: Birch Lane Press, 1996); Hugh A. Wilson, "Does Affirmative Action for Blacks Harm Whites?" *Western Journal of Black Studies* 22, no. 4 (Winter 1998): 218–225; and Clay J. Smith, "Open Letter to the President on Race and Affirmative Action," *Howard Law Journal* 42, no. 1 (Fall 1998): 27–58.

46. The first wave had been in the 1920s, called the Harlem Renaissance. The second wave occurred in the 1960s and 1970s with the Black Nationalist Movement and the civil rights movement.

47. Sam Fulwood III, "An Identity," *Los Angeles Times Magazine,* April 9, 1995, 12.

48. This number includes Delegate Donna Christian-Christensen of the U.S. Virgin Islands.

49. These companies include conglomerates like Time Warner (owner of HBO; America Online; Time, Inc.; Warner Bros.; Warner Music Group; New Line Cinema; El Television; Turner Broadcasting; CNN; and the Cartoon Network), Disney (owner of ABC Television, ABC Radio, ESPN, ESPN2, ESPN Classics, ESPNews, and Disney Enterprises), and Viacom (owner of CBS, TVLand, Blockbuster Video, Showtime, VH1, MTV, Nickelodeon, Comedy Central, KingWorld, Simon and Schuster, TNN, Paramount, CMT, Infinity, CBS Internet Group, UPN, and Black Entertainment Television).

50. David Atkin, "The Evolution of Television Series Addressing Single Women, 1966–1990," *Journal of Broadcasting and Electronic Media* 35, no. 4 (Fall 1991): 522.

51. Tim Brooks and Earle Marsh, *The Complete Directory to Prime Time Network and Cable TV Shows: 1946–Present* (New York: Ballantine, 1995), 1202. Although *Hill Street Blues* did not feature an all-black cast, nor was it a comedy, it hosted a large number of Colored actors, extras, and themes.

52. With programming and counterprogramming among all the networks, either Thursday or Sunday night became the fixed space for black comedy. All situation comedies with black casts aired before ten o'clock P.M., after which dramatic programming, serious people with serious lives, appeared. This narrowcasting pattern has been subsequently followed by both Warner Bros. Television (WB) and United Paramount Network (UPN).

53. Quoted in Patricia Mellencamp, *High Anxiety: Catastrophe, Scandal, Age, and Comedy* (Bloomington: Indiana University Press, 1992), 39.

54. Julianne Malveaux, section introduction in *Slipping through the Cracks: The Status of Black Women,* ed. Margaret C. Simms and Julianne M. Malveaux (New Brunswick, NJ: Transaction, 1987), 8.

55. John M. Jeffries, "Discussion," in *Slipping through the Cracks: The Status of Black Women,* ed. Margaret C. Simms and Julianne M. Malveaux (New Brunswick, NJ: Transaction, 1987), 131–32.

56. Ibid., 139.

57. Ibid.

58. Very few African-American women appeared in prime time outside of situation comedy. Full cast members in some dramatic series included Regina Taylor in *I'll Fly Away* (1991–1993); Diahann Carroll (1984–1987) and Troy Beyer (1986–1987) in *Dynasty*; Anne-Marie Johnson, Denise Nicholas, and Dee Shaw in *In the Heat of the Night* (1988–1994); Lisa Gay Hamilton in *The Practice* (1997–present); Gloria Reuben (1996–1999) and Michael Michele (1999–present) in *ER*; Vivica A. Fox, Viola Davis, and Gabrielle Union in the short-lived *City of Angels* (2000); and Lisa Nicole Carson in *Ally McBeal* (1997–2001). Lorraine Toussaint served as a co-lead in Lifetime's *Any Day Now* (1998–2002). And Vanessa Williams, Nicole Ari Parker, Malinda Williams, and Irma P. Hall appear in Showtime's *Soul Food* (2000–present). A handful of black female characters also worked in daytime soap operas.

59. bell hooks, *Yearning: Race, Gender, and Cultural Politics* (Boston: South End Press, 1990), 91.

60. bell hooks, *Talking Back: Thinking Feminist, Thinking Black* (Boston: South End Press, 1989), 42.

61. This situation changed slightly in 2001 when President George W. Bush appointed Condoleezza Rice national security advisor and General Colin Powell secretary of state. These two alone receive validation in the foreign affairs arena.

About the Editor

Alma M. García is professor of sociology and director of the Latin American Studies Program at Santa Clara University, Santa Clara, California. Her publications include *Ethnic Community Builders: Mexican Americans' Search for Justice, Power and Citizenship Rights* (coauthor, 2007); *Narratives of Second Generation Mexican American Women: Emergent Identities of the Second Generation* (2004); *The Mexican Americans* (2002), and *Chicana Feminist Thought: The Basic Historical Writings* (1998). Her article, "The Development of Chicana Feminist Discourse, 1970–1980," *Gender & Society* (1989): 217–228, was selected by the University of Memphis Center for Research on Women as one of the fifty "Classic Articles on Race and Gender" (fall 1997) and has been reprinted in fourteen anthologies. She is preparing a book on Latina day workers and is also conducting an oral history project of Latino/a entrepreneurs in Silicon Valley.